The Visitor's Guide
to
GERMANY:
BLACK FOREST

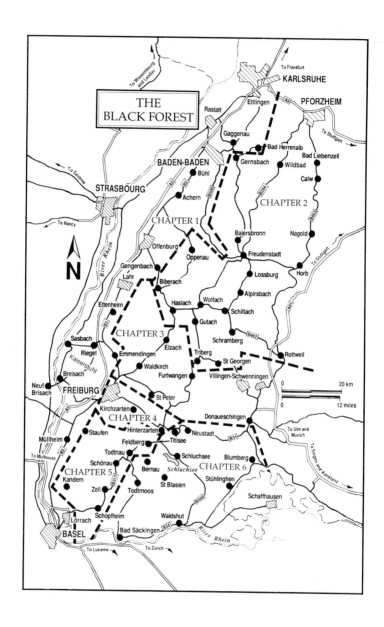

THE VISITOR'S GUIDE TO GERMANY: BLACK FOREST

GEORGE WOOD

MPC

HUNTER
PUBLISHING INC

Published by:
Moorland Publishing Co Ltd,
Moor Farm Road,
Airfield Estate,
Ashbourne,
Derbyshire DE6 1HD
England

British Library Cataloguing in
Publication Data:
Wood, George, *1922-*
    The visitor's guide to Germany:
    The Black Forest.
    1. West Germany. Black Forest -
    Visitor's guides
    914.3'4804878

ISBN 0 86190 343 9 (paperback)
ISBN 0 86190 342 0 (hardback)

Published in the USA by:
Hunter Publishing Inc,
300 Raritan Center Parkway,
CN 94, Edison, NJ 08818
ISBN 1 55650 238 9 (USA)

Colour and black & white
origination by:
Scantrans, Singapore

Printed in the UK by:
Richard Clay Ltd, Bungay, Suffolk

Cover photograph: *Gengenbach*
(MPC Picture Collection)

Illustrations have been supplied as
follows: H. Alcock: pp 30, 79, 87,
98, 102, 103 (top), 118 (top), 126,
143, 182 (both), 186 (top), 191, 214
(centre & bottom), 215; Stadt
Blumberg: p 210 (bottom); MPC
Picture Collection: pp 46, 47, 103
(bottom), 110 (both), 111 (both),
114, 115 (both), 118 (bottom), 179
(both), 207 (bottom), 214 (top).

All other illustrations are from the
author.

ACKNOWLEDGEMENTS
I would like to acknowledge the
assistance given by many people in
Britain and Germany in the preparation of this book. My wife and other
members of my family have cheer-
fully followed me in my explorations and have made many helpful
suggestions along the way.
Wolfgang Winter in Heidelberg
kindly checked the details of Alle-
manic history and customs for me.
The *Fremdenverkehrsverband* in
Freiburg was most helpful in providing background material and in
placing a number of photographs at
my disposal.

G.W.

CONTENTS

Key to Symbols Used in Text Margin and on Maps

 Recommended walk

 Parkland

 Archaeological site

 Nature reserve/Animal interest

 Birdlife

 Garden

 Skiing facilities

 Caves

 Church/Ecclesiastical site

 Building of interest

 Castle/Fortification

 Museum/Art gallery

 Beautiful view/Scenery, Natural phenomenon

 Other place of interest

 Sports facilities

 Interesting railway

Key to Maps

 Main road

 Motorway

 Railway

 River

 Town/City

 Town/Village

 Lake/Reservoir

 Canals

Country Boundary

PREFACE

Before and between the world wars and prior to the days of mass tourism, the Black Forest was highly regarded by the discerning traveller; indeed, the British were in the forefront in encouraging the promotion of modest tourist developments. Since 1955, this part of Germany has been an officially recognised holiday and recreation area and most of the amenities found today have been introduced during this time. Unchanged, however, are the scenery, the good food, drink and accommodation, as well as the friendly hospitality of the inhabitants. A noticeable development in recent years has been the increase in the number of English-speaking visitors enjoying the undoubted delights of the Black Forest. To a great extent, this is due to the large numbers of British and American forces personnel stationed with their families in Germany.

It is hoped that this updated and enlarged edition of the Visitor's Guide will prove useful to those who have already made plans to visit the area and that it will encourage others to do so. The Black Forest is very much a place in which to follow one's own inclinations and this guide aims to show just how easy it is to do that. Above all, it is a place in which to unwind from the trials and tribulations of the daily round, whether by relaxing beside a swimming pool, discovering the secrets of nature in the valleys and on the mountains, or by examining the treasures in the many museums.

INTRODUCTION

The 'Black Forest' (Schwarzwald) is usually regarded as the area measuring over 160km (100 miles) from north to south and some 65km (40 miles) from east to west which nestles neatly into the angle formed by the Rhine (Rhein) where the river also marks, broadly speaking, the borders with Switzerland and France in the south and west respectively. These boundaries are fairly obvious, but those on the east and north sides are much less precisely defined. However, for the purposes of this book, they may be taken as the Stuttgart-Lake Constance *Autobahn* 81 and the Stuttgart-Karlsruhe *Autobahn* 8.

The forest's name may be derived from the dense growths of pine trees which clothe many of the mountain slopes but the newcomer to the area should not expect from this that he will find mile upon mile of forest interrupted only by the occasional habitation. Of course, forestry is of great importance to the economy but there are large stretches of arable land, especially in the north and east, while dairy-farming is the main livelihood of many rural families. The huge traditional farmhouses provide shelter, not only for the family but also for the livestock, as well as accommodation for farm implements, vehicles and winter feed.

Today, space will often have been found to construct one or two very comfortable holiday flats as well. Most of the farmhouses have been modernised internally and the family enjoys the amenities of central heating, luxurious bedrooms and well-appointed bathrooms and kitchens. Such creature comforts will extend to, or may even have started in, the accommodation provided for paying guests. The life of the Black Forest farmer can be hard and members of the family often find employment in a nearby town to ease the financial burden.

The modest income from tourism is obviously an important factor too. Those family members with a paid job are not excused their share of farm work and find their evenings and weekends taken up with such tasks as milking, hay-making and repairing fences.

Another significant contribution to the rural economy comes from the wine industry. The great vineyards of Baden (this part of Germany is in the state of Baden-Württemberg) are mainly to be found along the sunny western slopes facing the Rhine. The wines of Baden are highly esteemed and the interested tourist can explore the wine country by following the Baden Wine Road (*Badische Weinstrasse*) which runs almost the entire length of the Forest, from Baden-Baden in the north to Basel on the Swiss border. Opportunities for sampling the product (*Weinproben*) abound.

The mountains of the Black Forest are fairly modest, rarely exceeding 1,000m (3,300ft) in the north. The main peaks are in the south but even the highest of these, the Feldberg, does not quite reach 1,500m (5,000ft). In clear weather, some of them offer superb views of the snow-covered Swiss Alps to the south. However, one should not expect too much of such distant views because a heat-haze frequently intervenes, particularly in summer. Nevertheless, the mountain tops are nearly all delightful in their own right and some of them will be mentioned in more detail later.

Apart from the Rhine on the southern and western boundaries, there are no big rivers in the Black Forest but there are many small ones which contribute greatly to the scenic interest. Indeed, one might say that the bubbling streams and numerous waterfalls are as typical of the Black Forest as the woodlands themselves. The famous Neckar rises near Schwenningen and then meanders northward out of the Forest, through Stuttgart and Heilbronn, before turning west towards Heidelberg and the Rhine. As it grows it becomes, like the Rhine itself, an important traffic artery for water-borne goods. An even better known waterway, the Danube (Donau), originates near Donaueschingen and leaves the Black Forest as a modest little river to continue its lengthy journey eastwards to the Black Sea. Similarly, although there are no very large lakes, a number of small ones provide boating facilities. The largest and best-known of these are the Schluchsee and the Titisee, both in the south-east.

There are no wholly industrial towns in the Black Forest. The busy cities of Stuttgart and Karlsruhe lie just outside its borders, as do Strasbourg, on the French side of the Rhine, and Basel which is mostly in Switzerland. Freiburg (im Breisgau, to distinguish it from any of several other towns of the same or similar name) is regarded as the capital of the Forest, with a population of some 180,000. Apart from Pforzheim (population 97,000), few other towns reach 50,000 and the vast majority are much smaller.

While discerning tourists have patronised the Black Forest for many years, it is only in about the last thirty years that it has developed into a proper holiday area. It has all the facilities modern visitors expect but there is also an emphasis on the features for which the area is renowned. There are well-marked and cared-for footpaths, long-distance paths, nature parks, health resorts and varied winter sports possibilities. This defined holiday area, embracing the 5,000 square miles of the 'forest', is now the most visited of Germany's many holiday regions.

It is the Black Forest's geographical nature which makes it unique. Some 50 million years ago, there occurred the literally earth-shattering developments which produced the remarkable contours of this part of Europe. The Alps were folded up and with them a mountainous chain stretching from the Massif Central of France, through the Vosges (Vogesen) and Black Forest, to the Erzgebirge in far-off Saxony. There was, at that time, no real division between the Vosges and the Black Forest, and it was not until about 42 million years later that another natural upheaval occurred. The middle section of the range broke free and plunged some 1,000m (3,300ft) into the earth's crust, creating what eventually became the Rhine plain — the mighty river flowing northwards through it from its source in the snows of the Swiss Alps to the North Sea. Further modifications of the landscape were caused by volcanic eruptions and the arrival of the Ice Age. The ice-cap was responsible for planing some 1,000m (3,300ft) from the tops of the mountains on both sides of the plain before it withdrew about half a million years ago to leave the generally rounded summits which distinguish these mountains from the craggy outlines of the Alps.

The original rocks consist of granite and gneiss, as can clearly be seen in a number of places in the southern Black Forest, in the rock wall of the Feldberg above the Feldsee for example . Gneiss can also be seen in the central and northern parts of the Forest, as well as in the stone terraces of the waterfall at Triberg or the rock walls of the Murg valley. In other places the rock is hidden by a thick layer of red sandstone or by yellow-white chalk. The area is rich in minerals, and in earlier days iron, felspar and silver were all mined. Until the beginning of this century, coal was obtained near Offenburg and Baden-Baden. Significant deposits of uranium exist at the foot of the Feldberg but conservationists have so far hindered its exploitation on any large scale. Lead, zinc and salt have also been worked in various places, but no longer. These earlier activities may, however, explain the remains of various earthworks, excavations or buildings which the inquisitive wanderer may notice in the remoter parts of the forest.

Not surprisingly, the Black Forest is also rich in health-giving mineral waters, as is reflected in the number of spa towns which still provide specialised treatment for various ills. Few readers are likely to make a point of travelling to Baden-Baden, Bad Liebenzell or Wildbad to take the waters, but the bottling of these spas' products is a major industry and they are to be found in restaurants all over Germany and, indeed, much further afield.

In several respects, the Black Forest is an ideal place for children. They are welcomed everywhere and frequently singled out for special treatment. It is very much an area for family holidays and, as such, considerable provision is made everywhere for the entertainment and enjoyment of all age groups. Naturally, the emphasis is on activities calling for a measure of physical exertion.

There are many splendid playgrounds (*Kinderspielplätze*), their equipment constructed, as one might expect, mainly of wood. Every centre of any size has one or more of them and even the tiniest village usually has a small play area. It is by no means unusual to find these attractions for children far from any habitation at all, deep in the woods or beside a small lake. Sometimes a little sign saying '*Waldspielplatz*' is the only clue to their presence.

Reduced prices for children are fairly usual in hotels and guest houses while most restaurants, including those on the motorways, have a special children's menu or are prepared to serve smaller portions for children on request. The family seeking a good, inexpensive holiday could hardly do better than select the Black Forest.

As is to be expected in an area where there are significant variations in altitude, there can also be great variations in the weather. The Rhine valley north of Basel is the warmest and driest part of Germany and this fringe of the Black Forest benefits accordingly. In the mountains the prospect of rain increases but during the summer months the chances of wet weather are certainly no greater than in other mountainous regions. Summer temperatures are, on average, significantly higher than in the British Isles and this is emphasised by the large number of outdoor swimming pools, not to mention the vineyards.

Thunderstorms can occur quite frequently in the mountains. Away from the Rhine, average winter temperatures are low enough to make winter sports a realistic possibility. From April onwards, the Black Forest is warmer than other parts of Northern Europe and remains so until about the end of October. In the Rhine valley, however, reasonably mild weather is likely to persist throughout the winter. There are invariably long periods of fine weather during the autumn which makes this the ideal season for walking holidays.

For the visitor from Britain, there are really only two practical methods of travelling to the Black Forest after the sea crossing — by rail or by car. If the journey is made by train, nearly all the main resorts may be reached without difficulty. The more remote parts require the use of a bus service, probably infrequent, for the final stages of the journey, and the rail traveller would do well to select his destination from the many towns and villages having a station. The motorist has the advantage of being free to choose his base from any spot which appeals to him and there is much to be said for having one's own transport available for general touring and excursions.

While other routes may also be used, the vast majority of rail travellers will proceed via London and then make the sea crossing from Harwich to the Hook of Holland or from Dover to Ostend. If the overnight sailings are used, most parts of the Black Forest can be reached by late the following afternoon.

Motorists travelling from Scotland or Northern England will find the North Sea Ferries services from Hull to Rotterdam or Zeebrugge (14 hours) very convenient. Dinner and breakfast are included in the fares on these routes. On the east coast too, there are the Felixstowe to Zeebrugge and Harwich to the Hook of Holland routes (7-8 hours) operated by P&O Ferries and Sealink respectively. South of the Thames there are 'long' overnight crossings from Sheerness to Vlissingen (Flushing) (about 8 hours) by Olau Lines and from Ramsgate to Dunkirk by Sally Viking on which, although the actual distance is short, passengers may remain in their cabins until about 7am in the outward direction.

Finally, there are crossings both day and night from Folkestone or Dover to Ostend and Zeebrugge (P&O Ferries), each taking about

4 hours. There are also, of course, many sailings on the traditional short sea routes from Dover and Folkestone but apart from Dunkirk and Calais, the Continental ports concerned cannot be regarded as ideal starting points for the journey to the Black Forest. Hook of Holland, Rotterdam, Vlissingen, Zeebrugge, Ostend and Dunkirk all have good connections into the European motorway system which takes one without any break to the fringes of the Black Forest. Distances from the various ports do not differ sufficiently to make this a factor in the choice of route. Baden-Baden, at the north end of the Forest, is about 713km (443 miles) from the Hook of Holland. Forty-five kilometres (28 miles) or 110km (69 miles) further are Freudenstadt and Freiburg respectively. There is a variety of motorway routes across the Low Countries but eventually one should cross the German border at Aachen and continue about 40km (25 miles) towards Köln (Cologne) to join the fine new A61 *Autobahn* which is much better than the older road east of the Rhine.

The transatlantic visitor will also find that his or her arrival in the Black Forest has to be completed by train or car. Arrival will probably have been by air at Frankfurt or at some other international airport and there is no difficulty then in reaching nearly all the main resorts by train. All the principal car hire firms have offices or agencies at the airports and the advantages of having one's personal transport for the duration of the holiday have already been mentioned.

Where, in the ensuing chapters, it is necessary to refer to distances or heights, the metric versions will be used, since these are what the visitor will find on signposts and maps. However, where appropriate, the imperial equivalents will also be given. Similarly, the local versions of place names will be used except where there is a well-established English version of the large cities or rivers. Incidentally, English is widely understood, particularly by younger people, who have often learnt it as their first foreign language.

In Germany, accommodation in private houses is widely available in tourist areas. Such accommodation will be recognised by a *'Zimmer frei'* (rooms available) sign at the roadside. Such rooms will invariably be found to be comfortable and spotlessly clean. The usual arrangement is 'bed and breakfast', and in this part of Germany the breakfast can be expected to be more substantial than the basic 'continental' and will perhaps include boiled eggs, cheeses, cold meat and a choice of breads. An advantage of using private accommodation is that one is more likely to have meaningful contact with local inhabitants than in larger establishments. It is fairly unusual for the private landlady to be able to provide an evening meal — the Germans often have their main meal at midday — but she will certainly know of a suitable inn or café.

Very good value can also be obtained in the village inns or in small hotels or pensions which will usually be able to provide an evening meal as well. The earlier practice of charging for room and breakfast separately has virtually disappeared. Half-board or full-board arrangements may not be available in private houses and one usually has to select a hotel or pension for these or, alternatively, one of the numerous farmhouses offering accommodation.

Farm holidays are, in fact, very popular in the Black Forest and a book *Urlaub auf dem Bauernhof* (Holidays on the Farm), available from German National Tourist Offices (GNTO) overseas, lists hundreds of addresses. Such accommodation is good value and allows the visitor to become acquainted with the people and the country. Of course, for children it is ideal. (Remember their wellington boots and old clothes if they are to be allowed to participate to the full). Milking time on the dairy farms is popular and the youngsters will usually be allowed to 'help' in some way. The book mentioned gives details of the activities of each farm and includes information on possibilities for riding, angling, skiing, etc, together with places of interest in the vicinity, distances to swimming pools and so on. Some of the farms are actually riding schools and others cater for unaccompanied children, usually from 10 years-of-age upwards. In vineyard areas, the information will often refer to wine-tasting in the house. Most of the farms have a common room where the family and guests can meet in the evening. Farm holidays are popular with both the Germans and their continental neighbours so the visitor may well find himself in a truly international gathering.

The Germans were pioneers of self-catering and there is a wide range of such accommodation in the Black Forest. Many farmhouses have one or more holiday flats built into the main building, while others have constructed a separate house for the purpose. Details of all these are to be found in the farm holiday book. There are also many holiday flats in and around the towns and villages. Most are in private houses and the proprietor usually lives on the premises. Lists are available from local tourist offices.

There is a growing number of holiday villages with self-catering houses or flats and with site amenities such as shops, restaurants and swimming pools, according to the size of the development. Some of these are run by religious or other institutions; a list of locations and addresses is given in the 'Useful Information' section of this book. The ferry companies also offer package holidays which include accommodation in holiday villages.

Camping or caravanning is the choice of many, and there are numerous sites to be found. Advance booking is essential for the summer months. There are also many youth hostels in the Black Forest and for these, too, advance booking at busy seasons is strongly recommended. Hostel-type accommodation is also available in around forty *Naturfreundehäuser*, while the *Schwarzwaldverein* has numerous *Wanderheime* along its routes. See the 'Useful Information' section for more details and addresses.

While there is no shortage of accommodation, it is not always easy to know what is available or where to get information. The GNTOs overseas will provide useful general information about any area and also accommodation lists for the main resorts. Alternatively, one can write direct to the Tourist Information Office (*Verkehrsamt*) of any place in which one is interested and ask for their accommodation lists. The material will invariably be more comprehensive than what is available in the overseas offices and will often include outlying villages. When writing to book accommodation, enclose an International Reply Coupon and expect to wait at least two or three weeks for a reply. Given an adequate command of the language, by far the most satisfactory thing is to telephone first — direct dialling is possible to all parts of Germany — and find out if the required accommodation is available. Incidentally, the farm holiday book includes references to the family's ability to speak English.

In general, there are no high season prices in the Black Forest, but there may be considerable reductions for the early and late season, commonly October or November until March or April. Places with winter sports potential often keep the same prices all year. A glossary of common terms and abbreviations encountered when seeking or booking accommodation is given at the end of this book.

Black Forest cooking is unlikely to offend the visitor's palate. Apart from boiled eggs, breakfasts are 'cold'. *Marmelade* is not marmalade but jam and the local honey is excellent. Lunch (*Mittagessen*) starts early; by noon on weekdays and as early as 11.30am on Sundays in restaurants, hotels and inns. Particularly good value is to be had on weekdays in the many modest inns which provide 'business' lunches. A sign announcing *'Gute bürgerliche Küche'* (Good home cooking) is usually an indication that the establishment can be relied upon to provide a satisfactory and reasonably-priced meal. In some places there will be several set meals, usually shown as *Gedeck I, II*, etc on the menu (*Speisekarte*), the lowest priced first. The main course of meat or fish will usually be preceded by soup of the day (*Tagessuppe*) and sometimes followed by stewed fruit (*Kompott*) according to season. Cooked puddings or desserts are rarely found, but ice cream of some sort will usually be available as an alternative to the *Kompott*.

The main course at lunch or dinner will often be some sort of *Schnitzel* or *Kotelett* (chops or cutlets of pork or veal). In addition to the set meals, there will be separately priced dishes and many Germans choose one of these and have only the main course. Snacks of the open sandwich type with some of the many varieties of German sausage (*Wurst*) or cheese (*Käse*) with bread (*Brot*) or a roll (*Brötchen*) will be shown on the menu as *Wurstbrot* or *Käsebrot* or *belegtes Brötchen mit* ... One can also try Frankfurters or the rather similar Vienna sausages, often described as *'ein Paar Wienerle'* (a couple of Viennas) or a substantial *Bockwurst* with mustard. There will be potato salad or bread with the sausages. Potatoes in many guises are popular but as an alternative one can try some of the delicious dumplings (*Knödeln*). Cooked green vegetables are rare and a side salad is more likely to be provided. *Salat* or *Kopfsalat* means lettuce; *gemischter Salat* means lettuce with cucumber, tomato, etc. The salad is always served in a dressing. Goulash and omelettes are often available too.

Afternoon tea becomes afternoon coffee (*Nachmittagskaffee*), taken in the *Kaffeepause* which can occur any time between 3 and 5 o'clock. It is an opportunity for indulging in a little pure gluttony among the cream cakes, fruit flans, pastries, etc. Most famous is the Black Forest cherry cake (*Schwarzwälderkirschtorte*). Portions of this and all other cakes are generous but even they can be supplemented by a large helping of whipped cream (*Schlagsahne*). Other specialities are *Zwetschenkuchen* (blue plums on a pastry base) in season, *Käsesahnekuchen* (creamy cheese cake) and *Johannisbeerenkuchen* (red currants on a sponge base).

The traditional drink at this time is coffee, which is fairly strong and with a little evaporated milk. This is not to everyone's taste and alternative beverages are tea (for which one has to use the evaporated milk), lemon tea (*Zitronentee*) or drinking chocolate (*heisse Schokolade*). Iced coffee (*Eiskaffee*) or iced chocolate (*Eisschokolade*) are refreshing drinks and there will be soft drinks, fruit juices or ice cream for the children. The usual German coffee cups are on the small side and it is preferable to ask for a pot of coffee (*Kännchen*) which will contain enough for two or more cups. Some establishments now only serve coffee in a *Pott* (a mug) which contains the same amount as a *Kännchen* but costs a little less. In the more fashionable resorts, the principal hotels or the *Kurhaus* or *Kurzentrum* may extend *Nachmittagskaffee* into a *Kaffeekonzert* and there may be a modest supplementary charge for the pleasure of an hour or so of light music with the coffee and cakes.

The evening meal is usually served from 6pm and much of what was said about the midday meal also applies to late dinner (*Abendessen*). The set meals will probably have disappeared, but an identical menu is likely to be available. Wine by the glass (0.2 or 0.25 litres) or $^1/_4$, $^1/_2$ and litre carafe (*offene Weine*) is readily available and is quite cheap, or one can enjoy a bottle of superior German wine. The prices displayed always include VAT (*Mehrwertssteuer*) and service (*Bedienung*), even if they do not say so. It is usual for the bill to be made out and the money collected by the waiter or waitress. While tipping is not necessary and not expected, most people wave away any small change left after paying the bill.

For the self-caterer, the advent of self-service shops has made the purchase of foodstuffs very simple. Each village has at least one small supermarket; the chains 'A & O', 'Edeka' and 'Spar', are among those most commonly found in this area. Larger supermarkets ('Aldi', 'Plus', 'Norma', etc) will be found in all the main towns. In addition, a baker's or butcher's shop will often have a small self-service area for general foodstuffs and drinks. Nearly all drink bottles, often including wine and plastic bottles, carry a deposit.

Fruit and vegetables are often found in street markets, or on individual stalls if there is no proper market. The butcher's shop (*Metzgerei*) is usually a place of cool and sparkling cleanliness. In addition to fresh meat, there is a bewildering display of sliced sausages (*Wurst*) and other cooked meats; for an assortment of different sorts of *Wurst* ask for *Aufschnitt*. A useful item, very popular with children, is *Fleischkäse* — literally meat cheese — a firm sort of pâté which can be sliced thinly for sandwiches or more thickly for frying.

There is no need for the self-caterer to carry a lot of foodstuffs from home because everything needed is readily available locally at very competitive prices. Those living on a dairy farm can buy milk very cheaply and have the pleasure of recalling or discovering how fresh pure milk really tastes. Needless to say, German quality and cleanliness controls are very strict.

Souvenirs from the Black Forest include the cuckoo clock. The traditional craft of clock-making still continues and the production of timepieces of every conceivable size and design is a major cottage industry. Today, many of the movements are mass produced but it is the attractive case which really sells the clock. At the lower end of the price scale a simple, spring-driven clock can be purchased very cheaply. A little more upmarket, there is an enormous range of weight-driven clocks for which one might pay between 40 and 120 marks. The largest and most expensive cuckoo clocks will cost upwards of 400 marks, for which sum one could acquire a truly magnificent example of the clock-maker's art.

In the ensuing chapters, an endeavour has been made to divide the Black Forest into areas which can be fitted into a logical touring pattern. Apart, perhaps, from the Baden Wine Road described in Chapter 1, each of the areas could be explored reasonably well by car from a single base but the Black Forest is best known for its walking possibilities and much has been done to encourage the walker to see the best of the countryside. Over a hundred years ago, Mark Twain wrote in glowing terms about the Black forest in *A Tramp Abroad*, having explored the region extensively on foot. The long-distance paths have been identified and marked by the *Schwarzwaldverein* (Black Forest Association), including such marathon hikes as the *Westweg* from Pforzheim to Basel, the *Mittelweg* from Pforzheim to Waldshut, the *Querweg* from Freiburg to Bodensee (Lake Constance) and several others. '*Weg*' means 'way', so the paths may be translated as West Way, Middle Way and Cross Way, etc.

The Association has marked about 22,000km (13,700 miles) of footpaths including some 7,000km (4,300 miles) of long-distance paths such as those mentioned above. Other routes have been marked by the local authorities or by tourist associations covering a particular geographical area. Inevitably, there is duplication of marking where, for example, one of the long-distance paths follows a locally marked one for a time; it is, therefore, a good idea to supplement the wayside markings by using a good map.

The 'Wanderkarte' series issued by Atlasco are very clear and easily followed. These are to a scale of 1:30,000 and the sheets covering the Black Forest can be readily identified by their distinctive yellow covers. In some popular resorts, the information office provides a map showing walks in and around the resort, some of which do not always appear on the more comprehensive maps. Such local walks are frequently marked by numbers rather than the more usual geometrical signs. The *Schwarzwaldverein* produces very good maps to 1:50,000 scale. Incidentally, the waymarking system used in the Black Forest has been highly regarded for many years and has been used as the pattern for marking footpaths in several other countries.

The motorist will often wish to use his or her vehicle to reach the starting point of a walk and will benefit from the many free *Wander-Parkplätze* (walkers' parking places) which have been established throughout the Forest. These provide good access to walks in the vicinity and each parking place has a map showing the various possibilities and an indication of the time required for each walk or the distance involved. All such walks can be completed in one day, the majority being less than 10km (6 miles). Some of the car parks are recognised by a distinctive blue 'P' sign with a pictogram of a couple of hikers, others by a rustic sign saying *Wander-Parkplatz* or *Wald-Parkplatz*. Car-park locations are clearly shown on the Atlasco maps.

The motorist also requires a smaller-scale map for his or her general movements about the Forest and those issued by the petrol companies will be found very suitable for this purpose. For example, Sheet 6 of the series issued by Aral covers the whole Black Forest at a scale of 1:400,000. The *Tourenkarten* issued by the same company are also recommended. These are to 1:200,000 scale and are designed for the tourist exploring the area. Sheets 13 and 16 cover the northern and southern parts of the Black Forest respectively. On the reverse of the sheets is a comprehensive catalogue of the various places of interest, etc. In addition to maps, there are many booklets obtainable locally giving detailed descriptions of walks. It will be easy for those with some knowledge of German to choose one which covers the part of the Forest they want to explore. These booklets complement the maps and sometimes prevent one missing a worthwhile feature or viewpoint.

A book of this size cannot give a comprehensive catalogue of Black Forest walks, but the chapters which follow include details of some which may be regarded as typical of the area.

1
THE BADEN WINE ROAD

North of Freiburg

The *Badische Weinstrasse* (Baden Wine Road) runs from north to
south along the western fringe of the Black Forest and passes
through almost all the important wine-producing areas. Most travellers, whether they come by road or rail, enter the Forest through
this narrow strip and may find more of interest here than expected.
The lover of good wine will certainly want to take time to sample the
products of the great vineyards facing the river Rhine in this mild
and dry part of Germany. The designated *Weinstrasse* is not quite
continuous but sometimes doubles back on itself or is divided in
order to embrace all the vineyards. For much of its length it follows
the main road No B3, the principal route to the south before the
construction of the nearby *Autobahn*. Road B3 enters the northernmost point of the Black Forest at Ettlingen just south of Karlsruhe and
it is from here that the journey southwards commences.

Ettlingen, virtually a suburb of Karlsruhe, is a place of considerable interest, especially for those interested in architectural treasures. The Catholic parish church of St Martin incorporates the
twelfth- to thirteenth-century tower choir and the high choir of 1459-
64. The rest of the original building was burned down in 1689. The
interior is now a plain, single space with some decorated wall
recesses. The striking façade is divided by three large pilasters.

The *Rathaus* (town hall) dates from 1737-8 and was built to the
plans of the Baden-Baden master stonemason, A. Mohr. The Roman
period in this area is recalled by a copy of the Roman Neptune stone
washed up from the river Alb in 1480 which has been incorporated

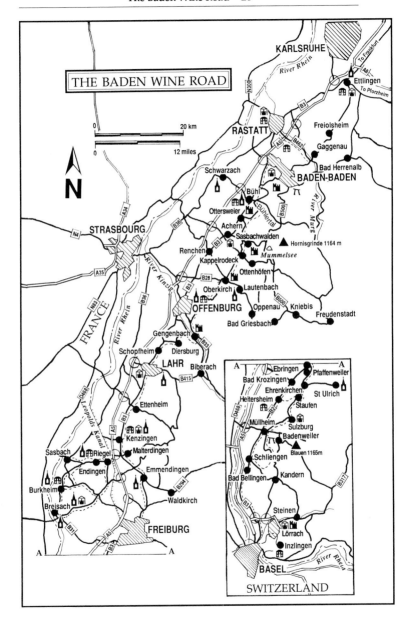

in the wall. The *Schloss* is a fine building with four wings and was built during the years 1728-33. In the courtyard there is the Delphin-brunnen (dolphin fountain) of 1612 and, in front of the *Schloss*, the Narrenbrunnen (fools' fountain) which dates from 1549.

In 1727, the Margravine Sybilla Augusta of Baden decided to move from the official *Residenz* in Rastatt and base herself in Ettlin-gen. The old sixteenth-century *Schloss* there had been burned out during the Palatinate war of succession. It had been a gloomy building and Sybilla Augusta decided to replace the remains with the building seen today. The architect Michael Ludwig Rohrer had to work to her very firm ideas as to what the building should look like and the south wing became her living quarters, decorated in the formal baroque style. Finally, the complex was completed by the construction of a chapel, also in baroque style, which was the equivalent of three storeys in height.

Sybilla Augusta originated from Bohemia and was anxious to have some reminder of her homeland incorporated in the new building. The famous Bavarian painter, Cosmas Damian Asam, was commissioned to produce a ceiling and wall fresco cycle in the chapel, depicting the life and martyrdom of Johannes Nepomuk, the patron saint of Bohemia; the work was carried out in 1732. With the death of Sybilla's second son in 1771, the Catholic line also died out and the significance of the *Schlosskapelle* was extinguished by the new Protestant masters.

In Napoleonic times, the *Schloss* was used as a hospital; the chapel was desecrated and the altars were sold. The chapel became a place of worship again from 1840 to 1876, this time for the little Protestant community of Ettlingen. In 1871, a school for Prussian non-commis-sioned officers was established in the *Schloss*; it demanded ever more accommodation and eventually took over the chapel in which addi-tional floors were built. Large parts of Asam's wall frescos were whitewashed over and only the ceiling painting and a few other remnants remained.

After World War II, it was realised that the ceiling in the *Schlosskapelle* was the only remaining example of Asam's work in the area, the others in the Mannheim *Schloss* and in the Bruchsal Hofkirche having been destroyed. It was decided to restore the chapel, the undesirable additions were removed and it became a splendid little concert hall in 1954. Since then it has been the venue of the famous Ettlingen chamber music festivals, the restored work of Asam beautifully complementing the baroque music often performed there under the auspices of Süddeutscher Rundfunk (South German Radio and TV). The rest of the *Schloss* complex now houses the Albgau and Albicker-Museum as well as the tourist information office.

Incidentally, the word *Schloss* frequently describes a building which in English would be called a residential palace, whereas a castle in the sense of a fortress is a *Burg* in German.

Today, Ettlingen is an important centre of the paper-making trade, an industry which goes back here to the year 1452 when the oldest paper-mill in Baden first produced acceptable writing paper for government offices. In fact, the Chinese had discovered the art of paper-making some 500 years earlier but it had been a closely guarded secret which only trickled slowly westwards through the reports and souvenirs of early travellers.

A picturesque road runs southwards through the villages of Schöllbronn, Völkersbach and Freiolsheim and, after 18km, reaches Gaggenau, a town of about 30,000 inhabitants. Here the little river Murg is met for the first time. The source of this river will be visited in a later chapter, but for the moment, it is necessary to go downstream for a brief visit to the town of Rastatt, a rather larger centre than Gaggenau. The lower reaches of the Murg support a considerable paper-making industry, one of the specialities being the fine quality, thin paper used for printing bibles, etc. **Rastatt** may well be the gateway town for the traveller arriving by train, for it is here that one must transfer to the so-called *Murgtalbahn* (Murg Valley Railway) to go towards Freudenstadt. The pretty little river Murg winds its way westward through Rastatt on its journey to the Rhine. The motorist may also find that the Rastatt exit from the *Autobahn* is the most suitable for his destination and it would be a pity to hurry through without spending a little time here.

Margrave Ludwig Wilhelm created a town of remarkable spaciousness for the period and after his death in 1707, his wife Sybilla Augusta, who has already been mentioned, continued his ambitious plans. The centrepiece is the magnificent *Schloss* which was the first baroque palace of such size to be erected in Germany. The owner and his architect wished to bring the splendour of Italian *palazzi* and French *châteaux* (such as Versailles) to the Upper Rhine and they succeeded in creating this outstanding example of the art in 7 years. The central section is the *Residenz* which dominates the wings grouped around a large courtyard. The interior staircases are among the finest to be found in a baroque *Schloss*. In the north wing, the Schlosskirche Heilige Kreuz (palace church of the Holy Cross) is entered through a magnificent portal and the visitor will be struck by the interplay of light and colours, to which great importance was attached, as in many churches built about this time. In addition to the large fresco of the vault, there are numerous smaller ornamental panels. The high altar has a silvered wooden crucifix and is particularly distinctive.

The Kapelle of Maria Einsiedeln was consecrated in 1717 and is now separated from the *Schloss* by a busy roadway. Its rather plain decoration is significantly different in character to that of the *Schloss*. The Pagodenburg (1722) next to the chapel was inspired by the pagoda in the grounds of Schloss Nymphenburg in Munich. The *Marktplatz* (market square) was part of the original concept for the town and is dominated by the Stadtkirche (town church) of St Alexander, which was consecrated in 1764, and by the *Rathaus* of 1750. The high altar in the church should not be overlooked and three large fountains complete the baroque townscape.

There are three museums in, or close to, the *Schloss*. The *Heimatmuseum* (*Heimat* means homeland or regional) concerns itself mainly with local history, while the Freiheitsmuseum deals with the various freedom movements which have featured in the national history of the country and is also a memorial to those who have died in that cause. Lastly there is the Wehrgeschichtliches Museum — West Germany's national war museum.

The Margravine Sybilla Augusta was also responsible for Schloss Favorite, 5km (3 miles) south-east of Rastatt at **Förch** near Kuppenheim. This was another link with Sybilla's homeland and an architect was actually brought from Bohemia to carry out the Margravine's wishes which she again expressed in no uncertain terms. However, the end result is delightful and reflects the owner's personality and charm. Built in 1710, this little baroque jewel now houses a fine collection of porcelain and antique furniture.

Excursions can readily be made from Rastatt to the ruins of two old castles which occupy fine vantage points. Altes Schloss Hohenbaden is quite near Baden-Baden and can be reached via the road from Gaggenau. Three kilometres (2 miles) to the west, Ebersteinburg has the advantage of having not only a splendid view over the Rhine plain, but also a very adequate restaurant and café.

The motorist using the A5 *Autobahn* between the Rastatt and Baden-Baden exits should stop at the Baden-Baden *Raststätte* (service area) to visit the unique *Autobahnkirche*. It is, of course, dedicated to St Christopher and was built to serve those using the motorway. It is a significant example of modern church architecture. The architect Friedrich Zwingmann and the artist and sculptor Emil Wachter have created a visual world embracing mankind's past, present and future. The church itself is in the form of a pyramid and the stained glass depicting the life of Christ makes an immediate impact upon the visitor as do the doors which are finished by an unusual enamel technique.

Between Gaggenau and Rastatt, the first signs of viticulture may be observed and these continue as road B3 is followed towards Baden-Baden where the *Weinstrasse* officially commences. **Baden-Baden** (population 50,000) is, of course, the classic spa and while it may lack the sparkle which it had in the days when it was frequented by the crowned heads of Europe, it remains an attractive town which may appeal to the less-active visitors in particular. It is served by the majority of the express trains on the main line to Basel.

Surrounded by hills and pine woods, Baden-Baden is a veritable sun trap and thus well-suited to the early or late season holiday. Royalty and oil sheikhs still frequent the elegant hotels which were built around the turn of the century. However, as the town is now the headquarters of the south-west German radio and television service, musicians, artists, journalists and the like from all over Germany are more likely to be one's neighbours. Baden-Baden is also the home of the oldest casino in Germany where, in earlier times, one might have rubbed shoulders with Kaiser Wilhelm I, Bismarck, Berlioz or Brahms. Today, well-heeled visitors from all over the world frequent the gaming rooms, where evening dress is still obligatory.

It was not, however, the attractions of the casino which gave Baden-Baden its position as an internationally famed spa. The reputation is due to the remarkable qualities of its healing thermal springs which gush out in the famous Friedrichsbad at a temperature of 69 °C, (156 °F) making them the warmest thermal springs in Europe. The Friedrichsbad was built in 1866; its modern counterpart, the Augustabad complex, includes gymnasia, a sun terrace and, on the uppermost of its seven storeys, an indoor swimming pool. The 'cure' is noted for its beneficial effects on sufferers from mental stress, heart and circulatory conditions. The area has been famed for the curative

Places of Interest In and Around Ettlingen, Rastatt and Baden-Baden

Ettlingen
Schloss
In town centre
Fine palace of 1728-33 with fountains.

Schlosskapelle
Former palace chapel with elaborately painted ceilings. Converted to concert hall.

Albgau and Albicker Museums
Located in the *Schloss* complex.

Church of St Martin
Sections dating back to the twelfth century.

Rathaus (1737-8)
In town centre.

Rastatt
Marktplatz
Huge market square with fountains, dominated by the church of St Alexander (1764) and the *Rathaus* (1750).

Schloss
In town centre.
The Schloss was the first baroque palace of such size to be built in Germany and with other buildings of the period forms the focal point of the town.

Freiheitsmuseum
History of national freedom movements and memorial to freedom fighters.

Wehrgeschichtlichesmuseum
West German national war history museum. (Above museums are in or close to the Schloss)

Schloss Favorite
In Förch 5km (3 miles) south-east of Rastatt.
A fine exhibition of porcelain and antique furniture in a baroque palace (1710).

Baden-Baden
Römische Badruinen
Römerplatz, in town centre.
Ruins of Roman baths.

Brahms Museum
Maximilianstrasse 85, in town centre.
Collection of manuscripts and other items connected with the composer.

Staatliche Kunsthalle
Lichtentaler Allee 8a, in town centre.
Works of art.

Kloster Lichtental
Hauptstrasse 40, in town centre.
Religious works of art, especially those connected with Cistercian Order.

Stadtmuseum
Küferstrasse 3, in town centre.
Collection relating particularly to the history of the town.

Autobahnkirche
On the A5 Autobahn at Baden-Baden *Raststätte.*
Modern church dedicated to St Christopher.

Ruine Yburg
6km (4 miles) south-west of town via Fremersbergstrasse
Outstanding viewpoint and marked walks.

Mummelsee
24km (15 miles) along road B500
Charming mountain lake.

Schloss Favorite, Förch

Kurhaus and casino, Baden-Baden

properties of the waters for more than 2,000 years, the Romans having carried out much development in the first 200 years AD. The ruins of the Roman baths are open for inspection from April to October.

Not much happened for some centuries after the Romans left but there was a revival of activity in the Middle Ages, especially after the illustrious Margrave Philipp I (1504-67) had taken the *Kur* from the distinguished Swiss physician Paracelsus, for the successful treatment of his rheumatism.

During this period, the thermal waters, welling up from a depth of 12-1500m (3,940-4,920ft) beneath the earth's crust, were led in channels through the alleys of the town for the steam to protect the inhabitants against the plague and cholera, though the level of success does not seem to be recorded. However, the turbulent times of the late seventeenth century did not leave Baden-Baden untouched and, when the town was sacked by the French in 1689, everything that would burn was set ablaze. Restoration took a long time and it was only after 1800 that the baths and healing streams became a significant part of the town's life again. Incidentally, the name really means Baden in Baden, and the present hyphenated form was adopted to distinguish it from numerous other 'Badens' throughout Europe. The town certainly revolves round its casino and the 'cure', but for the many visitors who are not attracted to these particular features, it is rich in well-kept parks, pleasant promenades and numerous buildings of historical or architectural interest.

The Lichtentaler Allee, a beautifully conceived sort of 'Rotten Row' close to the town centre, is a pleasant spot for a stroll. In addition to the Roman baths, there are no fewer than seven museums and art galleries in the town. Music lovers may enjoy exploring the archives of the Brahms Museum; others will find the religious works of art in the Kloster Lichtental of interest. (*Kloster* is another of those words which requires some explanation for there is no English word which exactly corresponds to it. It is a sort of omnibus German word meaning monastery, nunnery or convent. It seems to be used fairly loosely in describing religious buildings, even after their religious use has ceased.)

There are numerous possibilities for varied and attractive rambles within easy walking distance, such as in the idyllic Waldseetal with its trout pond, the climb to the 668m (2,191ft) high Merkur, or into the Wolfsschlucht (gorge) which provided Weber with the idea for a scene in his opera *Der Freischütz*. Six kilometres (4 miles) south-west of the town, the ruins of a castle called Yburg have splendid views of the countryside and make a worthwhile excursion. Beneath the Yburg is a *Wander-Parkplatz* with four short, round walks. The round walks based on the many *Wander-Parkplätze* need no detailed description as there is always a simple map at the parking place and each route is well-signed. The slight abbreviation *W-Parkplatz* will be used from now on.

Baden-Baden could be the place for an introductory Black Forest ramble of 14km (8$^1/_2$ miles) taking in the Ebersteinburg, which has already been mentioned. Start in the old town near the *Rathaus* and climb up the Staffelweg to the Neues Schloss for a view back over the town. Then follow the road for a few minutes until a marker stone points the way to the left along a shady footpath to the Altes Schloss, which can be reached comfortably in 1 hour. The extensive ruins date from the eleventh to fifteenth centuries and provide a broad vista over the Rhine plain.

Above the *Burgschenke* (inn), continue up through an arched gateway to the nearby Battertfelsen (rocks) and then follow the sign 'zum Oberen Felsenweg' and before long there is a view back over the castle ruins. When the path divides, do not take the left fork direct towards Ebersteinburg but keep to the right where it is possible to clamber up some of the many rocks and enjoy impressive views. These rocks are often used by climbers because they offer conditions seldom found in the Black Forest. The good track continues down some steps to a junction at the 'Hütte am unteren Felsenweg'. Here it is best to go along the route of (but not towards) the Engels - and Teufelskanzel (rocks — Angels' and Devils' pulpits), past some rather nice houses, direct into the village of Ebersteinburg. Go on to the ruin Alteberstein where there is a good outlook to the north.

From Ebersteinburg, go south beside the road towards Gernsbach or Gaggenau and at the end of the bus lay-by, immediately after the sign 'Zum Krankenhaus', walk to the right through the wood to the nearby Engelskanzel. Retrace your steps for about 20m (65ft) and follow a path (yellow bar waymark) through the woods and past more rocks to reach the obvious Hungerbergweg. Turn towards Baden-Baden and, after passing the Steinwaldhütte, one soon rejoins the outward route down to the Neues Schloss and returns to the starting point.

Another splendid tour is along road B500, the *Schwarzwaldhoch-*

A café in Baden-Baden

strasse (Black Forest High Road), which runs from Baden-Baden to Freudenstadt, a distance of rather less than 50km (31 miles), and one can make this slight deviation from the *Weinstrasse* if the weather is good. After climbing a series of steep, serpentine curves out of Baden-Baden, the road follows the crest of a ridge at a height of around 1,000m (3,280ft) until it descends into Freudenstadt. There are superb views on either side if the weather is clear.

After passing through Geroldsau, 5km (3 miles) from the start, there is no place of any size on this road. Hamlets such as Plättig, Sand, Hundseck and Unterstmatt are hardly noticeable unless one wishes to stop for a meal at one of the various hotels. One then reaches the large hotel at **Mummelsee** (*See* means lake) and may be astonished at the car parking space provided. The lake, 1,028m (3,372ft) above sea level, nestles at the foot of the 1,164m (3,820ft) Hornisgrinde in a delightful woodland setting. There are rowing boats for hire and an Old Father Neptune character tells the legends of the lake.

One story, recorded by the Jesuit Athanasius Kircher in his book of 1678, warns that any person throwing stones into the lake places his or her life in danger. Kircher tells how a Margrave from Baden came here with members of his court, including some religious advisers, and threw certain consecrated objects into the water. The reason for this action is not explained but a horrible monster suddenly emerged from the depths and chased the whole assembly from the shores. For seven days, the most violent storms imaginable raged around the spot. Needless to say, today's representative of the underwater world is a rather more benevolent character.

Apart from the summer scenery and the possibilities of walks along this ridge, the area also provides for winter sports; the settlements of Ruhestein, Alexander-Schanze and Kniebis are all devoted to skiing and associated activities. In fact, this area is at its busiest on fine winter weekends and what might have seemed in summer to be excessive car parking provision, is now filled to capacity as skiers converge upon the area from all directions. Both skiers and winter walkers make for the Vogelskopf 1,053m (3,454ft), the Schliffkopf 1,055m (3,460ft) and the Pfälzer Kopf 1,013m (3,322ft). There are also the less popular areas away from the main ski-runs where ramblers can soon find themselves totally isolated.

Down in the Rhine valley, there will be the first signs of spring while up here on the ridge, winter sports are still in full swing and the snow ploughs are still engaged in the task of keeping the roads clear. It is a delight on a cold winter's day to go into one of the many hostelries along the High Road for a bowl of warming soup or a glass of *Glühwein* (mulled wine) before continuing the outdoor activity. (A programme of winter sports package holidays is available from the German National Tourist Offices.)

The little resort of **Seebach** is not far from the Mummelsee, just off the ridge to the west on the road to Ottenhöfen. This is a popular place with nature lovers who can readily reach the various nature conservation areas along the *Hochstrasse*. Seebach and Ottenhöfen are both good starting points for a fairly strenuous ramble to the summit of the Hornisgrinde which is behind the Mummelsee. After Kniebis, the road descends towards Freudenstadt, which is to be visited in a later chapter.

The way must now be retraced to Baden-Baden to pick up the *Weinstrasse* again. In this area, the *Weinstrasse* never follows any one road for long but meanders to and fro in the best of the vineyard scenery. **Bühl** is reached 16km (10 miles) from Baden-Baden. The octagonal *Rathaus* tower and the nineteenth-century church of Saints Peter and Paul are worthy of inspection. The baroque church (1765) in the suburb of Kappelwindeck should also be seen.

A very worthwhile excursion can be made north-westwards from Bühl to **Schwarzach**, a distance of some 9km (5$^1/_2$ miles), where the former Benedictine Klosterkirche is to be seen. In the days long before the Rhine was as disciplined as it is today, a monastic cell was founded on an island in the river. Because the river changed its course or flooded new areas so often, the settlement had to move to firmer ground on the east bank in AD826.

Another move became necessary around 1200 when the present site was chosen. Following a fire, the present church was built in the then current Romanesque style in about 1220. The abbot allowed himself to be guided by influences from the *Klöster* at Hirsau and Gengenbach as well as from Alsace across the Rhine. Considering the resources available at the time, the resulting three-naved, cross-form basilica was a remarkable achievement.

In 1724, following periods of war and poverty, Peter Thumb, the distinguished architect and builder from the Austrian Vorarlberg region, was given the task of rebuilding the *Kloster* complex and improving the church. The interior was re-finished in the baroque style which was in vogue by then. The mighty high altar, now in the south transept, was built in 1752 by a Rastatt craftsman named Eigler. The choir stalls and the organ over the entrance are both eighteenth century, the latter having been supplied by the Strasbourg organ builder, Johann Andreas Silbermann.

In 1967, work started on a renovation of the church to remove some of the later additions and restore it to the more strict original form. The completion of this work has resulted in a church which is both dignified and exceedingly pleasing to the eye. Many of the eighteenth-century buildings survive and make the area around the church a pleasant backwater which certainly justifies the short diversion from the *Weinstrasse* or the *Autobahn* for a visit.

There is a fine ramble of 12km ($7^1/_2$ miles) from the Oberbühlertal up to the *Schwarzwaldhochstrasse* and back, taking in the wild and romantic Gertelbach waterfalls on the way. Just past the Hotel Schindelpeter, a little road goes down to the right to a car park in the valley. From there, follow the blue diamond waymark up the valley past the Café Waldhorn. The climb up steps and landings beside the waterfalls begins 20 minutes after passing the Restaurant-Café Gertelbach.

It takes about half an hour to reach the top of the falls, where there is a fork in the path. The waymark should be followed to the left to reach the imposing rocks, the Wiedenfelsen, in about 10 minutes. There is a hotel of the same name, immediately opposite which there is a sign 'Paradiesweg' pointing in the direction of Plättig. Follow the signs to gradually turn northwards and reach the Hotel Plättig on the Black Forest High Road in about half an hour. At the end of the car park, obey the sign 'Zur Hertahütte' but when the broad track goes right after about 5 minutes, keep straight on (sign 'Felsenweg'), climbing through the impressive labyrinth of the Falkenfelsen (rocks) to reach a good viewpoint at the Hertahütte. You will have been walking for some $2^1/_4$ hours.

Retrace steps towards the Falkenfelsen but now take a right fork past the massive Brockenfelsen. Just before reaching a wide track from Plättig, go down to the right at a sign saying 'Wiedenfelsen über Paradiesweg'. Then, almost immediately, on the edge of the wood, there is another sign indicating the way back down to the Bühlertal. This is along the so-called Briefträgerweg (postman's way). After a sharp left curve with a barrier and the sign 'Steinbruch' (quarry), leave the main track and climb up a woodland path marked with a blue spot and the number '10'. On reaching the first houses, go briefly right and then left down the road to the starting point. Total walking

Schwarzach, near Bühl

time for this circuit is around 3¹/₂ hours.

Returning to the *Weinstrasse* and continuing in a southerly direction, one reaches the ruins of Burg Altwindeck with a viewpoint back towards Bühl and over the Rhine valley. There is a *W-Parkplatz* at the castle with three round walks. The Burg Windeck hostelry lets a few rooms and there is a comfortable restaurant which is closed on Tuesdays. (Nearly all hotels and inns in Germany close on one day each week. This is the so-called *Ruhetag* or rest day.)

The *Weinstrasse* has wandered off to the vineyards in the Bühlertal (*Tal* means valley) east of the town but it comes down to touch Ottersweier briefly on main road B3 before returning to those behind Achern. In Achern itself there is a small museum which includes a collection of agricultural implements. However, it is only open on Sunday afternoons and not at all in January. The hotel Götz Sonne-Eintracht in the Hauptstrasse specialises in frogs' legs cooked in white wine and venison dishes in season. A modern railcar travels on the private Achertalbahn (Acher Valley Railway) which runs the 11km (7 miles) from Achern to Kappelrodeck and Ottenhöfen. However, on alternate Sundays from May to September, it is also possible to travel over this line in a carriage which may be 100 years old, hauled by a diminutive steam locomotive built at the turn of the century.

At Sasbachwalden, on a minor road east of Achern, there is a *W-Parkplatz* with five round walks. The walker will enjoy the splendid mixed woods with their many chestnut trees. **Sasbachwalden** is ✳ well-worth seeing anyway. It enjoys the title *Blumendorf* (flower village) and was picked out over twenty years ago as the most beautiful parish in the whole of Baden-Württemberg. It is now protected by a conservation order and when the flower-decked window sills of the old and new timbered houses are seen in summer, it is clear why the village achieved such renown.

The Brigittenschloss and the Burg Hohenrode (both eleventh- 🏰 century) occupy fine vantage points and, in clear weather, the granite hillocks provide a distant view of the tower of Strasbourg cathedral and of the mountain chain of the Vosges (Vogesen in German). The two little rivers, Sasbach and Brandbach, meet in the village and one can follow the course of the latter up through the rocky ravine called Gaishölle where there are many little waterfalls. 🦌 The famous *Spätburgunder* wine grapes are among those grown around the village with the greatest success.

Meanwhile, the *Weinstrasse* has reached the village of **Kappelrodeck** which is in a delightful situation; Rodeck castle was built in 🏰 the twelfth century. It is here that the Verein für Familienerholung in Deutschland (Assocation for Family Holidays) has one of its attractive self-catering villages. A little further on, Oberkirch (17,000 inhabitants) is reached and here the *Weinstrasse* crosses another of the named roads, the *Freundschaftstrasse* (Friendship road) running from Strasbourg across the Rhine to Freudenstadt and beyond. There are two *W-Parkplätze* near the main road (the B28) in the vicinity of Oberkirch. The first, called Moos, can be reached via the turning to Kalicutt and has five round walks of between 3 and 8km 🚶 (2 and 5 miles). The other is in Hubacker and can be reached over the railway bridge there. It too, has five walks, in this case of 2 to 6km (1 🚶 to 4 miles). Oberkirch is also the starting point for one of the marked long-distance paths, the 100km (62 miles) *Kandelhöhenweg*, which will be mentioned again in a later chapter.

Oberkirch is popular with wine connoisseurs who come to enjoy the local Renchtal wines — this is the commercial and cultural centre of the Upper Rench valley. The holiday visitor is well-catered for. There is a magnificent open-air swimming pool with sauna and solarium, the pleasant town gardens have a concert pavilion and there are children's playgrounds, as well as an animal enclosure. Tennis courts are also available and the ever popular mini-golf may be played.

The *Altstadt* — the old town centre — has been painstakingly restored and many of the streets are now for pedestrians only. The *Verkehrsamt* has produced a free, pocket-sized guide to the historic buildings and places of interest and the visitor should certainly make a couple of hours available for exploration of this charming old place. There is also ample accommodation in all categories.

Oberkirch lies right on the boundary between vineyards and forest. Downhill, into the Rhine valley, the vines appear to go on creating a gentle landscape as far as the eye can see; uphill to the east, the tree-clad slopes mark the start of the forest proper. The ruins of Schauenburg, high above the town, seem to be there to protect the idyllic scene. As the journey continues, this is a picture which will be constantly repeated.

There is a station at Oberkirch on the little branch line from Offenburg or Appenweier to Bad Griesbach so although the vineyards are soon left behind, it is appropriate at this stage to continue a little further up the Rench valley to the end of the line. Despite the presence of the railway and the rather busy B28, this is an entirely charming valley and the journey up it, especially by train, is one which can be recommended.

The village of **Lautenbach** is less than 4km (2^1/$_2$ miles) eastwards along the Friendship Road and has the Gothic pilgrimage church Maria Krönung (coronation of Mary) which was consecrated in 1493. Its origin can be traced back to a fourteenth-century pilgrimage. Two additional bays and the tower were added in 1895-7. The interior is lavishly decorated and has a net vault. A large lectern is supported by four columns and dates from 1488 while the Gnadenkapelle, from 3 years earlier, is where the sixteenth-century wooden image of the Blessed Virgin was kept. These are both noteworthy features, as are the pictures in the choir altar (1483 and 1510-20) and the fifteenth-century stained-glass windows. The choir stalls are the original ones from the time the church was built.

Just past Lautenbach, a minor road to the left leads to the tiny spa of Bad Sulzbach but the main road continues through pleasant scenery to reach the *Luftkurort* of **Oppenau** (population 3,000) in about 6km (4 miles). This little town, now slightly industrialised around the station, was developed by the Prämonstratensian monks from nearby Allerheiligen during the period from 1299 to 1319. Much of the place was later destroyed by fire but it was rebuilt in the years up to 1617 by a master builder named Schickhardt. Local history is on display in the *Heimatmuseum*.

From Oppenau, a minor road leads up through the Maisachtal and through Maisach to the little spa of Bad Antogast. Even today this is a pretty remote spot but the Romans discovered the healing springs here nearly two thousand years ago, making this the oldest of the several spas in this vicinity. A great peace reigns here and the visitor, whether he or she is taking the *Kur* or on holiday, will remain undisturbed by the noises usually associated with modern life.

This is perhaps the point at which to explain some of the terms used to describe the German resorts. A *Bad* is a spa at which curative treatment (the *Kur*) is based on the properties of thermal springs; a *Kurort* is also a place where treatment is available; a *Luftkurort* is a place where the air is particularly beneficial and a *Heilklimatischerkurort* bases the *Kur* on the healing properties of the climate generally. At a *Kneippkurort* the water treatments of Sebastian Kneipp are adopted. An *Erholungsort* specialises in recreation, recuperation and convalescence while a *Ferienort* is a general holiday resort.

Back on the B28, as it climbs towards the *Schwarzwaldhochstrasse*, is the double spa resort of **Bad Peterstal-Griesbach**, a well regarded convalescent centre. The mineral springs in Peterstal were also discovered in early times and the first documentary reference to what was then called 'St Peter im Tal' dates from 1290. The therapeutic qualities of the waters are valuable in the treatment of heart trouble, circulatory diseases, rheumatism, etc and the first spa hotel opened in 1584.

In order to protect the early aristocratic guests, a citizens' militia was founded and today the historic costumes of the little army are a great attraction at the various festivals in the Rench valley. Peterstaler Mineralwasser is excellent for table use and is bottled and exported all over the world. One would not, however, drink water from the associated sulphur spring for pleasure, although it is still used for medicinal purposes. The springs in **Griesbach** were discovered at about the same period, the first *Kurhaus* was built in 1579.

The bottling plant for the Griesbacher Mineralwasser is a short distance from the entrance to the valley of the Wilder Rench which leaves the main road at the east end of the village. There is a drinking

Places of Interest In and Around Bühl, Achern, The Rench Valley and Offenburg

Bühl
Rathaus (Town Hall)
Unusual octagonal tower.

Church of Saints Peter and Paul
Fine nineteenth-century building.

Baroque Church (1765)
In Kappelwindeck 3km (2 miles) south-east of Bühl.

Burg Altwindeck
4km (2$^1/_2$ miles) south-east of Bühl. Views of the Rhine valley.

Former Benedictine Klosterkirche
In Schwarzach 9km (5$^1/_2$ miles) north-west of Bühl
Romanesque church (1220) with later baroque treatment. Fine organ.

Achern
Sensen and Heimatmuseum
Berlinerstrasse 31.
Local relics with a collection of agricultural implements.

Achertalbahn
Steam railway from Achern to Kappelrodeck and Ottenhöfen.

Sasbachwalden
First floral village of Baden-Württemberg.

Brigittenschloss and *Burg Hohenrode* (Eleventh-century)
Splendid viewpoints above village.

Renchen
Memorials to famous writer J.J.C. von Grimmelshausen (1622-76)

Oberkirch
Altstadt
Well-restored old town centre with half-timbered houses.

Zum Silbernen Stern
North-east of town centre near church in Gaisbach
Traditional hostelry once owned by J.J.C. von Grimmelshausen.

Schauenburg
Castle ruins above town, with excellent views.

Lautenbach
Maria Krönung
Gothic pilgrimage church (1493). Lavishly decorated interior.

Offenburg
Catholic parish church of the Holy Cross
Consecrated in 1791. Splendid high altar and other furnishings.

Rathaus (1741)
Hauptstrasse
Baroque Town Hall with striking façade.

Königshof (1717)
Hauptstrasse
Another building with a fine baroque façade.

Former Franciscan Monastery Church
Lange Strasse
Beautifully maintained baroque church with fine Silbermann organ and furnishings.

Ortenberg
Schloss Ortenberg
4km (2$^1/_2$ miles) south-east of Offenburg
Ruins of twelfth-century castle rebuilt around 1840 in 'English' style.

Gengenbach
Medieval town in Kinzig valley 11km (7 miles) from Offenburg Many half-timbered houses, fountains and former *Klosterkirche* with baroque tower.

The Rench valley

fountain outside the little factory where the passer-by can sample the water. The traditional local costumes are often worn at weddings and other festivities in Bad Griesbach. The tiny St Antonius Kapelle can be reached by a path which goes up the hillside opposite the modern *Kurhaus*. From there one can wander gently upwards to the *Sprungschanze* (ski-jump) and there are open-air tennis courts close to the top of this, found by following signs for 'Tennis-Hütte'.

This resort in the popular Rench valley has excellent visitor facilities including indoor and outdoor swimming pools and a wide range of accommodation with many *Ferienwohnungen* (holiday flats). On the first Saturday in August the Summer Nights Festival is held, with illuminations and fireworks. There is also an easy and exceptionally picturesque walk of $4^1/_2$km ($2^3/_4$ miles) between the two parts of the resort.

At Griesbach station, go round behind the buffer stops and turn left, parallel with the line. Beyond the station area the path goes down to the bank of the river Rench — the waymarks to follow read 'Renchtalweg'. After a short while, the river and path pass beneath the railway under a fine arch. If one looks back from time to time, there are pretty views. On the outskirts of Peterstal, turn right over the river, cross the main road and go under the railway again to climb rather steeply up the slope the other side of the valley. After a short distance, turn left to follow a path through the woods along this slope with views down on to Peterstal. Watch for the sign 'Bahnhof' and turn left down the hill to Peterstal station.

The Wine Road route must be rejoined in Oberkirch but before going further south, it would be a good idea to follow the Rench valley a few kilometres down to **Renchen**, a little town on the B3, more concerned today with its breweries and timber workshops than with the tourist trade. However, the visitor will soon note that it is quite an attractive place and some of the surrounding villages are very pleasant indeed. The most famous son of Renchen is Johann Jakob Christoffel von Grimmelshausen (1622-76) the noted chronicler of the Thirty Years War, who told the story mainly through the adventures of his anti-hero, Simplicius Simplicissimus.

Grimmelshausen had a varied if not very long life, serving often in the rôle of writer or secretary to various military units. He came to Offenburg in 1649 after one period of service and married the 22-year old daughter of a cavalry sergeant-major from Saverne in Alsace and, as a result of this union, adopted the Catholic faith. He settled in Gaisbach on the outskirts of Oberkirch, where he was the official in charge of the Schauenburg properties but, perhaps partly because of his change of faith, his masters came to distrust him and he was dismissed. He then leased a fine manor-house and converted it to a wine hostelry called *Zum Silbernen Stern* (the Silver Star), an identity which the charming building beside the Gaisbach church has retained to this day.

Grimmelshausen was born and is buried in Renchen where he was the village mayor for the last 9 years of his life. An obelisk was erected in 1879 at his final resting place near the church; it looks more like a war memorial of the period with its stone palm branches and wreath of oak leaves. A more modern memorial is the bronze fountain cast by Giacomo Manzu of Rome and presented by one Dr Franz Burda (of the extensive Burda magazine empire) in 1977. Further reminders of the writer are to be found in the Renchen restaurant 'Zum Bären' (the Bear) where one room has been named the Grimmelshausen-Stube. His *Adventuresome Simplicissimus* was first published in 1668 and Simplicissimus has been adopted as the title of a German satirical periodical published in Munich since 1896.

The *Weinstrasse* winds down from Oberkirch towards Offenburg, into the heart of the vineyards. **Durbach** (population 3,700) is an important vineyard village with several hostelries serving good food which is complemented by the local wines. In particular, the tastefully decorated Gasthaus 'Zum Ritter', at the foot of Burg Staufenburg, is noted for its cuisine with Baden specialities — it has a Michelin 'star' — and wine from its own vines.

Staufenburg castle was originally built in the eleventh century. It was destroyed in 1689 and a new building was erected on the site in the nineteenth century. The Duke of Edinburgh is occasionally here as the guest of the Duke of Baden, who is the present owner of Staufenburg castle, much of which is normally open to the public. There are some rather good half-timbered houses in the main street, along which there is a pretty little river. In summer the bridges are a blaze of colour with boxes of flowers along the balustrades. Look out for some fine traditional farmhouses in the vicinity. For the guest there is fishing, tennis and mini-golf at hand.

Offenburg (population 50,000) is yet another fringe town, standing, like Rastatt, astride a Black Forest river flowing westwards to the Rhine. The river Kinzig has come through the beautiful Kinzigtal from Freudenstadt. Offenburg is a stopping place for many of the trains on the main line south to Basel and is also an interchange station for trains up and down the Rhine valley, into the Rench valley, and over the Rhine to Strasbourg (half an hour). It forms the western extremity of the *Schwarzwaldbahn* (Black Forest Railway) which runs through the Kinzig and Gutach valleys eastwards to Donaueschingen, with many trains going through to Konstanz on the Bodensee (Lake Constance). There are also many bus routes to outlying villages. All this makes it an ideal centre for the traveller reliant upon public transport.

Offenburg itself has numerous places of interest and the first-time visitor would do well to arm him- or herself with the English language guide and town map obtainable free from the *Verkehrsamt* at Gärtnerstrasse 6, just behind the Hauptstrasse. The Catholic parish church of the Holy Cross, with its dominant three-storey tower, was erected under the influence of the Vorarlberg architectural school. After a period of building lasting nearly 100 years, it was

Church of the Holy Cross, Offenburg

consecrated in 1791. The splendid high altar was created by Franz Lichtenauer in 1740 and the left side choir houses a Renaissance crucifix dating back to 1521. The Protestant town church in the Hauptstrasse has an ornate steeple and was built in neo-Gothic style between 1857 and 64.

At the south end of the Hauptstrasse are several places of interest in close proximity. The baroque *Rathaus* of 1741 has a fine façade; above the balcony are the town coat of arms and the Austrian double-headed eagle, reflecting the allegiance of the town at the time of its construction. Opposite, in the little square called Fischmarkt, the painted front of the Hirsch Apotheke has many amusing features; the lion fountain outside dates from 1599.

The old coaching inn 'Hotel Sonne', next to the *Rathaus*, dates back to 1350 but, like nearly everything else in the town, it was completely destroyed at the hands of the French in the great fire of 1689. It was reconstructed almost at once and is, therefore, the oldest existing hotel in Offenburg. The courtyard where the horses were changed now serves as the hotel car park and the former stables are now garages and store rooms. Inside there is a fine baroque staircase and the main public rooms have magnificent tiled stoves which are still in regular use, although today they are supplemented by modern central heating. A small picture is a reminder that von Grimmelshausen was a guest here at one time.

Immediately after the 'Sonne' is the Landratsamt or Königshof, a fine baroque building with a very ornamental façade. It was built in 1717 under the instructions of the Margravine Sybilla Augusta, of whom mention has already been made, and it now houses the police headquarters. Nearby, in the centre of the street, is the Ursula Column, one of several modern sculptures in the town. It was created in 1961 by the sculptor Emil Sutor and was a gift from Dr Franz Burda, who is an honorary citizen. St Ursula is the patroness of the town and is said to have appeared on the walls in 1638 to ward off an attack by the troops of Duke Bernhard of Weimar.

At the other end of the town, not far from the station, the former Franciscan monastery now houses a girls' school. It too was rebuilt after the great fire of 1689. The beautiful baroque church has a massive wooden altar, a Silbermann organ and carved choir stalls. In St Mary's chapel there is a late-Gothic wooden Madonna. The church is attractively decorated inside and should be included in every visitor's itinerary. Access is through the entrance hall, beyond which there is a wrought iron screen with a bell-push. One of the girls acts as doorkeeper and, upon being summoned, will open the gate in the screen for the visitor to pass through into the church itself. There is no charge.

This only represents a small selection of the places of interest in a compact town. Most of the Hauptstrasse (main street) is a spacious pedestrian zone lined with departmental stores and other shops. The accommodation in the town itself is almost entirely in the hotel category. There is a pleasant little park outside the walls alongside the river Kinzig and this leads into the Bürgerpark where the *Freibad* and *Hallenbad* are situated. The Stadtwald (town forest) just west of the town has several parking places, one of which is adjacent to a *Trimm-Dich* (keep fit) circuit. There are many pleasant walks through the woods; the visitor without his or her own transport can walk from the town centre (a detailed description of the route in English is available from the *Verkehrsamt*) to the far side of the Stadtwald and back in about 4 hours, or make the journey one way by bus.

Offenburg, like other towns of its size, can pose car-parking problems. Although most of the Black Forest towns which the visitor will visit are comparatively small, narrow streets, markets and agricultural activities can contribute to a significant traffic problem. The casual motoring tourist is advised to leave the car on the outskirts rather than face the harassment of parking in the centre.

Since starting the journey down the *Weinstrasse*, the visitor has had ample choice of fairly short walks, mostly demanding no more than modest effort. For those who require something more exciting, a 5-day ramble is organised by the Ortenauer Weinseminar, Gärtnerstrasse 6, 7600 Offenburg (the *Verkehrsamt*). The tour, called *'Fröhliche Weinwanderung'* (merry wine ramble), starts in Baden-Baden. It follows the Ortenauer Weinpfad (Ortenau Wine Path), more or less parallel with the *Weinstrasse*, by way of Unterbühlertal, Sasbachwalden, Kappelrodeck, Oberkirch, Offenburg and Gengenbach to Diersburg.

The walkers travel light, their luggage being forwarded between the good hotels used by the organisation. Walking time is between 4 and 6 hours each day, leaving ample time to sample the various wines along the way. The total distance to be covered is about 100km (62 miles) and the terrain traversed does not exceed the 'moderately strenuous' category. The route is full of interest; the vineyards as well as picturesque castles and historic towns are visited en route.

Not every walker will wish to commit him- or herself to the whole of the ramble mentioned but a most pleasant 1 day walk of 16km (10 miles) along the *Weinpfad* can be started in Offenburg. Go south from the *Rathaus* along the Hauptstrasse and at the end turn left through the rose garden until reaching the end of Lange Strasse. Here, in a fine
 group of trees, is a memorial to Carl Isenmann who set Ludwig Auersbach's poem *O Schwarzwald, o Heimat* to music.

Go forward over the railway bridge and cross the road to go to the right along Ortenberger Strasse for about 700m (765 yards) to the junction left to Fessenbach. Follow this road for about 1km ($^1/_2$ mile) and about 200m before the first houses of Fessenbach turn right onto a surfaced track rising slightly for about 500m (547yd) to reach the *Weinstrasse*. Cross this road and go straight ahead into Senator-Burda-Strasse, past a *Kloster* and the vineyards and estate house of Dr Burda. Then turn sharply right into the heart of the vineyards, following the Ortenau Wine Path (bunch of grapes waymark) along surfaced roads until Schloss Ortenberg is approached.

The castle is now a youth hostel and the experimental station for vine cultivation in the Ortenau district. Turn left 150m (164yd) before the castle and continue through the terraces until, descending slightly, one passes through a pair of former gate pillars marking an estate boundary. Keep to the left here and almost at once turn back to the right, up through woods and before long on to an unsurfaced track which goes round the top of a quarry. Continue down towards the hamlet of Büchen and then follow waymarks '5', which pass mostly through woods, until coming out into the vineyards of Ohlsbach, which is the village below. Ahead will be seen a little red- roofed chapel called Maria im Weinberg, built as recently as 1985 by the Karl Wacker family in fulfilment of an old vow. Visit the chapel and then walk straight down into the village.

It will have taken $2^1/_2$ to 3 hours from Offenburg so this is a good place to stop for refreshment in one of several hostelries. Leave Ohlsbach via Weissenbachstrasse to the Waldcafé, past the recrea- tion area to footpath No 1. The route forks to the right above the cemetery down via 'Holzer Eck' to the Reichenbach school. Cross the valley road and continue past the sports field to the few houses at a corner called Sanktis Klaus and turn right. Continue on the path parallel with the road as long as possible but eventually walk on the road itself down into Gengenbach past the Geschwister-Scholl- Schule and into the old town through the Oberer Tor. The total time from Offenburg is 5 to 6 hours. There is a reasonably frequent train service from Gengenbach station back into Offenburg and buses are also available.

From Offenburg, the *Weinstrasse* now swings up into the Kinzig- tal, following the north bank of the river to reach the village of **Ortenberg** in 4km ($2^1/_2$ miles). The impressive Schloss Ortenberg overlooks the valley and occupies the site of a twelfth-century castle. It was reduced to ruins when this part of the country was overrun by French soldiers in 1678, suffering the fate of many similar fortifica- tions which originally guarded the valley entrances. The rubble lay around until 1840 although much of it was removed to be used as building material by the local population. However, funds were then made available for the building of a new 'English' style castle which, after many changes, eventually became the youth hostel and experi- mental station which it is today.

The *Schloss* provides a wonderful viewpoint. Immediately below

The town hall,
Gengenbach

The main square,
Gengenbach

are vineyard slopes and the village; towards the Rhine are extensive orchards and the city of Offenburg with its housing and industrial areas, while across the Rhine, the distant tower of Strasbourg cathedral may perhaps be seen.

In another 7km (4 miles), **Gengenbach** is reached; an immediately attractive, medieval town which makes a pleasant overnight stop or a longer stay. The centre of the walled town makes visitors feel as if they are back in the Middle Ages. The market place is surrounded by delightful timbered houses, and a fountain is a reminder that until 1803 this town had 'free' status; it had bought itself out of obligations to local dukes and sundry other noblemen and owed allegiance only to the crown. The nobility frequently used this as a means of raising capital when times were hard, but all such 'arrangements' were finally cancelled by law in 1803. Roman remains have been found in the area and a Benedictine Kloster was founded here in the eighth century. The building itself, rebuilt in 1695 after a fire, today houses an educational establishment.

The former Klosterkirche, now the main church of Gengenbach, has a fine baroque tower but the garish interior decor is somewhat disturbing. The writer and folklore researcher Ernst Sutter lived here in the house 'Zum Löwen' which now, appropriately, houses the *Heimatmuseum*. It is through Sutter's efforts, ably supported by the *Bürgermeister* of the day, that the historic townscape has remained unsullied by obtrusive advertisement hoardings and the like, to charm us today. This delightful little town has an air of sparkling cleanliness, with carefully restored buildings and a riot of flowers, making it a much photographed place. It is a centre of pre-Lenten festivities when the masked fools take over the town.

Leaving Gengenbach, one travels back down the other side of the river on road B33 towards Offenburg, but before then the *Weinstrasse* leaves the main road to turn south through the vineyard villages of Zunsweier and Diersburg to rejoin road B3 at Schopfheim. This main road is now followed for some 40km (25 miles) but the unchanging landscape and succession of villages devoted to the wine industry does not provide very much new interest.

There are few walking opportunities along this section of the route. However, Lahr, a town of about 36,000 inhabitants, has a *W-Parkplatz* which is the starting point for a walk through the vineyards and around the Schutterlindenberg, a modest hill with a splendid outlook. The Protestant church in **Lahr**, the former St Peter's Church,

stands on a site where there has been a religious building of some
kind since the eighth century. The former collegiate church in the
same town was spoiled by unsympathetic restoration work in the
middle of the nineteenth century but a choir from the original
thirteenth-century building has survived.

The *Neues Rathaus* has a beautiful colonnaded hall in the upper
storey. It was originally built in 1808 as a town house for the Lotzbeck
family. There are late baroque, rococo, classical and Biedermeier
houses in the town, one of the most important being the Stoessersches Haus (1783) at No 41 Kaiserstrasse. The Geroldsecker Museum
is in the Storchenturm which is all that remains of the *Burg* which
Walter von Geroldseck built in 1250.

Road B415 runs eastwards from Lahr through the Schuttertal
and, after a couple of kilometres, it reaches the little village of
Kuhbach which contains a sight worth seeing in its tiny old church
of St Gallus. It was built about 1300 and has the remains of medieval
wall paintings in the choir. At some later date the original tower was
removed, probably because it was unstable, and it was replaced by
the pretty little turret seen on the roof today. Used for some time for
school children's services only, the church authorities now seek to
obtain financial support from the state in order to protect and
preserve this historic building and restore it to its original use as a
cemetery chapel. Twelve kilometres ($7^1/_2$ miles) south-west of Lahr
between the *Autobahn* and the Rhine, there is the leisure centre called
Europapark Rust which has many attractions for children.

Ten kilometres (6 miles) south of Lahr, it is necessary to leave the
main road for a kilometre or so to visit **Ettenheim** (population 8,000).
This is a former place of residence of the Prince-Bishops of Strasbourg. A brief visit here would be particularly rewarding; there is an
imposing baroque church, splendidly flanked by a number of attractive Renaissance and rococo buildings.

If the picturesque road is followed for a further 6km (4 miles)
beyond Ettenheim, one reaches **Ettenheimmünster** which is situated in grand rambling country with at least four *W-Parkplätze* within
2km ($1^1/_4$ miles) of the village. The first of these is reached 1km ($^1/_2$
mile) up a road which goes south for 1km before reaching the village
and has three round walks. Near the *Kloster* at the west end of the
village, take the Lautenbachstrasse for 1km to a parking place with
a marked walk of 8km (5 miles). A kilometre past the *Kloster* and at
the east end of the village, a minor road goes due east alongside a

stream to a car park with a round walk of 4.5km (3 miles).

Yet another easily accessible *W-Parkplatz* is on the main road beyond the village close to the first sharp bend of the zig-zag road which climbs into the hills and has numerous further opportunities for *parken und wandern* along the next 8km (5 miles). This is an area which will be dealt with in more detail in a later chapter.

Kenzingen, 10km (6¹/₄ miles) south of Ettenheim, has the typical oval layout of many towns in this area which were planned by, or in imitation of, the towns founded by the dukes of the Zähringen dynasty in the twelfth century. This delightful little town — the population is only about 8,000 — presents a medieval face to the world and it is not easy to detect that many of the buildings were, in fact, only built or rebuilt following a disastrous fire in the nineteenth-century. However, the seventeenth-century building styles were faithfully reproduced so that the new and old blended together harmoniously.

The *Rathaus* was built in 1550 and there are three pretty fountains nearby, typical again of the 'Zähringen' towns. At No 20 Alte Schul-strasse, the Verbande Oberrheinischer Narrenzünfte (Association of Upper Rhine Fools' Clubs) has a colourful exhibition of the artefacts of the Alemannic *Fasnet* — masks and costumes as well as 230 life-size 'fools' figures. The parish church of St Laurenzius was built about 1275; it has wall paintings dating from about 1300 and some viewable sixteenth-century gravestones.

Because so much of Black Forest folklore, particularly the pre-Lenten *Fasnet* or carnival celebrations, is bound up with the Aleman-nic origins of much of the population, some words of explanation may not come amiss. There is a distinct Alemannic dialect which crosses national and ethnic boundaries and is to be found in Alsace, in German-speaking Switzerland and in the Vorarlberg of Austria as well as in the south-western corner of Germany which includes the Black Forest.

All this results from the history of the Alemannians, which goes back to the third century. About that time, tribes known as the Sueben (or Sweben) banded together with others as the *'alle Mannen'* (all men), and this was the title by which they were known until about the year 1000. In AD213 they started to move against the Roman garrisons on German soil and, 47 years later, finally suc-ceeded in ending Roman domination. From the year 1000, the term *Alemannen* ceased to be used in German speaking regions but was

Places of Interest In and Around Lahr, Ettenheim and Kenzingen

Lahr
Neues Rathaus (1808)
Former family house. Colonnaded hall in upper storey.

Stoessersches Haus (1783)
Kaiserstrasse 41
One of several fine town houses representing the baroque, rococo, classical and Biedermeier styles.

Geroldsecker Museum
In the Storchenturm
All that remains of the castle of 1250.

St Gallus' Church
In Kuhbach, east of Lahr town centre. Built about 1300; medieval wall paintings.

Europapark Rust
12km (7½ miles) south-west of

Lahr
Modern family leisure centre.

Ettenheim
'Baroque' town with church and attractive Renaissance and rococo buildings.

Kenzingen
Typical Zähringen dynasty town.

Rathaus (1550)
Three attractive fountains nearby.

Exhibition of masks, costumes, etc of 'Fasnet'
At Alte Schulstrasse 20

Parish church of St Laurenzius (about 1275)
Several items of interest with wall paintings from about 1300.

adopted in the Latin languages as the general name for the whole German area. This has persisted until today as in Allemagne (French) and Alemania (Spanish).

The great dialect poet, Johann Peter Hebel (1760-1826) re-awakened interest in the old language and in the unity of the people able to converse in it. The old customs and language are now safeguarded by several dedicated organisations and the museum in Kenzingen is a fine place in which to find out more about this interesting background; a visit there is especially rewarding.

Continue following road B3 to Malterdingen, where it is necessary to leave it and turn west towards Riegel; here the Leopoldskanal connecting Freiburg with the Rhine is crossed. Ahead there is a fantastic conglomeration of vineyards on the hill, or rather cluster of hills, called the Kaiserstuhl. This is a volcanic hump rising abruptly from the Rhine plain to a height of 557m (1,827ft), encircled by a loop of the Wine Road and dotted with numerous small communities, all working feverishly to produce what they claim are the best wines of the *Weinstrasse*. One thing is certain; the remarkable climate experienced here does give them a very good chance of achieving their aim.

Riegel is the starting place for a leisurely journey in the *Rebenbummler*, a train — complete with well-stocked wine bar — which potters through the vineyards to Breisach. In the *Rathaus*, which dates from 1784, there is an exhibition of finds from the area, principally from Roman times. The baroque St Martin's-Kirche is also worth seeing.

Going round the Kaiserstuhl in an anti-clockwise direction, one soon reaches the very attractive little town of **Endingen**, its fine towers straddling the road. This is an excellent place for an introduction to rambling on the Kaiserstuhl, for not only is the *W-Parkplatz* the starting point for round walks of 2-10km (1-6$^1/_4$ miles) but there are five further parking places on the circular footpath network. With Breisach, Burkheim and Endingen represent the urban element of the Kaiserstuhl.

The Gothic and baroque citizens' houses of Endingen fit comfortably into a townscape with charming squares and streets. The main public buildings are of a high quality; the early Renaissance *Kornhaus* (1417), the old *Rathaus* (1527) in Gothic and baroque and the new *Rathaus* in rococo style are grouped around the market place with its *Ratsbrunnen* (fountain) in the centre of the town. Architectural styles from late-Romanesque to that of Louis XVI are incorporated in the Peterskirche while St Martin unites Gothic elements from the fourteenth century with nineteenth-century replicas. There is a *Gnadenbild* (miraculous image) of the weeping Mother of God. A recommended short ramble is to the Katharinenkapelle on the Katharinaberg 492m (1,615ft) — a distance of 8km (5 miles) there and back.

The Katharinenkapelle may also be visited during a rather more ambitious, circular walk of 15km (9$^1/_2$ miles) starting in the village of Oberbergen, and taking in a good selection of Kaiserstuhl scenery and several fine viewpoints in an area that is not so dominated by the vineyards. Leave Oberbergen by the church on the road to Kiechlinsbergen and, after about 15 minutes, reach the first big serpentine curve and look for a path to the right near the 100m stone '4'. This leads up to the Waldparkplatz 'Auf dem Eck' and from here the waymark of the long-distance Querweg Schwarzwald-Rhein (red diamond on yellow ground) can be followed eastwards. The path goes gently up and down with pretty views and, in about 1 hour from the 'Eck', the Katharinenkapelle 492m (1,615ft) is reached, with the first view to the north.

There is a kiosk here where it may be possible to buy drinks but apart from this, provisions for the whole tour should be carried. Go down to the right following signs 'Eichelspitze-Neunlinden-Toten-kopf' and in 15 minutes, on the grassy ridge called Schönebene, there are views left to the Black Forest and right to the Vosges across the Rhine. From the slopes of the Eichelspitze 500m (1,640ft), can be seen the Naturschutzgebiet Badberg which lies to the right. The Parkplatz Vogelsang is soon reached and this marks the start of a climb through woods to the Neunlinden tower at 555m (1,820ft) which may be ascended for an even better vista.

Leave the north-south way in the dip between here and the television mast on the nearby Totenkopf, and follow a path marked by a green spot until you return to the starting place in 45 minutes. Although no great altitudes are attained, the undulating nature of this walk means that there is a total climb of more than 500m (1,640ft) and this should be borne in mind when planning the outing. Because of the exposed nature of much of the route, this walk is not recommended during stormy or very hot weather.

The next place of interest is **Sasbach** on the banks of the Rhine. The ferry which formerly provided the link across the river to France was replaced by a temporary Bailey bridge after the war. After many years of service, this has been replaced in its turn by a fine, modern road bridge, the frontier formalities being on the French side. The natural river here is bypassed by the Rhine-Rhône Canal in France which is used by all through shipping traffic, leaving the noble Rhine to become a rather forlorn lagoon with boats for hire and steamer trips. Pictorial displays near the riverside car park describe the history and progress of the canalisation.

Throughout its length, the *Weinstrasse* is identified by special signs at junctions and from time to time by small plaques bearing the symbol of a bunch of grapes. The section round the Kaiserstuhl is no exception and there is no difficulty in following the route. There are several *W-Parkplätze* along the way but the similarity of the vineyard landscape does not make this very attractive walking territory — it is more suited to mechanised touring. Although the Kaiserstuhl may

Places of Interest on the Kaiserstuhl and in Emmendingen

Riegel to Breisach
Railway with historic steam train, *Rebenbummler*

Endingen
Attractive town with fine towers.

Kornhaus (1617)
Early Renaissance style.

Altes Rathaus (1527)
Gothic and baroque

Neues Rathaus
Rococo style.

All these buildings grouped around the *Ratsbrunnen* (fountain) in the town centre.

Churches of St Peter and St Martin
Both buildings combine a variety of architectural styles.

Sasbach
Rhine bridge to France. Boating on the river.

Bischoffingen
Protestant church
Excellent wall paintings.

Burkheim
Rathaus
Renaissance building comple-mented by timbered houses.

St Pankratius-Kirche
Wall paintings and stained glass.

Schwendi-Schloss
Mighty Renaissance ruin.

Niederrotweil
St Michael's Catholic Church
Very impressive late-Gothic high altar. Important wall paintings from about 1500.

Achkarren
Museum of vine culture

Breisach
Minster with outstanding high altar. Oldest parts from about 1200. Views over Rhine.

Oberschaffhausen
Church of St Alban
Outstanding fifteenth-century frescos.

Emmendingen
Parish Church
Fifteenth-century altar.

Alten Friedhof (Old cemetery)
Graves of Goethe's sister Cornelia and the aviator Carl Friedrich Meerwein.

Heimatmuseum
Housed in former *Schloss* Town history and memorabilia of Goethe and works of painter, Fritz Boehle.

Rathaus (1729)

Museumbahnhof
Wolfratsreuter Strasse
Small collection of historic rail vehicles.

Endingen, on the Kaiserstuhl

not be ideal for general rambling, it is an area of great significance to geologists and naturalists who find much here to stimulate their various interests.

Abandoned quarries are a rich source of finds for the amateur mineral collector and have been described by one writer as providing a window on earth history. The geological diversity also gives rise to variety in the flora and fauna; unusual species are found in quantities rarely seen in Germany. Of the fifty-five types of orchids known in the Federal Republic, no less than thirty-three are to be found on the Kaiserstuhl. Birds and butterflies more common in a Mediterranean environment can also be found here.

The visitor wishing to see a selection of the many places of interest on the Kaiserstuhl could hardly do better than to follow the 40km (25 miles) *Weinstrasse* circuit and what follows could provide the basis for a suitable itinerary.

Continuing southwards parallel with the Rhine, the visitor will pass through many pleasant vineyard villages and may often be tempted to stop and take photographs or sample the local wine. The very fine wall paintings in the Protestant church in **Bischoffingen** include scenes from the childhood and suffering of Christ, with portrayals of the prophets and apostles.

Burkheim stands lovely and romantic on a spur of the Kaiserstuhl running towards the Rhine and is dominated by the mighty Renaissance ruin of the Schwendi-Schloss. The town has some fine timbered houses and a Renaissance *Rathaus*. In the St Pankratius-Kirche, the vault under the late-Gothic tower has evangelical symbols from the mid-sixteenth century, with St Michael and the martyrdom of St Ursula in the windows.

A stop should certainly be made in **Niederrotweil** to visit the Catholic church of St Michael where the late-Gothic high altar is an outstanding work by an anonymous master craftsman known only by his initials, H.L. The altar depicts the coronation of Mary who is flanked by St Michael and John the Baptist. The inner panel reliefs include St Michael with a balance for weighing souls, the fall of the damned and the beheading of John the Baptist. The wall paintings in the choir date from about 1500 and show Christ with the four evangelical symbols and St Michael again, while the side walls have the figures of the apostles and scenes from the New Testament. The paintings represent the start of important fresco cycles in the churches of the Kaiserstuhl.

Achkarren is a typical wine village in an excellent location. Nearby is the Schlossberg 352m (1,155ft), with the ruins of Höhingen castle. At the foot of the south-west corner of the Kaiserstuhl is the little town of Breisach with Neuf Brisach across the Rhine in France. The main road (B31) eastward from Breisach is the *Grüne Strasse* (green road) and this runs west to east from the Rhine to the Bodensee (Lake Constance).

The Minster in **Breisach** occupies a commanding position with a fine view. Despite having survived many wars and political upheavals, the church, which is dedicated to St Stephan, had to be completely rebuilt after World War II. This was done so skilfully that it is impossible to distinguish between parts which are original and those which are of modern construction. For practical purposes, the building which can be admired today is that which dates from about 1200, when the nave, transepts and east towers were built. The choir and the west bay date from 1300-30 while the vaulting, sacristy and interior furnishings are fifteenth-century. The addition of the choir made the *Münster* into a hall church.

Rebuilding in the fifteenth century accentuated the Gothic elements and each of the symmetrical towers has a Romanesque and a more elaborate Gothic section. In addition, a North Italian influence can be detected in the Romanesque nave. The late-Gothic choir screen (about 1500) and the monumental fresco by M. Schongauer in the west hall are of note but the most valuable interior fitment is the famous Breisach altar, another work of that master known simply as H.L. It dates from 1523-6 and the Madonna appears on the central shrine between God the Father and Christ. The martyrs Stephan and Laurentius can be seen on one side panel and the town's patrons, Gervasius and Protasius, on the other. Their bones are in a silver shrine in the church treasury.

From Breisach, the circuit of the Kaiserstuhl is continued by travelling north-eastwards through Ihringen, a wine community with a history documented back to AD962. Fruit trees grow here as well as vines and it is a favourite place to visit in spring when they are in blossom. The outwardly homely little church of St Alban in **Oberschaffhausen** is the place where the artistic pinnacle of the early wall paintings was reached. The frescos were created between 1477 and 81 and the portrayals are the most extensive in the region of the Kaiserstuhl. The realistically carved *Pestkreuz* (plague cross) above the altar is most impressive. It is also worth making a final stop in the village of **Eichstetten** which has some fine timbered houses and a bridge dating from 1556.

The first-time visitor may have been surprised by the vastness of the Kaiserstuhl vineyards and a few words about the wines of the area may not come amiss. It is not known exactly when viticulture was started on the Kaiserstuhl and the nearby sunny slopes on the east side of the Rhine. It seems probable that the Romans were responsible for introducing the vines but the first documentary evidence on the subject does not appear until the eighth century. The traveller who has been following the Wine Road may have become aware by now of the great variety of wines produced. This is due mainly to the number of grape varieties used but is also influenced by the nature of the ground in which they are grown, the varying climatic conditions from place to place and the methods employed by the various growers.

There are eight classic grapes and numerous new crosses; of the former, the *Riesling* is widely grown and produces an elegant white wine. The *Ruländer* is also very common and from it comes a fiery wine with a fulsome bouquet. A light, slightly prickly wine comes from a *Ruländer* mutation known as *Weisse Burgunder* while earthy wines, with almost a hint of rose-scent, stem from the *Traminer* and *Gewürztraminer* varieties. However, it is the *Müller-Thurgau* which is grown most extensively and produces a light wine with a hint of nutmeg which should be drunk young. The *Silvaner* grape, on the other hand, is not as widely grown as it used to be. The *Gutedel* is only grown in the Markgräflerland south of the Kaiserstuhl and produces grapes for dessert as well as for wine.

So much for white wines; the growers claim that the wine made from the grapes of the blue *Spätburgunder* is the finest red wine in the world. Newer grape varieties which may be found on bottle labels include *Scheurebe, Nobling, Huxel* and *Bacchus*. The visitor will find plenty of opportunities for tasting and buying wine. The signs to look for are *Weinproben* (tastings) and *Weinverkauf* (sales); many vineyards and wine co-operatives have facilities for tasting on weekdays (only in the morning on Saturday). One should not expect wine from these sources to be appreciably cheaper than in the supermarkets but the prospective purchaser will have a greater variety from which to choose and the satisfaction of trying before buying. The previous notes may give him or her a little help in deciding what to taste.

A selection of addresses for tastings and sales which are readily accessible from Freiburg is given in the Useful Information section of this book. Wine festivals take place from about the end of June (Freiburg) through into September. The visitor here during the wine harvest should certainly try the new wine, with which it is the custom to eat warm onion-cakes.

Leave the Kaiserstuhl area by continuing to Teningen just beyond the north-south *Autobahn* A5. Rejoin the main route of the *Weinstrasse* (B3) and turn right towards **Emmendingen**. Here it is worth pausing to visit the parish church and inspect the *Flügelaltar*. This is a carved altar piece in three sections with folding wings, dating from about 1470, although the church itself is nineteenth century. In any event, Emmendingen is a good centre with excellent tourist facilities and provides a suitable base for exploring the area. Goethe was particularly fond of this district and wrote about it in glowing terms. His sister Cornelia lived and died here; her grave can be seen in the *Alten Friedhof* (old cemetery), which is also the resting place of the German flying pioneer Carl Friedrich Meerwein.

The former *Schloss* was the *Residenz* of the Margraves of Baden and now houses the *Heimatmuseum* which deals with the history of

The town centre of Emmendingen

the town and has memorabilia of Goethe and works of the painter, Fritz Boehle. The *Rathaus*, dating from 1729, and the eighteenth-century town gate are also worth seeing. The nearby Hochburg is one of the best preserved castles in the area. The *Weinstrasse* continues as the B3 towards Freiburg and soon becomes a very busy highway leading into the city centre.

South of Freiburg

Freiburg is described fully in a later chapter and the city can be bypassed by using the *Autobahn* between the Freiburg *Nord* and *Süd* junctions, resuming exploration of the Wine Road south of the city on road B3 at Ebringen. The vineyard route soon leaves the main road and saunters off past Pfaffenweiler to the little town of Ehrenkirchen.

The *Weinstrasse* may be left here for an excursion 4km (2½ miles) to the south-east of Bollschweil where there is an entrance to a narrow, steep-sided valley. The little river Möhlin can be followed through this to the hamlet of **St Ulrich**, a further 4km away. This picturesque journey is worthwhile in its own right but there is a bonus at St Ulrich in the rich stucco work of the baroque church of the former Benediktinerkloster, another work of the Vorarlberger, Peter Thumb. A Romanesque font can also be seen; this was formerly in the parsonage garden and is now to be found inside an ornamental gate just to the left of the church.

The next place of interest is **Staufen,** at the entrance to the Münstertal. This little town has a folk and costume museum worthy of a visit. The old Gasthaus 'Löwen' (Lion) has tales of the legendary Dr Faustus and even a Faust room to substantiate them. The death of this mysterious character is colourfully portrayed on the front wall of the 'Löwen' where there is a brief description of the event. The area around Staufen was already settled in prehistoric times from which there have been some interesting finds indicating early defensive works.

Already, in AD770, there was a documentary reference to the place but the formal founding of the town only took place in 1280. Later inhabitants had to put up with the plague, famine and witchcraft as well as the warlike activities of their neighbours, who were often anxious to get access to the silver mines in the Münstertal. The ruins of the Staufenburg are now surrounded by vineyard slopes. It was erected to discourage this pillaging but the castle was burned down in 1632 by the Swedes, who then went on to plunder the town. In the period 1689-90, the French virtually pulled the town apart and set it on fire. Later, the French Revolution and World War II both left their marks and it is clear that the beautiful façade of the *Rathaus,* built in 1546, is only there today because of painstaking restoration after all these damaging events.

Even before receiving its charter, this was an important settlement on one of the main routes eastwards into the Forest and the little man on the octagonal market fountain is a reminder of the market rights once held here. The late-Gothic church of St Martin is worth seeing and there is an international music festival each summer. On the south-eastern outskirts of Staufen along the Münstertal road, there is a camping and caravan site popular with English-speaking visitors, and a pleasant but unheated open-air swimming pool nearby.

In the village of **Grunern** near Staufen, at the vineyard of the Koeppler family, there is a private museum which has an interesting collection of historic tools and equipment associated with winemaking. The vineyard has been owned by the same family for seven generations but some of the items on display go back to the sixteenth century. The most impressive item is the 4m (13ft) high and 10m (33ft) long *Torkelbaum* (wine press) with massive stone weights bearing the date 1578. This machine was in use pressing the local grapes until after World War II.

After Staufen, the *Weinstrasse* divides, the left fork leading to the village of **Sulzburg**. In fact, it rather likes to think of itself as a 'town', having received its town charter as far back as 1250. It has not grown much since and has the distinction of being known as the tiniest town in the state.

Sulzburg is a surprise, for here in this quiet valley — the Sulzbachtal — is a spot with more than its fair share of historical associations. There is little traffic as there is no way out of the valley beyond the village and the road finally peters out after a few kilometres. The visitor, therefore, has peace to explore the charming market square with the colourful centuries-old houses around it. Here there is the mining museum of Baden-Württemberg, although mining activities in the area have long since ceased. Knowledgeable campers speak highly of the camping place at the *Alte Sägemühle* (old sawmill) beyond the village. Through the camp site, one can reach the gold-lettered gateway at the entrance to a Jewish cemetery, a very old burial place which served a wide area and is still kept in remarkably good order. The visitor may also learn of other Jewish associations with Sulzburg and can see the restoration work done on the synagogue which was built in 1823.

In contrast to their Austrian neighbours, the Margraves of Baden were kindly disposed towards the Jewish communities and this is reflected in the numerous Jewish cemeteries and places of worship throughout the former state of Baden. The charming little church of St Cyriak was originally built in 1510 but has been virtually rebuilt on several occasions.

In a sheltered spot, a little way past the camp site, is a natural woodland swimming pool fed by crystal-clear mountain streams and surrounded by a spacious playing and sunbathing area. Going on up the valley, the visitor comes to the Waldhotel at Bad Sulzburg, surrounded by tall pine trees. This, in fact, is just about all this miniscule spa has to offer. There are useful parking areas here and at the swimming pool, which provide the rambler with access to 100km (60 miles) of marked paths around the valley. From 20 to 22 August each year, there is an event called *Weinkurtage*, a word which cannot really be translated but refers to three days devoted to festivities

Places of Interest South of Freiburg

St Ulrich
Church of former Benedictine Kloster
Beautiful baroque church by Peter Thumb.

Bad Krozingen
Historic Keyboard Instrument Collection
Housed in the *Schloss*.

Staufen
Gasthaus Löwen
Fine old inn with Faust room and tales of Dr Faustus.

Museum of Wine Presses and other Equipment
At the vineyard of the Koeppler family in Grunern.

Sulzburg
Landes-Bergbaumuseum
Former silver mine. Underground tours for visitors.
Relics dating back to the eleventh century.

Jewish Cemetery
Very old, well-kept resting place.

Synagogue
Built in 1823 and now restored.

Heitersheim
Schloss (sixteenth- to eighteenth-centuries) and baroque Chancery (1740)

Badenweiler
Roman bath ruins
Very well-preserved remains in the Kurpark.

Schloss (1811)
Former *Residenz* of grand dukes of Baden.

Bad Bellingen
Gasthaus 'Schwanen' (1716)
Baroque hostelry in the old village.

Lörrach
Museum am Burghof
Medieval history of town.

Burg Rötteln
3km (2 miles) north of Lörrach near road B317.
Impressive ruins and fine views.

Inzlingen
Wasserschloss Reichenstein (1563-4)
6km (4 miles) south-east of Lörrach. Charming moated palace now serving as the *Rathaus*.

associated with the grape. Regional food specialities are served, accompanied by wine and music, in the historic cellars around the Sulzburg market place. The sleepy village today has a population of no more than 1,700, although it is said that, in their heyday, no fewer than 500 people were employed in the mines alone.

The distance from Sulzburg to Müllheim is only about 15km (9

Staufen with Schlossberg

Markgrafenbad, the centre of spa treatment in Badenweiler

miles) but before reaching the latter town, bear to the left to visit the distinguished spa resort of **Badenweiler**. Compared with the better-known Baden-Baden, it is a rather reticent sort of place. It is peaceful and quiet, mainly because traffic is not permitted to enter the streets of the little town (population 4,000) except for access to the hotels, etc. As with Baden-Baden, this is a resort much favoured by prominent international personalities, but here they are rarely seen, favouring a domicile with friends or in private villas hidden from the curious by flower-covered walls.

The town, with its parks and villas, occupies a sunny slope which falls towards the Rhine and there is a wide vista of vineyards and orchards to charm the eye. The Celts already knew of the thermal springs here but the first bathing complex was that developed by the Romans during the first century AD. There is a saying that where the Romans came they built and where they built they bathed — that is certainly true here. A holy place was declared and a temple was erected to honour the favours of the spring goddess Diana Abnoba. Badenweiler is proud to possess the best preserved Roman bath ruins north of the Alps and the visitor is able to get a very clear idea of the ancient Roman bathing customs.

The ruins have been integrated into the *Kurpark* and the modern (1874) Markgrafenbad was built on the pattern of the Roman original and is the centre of spa treatment today. There is nothing left of the medieval bath installations although there is little doubt that these did exist. A castle of the Zähringer dynasty was built in 1122 on the remains of a Roman fort but this was destroyed in 1678 by French troops under General Mélac. All that is left is the fine view from the ruins. The *Schloss* was the *Residenz* of the grand dukes of Baden. It was built in 1811 by the court architect Friedrich Weinbrenner for the Grand Duchess Stefanie, an adopted daughter of Napoleon. Hilda, the last grand duchess, died here in 1952.

The Protestant church (1897) is worth seeing and has the earliest German representation of the 'dance of death' (1413) in the choir. The Catholic chapel was built in 1862 in the Byzantine style. Many well-known names feature in the catalogue of those who have come to Badenweiler for their health. They include the Russian dramatist Anton Chekhov and the American writer Stephen Crane, both victims of tuberculosis and both of whom died here. The relatively new *Kurhaus* — now more of an entertainment centre than a place for medical treatment — is a remarkable piece of modern architecture.

The resort has a daily programme of walks, with leisurely local strolls in the mornings and more energetic rambles in the afternoons, often to vineyard villages where there is wine-tasting.

The Wine Road divided at Staufen, the right fork going down towards Bad Krozingen and through Heitersheim where it rejoined the B3. **Bad Krozingen**, one of the trio of south Black Forest spas, is comparatively modern and, as at Bad Bellingen, its thermal springs were revealed during a vain search for oil. It was in 1910 that, at a depth of 500m (1,640ft), the hopeful oilmen struck water instead of oil and a new spa was born. What is more, the water was found to have properties similar to those at the 2,000-year-old, third member of the group, Badenweiler. Over the years, a very pleasant and well-kept spa complex has grown up on land which, until the turn of the century, was no more than fields and meadows.

The so-called *Schloss* was built in 1579 for the priory of St Blasien and today houses a collection of some fifty historic keyboard instruments. The collection belongs to Frau Klaraliese von Gleichenstein, one of whose predecessors, Ignas von Gleichenstein, appears in the annals of musical history as a friend of Beethoven. The instruments are kept in working order and each month a concert is given in the Gobelin tapestry-hung hall of the *Schloss*, where the music of previous centuries is played and wine and food is served. The little Glöcklehofkapelle (court chapel) has frescos which date from around the eleventh century or even earlier.

Heitersheim, a little south of Bad Krozingen on the B3, deserves a brief mention. Although having less than 4,000 inhabitants, it was granted its town charter in 1810. This little town sparkles with cleanliness and has an impressive Hauptstrasse — a charming baroque street — with its several old *Gasthäuser*, including the 'Löwen' and the 'Krone', with the 'Ochsen' round the corner in Eisenbahnstrasse.

Heitersheim may lack the natural landscape of some other places along the *Weinstrasse* but this is more than compensated for by the historic buildings which go to make up the town on the little river Sulzbach. In 1428 it became the seat of the grand prior of the Order of the Knights of St John. The *Residenz* was gradually converted into an imposing palace with mighty walls and vast courtyards which has become a landmark of the town, an honour it shares with the parish church erected in 1825. The palace houses the Johanniter and Malteser Museum but even if this is not visited, a stroll through the courtyards is very pleasant. On the third Wednesday in each month there is a guided tour of the whole complex.

The two Wine Road routes both touch Müllheim but then continue on their separate ways as far as Schliengen. **Müllheim** (population 13,000) is only 8km (5 miles) south of Heitersheim. It is a busy border town with an important crossing over the Rhine to French Alsace. There are a number of good hotels but, for the general holidaymaker, some of Mullheim's satellite villages such as Britzingen, Feldberg or Hügelheim, would be more pleasant places to stay in, rather than the town itself which is at the junction of two busy roads. Facilities in the area include an open-air pool heated to 24°C (75°F) by thermal water.

Seven kilometres (4 miles) further on, **Schliengen**, with its stately baroque houses and interesting *Rathaus*, invites a short stop. The nearby moated palace, Wasserschloss Entenstein, originated in about 1400 but was extensively rebuilt in the sixteenth century. It stands in a park laid out in the so-called 'English' style. A *Weinlehrpfad* (vineyard nature trail) starts at the Winzergenossenschaft (wine-growers' co-operative) building.

The main road is now left for a quieter route closer to the Rhine for the final 24km (15 miles) of the named road to its end at Weil am Rhein, just 6km (4 miles) from the centre of Basel. The *Weinstrasse*, the railway, the *Autobahn* and the Rhine are confined to an ever narrowing strip and there is a temptation to hurry on. However, if time permits, the traveller should meander through the many delightful villages which lie to the east between the main road and the mountains, or spend some time in the well-appointed modern spa of **Bad Bellingen**, close to the Rhine.

As already hinted, this resort has a history similar to that of Bad Krozingen a little further north. In 1955, oil exploration was taking place near the sleepy and homely little village of Bellingen. Once again, when the trial bores reached a depth of about 500m (1,600ft), the drillers struck water. The oil men left the site in disgust and Herr Ruf, the *Bürgermeister* (mayor) of the day, did not have too much difficulty in persuading his council to take over the well for the benefit of the community. By the following year, the place was known as 'Bad' Bellingen, even though the facilities for guests were extremely primitive at first. But the water, shooting from the depths at more than 38°C (100°F), proved to be very effective in the treatment of certain ailments and it was not long before patients, especially from nearby Basel, were making their way here in considerable numbers.

The years of development are now long past and Bellingen today has nothing to fear from comparison with its older neighbours. Needless to say, all the facilities one expects in a modern resort are to be found here. In the old village, the baroque Gasthaus 'Schwanen' (1716) makes a worthwhile stop for a drink or a meal. Near the Rhine, just south of Bad Bellingen, is a little place called **Blansingen** which has a Romanesque church with a late-Gothic choir, restored in 1955, and superb wall paintings from about 1440. The Swiss border and the city of Basel lie ahead. The towns of Weil am Rhein and Lörrach, reached before the frontier, are both mainly industrial centres within the orbit of Basel itself.

Lörrach was a favourite place of the dialect poet Johann Peter Hebel who was a teacher at the Pädagogium here from 1783 to 91. A monument has been erected in his memory and the Hebel society is based here. St Fridolin's church was built in the district of Stetten, in 1821-2. Inside, the neo-Classical lines are broken by J. Wilhem's stucco imitation of the late baroque style. The west tower dominates the exterior. The tower of the Protestant Stadtkirche was built in 1514 but everything else was rebuilt in 1815-7. The result is quite pleasing; there is a classical hall inside with a gallery supported by Doric columns. On the other hand, four of the pillars in the Catholic parish church of St Peter are in concrete relief — an unusual use of a modern material.

The Museum am Burghof (*Heimatmuseum*) gives the history of the town and of nearby Burg Rötteln. There are seventeenth- to twentieth-century paintings, sculptures, prints and maps as well as displays showing domestic interiors of former centuries. The museum is partly housed in a former cooper's workshop. In the town there are several beautiful fountains built of white limestone from Solothurn in Switzerland.

The imposing ruins of Burg Rötteln can be found about 3km (2 miles) north of Lörrach near road B317, and from here the way up to the castle is clearly signed. The oldest parts, including the keep, are Romanesque but many important sections were added in the period up to the sixteenth century. It is another fortress which was destroyed in 1678 when the French overwhelmed this part of the world. Rötteln commands the finest viewpoint in the lower Wiesental. However, the charming moated palace, Wasserschloss Reichenstein, is still intact and is situated in the little town of **Inzlingen**, about 6km (4 miles) south-east of Lörrach and virtually on the Swiss border. The palace was built in 1563-4 and now serves as the *Rathaus*. The stucco coats of arms on a ceiling of the upper floor are reminders of the Reichenstein family's history.

The *Badische Weinstrasse* then, is a route of considerable interest which is very largely associated with the wine industry. From a layman's point of view, one vineyard is very much like another — a determined effort to explore the road from end to end could become boring. The visitor is advised to combine part of the *Weinstrasse* with some of the other areas covered in later chapters: two sections being particularly suitable; the first at the north end, between Baden-Baden and Offenburg, and the other the Kaiserstuhl. Of course, all the towns and villages have their wine festivals, mostly between the last week in August and the end of September. This is the time to visit the *Weinstrasse* if eating and drinking, together with music and general jollity, have an appeal.

2
VALLEYS OF THE NORTH

Pforzheim to Freudenstadt

A pleasant road leads eastwards from Ettlingen (see Chapter 1) towards Pforzheim. After a few kilometres, it divides in Busenbach, the right-hand fork going southwards towards Bad Herrenalb through the Albtal. That route will be explored later but, in the meantime, continue east through the villages of Waldbronn, which is a *Luftkurort* with thermal bath, Langensteinbach, Ellmendingen and Dietlingen. The road crosses numerous streams carrying water down from the northern hills towards the Rhine at Karlsruhe. After about 20km (12¹/₂ miles), **Pforzheim** is reached. It has a population of 97,000 and lies on the northernmost fringe of the Forest.

The city boasts the title 'Gateway to the Black Forest' and in many ways it is justified, for it has excellent road and rail connections. On 23 February 1945, the city was devastated by the Allied forces and an estimated 80 per cent of the buildings were destroyed, including many historical sites which are now remembered only in name. The Waisenhausplatz, now a large par park, was formerly the site of an orphanage which had been housed in an old Dominican monastery. Apart from the name, all that remains of this historic building are some remnants of a wall, preserved near the river Enz. The Enz is one of two formerly important northern Black Forest rivers, the other being the Nagold, which meet here to continue as the Enz until finally disappearing into the Neckar north of Stuttgart.

Until the beginning of this century, rafts of logs from the forests up-river were floated down the Enz and Nagold to Pforzheim, where they would be combined into larger units to continue their journey northwards. The last timber raft went down the Enz in 1913 and this mode of transport was never revived after World War I. However, the floatage of timber on these rivers had been the principal factor in the economy of Pforzheim for about 300 years.

Together with buildings, the old town walls and their towers disappeared in the destruction of 1945; this and other rubble provided sufficient material to raise the general level of streets in the town by about 2m (6$\frac{1}{2}$ft). Today a spacious modern city has risen from the ashes. Pforzheim is the home of an important gold and jewellery trade, the secrets of which are jealously guarded by the firms engaged in this work. Its so-called Industriehaus holds what is probably the most significant collection of jewellery in the world but this is not for the eye of the casual tourist. However, the interested visitor may have the consolation of a visit to the Reuchlinmuseum (also known as the Schmuckmuseum) in the *Stadtgarten* (town park) where he or she will find a worthwhile collection of examples of the jeweller's art through the centuries.

The museum is actually part of the cultural centre which also houses the town library and a lecture hall. The name comes from that of a famous son of Pforzheim, Johannes Reuchlin (1455-1522). He was a contemporary of Martin Luther (1483-1546), many of whose ideas he shared, if not with such obvious fervour. Reuchlin was a humanist and is famed for his work as a Hebraist and as a statesman.

Close to the *Hauptbahnhof* stands the Protestant Schlosskirche of St Michael. All but the outer walls were destroyed in the bombing of 1945 but it was rebuilt in exemplary fashion in the years 1949-57. Building originally began in 1225 and the reconstructed church faithfully portrays the style of that period, with a fine porch and rose window on the south gable. The rest of the building is early-Gothic; the massive collegiate choir is significantly higher than the nave and has outstanding stellar vaulting. The church contains the wall-tombs of the Margraves of Baden-Durlach, for whom St Michael's has been the funerary chapel since 1535.

At the Protestant parish church of St Martin in Altstädterstrasse, there is an interesting portal in the west tower porch which has survived from the Romanesque basilica. On the tympanum, symbolic figures depict the Threat of Evil to Mankind and its salvation through the Church. The choir of 1340 has late-Gothic wall paintings with the Last Judgement, Sheltering Mantle of the Virgin Mary and saints (1430-50). The *Heimatmuseum* at the west end of the long Karl-

Friedrich-Strasse (No 243) has a collection which includes scientific instruments and goldsmiths' tools.

A pleasant walk through the *Stadtgarten* leads to Kupferhammer, where the little river Würm joins the Nagold and where a restaurant is now housed in a smithy and sawmill dating from 1663. Kupferhammer has one of the ten *W-Parkplätze* in and around Pforzheim. This one has three round walks but, more importantly, it is the starting point for three long-distance paths, to Basel, Waldshut and Schaffhausen, as well as for a nature trail into the Erzkopf, an *Erholungsgebiet* or recreation area. Despite the ravages of war, there is still much of interest to see in Pforzheim but its gateway role has the greatest significance for the tourist. The countryside meets the town on all sides and the shortest of excursions leads into areas of the utmost beauty and tranquillity.

Continuing south-eastwards, the river Würm may be followed from Kupferhammer to the little town of Würm where a delightful alpine garden has been laid out and has become a popular goal of summer excursionists. A little later, the Gasthaus Liebeneck is reached, formerly the water mill belonging to the castle of the same name, the ruins of which are hidden in the woods above.

A stiff, 15 minutes' climb will bring the visitor up to the castle and the effort is certainly worthwhile. Such well-concealed castles are rare and one could be forgiven for thinking that this might just have been the original retreat of the Sleeping Beauty. The reality is less romantic for this was one of the haunts of the robber-knights who preyed upon travellers and merchants passing along the valley below. In this case, they received their just deserts, for, in the war with the French, the castle was captured by the troops of General Mélac in 1692 and robbed of the valuables found there.

Not far away, a little up a side valley, may be glimpsed yet another castle, Burg Steinegg. This is a much more extensive complex which, perhaps because of its location, remained more or less intact until the 1840s. Then the state of Baden decided to turn the place into a factory to provide employment for the local populace. This had been done with some success in a number of disused monastery buildings following the 1803 Secularisation. However, the idea did not appeal to the owners, the Lords of Gemmingen, who removed the roofs, took out the doors and windows and left the elements to take their toll. After World War II, youth groups from Pforzheim worked together to create a hostel in part of the buildings

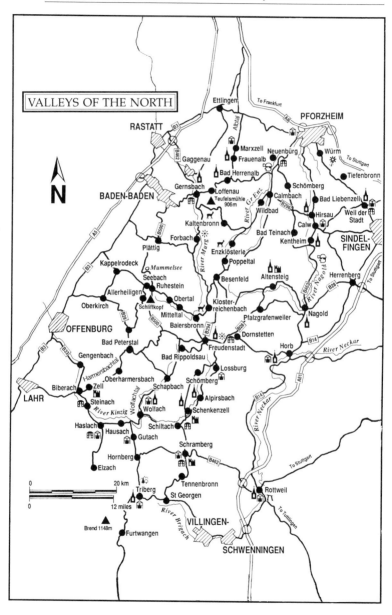

still in reasonable repair.

The village of **Tiefenbronn** (population 3,500) lies about 2km ($1^1/_4$ miles) across the valley and has in its Catholic parish church of St Maria Magdalena, a remarkable altar painting, the only known work of one Lukas Moser, which bears the date 1431. The church itself is a Gothic basilica dating from around the same time.

Continuing through the Würm valley, **Weil der Stadt** is reached about 20km ($12^1/_2$ miles) from Pforzheim. This little town with its towers and gables is a medieval gem, an exciting discovery in rural surroundings yet only a dozen miles from the centre of sprawling Stuttgart. The famous astronomer, Johannes Kepler (1571-1630), was born here in the house at Keplergasse 2 which is now the Kepler-Museum. A monument to the great man is in the market place, where one of the fountains has the figure of Emperor Karl V.

The *Rathaus*, dating from 1582, is a fine building with arcades which has survived almost unchanged. The Catholic parish church of St Peter and St Paul has a west tower which not only dominates the church, but has become the emblem of the town. The architect Albertin Jörg incorporated the twelfth- and thirteenth-century east towers when he rebuilt the church, this work being completed in 1492. The choir, which has stellar vaulting, was added in 1519, as was the Renaissance tabernacle in 1611, and the interior was partly re-decorated during the baroque period. The *Stadtmuseum* is to be found at No 12 Marktplatz and there is a Narrenmuseum (Fools' museum) at Stuttgarter Strasse 60 which is occasionally open. One of the old defensive towers, the so-called Storchenturm, is no longer visited by the storks although the locals are always hopeful that the birds will return some day.

The river Würm has its sources beyond the Black Forest boundary but the visitor prepared to travel another 10km (6 miles) or so in this direction could spend an hour or two in the large town of **Sindelfingen**. Here, the former canonry church of St Martin is a basilica with a nave, two aisles and no transept, which was consecrated in 1083. It was authentically restored in 1933 and in 1973-4. The arches and pillars show Lower Saxon influence, the apses that of Lombardy. The Romanesque strapwork of the west door should be noted as should a late-Gothic relief slab dating from 1477.

The *altes Rathaus* is from the following year and is connected to the Salzhaus of 1592. Both buildings are half-timbered as are several others in the town. The *Stadtmuseum* has interesting collections

Places of Interest In and Around Pforzheim and The Würm Valley

Pforzheim

Schlosskirche of St Michael
Near the station
Parts dating from 1225. Extensively rebuilt after World War II.

Parish church of St Martin
In Altstädterstrasse
Romanesque and Gothic. Wall paintings from 1430-50.

Heimatmuseum
At Karl-Friedrich-Strasse 243
Collection includes scientific instruments and goldsmiths' tools.

*Reuchlinmuseum
(Schmuckmuseum)*
In the *Stadtgarten* close to town centre.
Outstanding collection of jewellery.

Kupferhammer
Short walk south from *Stadtgarten*
Restaurant in seventeenth-century smithy and sawmill. Nature trail.

Würm

Alpine garden

Gasthaus Liebeneck and castle ruins
The *Gasthaus* is the former water mill of Burg Liebeneck.

Tiefenbronn

Burg Steinegg
Partly ruined castle now a hostel for young people of Pforzheim.

Church of St Maria Magdalena (1430)
Gothic basilica with notable altar painting (1431).

Weil der Stadt

Charming medieval town, birthplace of astronomer Johannes Kepler (1571-1630)

Kepler Museum
In the house at Keplergasse 2, where the famous astronomer was born.

Rathaus (1582)
A fine building which has hardly been changed over the centuries.

Church of St Peter and St Paul (1492)
Towers from twelfth and thirteenth centuries.
Some interior baroque treatment.

Stadtmuseum
At Marktplatz 12

Storchenturm
An old defensive tower.

dealing with town history while the Haus der Donauschwaben is a museum housing the central collection and library of the Swabian Danube.

The next route to be explored starts along the valley of the river Nagold from Kupferhammer. Bad Liebenzell, Hirsau, Calw, Nagold

Hirsau

and Horb are small towns along the lesser of the two routes south from Pforzheim (road B463) and it is convenient to consider them collectively in the order that the traveller entering by the Pforzheim gateway will reach them. All except the last lie on the pretty river Nagold; Horb is on the Neckar. Similarly, all are served by the Pforzheim-Freudenstadt railway line except Horb, which has a direct link with Stuttgart. **Bad Liebenzell**, only 24km (15 miles) from Pforzheim, provides a favourite excursion for the citizens of the big cities of Karlsruhe and Stuttgart who find it ideal for a couple of hours in the spa centre known as the Paracelsusbad, a walk in the woods or a climb up to the castle (1363) for coffee and cakes in the clean air.

Bad Liebenzell boasts a large camping and caravan site close to the outdoor heated swimming pool with its exciting waterchute. During the summer months there are frequent concerts in the *Kurpark* but there is an admission charge unless one is staying in the area and holding a *Kurkarte*. In earlier years the river Nagold had a history of serious flooding and, on a few houses in Bad Liebenzell and other towns in the valley, old high-water marks may be seen.

Bad Liebenzell station is the starting point for a modest ramble of 10km ($6^1/_4$ miles) which includes the attractive Monbachschlucht (ravine) and is suitable for warm days. Leave the station northwards, following the bank of the river Nagold for about 45 minutes to reach Monbachtal. Turn right by the kiosk here, following the signs up along a little stream, cross the mini-golf area and then climb up through the ravine for about 45 minutes. A junction is reached where there are many signs; the red square with letter 'L' should be followed steeply upwards to the Monakam 541m (1,775ft).

Pass the church and the school-house to reach the edge of the woods nearby. Go briefly to the left then follow the signs to the right on a field path which soon joins a steep forest track. In a good 15 minutes, the road by the markers 'Layle' and 'Hehren' will be reached. The forest track continues to drop and the return to the starting point at Liebenzell station takes barely 45 minutes from Monakam. Because of the terrain through the *Schlucht*, good footwear and a degree of sure-footedness are necessary on this walk.

Hirsau, 4km ($2^1/_2$ miles) further along the road, is one of the most significant places in terms of south German culture and the train traveller has an advantage over the motorist here in having a splendid view of the ruins of the famous Benedictine Kloster and the hunting castle of Duke Ludwig of Württemberg in the Kloster precincts.

The cultural history of Hirsau goes back to AD770 when workers from Kloster Lorsch in Hessen erected a house here which soon, however, fell victim to the repeated floods. Then, in AD830, a small group of monks founded a cell here which was dedicated to St Laurentius. In the eleventh century, this developed into the Benedictine monastery and the monks set out from here on their missions to found a number of other religious houses on the pattern of that at Hirsau. Religious life in the building ceased at the time of the Reformation in 1534 and Ludwig then built his castle in the grounds. Both were destroyed by French troops under General Mélac in 1692 but, after nearly 300 years, the remains are still worth a visit. The only part of the *Kloster* which survives intact is the north-west tower, the so-called Eulenturm (owl tower) built around 1100.

One should not leave Hirsau without seeing the St Aurelius Church, a triple-naved basilica dating from 1071, the only remaining building pre-dating the monastery. From the outside the church appears more like a barn and it was, in fact, used as such for many years. However, in 1955 the restoration of the church was begun and now worshippers stand again in the dark interior between the Romanesque columns.

Another 2km (1¼ miles) upstream is **Calw** (pronounced Kalb), the principal town in this valley and the home town of the writer Hermann Hesse (1877-1962). He was very fond of Calw and wrote that although his travels had taken him to beautiful towns in all sorts of situations; in the mountains, on the coast and in the countryside, there was none to compare with Calw, 'a little old Swabian Black Forest town.' Several old buildings are evidence of the one-time importance of Calw in the international textile trade. It was also a centre for timber floatage on the Nagold and the town derived much of its prosperity from these two diverse activities. Today the interest of the visitor may be caught by the many reminders of Hermann Hesse, mainly collected in the old house which serves as the folkmuseum

In recent years, the old town centre in Calw has been transformed by adoption of an imaginative pedestrianisation scheme. Most of the fine, half-timbered houses around the Marktplatz and elsewhere have been renovated and, where appropriate, provided with a discreet plaque outlining their history. The majority were erected

Calw

following the great fire which devastated the town through the action of the French troops in 1692. The *Rathaus* of 1673 had its upper storeys added in 1726 and the fine market place fountain was erected in 1686.

The oldest building in Calw is the tiny Gothic St Nikolaus chapel, built above the middle pier of the old Nagold bridge in the fourteenth century. Near the door are two niches in which one might expect to see biblical figures portrayed. In fact, the statues are of a man in medieval dress unrolling a bolt of cloth and of a *Flösser*, a man responsible for floating timber down the river, thus reminding the visitor of the two most important economic influences in the history of Calw. The stained-glass windows portray prominent citizens with their coats of arms.

It is worth pausing in **Kentheim**, three kilometres (2 miles) south of Calw, to visit one of Germany's oldest churches, dating from the ninth century. Shortly after Kentheim, the road from Bad Teinach and Zavelstein comes down from the west. The tiny health resort of **Teinach**, with no more than about six hundred residents, has been known for its mineral springs since the fourteenth century. It was the

Calw market

summer residence of the former Dukes of Württemberg and the building of hotels only dates from the eighteenth and early nineteenth centuries. Whether for health reasons or otherwise, this is a place where the visitor should be able to unwind in peaceful surroundings. There is the usual range of resort facilities on a modest scale, including a *Freibad* heated to 24°C (75°F). The Bad Teinach spring water is bottled and distributed widely as table water.

The valley is dominated by the imposing ruins of Burg Zavelstein, another castle which succumbed to the attentions of General Mélac's troops in 1692. One can walk from Bad Teinach to **Zavelstein** in about 45 minutes. Zavelstein claims the distinction of being the smallest town in Baden-Württemberg but the reader will note that it is not the only such claimant. Despite having only about five hundred inhabitants, it is a town as distinct from a village, having been granted *Stadtrecht* (town status) in 1367 by Count Eberhard II in recognition of the protection given him in the castle when fleeing from his enemies.

Around Easter time, the fields of Zavelstein are ablaze with the colour of thousands of crocuses and the area is much visited in the spring for this reason. How the bulbs came to be here in the first place is not really known but one theory is that they were introduced in Roman times to provide saffron flavouring.

Returning to the valley, continue the remaining 23km (14 miles) to **Nagold**, an important transport centre and a town with more industrial activity than is usual in the Black Forest. Fortunately, the important main road (B28) which crosses the Forest on its way eastwards from Strasbourg towards Munich, now bypasses the town and the tourist is unlikely to notice the industry as he wanders through the old streets with their many fine timbered buildings. Standing near the bypass, and worth a visit, is the eighth-century Remigiuskapelle with its fourteenth- and sixteenth-century frescos. It is also worth finding the *W-Parkplatz* at the Schlossberg where the round walk is, in fact, a nature trail.

If one were to follow the river now, one would turn a complete half-circle to find oneself heading north again and eventually turning towards Freudenstadt. However, that is not the intention and the valley is left to follow the road 15km (9 miles) south to **Horb** where the Neckar flows north from its source near Schwenningen. Horb is a pleasant little town with a number of timbered houses and some interesting paintings on the *Rathaus*. The collegiate church, with an attractive coloured altar-piece and a pretty baroque organ, is sufficient reward for the modest climb. Interest along this route from Pforzheim has mainly centred upon the charming little towns. However, a pleasant 12km (7¹/₂ miles) excursion from Horb lies eastwards along the Neckar valley to Schloss Weitenburg, which dates from 1585. There are good views over the valley and the quiet hotel of the same name provides an opportunity for a leisurely meal.

The main road south from Pforzheim, B294, follows the valley of the river Enz and is pretty for most of the way through this fairly sparsely populated area. Reached after a few kilometres, **Birkenfeld** is an *Erholungsort* surrounded by forest and in nearby **Gräfenhausen** the Wehrkirche (a fortified church) has early Gothic frescos. Twelve kilometres (7¹/₂ miles) from Pforzheim, the houses of the little town of Neuenbürg are crowded into the narrow strips on either side of the river, which has to make a wide sweep around the Schlossberg above the old town. Through traffic no longer has to negotiate the old streets but passes beneath a spur of the Schlossberg through a short tunnel. The town was rebuilt after seventy houses had been destroyed in a disastrous fire in 1783. On the Schlossberg today, there is a Renaissance *Schloss* of the fifteenth to sixteenth centuries which houses the local forestry office but, unfortunately, the interior cannot be visited. An earlier *Burg* on the site was destroyed in the Thirty Years' War. This area around the *Schloss* is a protected nature reserve and the visitor can see the many exotic trees which have been planted. The former *Schloss* church of St George — earlier a Gothic building — was altered in 1557. The decoration includes early fourteenth-century wall paintings which were only revealed in 1952. The Protestant parish church is a neo-classical building with a rare pulpit altar.

Schwann, six kilometres (4 miles) westwards, is a tiny village on the hill road from Pforzheim to Dobel. Gasthaus Hirsch is noted for its good value meals with large portions, and home-made *Wurst* may be purchased in the adjoining *Metzgerei*. Above the village, near the Schwann observatory, the Hotel Adlerhof has a restaurant, a café, and splendid views over the countryside. Although quite a modern building, it is furnished in a rustic style.

Ten kilometres (6 miles) further on at Calmbach, the river divides, the main road following the minor leg known as the Kleine (little) Enz while a lesser road follows the Enztal proper and leads to the little spa town of **Wildbad**. Apparently, the waters here were

Places of Interest In and Around The Nagold and Enz Valleys

Hirsau
Ruins of Benedictine Kloster and Duke Ludwig's hunting lodge.

St Aurelius Church
Triple-naved basilica dating from 1071.

Calw
Heimatmuseum
Local and regional items, especially reminders of writer Hermann Hesse.

St Nikolaus Chapel (fourteenth-century)
Stands on old Nagold bridge.

Kentheim
Ninth-century church
3km (2 miles) south of Calw. One of the oldest churches in Germany.

Nagold
Remigiuskapelle
Just south of town, near bypass (road B28). Eighth-century chapel with important frescos.

Horb
Collegiate Church
Painted altar and baroque organ.

Heimatmuseum
In Neckarstrasse. Mainly items of local interest.

Excursion from Horb:
Schloss Weitenburg, 12km (7$\frac{1}{2}$ miles) east along Neckar valley. Sixteenth-century Schloss, with good views and pleasant hotel.

Neuenbürg
Schlossberg
Fifteenth-sixteenth-century *Schloss*
Interior not open to the public. Nature reserve with exotic trees.

Schloss Church
Originally Gothic. Fourteenth-century wall paintings.

Wildbad
Spa
Thermal springs up to 40˚C and outdoor pool open all year.

Funicular railway to Sommerberg, 836m (2,743ft)

Kaltenbronn
15km (9 miles) south-east of Wildbad in direction of Gernsbach. Particularly beautiful woods in summer. Deer park.
Unique moorland plateau around Hohlosee and Wildsee

Enzklösterle
Red-deer park and nature trail.

Poppeltal
5km (3 miles) south of Enzklösterle.
Source of river Enz.
Giant summer 'toboggan' run.

Half-timbered houses in Horb

Carved signpost in Calmbach

discovered not by the Romans, who developed so many spas, but, according to legend, by a lone hunter who shot and injured a wild boar which fled through the forest. The hunter caught up to find it bathing its wounds in a hot spring, thus giving justification for the name Wildbad. Records show that the spa was founded in 1367; the thermal spring here has a temperature of up to 40°C (140°F), having come from a depth of about 1,000m (3,280ft). Each year it gives forth 1¹/₂ million litres (330,000 imperial gallons) of healing water which is used in the treatment of, among other things, rheumatism and accident injuries.

In winter, the snow and the thermal bath provide a novel combination for skiers. After winter sports on the Sommerberg above the town, a long swoop down to the very doors of the thermal bath, a quick trot across the snow and into the steaming water, one can relax in comfortable warmth while breathing the clear winter air. There are many good hotels and inns to provide for the needs of the visitor in both summer and winter. There is a camp site nearby and plenty of places for modest strolls but there are no designated *W-Parkplätze* in the immediate vicinity.

Wildbad is the terminus of a branch line from Pforzheim and a funicular railway will carry one swiftly from the centre of the town up to the Sommerberg, the summit of which is at a respectable 836m (2,743ft). In earlier times, the town was much favoured by the nobility, especially the princely houses of Württemberg, of whom the baths are a constant reminder.

Today, anybody with sufficient resources can visit the Graf Eberhard-Bad and bathe in the tub that has been used by, among others, Czar Nicholas of Russia, Kaiser Wilhelm I, the Rothschild brothers and Count Bismarck. If this does not appeal, there is no shortage of other attractions for the visitor and it is also worth taking a stroll along the pleasant shopping streets which front both sides of the Enz. Then on, perhaps, into the Kurpark at the end of the town for easy walking or by the funicular to the Sommerberg, where there are many near level paths through the woods for summer or winter exercise. The Sommerberg skiing area can also be reached easily by the same means.

Wildbad is the second stop on another hotel-based walk similar to that described in Chapter 1. Whereas the earlier walk centred on wine, this one, named *Auf Spätzlespfaden*, (*Spätzle* is a kind of dumpling, a favourite dish of this region), is more concerned with its gastronomic delights. It starts in Bad Herrenalb and calls at several places on the *Badische Bäderstrasse* (the spa road). Seven hotel nights are included and luggage is transferred from place to place. The total distance is around 90km (55 miles). (Information in this case from the Herrenalber Reisebüro.)

On the fifth day of this walk, one of its highest points will have been reached — the very attractive *Heilklimatischer Kurort* of **Schömberg**. This is at an altitude of around 650m (2,130ft) on the ridge between the Nagold and Enz valleys. Here one is away from major roads in a resort which does not appear to have developed too rapidly but which has an excellent choice of good accommodation in all grades. The visitor who is staying will find a full measure of peace and quiet; he or she will be able to explore many kilometres of woodland paths starting virtually at the door of the hotel or guest house. There is a heated swimming pool with a giant chute which will entertain the youngsters for hours, and a *Hallenbad* with artificial waves.

Past Wildbad, the valley varies in width but there are no large settlements — merely single farms, hostelries and sawmills. At the Christophshof, a farm just before the turning to Kaltenbronn, there is a large camp site. From here the visitor is urged to make a side excursion up to **Kaltenbronn**, situated at about 900m (2,950ft) on the ridge between the Enz and Murg valleys. If there is enough time, the ascent can be made on foot through the attractive pine woods where the ground is carpeted with bilberries. There are six or seven car parks near the top, three of which — called Seeloch, Wildsee and Schwarzmis — have marked, round walks of 3.5-7km (2-4 miles).

In winter this is a popular skiing area, hence the car parking provision, but in summer the paths can be used to visit a unique nature conservation area around the Wildsee and the Hohlosee. This is a moorland plateau and at first sight, the tiny lakes appear to be of little interest. However, the processes of nature have caused a large area which was once open water to gradually become a spongy mass supporting a variety of wild life and plants more suited to a tundra environment.

The water up here derives entirely from rain or snowfall and, because of the ground conditions, cannot readily drain away. After the Ice Age, small ponds gradually increased in size, then reeds took a hold around their edges and sphagnum started to spread and form a mossy blanket over the area. Sphagnum dies from beneath but grows quickly above so the surface gradually became ever thicker with the lower parts now turned to peat. Gardeners will know of the water-holding property of sphagnum and this is what has given this area its unusual character. Alongside the lakes, walkways have been formed from old railway sleepers and the unwary visitor who steps off, quickly discovers, to his or her discomfort, just how much water is held in the moss. This environment cannot support much tree life except for silver birches and some pines, nor are there fish to be found in the waters. Other similar moors in the northern Black Forest have been destroyed by drainage, peat cutting or afforestation but fortunately this one was placed under protection in the early part of this century and so has survived.

Not far from the Hohlosee there is a 28m (92ft)-high tower, from which an extensive view may be obtained in all directions. Detailed walking directions are unnecessary here. Follow the very adequate signs from the car park opposite the *Kurhaus* and reach the plateau after about half an hour's fairly steep climb; a circular route taking in the Hohlosee and the tower (Hohloturm) could be completed easily in $1^1/_2$-2 hours.

Kaltenbronn is actually an outlying part of Wildbad but appears to consist of little more than the *Kurhaus* (hotel, restaurant and café), a forester's house and the former hunting lodge of the Grand Duke of Baden. The *Kurhaus* is a comfortable rural hostelry and the restaurant is noted for its venison and other game specialities; there is also a deer park across the road.

Back in the Enztal, 12km ($7^1/_2$ miles) from Wildbad, is the resort of **Enzklösterle**. This is described as a *Luftkurort*; a place which is recognised as having particular climatic qualities due to its altitude and geographical situation, qualities considered to be helpful to sufferers from certain health problems. Already a summer holiday centre, it has also developed quickly in recent years into a first class winter sports resort. There are many kilometres of footpaths for summer walks and there is a red-deer park through which the visitor may be conducted personally by the forester. The deer park has a *W-Parkplatz* with a woodland nature trail and four round walks. Five kilometres (3 miles) further on, at **Poppeltal**, one reaches the source of the Enz, surrounded by dark, stately pines. Nearby, there are signs to the *Riesenrutschbahn*, a long summer bob run and a popular venue for holidaymakers, especially family groups. There is a large, free car park. Originally, *Riesenrutschbahn* was the name given to the long wooden chutes constructed to enable the foresters of bygone days to slide the timber down the hillsides to the nearest waterway suitable for floatage.

The road leaves the valley to rejoin the B294 shortly before the village of Besenfeld. The remaining 21km (13 miles) into **Freudenstadt** are not of outstanding interest. However, this town, with a population of 19,700 is a bustling little place and a popular goal for visitors to the northern part of the Forest, for whom it is a delight to wander through the arcades which surround the main square with their miscellany of attractive shops. Incidentally, visitors from the United Kingdom compose the second highest number of foreign guests here.

Protestant church in Freudenstadt

Freudenstadt is the highest northern Black Forest town, lying at around 735m (2,415ft), and its sub-Alpine climate and near fog-free atmosphere have made it a suitable place for numerous clinics and nursing homes. It is not a 'spa' in the accepted sense of the word but it is an officially accredited *Luftkurort*. Surprisingly, Freudenstadt was founded in 1601 by Duke Friedrich I as a home for miners. Minerals, particularly silver, had been won in this area since at least the thirteenth century but it was to develop the industry and fill his coffers that Friedrich decided to supplement the local labour with experienced silver-miners brought from Austria. The present town plan mainly stems from that time.

Looking at Freudenstadt today, one can only wonder what possible military significance the town centre can have had for it to have been almost destroyed by Allied bombing on 16 and 17 April 1945. As a result of these bombings, picturesque though the town centre undoubtedly is, almost all the buildings are of post-war construction. The town church at one corner of the square is beautifully restored, a remarkable L-shaped building with an identical tower at each end and two naves at right-angles to each other. In providing for the segregation of the sexes in earlier times, it was arranged that the men and women could not even see each other. Both parties, however, could hear the sermon, from one central pulpit at the point where the naves converge. There is a valuable sixteenth-century crucifix near the pulpit and other precious relics to be found in the church include a carved lectern dating from about 1150 which came from the *Kloster* in Alpirsbach, and a font, also from the twelfth century, which may have originated in Hirsau.

At the opposite corner of the square stands the town hall, which has a tower with a wonderful panoramic view over the town and the surrounding countryside. The splendid modern *Kurhaus* also faces the square and is the place where much of the entertainment can be found. Tea dances are popular and concerts are given by the spa orchestra and by visiting artists. All the usual facilities of a holiday resort are available including a heated *Freibad* and a *Hallenbad*. The Panoramabad is a fun swimming centre for the whole family with six water chutes, fountains, a hot whirlpool, and a mother and toddler pool. There is also a solarium gallery with fifteen sun beds. As well as this, visitors are welcome at Freudenstadt's nine-hole golf course.

The town lies at the junction of several important roads but most through traffic is now diverted from the centre by a recently built bypass. Parking, which has been a headache for years, is now alleviated by the opening of an underground park for over four hundred cars beneath the part of the huge central square which forms the market place, close to the town hall. The forest marches uncompromisingly up to the very edge of the town and there are 150km (93 miles) of footpaths to be found in the so-called Parkwald, the biggest nature reserve in Germany. In Freudenstadt one can join the ten-day ramble called '*Auf der Fährte des Rothirsches*' (roughly translated; 'On the track of the red deer') organised by the Kurverwaltung between April and October. Included in the itinerary is a large part of the ridge along which the *Schwarzwaldhochstrasse* runs.

Baiersbronn, which lies 7km (4 miles) north of Freudenstadt, is also served by the branch line from Rastatt. Here the river Murg makes a sharp left-hand turn after flowing south-eastwards from its source on the Schliffkopf in order to make its way in precisely the opposite direction and join the Rhine near Rastatt. Like Freudenstadt, Baiersbronn is a *Luftkurort* and in this case the air is said to be particularly suited to those with respiratory conditions.

There is no great outward similarity between the two towns, for there is no magnificent central square here nor any very coherent pattern of shopping streets. Baiersbronn, in fact, is made up of a number of individual hamlets which straggle some way into the many side valleys which open out here into the main valley. This is a good starting place for excursions on foot or by car, while the railway makes for easy access, northwards into the Murgtal or southwards to Freudenstadt and the Kinzigtal.

Baiersbronn lies on the Black Forest Valley Road (*Schwarzwaldtälerstrasse*) and is now making a new name for itself as a skiing resort with a chairlift to the 730m (2,394ft) Stöckenkopf. The long-established skiing resorts along the Black Forest High Road are also within easy reach. The Valley Road, which started in Rastatt, continues to Freudenstadt and to Wolfach, some 50km further south.

Before leaving this area, one can visit the official source of the little river Murg and then go on to the summit of the Schliffkopf. The starting point for this 11km (7 mile) walk is at the *W-Parkplatz* in Buhlbach at the end of the road which leaves the main Ruhestein road at Obertal, 6km (4 miles) from Baiersbronn. This point can be reached by bus and the walk to Buhlbach adds about 2km (1$^1/_4$ miles) to the start of the ramble.

The Murg proper has been created by the confluence of the

Rotmurg and the Rechtmurg close to the road junction at Obertal and it is the Rechtmurg which is to be followed. Motorists, having parked in the *W-Parkplatz*, must go back along the road for about 400m ($^1/_4$ mile) to cross the river by a little bridge. The track is marked with a red spot, but very shortly a small road is joined and a turn to the right is taken. From here the marking is red 'T'; almost immediately the road divides, both branches having the same marking. The left fork runs higher up the hillside through the tiny settlement of Unterer Sand, while the right fork stays closer to the river and climbs more gently. After about 3km (2 miles) the routes reunite to cross back over the river. There is a hut here — one of several passed in the course of this walk — which provides useful shelter in the event of a sudden shower. Turning left along one of the marked paths of the *Schwarzwaldverein* (blue diamond) one now commences to climb up towards the *Schwarzwaldhochstrasse*, described in Chapter 1. It should be mentioned that the whole of this ridge is a nature conservation area (*Naturschutzgebiet*) in which it is forbidden to interfere with the plant life.

The forestry road, which has been followed since the hut, stays close to the Murg and having crossed the now tiny stream for the last time, ends close to the source about 1.5km (1 mile) from the hut. This is a good spot for rest and refreshment, for the steepest part of the climb is yet to come. Those not wishing to continue should retrace their steps to the hut and follow the direct track along the other bank of the river to the car park, making a total distance of about 7km (4 miles).

To continue to the summit, it is necessary to go back across the final bridge, pick up the blue diamond marking again, and follow this for 400m ($^1/_4$ mile) until the main road is reached and crossed. Still following the signs, now climb to the summit of the Schliffkopf, at 1,055m (3,360ft), before continuing in a north-westerly direction to another splendid viewpoint. From here one can see the mountains of the middle and south Black Forest, the Vosges, Strasbourg cathedral and, in the most favourable conditions, the Swiss Alps.

Nearby, the track divides and the left fork (red diamond) would, in another 3km (2 miles), bring one to Ruhestein for a return to Obertal or Baiersbronn by bus. Returning on foot to Buhlbach, however, the right fork is followed to recross the main road and descend to a junction of half a dozen forest roads or paths known as Roter Schliff. The way lies along the second turning to the right to

Places of Interest In and Around Freudenstadt, Baiersbronn and The Valley of the Northern Alb

Freudenstadt
Stadtkirche
Church of unusual L-shaped design.
Lectern from 1150, sixteenth-century crucifix and other valuable relics.

Stadthaus (Town Hall)
Views from tower.

Panoramabad
Fun swimming centre for all the family with chutes, fountains and whirlpool.

Parkwald
On the fringes of the town. Said to be the biggest nature reserve in Germany, with 150km (93 miles) of footpaths.

Baiersbronn
Stöckenkopf
730m (2,394ft) hill, 1km ($^1/_2$ mile) from Baiersbronn with chairlift.

Mummelsee
20km (12$^1/_2$ miles) north-west on Schwarzwaldhochstrasse B500. Charming mountain lake. Boating.

Schliffkopf
15km (9 miles) west on

Schwarzwaldhochstrasse B500.
Views over Forest, to Strasbourg and the Alps.
Nature conservation area.

Allerheiligen
20km (12$^1/_2$ miles) east on Ruhestein to Oppenau road. Waterfall and ruins of Kloster founded in 1196.

Deer Enclosures
At Sankenbachtal, Klosterreichen-bach, Schönegrund and Langen-bach.

Marxzell
Albtal Transport Museum
Collection includes early vehicles from Alb Valley Railway.

Frauenalb
Ruins of Benedictine Kloster Church (1727)

Bad Herrenalb
Ruins of Kloster and Church

Loffenau
Important hang gliding centre on the Teufelsmühle 906m (2,972ft). Look-out tower.

descend fairly steeply and soon follow a small river, the Wolfach. After about 2km (1$^1/_4$ miles) this joins the Murg, and Buhlbach is reached after 1.5km (1 mile). This walk is suitable with or without a car and even a visitor dependent upon public transport will find no difficulty in reaching the starting points of walks in this area. There is a multitude of marked paths in the vicinity of Baiersbronn itself and the tourist information office will be able to give details of conducted rambles either starting from the centre or using public transport.

Deer are quite numerous in the Forest and wild boar are also to be found. Both are difficult to see in their natural habitat and in many places enclosures have been constructed so that they may be observed and preserved at the same time. Most of these enclosures are accessible at all times without formality. The signs to look for are *Saupark* or *Wildgehege*. There are several deer enclosures in and around Baiersbronn; the nearest is that in the Sankenbachtal, a pleasant 3.5km ($2^1/_4$ miles) stroll from the centre. Others are to be found in the Ailwald at Klosterreichenbach, 4.5km (3 miles) away, in Schönegründ, 9km ($5^1/_2$ miles) away, and through Schönmünzach to Langenbach, 24km (15 miles). Exact locations vary from time to time and it would be advisable to check with the *Kurverwaltung* before setting out.

Another interesting excursion from Baiersbronn is to **Allerheiligen**, on the road between Ruhestein and Oppenau. There is a very fine seven-stage waterfall, beside which a steep stairway descends from the parking place near the main road. Here too, are the ruins of the Kloster Allerheiligen which was founded in 1196 and burnt down three times — in 1470, 1555 and 1803 — after being struck by lightning, if one can give credence to such a remarkable history of disaster. The few buildings which survived the last fire are now used as a forestry office and a *Gasthaus*.

From Ettlingen, the visitor without his or her own transport can take the little train for the 20km ($12^1/_2$ miles) or so through the Albtal to Bad Herrenalb. This valley is often described as the *nördliches* Albtal for there is another of the same name in the southern part of the Forest. Soon after leaving Ettlingen's industry, one is in a genuine Black Forest atmosphere with densely packed pine trees and, in some places, pleasant meadows beside a merry little river.

When **Marxzell** is reached, it is worth pausing to visit the church of St Markus (1772-82) with its colourful sandstone tower. Across from the Marxzeller Mühle Hotel, there is the little Albtal Transport Museum which has an interesting collection of vehicles, including some early ones from the Alb Valley Railway.

As the journey progresses, the ruins of the *Kloster* at **Frauenalb** soon come into view. Nuns of the Benedictine Order were already

resident here in the twelfth century. In 1727, the famous architect
Peter Thumb was responsible for the design of a church whose two
towers still stand. Some parts of the main aisle also survived a
devastating fire in 1853 but the religious establishment itself had
been disbanded 50 years earlier as part of the Secularisation process.
The extensive ruins are in stark contrast to the traditional spa hotel,
the 'König von Preussen' (King of Prussia) which is nearby. The
monastery garden has three terraces and usually a colourful display
of flowers and shrubs.

Frauenalb seems almost to live in the past but **Bad Herrenalb**, the
most important place in the valley, has developed into a modern
Kurort with a wide range of facilities for guests convalescing after
illness or just seeking relaxation from the trials of everyday life. The
monastery at Herrenalb was also founded in the twelfth century to
complement nearby Frauenalb. Both establishments were wealthy
and the monks had the privilege of calling themselves *Herren* (gentlemen). Their lives were occupied solely with religious observance, in
great contrast to the hard-working lay brothers.

In the fifteenth century, the religious zeal of the gentlemen monks
began to cool and they started to take interest in more earthly
pleasures. There was, for example, Abbot Georgius Trippelmann.
He had certainly encouraged the revival of life in the Catholic
establishment following the doldrums of the Reformation but he did
not conduct himself with the expected monastic virtues. In the end,
two of his monks complained to higher authority that, among other
misdemeanours, the Abbot 'consorted with a female person'. As a
result, Trippelmann had to lay down his abbot's staff in 1555;
perhaps he had the last laugh though, for he married the lady in
question! If one sits in the porch of the former Klosterkirche, two
meditating monks can be seen standing in niches to the right. Are
they, perhaps, praying for the soul of the sinning Trippelmann? Of
the church itself, only the choir of 1427 and its side chapel remain. An
exhibition of the history of the monastery and a collection of handmade roof tiles can be seen in the *Heimatstube* of the *Kurverwaltung*
building on Saturdays from 10am to 12noon.

Herrenalb is at the convergence of seven little valleys. About 5km
(3 miles) along one of these, to the north-west, is the little village of
Moosbronn which has a pretty baroque church. Here, in 1626, the
glass-maker Franz Kunard and his sons established the first
Glashütte (workshop) in this district. Several others were to follow

but as they relied on large quantities of wood for their processes, they fell into disuse when the nearby forests were felled and had to be re-established elsewhere, nearer new supplies of the essential commodity. In those days, transport of timber for any distance without a convenient waterway was a virtual impossibility.

There is a road from Bad Herrenalb to Gernsbach, in the neighbouring Murg valley, which passes through the *Erholungsort* of **Loffenau** (population 2,500). There are some half-timbered houses and several old water mills are within walking distance. The nearby Teufelsmühle has a deceptive name, for it is not a mill at all but a 906m (2,972ft) high mountain with a lookout tower. This is the principal hang gliding centre in the northern Black Forest and the school here prepares the fliers for international certificates of competency.

A walk of 12km (7½ miles) can be started in this area at the *W-Parkplatz* Talwiese in the upper Gaistal, 4km (2½ miles) south of Bad Herrenalb. This is a varied ramble for sure-footed walkers and begins at the Raststätte Talwiese along the so-called Brudes-Weg, marked by blue diamond and the number '11'. Climbing continuously through the wood, the Hahnenfalzhütte is reached in about 45 minutes and, after a few more minutes' climb, the long-distance *Westweg*, with its red diamond waymark, is encountered at Langmartskopf. However, the sign to follow remains the blue diamond and there is a notice 'Zur Teufelsmühle'. Some fine, long-distance views enhance this section and the highest point of the walk, at 942m (3,018ft), is soon passed.

Continue towards the Teufelsmühle which has an observation tower at 906m (2,972ft) that can be climbed for even better views into the Enz and Murg valleys and to the mountains along the *Schwarzwaldhochstrasse*. The nearby Gasthof provides rest and refreshment but it is closed on Tuesdays.

Commence the return descent by following route number '43', still marked by the blue diamond, along a little road at first but then bearing left towards a good viewpoint, continuing from here to follow the waymarks steeply down to the Grosses Loch. Thereafter, path '43' leads to the right and there is a sign 'Herrenalb'. But take care — after just 5 minutes, leave the '43' and now follow '44' and the signs 'Zur Plotzsägemühle'. First of all, follow this for about 200m (217yds) along a little road and then turn right, down through the woods until the old sawmill on the river Alb is reached. Refreshments are available here at weekends.

Alb Valley Railway at Bad Herrenalb

The mill is at 540m (1,650ft) and the whole descent will have taken about 1 hour. Now go uphill for a short while on a little road; follow the *Naturfreundehaus* sign and pass the *Spechtschmiede* (refreshments) up to an open area. Take the level road 200m (650ft) to the right and into the wood in order to get back to the starting point at Talwiese.

Rastatt (see Chapter 1) is left in a south-easterly direction to follow the *Schwarzwaldtälerstrasse* (Black Forest Valley Road) through the valleys of the rivers Murg and Kinzig. Schloss Favorite is passed on the outskirts of Rastatt and the road goes on through Kuppenheim and **Bad Rotenfels**. The latter has a baroque church and a thermal spring delivering water at 34°C (93°F). The B462 is joined and **Gaggenau** is reached in about 7km (4 miles).

By Black Forest standards, this is quite an industrialised town and there was an ironworks here as early as the seventeenth century. The first *Glashütte* was established in the eighteenth century and these activities continued to flourish through the nineteenth and into the twentieth centuries. Now the most geologically and scenically interesting of all the northern valleys truly begins. This is especially true of the section from here to Raumünzach in which there are several interesting small towns and villages as well as numerous places to *parken und wandern*.

✳ **Gernsbach**, only 5km (3 miles) from Gaggenau, should be singled out for special mention — a town of old timbered houses and medieval fortifications. An impressive fountain graces the pretty market place, and the Renaissance *Rathaus*, originally the home of a Gernsbach merchant, should not be overlooked. The Liebfrauen-

⌀ kirche, the oldest church in the town, dating from 1378, is noted for its fine windows and an artistic altar. The railway traveller from Rastatt to Freudenstadt can enjoy a constantly changing scene as the train winds its way up the valley, frequently crossing and recrossing the river.

Two kilometres (1¼ miles) upstream on a rocky outcrop is

🏠 Schloss Eberstein (1150). The Schloss-Restaurant is worth visiting but, apart from this, the inner courtyard of the palace has a crucifixion group (1464) which originated in Kloster Herrenalb. Four kilometres (2½ miles) from Gernsbach, the road from Kaltenbronn descends into the valley at **Weisenbach**, an *Erholungsort* which is in a good rambling area with ready access to the Kaltenbronn upland already described. Here the valley is a little wider and the river bank

⌀ is lined with attractive houses.

The pretty church is prominent on a small hill and was built in 1845 in the colourful local sandstone. The cultivation of vines is not possible any further up the valley than this and from now on the scenery changes dramatically. The traveller will note the several large paper mills in the narrow valley bottom, this being one of the most important areas for the production of newsprint in the Federal Republic.

✳ **Forbach** is 14km (9 miles) from Gernsbach and is worth a stop for the benefit of the photographer. The covered wooden bridge is outstanding; it was built originally in 1778 and roofed with Canadian red cedar shingles. At 40m (131ft), it is the longest bridge of this type in Germany. The Catholic parish church with its two neo-Roman-

⌀ esque bell towers is in a picturesque setting too. The Murg has been dammed between Forbach and Raumünzach to form a 600m (650yd)-long lake and at Raumünzach a road leads westwards up a steep, twisty road to another man-made lake. This is the Schwarzenbach-Talsperre, about 4km (2½ miles) distant, where a popular recreation area has been created.

It was difficult to find space in this part of the valley for road and railway alongside the river and the line often cuts through rocky outcrops by means of short tunnels. For a long time, the Baden State Railway from the north had its terminus at Raumünzach for this was the frontier with Württemberg; the traveller then had to find his way 10km (6$^1/_4$ miles) to Schönmünzach where the Royal Württemberg railway took over for the remainder of the journey into Freudenstadt.

Before arriving in that town, the *Luftkurort* of **Klosterreichenbach** is reached. There was once a monastery here which had been founded by the monks from Hirsau. Part of the west wing, the bath house and a tower survive. The restored Klosterkirche has two early Romanesque towers which date from the eleventh century. The *Kloster* garden is beautifully maintained and there is a modern outdoor swimming pool. In the nearby Ailbachtal there is one of the deer enclosures suggested as an excursion from Baiersbronn.

Before going further south, it is worth making a tour towards the east in order to explore the upper part of the Nagoldtal. A picturesque road goes south-east at first from Besenfeld for about 7km (4 miles) to Erzgrube, a name which recalls the seventeenth- and eighteenth-century iron-ore mining in this area. One of the countless streams originating near Besenfeld is the official source of the Nagold which turns east at Erzgrube and almost immediately enters the Nagoldtalsperre, two man-made lakes constructed between 1965 and 70. The dams are respectively 11.5 and 32.1m (38 and 105ft) high and the total length of the lakes is some 3km (2 miles). This has become another favoured recreation area, with water activities and an extensive network of footpaths around the lakes.

The little *Erholungsort* of Kälberbronn is just a few kilometres to the south. The valley road can be followed in a generally westerly direction for the 8km (5 miles) to **Altensteig** where the old town clings precariously to the steep slopes on the north flank of the Nagold. The old castle dominating the skyline dates from the thirteenth century and the attractive rococo church nearby dates from the eighteenth. The little church in **Altensteigdorf** was built around 1200 and contains some beautiful wall paintings. Altensteig is one of the most photogenic towns in the northern part of the Forest and although it does not lie directly on one of the main tourist routes, it is well worth a visit.

From Altensteig, the rather busy B28 continues down the valley and soon passes near the *Luftkurort* of **Berneck** where the many facilities for the visitor include a *Hallenbad* and a heated *Freibad*. The

Thirteenth-century inn, Gernsbach

main road continues through the attractive landscape and passes through the *Erholungsort* of Ebhausen before the final descent into Nagold, which was visited earlier in this chapter. To return towards Freudenstadt, turn right upon reaching the B463 and, after about 2km (1¼ miles), turn right again into a pretty road going eastwards and signposted Pfalzgrafenweiler.

At **Haiterbach**, an *Erholungsort* just south of this road, there is the ruin of Mantelberg castle with a 30m (98ft) high tower. **Egenhausen**, also just off the through road, is reached about 14km (9 miles) after leaving Nagold. It is a little market town and makes a peaceful base, equally ideal for exploration of the immediate vicinity or for excursions further afield. The church has some interesting early-Gothic wall paintings. Altensteig is only a few minutes' journey to the north.

The important *Luftkurort* of **Pfalzgrafenweiler** is about 8km (5 miles) further on. This is a summer and winter resort with several attractive satellite villages grouped around it. The total population of the area numbers only some 4,000. Close nearby, another *Luftkurort* consists of the twinned communities of **Waldachtal** and **Lützenhardt**, which also have a group of surrounding villages. The

Places of Interest In and Near The Murg and Upper Nagold Valleys

Gernsbach
Old timbered houses and medieval fortifications.

Liebfrauenkirche (1378)
Fine windows and artistic altar.

Schloss Eberstein (1150)
2km (1¼ miles) south.
Good restaurant.

Forbach
Covered wooden bridge (1778)
Longest example of this type in Germany.

Catholic parish church
Two neo-Romanesque bell towers.

Klosterreichenbach
Remains of former Kloster
Restored church (*Klosterkirche*) with early Romanesque tower.

Nagoldtalsperre
7km (4 miles) to the east.

Man-made lakes 3km (2 miles) long.
Recreation area.

Waldachtal-Lützenhardt
Old sawmill
Has biggest mill wheel in Black Forest.

Altensteig
Picturesque medieval town on steep hillside.

Thirteenth-century castle and eighteenth-century rococo church

Church (1200)
In Altensteigdorf
Beautiful wall paintings.

Dornstetten
Outstanding old town centre. Many half-timbered houses, late-Gothic church and old fountain.

Heimatmuseum is worth a brief visit and an inspection of an old sawmill which has the biggest mill-wheel in the Black Forest, is recommended. At **Heiligenbronn** there is an old *Wallfahrtskirche* (pilgrimage church) which may be visited.

Finally, nearing Freudenstadt, the little town of **Dornstetten** (population 6,000) should on no account be missed. It has had 'town' status since 1276 and is thus about three centuries older than Freudenstadt, by which it is now rather over-shadowed. Silver and lead used to be mined here but these activities have long since disappeared. Many beautiful half-timbered houses line the main street and market place and complement the elegant late-Gothic church of St Martin. The fountain in the market place is almost 500 years old.

South of Freudenstadt

The *Tälerstrasse* south of Freudenstadt is road B294 which was the main route out of Pforzheim. The Kinzig valley is now the one to be followed. As all the principal places in the 70km (44 miles) of the Kinzigtal can be reached by train, this is a particularly suitable area for the visitor without his or her own transport.

Only 8km (5 miles) from Freudenstadt, the small, modern *Luftkurort* of **Lossburg** makes no claim to architectural splendour or historic assocations. But it does have a fine climate and quite a lot of attractions for the twentieth-century holidaymaker. Accommodation ranges from the traditional old Gasthof 'Bären' (The Bear) to simple bed and breakfast accommodation and self-catering flats, mostly in modern houses. There is a splendid heated swimming pool with grassy slopes for sun-bathing and a children's play area. There is also a *Hallenbad* (indoor pool); an open-air pool is usually called a *Freibad* — *beheiztes Freibad* if it is heated, as most of them are . A more natural bathing place may be called a *Waldbad* but this may equally be just a *Freibad* which happens to be in the woods. Other names such as *Schwimmbad* or *Schwimmhalle* are also used.

Near the outdoor pool at Lossburg, there are tennis courts and a small *Kurpark* where band concerts take place during the summer months. Lossburg has a good musical reputation and the brass band of the *Musikverein* is well thought of. The Schwarzwaldmuseum (Black Forest Museum) houses a comprehensive collection of objects from the Kinzigtal including a number of unusual Black Forest clocks.

Alpirsbach, a busy little town with useful shopping facilities, is one of the places in which the Benedictine monks founded a monastery on the pattern of Hirsau and the Klosterkirche (1125) still dominates the town. If it appears to be somewhat unbalanced, this is because a planned second tower to match the present one was never built. The church has much of interest and in the summer season is used as the venue for popular serenade concerts. There are a number of impressive half-timbered houses and the stately *Rathaus* (1566) is well-worth inspection. Many cosy hostelries offer the traveller a wide choice of meals or just a drink and a snack. Alpirsbach is yet another *Luftkurort*, noted for the mild climate experienced in its steep-sided valley. There are three *W-Parkplätze* in and around the town with nine round walks in pretty surroundings.

Schenkenzell stands at the junction of the Kleine (little) Kinzigtal with the main valley and is consequently somewhat more open and airy than Alpirsbach. The ruins of the Schenkenburg, 1km ($^1/_2$ mile) south of the town, provide a modest excursion while a tour or a walk in the peaceful and beautiful Kleine Kinzigtal should not be missed. One could start from the *W-Parkplatz* at the edge of the town on the road leading into this valley (signposted Reinerzau) and take one of the three walks shown on the map there. Alternatively, one could continue northwards up the valley and, after about 7km (4 miles), take the minor road on the left to Berneck, which should not be confused with the Berneck in the Nagoldtal that has already been mentioned.

After parking beyond this hamlet, continue forward less than 0.5km ($^1/_3$ mile) to reach the south end of a *Stausee* (reservoir). Following waymarks '21', there is a fine 5km (3 miles) ramble right round this man-made lake. The motorist may go on up the main valley to Schömberg and choose one of several routes for a modest round tour. This Schömberg is a village and not to be confused with the resort of the same name mentioned a little earlier. Nevertheless, it is the focal point of six marked walks of varying grades but presenting little difficulty.

Another interesting excursion in this area is that to the remains of the former nunnery at Wittichen. From Schenkenzell one travels a few kilometres up the valley of the Kleine Kinzig and at Vortal leaves the Reinerzau road in favour of a more westerly one leading up into the hills. This is part of the long-distance *Wanderweg* from Gengenbach to Alpirsbach and, if followed in this direction, would eventually allow one to drop down to Schapbach in the Wolfach valley.

The nunnery at **Wittichen** was founded in 1324 and, among the other difficulties experienced over the centuries, managed to survive the Reformation in the Upper Kinzig valley in 1540. Only with Secularisation in 1803 was the life of the abbey ended; the last abbess, Antonie Schmitt of Kaltbrunn died in 1840. Some of the church vestments made by the nuns are still to be seen in the old baroque church. In the cool, quiet interior one could be in another world unless, that is, one has come on a modest bus tour from Schenkenzell for a guided tour of the nunnery, or happens to be there when an excursion arrives.

On the hill to the east above the *Kloster*, there are a few remains of a castle called Wittichenstein. It was built to protect the numerous silver and cobalt mines that once existed here, traces of which may

Alpirsbach church

The river at Schiltach

*A narrow
street in
Schiltach*

also still be found. A mine called Sofie is reputed to have produced the best silver in the whole Kinzigtal.

Schiltach also stands at a junction of valleys, this time the main Kinzigtal and the Schiltachtal running south to Schramberg. A photographer's paradise, with a beautiful unspoilt market place surrounded by tall, timbered houses, it is a riot of colour in the summer months, almost every window ledge bearing a box of vivid geraniums or petunias. The *Rathaus*, built in 1590, carries colourful pictorial reminders of calamitous fires and floods which have destroyed the town in the past. In the market place there is a beautiful fountain of red sandstone (1751) on the column of which is a double-tailed lion, a creature which also appears on the town's coat of arms.

Schiltach's important strategic position means that it has been inhabited for a very long time. Indeed, Roman troops were stationed here to secure a route between the Rhine and the Danube. Excavations near the Brandsteig pass have revealed parts of the Roman settlement and Roman gold coins, including one with the likeness of Emperor Trajan (53-117), have been found in the vicinity of the town. Today, Schiltach is a *Luftkurort* with well under 4,000 inhabitants; a delightful base for those seeking a peaceful holiday without the trappings of the more fashionable resorts.

It is worth leaving the Kinzigtal briefly in Schiltach to drive the 9km (5^1/$_2$ miles), to **Schramberg,** one of the most important towns in the Black Forest, primarily resulting from its flourishing watch and clock industry. There is no settlement in the valley between these two towns except for a few isolated farmhouses and an occasional sawmill. Just before entering the town, an imposing rocky barrier of granite known as the Rappenfels can be seen. The ruins of the Burg Schilteck, built around the year 1200, stand opposite. Five valleys meet in Schramberg, but the place is still cramped because the steep and wooded valley sides give little scope for expansion. Towering above the town, the Burg Hohenschramberg dates from 1457 and is one of five medieval fortresses surrounding Schramberg. There is a significant production of good quality furniture here, and Schramberg pottery should not be overlooked by those seeking a worthwhile gift or souvenir. The Junghans family founded the clock business in 1860 and the visitor should inspect two fine examples of their craftsmanship: the decorative clock in the town museum and the complicated astronomical one at the *Rathaus*.

The clock in the museum, which is almost 5m (16ft) high, was built as an example of the work of the Junghans' factory for display at the Paris exhibition in 1900. The art work consists of themes from the Old and New Testaments, including a sequence of moving scenes depicting the sufferings of Christ. The *Rathaus* clock, built in the factory of Philipp Horz in Ulm, and installed here in 1913, shows a ✳ full astronomical calendar made up of twelve different functions. Visitors can obtain a free explanatory booklet in the information office situated in the *Rathaus* immediately beneath the clock.

This is perhaps the place to make reference to the history of clock-making in the Black Forest, for not only in Schramberg but in nearby towns such as Hornberg, Triberg and Furtwangen this activity has long played an important part in the rural economy and still continues to do so. In the seventeenth century, settlements were established deeper and deeper into the forests but this resulted in great poverty and deprivation, because of which trade came to a virtual standstill.

The plentiful timber led first to a charcoal burning industry and later to glass-making. Glass carriers conveyed the products across Europe on their backs and it is thought that one of them brought a primitive clock back from Bohemia which aroused great interest. The forest inhabitants pondered over the possibilities of this new idea and soon contrived to make simple timepieces using the materials readily available — wood, stone and glass. The wooden cog-wheels all had to be cut by hand. Some examples of these early clocks may be seen in the clock museum in Furtwangen.

Later came metal for the mechanisms, at first imported from afar but in 1787, Leopold Hofmayer succeeded in setting up a brass foundry in Neustadt. The painted clock faces of the early timepieces were succeeded by artistically carved cuckoo clocks, the better ones having complex musical movements. Coming right up to date, the mechanical parts are often now replaced by modern quartz electronic movements but the traditional 'Black Forest clock' appearance is still often maintained.

There is an adequate selection of eating places in Schramberg. The hotel-restaurant 'Hirsch' (stag) in the Hauptstrasse (closed for four weeks July/August, from 2pm Sunday and all day Monday) has a pleasant restaurant and selection of specialities including home-made pies, loin chops 'Florence' and Swabian roasts. Table reservations are advisable.

South of Schramberg, followed by the road towards St Georgen, is the so-called upper Schiltachtal or Bernecktal. The ruins of the eleventh-century Burg Falkenstein (one of the many with this name in Germany) are surrounded by dark pines. There are many stories of the treacherous deeds centred upon this castle in the eleventh century, in the course of which both Duke Ernest of Swabia and his friend Count Werner of Kyburg met their deaths. The road climbs to the plateau where the sunny summer resort of **Tennenbronn** has an attractive setting. From 1500 until 1902, this village was politically and denominationally divided, with one half belonging to Catholic Austria and the other to Protestant Württemberg.

In winter, Tennenbronn is a popular centre for *Langlauf* or cross-country skiing. The time when downhill skiing was the only way of enjoying the sport has long since passed, especially in the Black Forest. Indeed, there are none of the lengthy *pistes* which generally characterise the Alpine ski resorts. On the other hand, cross-country skiing is very much at home in this terrain — there are few resorts in the Black Forest's higher altitudes which do not have the appropriate facilities and there are many specialist ski schools. There are *Langlaufloipen* (the marked tracks to be followed by cross-country skiers) nearly everywhere and they range from modest circular routes round a resort to lengthy tours for which it is necessary to arrange overnight accommodation away from one's base.

The great advantage of cross-country skiing is that it can be a family activity in which all members can participate regardless of their degree of proficiency. Several places are mentioned in this book in this connection and those wishing to try this sport for the first time might well write to these for details of what is available, including any 'package' holiday offers. Two words of warning though; the winter walker should avoid the *Loipen*; the summer walker should not assume that because a *Loipe* is marked on the map, it is necessarily a route along which he or she may walk. Walking routes are separately waymarked.

Continuing eastwards on the B462 from Schramberg, one would come, in 24km (15 miles), to the town of Rottweil which lies at the south end of the picturesque Neckar valley road from Horb. With 24,000 inhabitants, **Rottweil** is an important centre, right on the fringe of the Black Forest and there are fine views through the streets towards the Schwäbische Alb, another area of outstanding beauty to the east. The Heiligkreuzmünster (Holy Cross Minster) has altars and a crucifix of particular interest. The fourteenth-century

Places of Interest In and Around The Upper Kinzig Valley, Schramberg and Rottweil

Lossburg
Schwarzwaldmuseum
Clocks and other items from the Kinzigtal.

Alpirsbach
Klosterkirche (1125) and former Kloster.
Numerous relics of note. Serenade concerts in summer.

Rathaus (1566)

Schenkenzell
Schenkenburg
1km ($^1/_2$ mile) south.
Ruins of typical hilltop castle.

Church and remains of former Nunnery (1324)
At Wittichen, 4km ($2^1/_2$ miles) north-west.

Schiltach
Colourful market place with impressive timbered houses.

Rathaus (1590) with interesting murals.

Beautiful sandstone fountain (1751).

Schramberg
Stadtmuseum (Museum fur Sozial- und Technikgeschichte)

In town centre. Social and technical history. 5m- (16ft-) high decorative clock and many other treasures.

Rathaus
In town centre. Remarkable astronomical clock.

Ruins
Ruins of five castles around the town on the heights between the valleys.

Rottweil
Heiligkreuzmünster
Dating from fifteenth and sixteenth centuries with some older sections. Interesting altars and crucifix.

Kapellenkirche Unserer Lieben Frau (fourteenth-century)
Tower and rich stone sculpture.

Lorenzkapelle
Museum with art collection and late-Gothic sculptures.

Wolfach
Rathaus with painted façade and Fürstenberg palace (1631)

St Laurentiuskirche (sixteenth-century)

Glass Museum
Glass-blowing demonstrations.

Kapellenkirche has a noteworthy tower and stone carving said to be the best of its period; the Lorenzkapelle is now a museum housing a fine art collection. The old town centre is very attractive; there is a

Roman bath to be visited and an open-air exhibition of modern art.

Back in the Kinzigtal, the final 10km (6¹/₄ miles) of the officially designated Valley Road lead to **Wolfach**, where several typical valleys come together. The painted *Rathaus* and the Fürstenberg Palace (1631) are worthy of inspection, together with the sixteenth-century church of St Laurentius. During World War II it was intended that the Schlosskapelle should provide office accommodation but it actually became a prison. It was later used as stables and during the French occupation from 1945 it became a coal store! It was restored by local tradesmen in 1965. Although this pleasant little town is not developed on tourist lines to the same extent as, say, Lossburg, there is plenty of accommodation, including a camp site, and there is a fine outdoor swimming pool.

As has already been noted, glass-blowing is another typical Black Forest craft and here in Wolfach there is a fine example of a *Glashütte* where one may see the skilled craftsmen at work, admire the results and, in the associated museum, be taken through the 2,000 year history of glass-making. The *Heimatmuseum* houses a good collection of minerals, splendid crystals beautifully worked into a multitude of geometrical forms. The eye is delighted by this colourful display of nature's treasures. There is a natrium-calcium-sulphur spring in the *Kurgarten* whose waters are claimed to be beneficial for stomach and intestinal disorders.

From Wolfach, a side valley follows the river Wolfach in a northerly direction towards Freudenstadt and the *Schwarzwaldhochstrasse* at Kniebis. From its name, one might imagine the Wolfachtal, or Wolftal, as it is sometimes called, to be a way through rough country where wolves had lurked in the past. The reality is quite the contrary as it is a remarkably beautiful valley throughout. After Oberwolfach, the valley is sparsely populated for about 10km (6 miles) — just the occasional farmhouse or tiny settlement where the valley widens a little. A twisty road climbs away to the left to Bad Peterstal and Griesbach, already described in Chapter 1. The valley road then enters the resort of **Schapbach**, now united with **Bad Rippoldsau**, 10km (6¹/₄ miles) further on. For all that, the resident population numbers little more than 3,000 so the place is hardly overcrowded. Traditional costumes are still worn sometimes in Schapbach.

The big farmhouses in the area are sometimes called *Zinken* and their underpart and doorways are built out of the local red sandstone, an unusual feature in the Forest. Ample provision is made for the accommodation of the holiday visitor and many facilities are available for those coming to 'take the waters' as there are numerous mineral springs here. Much of the output is bottled and exported as table water. In the *Kurmittelhaus* the facilities include a *Hallenbad* and a *Freibad*, both heated to 30 °C (86 °F) by the natural waters. There is also a heated *Freibad* for more general use, all the other leisure appointments expected of a modern resort and a camp site which is open all year round.

From the hamlet of Vorseebach, 3km (2 miles) north of Schapbach, a narrow road climbs up through a mysterious landscape where elves and goblins are said to live and where ancient superstitions abound, to the Glaswaldsee 839m (2,748ft) above sea level. There are three parking places as one approaches the little lake with access to nine circular walks ranging from 2.5 to 11km (1¹/₂ to 7 miles). The lake and surrounding countryside are in a *Naturschutzgebiet* (nature conservation area). At Klösterle, as one is approaching Bad Rippoldsau, a church with two towers appears to bar the way but the road divides, the right hand fork climbing steeply out of the valley to Freudenstadt and the left hand one to Kniebis near the point where the 'Wolf' river has its source.

The journey through the Kinzigtal brings one, 4km (2¹/₂ miles) from Wolfach, to the road running due south into the Gutachtal, probably the best-known of all the Black Forest valleys and the opportunity for yet another side excursion. In 20 or 30km, the Gutachtal offers a selection of everything that the visitor may consider to be genuinely 'Black Forest'. Not least, the traditional costumes of the area, with the women's red *Bollenhut* being the most distinctive feature. Throughout the Forest, the tourist will be offered dolls dressed in a sort of traditional garb with a red *Bollenhut* and this has become perhaps the most familiar worldwide symbol of the Black Forest. However, it should be remembered that it is only at home in the area of the Gutachtal and that other areas have their own equally significant, if less flamboyant, costumes.

The *Bollenhut* is difficult to make and is therefore stored most carefully when not being worn. An Italian straw hat is treated with plaster so that it becomes snow white (and very heavy). The fourteen red woollen balls or pompoms are made exactly according to tradition and fastened to the hat in the correct numbers and positions. The finished article weighs some 1.5kg (3lbs). By the way, not all the

Oberwolfach

Procession through the streets of Wolfach

Wayside shrine in Wolfach

*Wrought iron sign and
window boxes in Wolfach*

woollen balls are red — the hats
of the married women are
adorned with black ones.

There is an open-air mu-
seum in the village of Gutach which
consists of a collection of typical farmhouses
from all over the Forest. These have been re-assembled here,
complete with their furnishings, implements and vehicles. The original farm on the site was apparently the Vogtsbauernhof, which is still
standing and from which the museum rightly takes its name, since
this is the most imposing of all the houses.

It is possible to start a fairly strenuous ramble of 14km (8^1/$_2$ miles) in the centre of Gutach by the 'Krone' where there is ample parking space. Leave the village by the Sulzbachweg opposite and follow the blue diamond waymarks. After the Café Höflihof there is a big farm and a sign points uphill to 'Zum Michaelsberg und Farrenkopf'. The route is now well-marked and mostly shady and in about 1^1/$_2$ hours one reaches the Hasemannhütte on the summit of the Farrenkopf 789m (2,588ft). Refreshments are available here at weekends and the view makes the climb worthwhile.

The route now continues southwards on part of the long-distance *Westweg* whose red diamond should be followed on an undulating path to Büchereck, reached in about 45 minutes. Now the road coming up from Elzach must be followed downhill for about 20 minutes when, just past the second *Hütte*, a waymarked path will be seen coming up from the right. Go 50m (54yd) further and then leave the road to join a pretty, unmarked track going left. Follow this round great curves, first to the left, then to the right, after which it becomes the surfaced little road down the Sulzbachtal, past several picturesque farmhouses back to the starting point.

Next is **Hornberg**, a tiny town which impresses initially with a feeling of spaciousness, although this may not be confirmed by closer acquaintance with the place. There is plenty of good, fresh air in this favourite holiday centre in a deservedly popular valley. An eleventh-century castle provides a splendid view over the town — the church, with murals dating from the sixteenth and seventeenth centuries, is worth a visit. There is also a short course on mushroom culture available nearby.

The so-called Black Forest Railway, now part of the Deutsche Bundesbahn (German Federal Railway) runs through the Gutachtal. The panoramic delights of this line deserve to be sampled and even the motorist should forsake his car and make the train journey over the most spectacular part of the route from Hornberg to St Georgen and back. Indeed, the Black Forest offers the railway enthusiast several exciting possibilities for indulging in his or her hobby and none is more exhilarating than the *Schwarzwaldbahn*. This runs from Offenburg in the Rhine valley to Donaueschingen on the eastern fringe of the Forest, a distance of some 85km (53 miles).

It was long thought that the technical problems involved in constructing such a line were so great as to make the project impracticable. However, detailed planning was started in 1862 with five possible routes in the starting list. In the end, it was decided to build the line through the Gutachtal despite the difficult terrain. For example, between Hornberg and Sommerau (today a journey of no more than 27 minutes), the line would have to overcome an altitude difference of 448m (1,460ft) in a straight line distance of only 11km (7 miles), and this through the notable Triberg granite. To do this, it was first proposed to introduce *Spitzkehren* which meant the altitude could be attained by a series of zig-zag movements. Such an arrangement persists today in the Andes and did, until recently, in Australia on the main line westwards from Sydney, where it is kept in operation as a museum piece.

The far-sighted railway pioneer Robert Gerwig realised that such cumbersome operations would soon prove unacceptable and he was responsible for the two great double horseshoes which the trains traverse to this day. Much of this section is in tunnels — in fact it has thirty-six of the thirty-nine on the whole line. Between the rapidly succeeding tunnels, the bewildered passenger catches tantalising glimpses of the spectacular scenery on either side. Gerwig was also responsible for building the tunnels big enough to take a double track even though only a single line was laid when the railway opened in 1873. Traffic developed quickly and the second track was laid piecemeal between 1888 and 1921.

Gerwig was later put in charge of the construction of the St Gotthard line in Switzerland and eventually returned home to become the general director of the Baden State Railways. So great was the impact of the new railway on the the territory through which it passed that, to this day, many places include 'Schwarzwaldbahn' in their postal addresses.

Soon after leaving Hornberg, the valley, which has hitherto been open and light, becomes narrow, dark and rocky, remaining so until **Triberg** is reached. The town is enclosed by the high mountains and a natural attraction is the famous Triberg waterfall, said to be the highest in Germany. There is a safe but somewhat exhausting walkway up beside the fall. This natural spectacle can, however, be seen with less expenditure of energy by taking the service bus in the direction of Schönwald and alighting at the stop known as 'Wasserfall' to follow the walkway downhill back to the town. In this busy resort of some 7,000 inhabitants, there is ample accommodation for the traveller but the town's restricted outlook makes it more suitable, perhaps, for an overnight stop only.

A traditional thatched farmhouse near Hornberg

Several large wood-carving shops, including the so-called 'House of a Thousand Clocks' make this a good place for the determined souvenir hunter. The *Heimatmuseum* in Triberg is held in high regard with its displays of costumes and clocks. An unusual exhibit is a relief model of the *Schwarzwaldbahn* complete with trains, the result of three years work by A. Fehrenbacher from Schramberg.

There are few really old buildings in Triberg for the town was almost completely destroyed by fire in 1826. All the same, there are a few sights of interest worth seeking out. The old *Amtshaus* (public office) with its timbered façade exposed in 1925 is one of these. Another is the simple *Rathaus* with its surprising council chamber decorated with beautiful carvings by the local craftsman, Karl Josef Fortwängler.

On the upper edge of the town, the interesting pilgrimage church known as Maria in der Tanne also survived the blaze. Already in

Hotel with window boxes in Triberg

Triberg waterfall

1645, there was a little chapel here with an altar painting of a miracle-working Madonna. The name is said to stem from the fact that someone had fastened the miraculous image to a *Tanne* (fir tree) in 1644. The picture was missing for some years but it is said to have been rediscovered by Austrian soldiers in 1692 when they suddenly heard singing as they were passing the tree.

The present church was built between 1699 and 1702 in order to accommodate the increasing number of pilgrims. The high altar, now incorporating the famous picture, was created by the sculptor, Anton Joseph Schupp from Villingen. He was also responsible for the side altars and the pulpit. Margrave Ludwig Wilhelm, who has been mentioned earlier, presented the artistic altar base in 1706. A memorial tablet of the citizens of Villingen (1715) is particularly interesting as it is the only known full picture of eighteenth-century Villingen. Triberg's modern spa centre is set in delightful gardens and embraces a concert hall, reading rooms, television room and a café with sun terrace.

The road divides at Triberg, the left fork going towards St Georgen which is also the direction of the railway. The European watershed comes between Triberg and St Georgen and the rivers, including the Gutach, which flow towards the west, the Rhine and ultimately the North Sea are now left. The first eastward-flowing stream, the Brigach, is met here. It is one of the sources of the Donau (Danube), which empties into the Black Sea.

Triberg is another place to start one of the organised walks already mentioned. This 9-day ramble follows the possible route of one of the old-time clock carriers who walked from place to place burdened with new clocks for sale. The territory covered is to the south and east of Triberg and takes in St Märgen, Titisee, Bonndorf and Villingen-Schwenningen. The going is a little easier than on some of the walks previously mentioned and this is emphasised by the distance of 187km (116 miles) covered. One does not need to undertake the whole route, however, and sections can be booked to suit the individual. In winter there is an alternative *Ski-Wandern* from Triberg to Titisee. (Details in both cases from Kurverwaltung, Triberg.)

St Georgen is another *Luftkurort* and winter sports centre. At an altitude of 800-1,000m (2,620-3,280ft), its chances of getting snow are fairly good while there are attractive walks around the town in all directions for the summer visitor. This is yet another place in which the Benedictine monks founded a monastery on the pattern of Hirsau, but in 1865 it was destroyed in a disastrous fire which also engulfed part of the town.

The present main shopping area is not particularly attractive, despite the excellent shops located there; modern architecture cannot compete with the old for charm. The beautiful town garden is worth visiting, and in the folk museum one can enjoy an educational display on the Black Forest way of life. The traditional costumes of the Forest are to be seen in many museums, but they are also still worn in many places for church-going and for special occasions such as weddings. St Georgen is one such place; here the headpiece worn by the women is the *Schäppelkrone*, an enormous decoration of glass pearls, coloured stones and tiny mirrors, the whole weighing 3kg ($6^1/_2$lbs).

It may be thought that the route to St Georgen described hardly falls within the scope of 'Valleys of the North' but it has been included here because of the continuous link from the Kinzigtal provided by the *Schwarzwaldbahn*. Other places in this area will be covered in Chapter 3.

For the purposes of this book, at least, one must retrace the route through the Gutachtal to the Kinzigtal, where the next town is **Hausach**. Its castle was destroyed during the Thirty Years' War, but the ruins remain and a good view is obtained along the valley. Once again, a history of fires means that there are no really old buildings in the town itself, but in the part known as Hausach-Dorf (village) there is an ancient church worthy of a visit. It is built on the site of a former Romanesque church which stood there in 1148. The late-Gothic choir, the tabernacle and the crucifixion scene from the twelfth century on the north outside wall all justify the visitor's attention. Hausach, together with **Haslach**, 6km (4 miles) further down the valley, attracts many visitors each year for its Shrovetide processions during which some of the participants wear historic wooden masks.

The pre-Lenten season of jollity is known in this area as *Fasnet* and its origins have something in common with *Karneval* in places like Cologne or Mainz and *Fasching* in Munich. However, the nature of the celebrations is quite different and there is less of the noisy and ostentatious revelry one associates with those places. The often grotesque masks conceal the identities of the participants in the various activities and the word *Narr*, meaning fool or jester, is used

Rathaus with colourful mural, Haslach

House in the Nordrachtal

Places of Interest In The Gutach Valley and Lower Kinzig Valley

Schwarzwaldbahn
This remarkable railway runs through the Gutach valley.

Gutach
Open Air Museum Vogtsbauernhof
Typical Black Forest farmhouses collected and reassembled with furnishings and implements.

Triberg
Highest waterfall in Germany.

Pilgrimage Church 'Maria in der Tanne' (1699-1702)
High altar incorporates the miraculous image.

Heimatmuseum
Excellent display of costumes and clocks and relief model of *Schwarzwaldbahn*.

Haslach
Heimatmuseum
Klosterstrasse 1. In former *Kapuzinerkloster* (1630)
The definitive collection of traditional Black Forest dress.

Rathaus (1733)
Paintings of traditional costumes on external walls.

Gasthaus 'Zur Sonne'
Birthplace of writer Heinrich Hansjakob (1837-1916).

Hansjakobmuseum
Hansjakobstrasse 17.
Memorabilia of the writer.

Steinach
Gasthaus 'Schwarzer Adler' (1715)
Regarded as the most beautiful half-timbered house in the Black Forest.

Zell am Harmersbach
Storchenturm (1402)
25m (82ft) high tower with basket for storks' nest.
Nearby are four Swedish cannon from Thirty Years War.

Hirschturm
Round tower, formerly part of defensive walls.

freely. Other places for seeing something of this seasonal letting down of hair include Zell am Harmersbach, Staufen, Rottweil, Villingen, Bad Dürrheim and Freiburg. Examples of the wooden masks will be found in the *Heimatmuseen* in these places.

In addition to the annual attraction of the Shrovetide processions, Haslach has several historic buildings for the traveller's delight, and the *Heimatmuseum* is in one of them, the former Kapuzinerkloster, which dates from 1630. The Zehntscheur (tithe barn) (1550), the town wall, the Sebastiansbrunnen (fountain) and the Gutleutbrücke (bridge) all contribute to a pleasant tour of inspection which should include the town church, with its Gothic west tower, a sandstone relief from the twelfth century and the tomb of Count Götz of Fürstenberg. As well as all these, there is the *Rathaus* (1733) which has unusual paintings of traditional costumes on the exterior walls.

The local writer, Heinrich Hansjakob (1837-1916), commemorates Count Götz in one of his Kinzigtal stories, *Der steinerne Mann von Hasle* (*The Stone Man of Haslach*). Hansjakob was born in the Gasthaus 'Zur Sonne'; this and another historic *Gasthaus*, the 'Zur Kanone' should not be omitted from one's exploration of this little country town.

The river, which flowed southwards from Freudenstadt then westwards from Schiltach, now completes its U-turn to flow in a northerly direction towards Offenburg. On its way, it meets several small places worthy of our attention.

There are those who contend that the Gasthaus 'Schwarzer Adler' (Black Eagle) in **Steinach** is the most beautiful timbered house in the Black Forest. Only the façade of this fine building is genuinely old, dating from 1715. The main structure of the house has been meticulously rebuilt behind, following 'clearance' of the site by the Royal Air Force during World War II. It was believed that the private railway saloon which was the headquarters of Nazi SS Chief Heinrich Himmler was being concealed in and moved between the various tunnels of the *Schwarzwaldbahn*; it was during attempts to sever the line by bombing, that the 'Adler' came to grief. Its restored *Flösserstube* (raft room) is like a little museum. A meal here could well be something to remember, as could one in another old *Gasthaus*, the 'Alte Bauernschänke' (literally translated: old public house for farmers), where the original interior has been preserved.

In the village of **Biberach** (population 3,000) there is a small *Heimatmuseum* and there is a *Waldparkplatz* about 1km ($^1/_2$ mile) east of the station adjacent to the attractive heated *Freibad* called the Terrassenbad, which has a big, curved chute. Numerous short round walks are indicated on the sign at the parking place together with a woodland nature trail to Zell am Harmersbach. The nature trail (*Waldlehrpfad*) makes for a pleasant 7km ($4^1/_2$ miles) ramble through the woods into the Harmersbach valley. The sign to follow is 'WL'; some signs also show Rebeck which is a point where paths meet.

Leave the car park past the swimming pool entrance and follow a broad, steadily rising track almost to the ridge, where care must be taken not to miss the narrow footpath going back sharply to the right. Climb a little more on this path until emerging on to wider tracks at Rebeck. Go straight forward down the one opposite and watch out for a diversion into another footpath going to the right and dropping steadily down towards Zell. Turn right on arriving at another broad track and, with the buildings of the town now clearly visible through the trees, go down a path which soon appears to the left and reach the first houses of Zell a few minutes later. Just before emerging from the woods, notice the entrances to two old mining galleries.

A path back to Biberach about 4km (2¹/₂ miles) along the slopes of the hill will be seen before reaching the town itself. Allow about 1¹/₂ hours each for the outward and return legs. There are also trains and buses from Zell to Biberach. Even if the ramble described has not been undertaken, most visitors will wish to leave the Kinzigtal at Biberach for an excursion into the Harmersbachtal and this is certainly to be recommended.

The former 'free' town of **Zell** is today a *Luftkurort* lying in a splendid holiday valley which, like the town itself, formed part of a 'free' farmers' republic until 1803. Prominent in Zell is the Storchenturm of 1402, which is 25m (82ft) high and still bears the basket intended to encourage storks to nest here although the birds have not made an appearance for many years. There is a small museum in the tower and four Swedish cannon are a relic of the Thirty Years War. They have survived more significant dangers since then, even the scouring of the land for scrap metal during World War II. Nearby is the smaller, round Hirschturm, a former strong point at a corner of the town wall, now standing in a peaceful little garden.

From Zell, a small road branches off to the north through the tiny Nordrachtal and an excursion through here is a pleasure no visitor to the area should miss. If the little river Harmersbach is followed up the main valley, note the fine old farmhouses along the way and several *Bildstöcke* (wayside shrines or memorials).

Yet another *Luftkurort*, **Oberharmersbach**, is reached in about 10km (6¹/₄ miles); this is a place for peaceful relaxation but it also has good facilities for visitors and ample access to the countryside. The Harmersbach comes down from Löcherbergwasen, the wooded upland between Oberharmersbach and the Renchtal. There is a W-Parkplatz up there with circular walks of 2-8km (1-5 miles) in length.

The visitor reliant upon public transport can readily explore the valley by using the little private railway, the *Harmersbachtalbahn*.

There is a fairly frequent service between Biberach station and Zell (5 minutes journey) and a less regular service on to Oberharmersbach. Many of the 'trains' are actually buses which start from just outside the station at Biberach.

The river Kinzig continues in a north-westerly direction from Biberach through Gengenbach and Offenburg (described in Chapter 1) and finally loses itself in the Rhine opposite Strasbourg.

3
THE CENTRAL AREA

Had the right-hand fork of the road been taken in Triberg, the traveller would have found him- or herself climbing through a series of sharp bends to the upland and the holiday area of **Schönwald**. It is not so many years since this was an enclosed village with old farms in a picturesque landscape; the development of holiday facilities has not been to the advantage of the general environment — a case of too much and too quickly perhaps.

Nevertheless, this is a most popular *Erholungsort* situated in the splendid rambling area of the Stöcklewald 1,067m (3,500ft) and Brend 1,149m (3,771ft). The nature conservation areas around the Blindensee and the Schwarzenbachtal are readily accessible. There are some big hotels here as well as accommodation in every other category. However, this is on the way to **Furtwangen** which, lying at 870m (2,854ft) above sea level, is the highest town in the southern half of the Black Forest.

It is not a beautiful town, despite its fine surroundings. After a disastrous fire in 1857 a decision was taken to only build in stone — in more recent times the 'stone' has become concrete, of course — and the resulting buildings are practical rather than charming. This is another clock-making town and one should visit the fine clock museum, which has more than a thousand examples of clocks of every kind. There are also mechanical organs which play from time to time, and models which can be operated by the visitor. Furtwangen stands on the young river Breg as it hastens eastwards to become one of the principal tributaries of the Danube.

Six kilometres (4 miles) north-west of the town is Brend where there is car-parking space to enable one to explore this 1,149m

(3,771ft) high formation on foot. There are outstanding views from its 46m (151ft) look-out tower in all directions over very typical Forest landscape. Close to the tower there is a *Gasthaus* as well as a youth hostel. Brend is the general name for the long-stretched ridge between Furtwangen and Elzach with summits running from south to north such as Brend itself, Rosseck 1,152m (3,781ft), Obereck 1,180m (3,872ft) and Rohrhardtsberg 1,155m (3,790ft).

An attractive little road runs along the ridge just to the east of these heights before descending to Schonach near Triberg. Near Brend is the ancient Martinskapelle, thought to have been built in about the year AD700. Many visitors go down the few steps to the source of the river Breg; the mighty Danube may thus be said to begin its 2,288km (1,430 mile) journey eastwards to the Black Sea here.

The great farmhouses in this area are well protected from the severe winter weather by their enormous roofs which reach almost to ground level in exaggerated, typical Black Forest style. Those same winters however, make the area a splendid playground for winter sports enthusiasts, for whom snow ploughs keep the road clear. The lives of these upland farmers have always been hard but now, at least, they have electricity, telephones and motor vehicles. More and more of them supplement their incomes by taking in paying guests.

An excursion of 10km ($6^1/_4$ miles) to the south-west through Neukirch takes a minor road towards St Märgen to visit the famous Hexenlochmühle (mill in the witches' hole). This is a working sawmill of unique design in the Black Forest because it has two contra-rotating waterwheels which can be operated simultaneously. Traditional cuckoo clocks are finished on the premises and there is a small, well-stocked shop where these and other souvenirs can be bought.

Westwards from Furtwangen, is the picturesque Simonswälder-tal, which contains the resorts of Gütenbach and Simonswald. The altitude decreases steadily as one drops towards the Elztal and road B294, which is still on its way from Pforzheim to Freiburg. **Güten-bach** is a small *Luftkurort* only 7km (4 miles) from Furtwangen and is an ideal resort for a quiet holiday. There is a fine network of marked footpaths allowing for walks of varying grades. The water-wheel no longer turns at the little old sawmill *Sägehäusle* on the outskirts of the village in the direction of Hintertal. However, this makes an excellent spot to start a typical round walk of 4km ($2^1/_2$

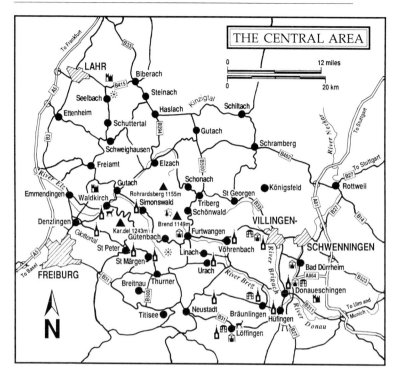

miles) which takes in the charming Hübschental.

There is parking space at the sawmill 859m (2,814ft) which is passed on one's left as the track is taken gently uphill in an easterly direction past isolated houses. At one of these, an attractive cluster of miniature houses stands beside the track for the passer-by to admire. After going past a small fish pond, the track curves round to the right at the end of the valley, to climb fairly steeply and complete a semi-circle for the return walk, which is mostly in woods, to the sawmill. As the whole route is on unsurfaced roads, the walk is fairly easy and can be completed comfortably in 1½ hours.

Although Gütenbach is quite small, the village has a fine, modern *Hallenbad*, and its other attractions include a fully automatic bowling alley (*Kegelbahn*) at the Park-Café 'Wendelbeck'. The well-known toy firm of Faller has a small factory here and music-lovers may be interested to know that the forefathers of Wilhelm Furtwängler, the

The Hexenlochmühle, near Furtwangen

famous conductor, lived and worked in Gütenbach.

The name **Simonswald** covers the hamlets of Ober-, Alt-, Haslach- and Untersimonswald, which straggle along the Simonswäldertal. An oddity here is that the valley does not take the name of its river, for the river is the Wilde Gutach. Gutach is a name which crops up many times in the Black Forest and this one has no connection with that mentioned earlier when the Gutachtal was explored. The Simonswäldertal, some 30km (19 miles) north-east of Freiburg, is within walking distance of several centres including St Peter and St Märgen. However, the less energetic will find it more comfortable to arrive in the valley by road and perhaps explore it on foot. There is no railway, but the valley is served by a bus service operating between the station at Bleibach and Furtwangen.

The church occupies a prominent position in Obersimonswald — another place to see traditional dress during Sunday churchgoing. The costumes in this valley are some of the most decorative that can still be seen in ordinary use. In the church there hangs a famous picture, *The Seven Holy Sleepers*, which tells of seven youths who were walled up alive in Ephesus and awoke when discovered 175 years later. The Gasthof 'Engel', closed in November and on Tuesdays, is a rural inn with stables and its own chapel. The walled church in Altsimonswald, a place of farms and sawmills, stands on a small hill and contains two artistic wooden sculptures from the sixteenth century. At Untersimonswald, a small side valley, the Haslachtal, accommodates the community of Haslachsimonswald. At the valley entrance there is a *Märchenwald* — a fairytale wood.

The scattered community of Simonswald constitutes yet another *Luftkurort* which has an altitude range of 300-1,200m (984-3,940ft). It offers all that the visitor seeking a peaceful holiday could wish for, including a heated swimming pool. The river Wilde Gutach is not usually particularly wild where it passes through the resort. However, to the south it parts company with the main road and enters a sombre valley which has many legends of witches, goblins and the like, eventually leading to the *Hexenloch* (witches' hole) and the famous mill mentioned earlier.

Continuing down the valley, road B294 is joined at Bleibach and a right turn here leads through the small *Luftkurort* of Elzach back to Haslach in the Kinzigtal. **Bleibach** has an old charnel house chapel with a Dance-of-Death frieze from 1733. The parish church dates from the sixteenth century. The visitor should spend a little time in **Elzach** (population 6,400), an old-world place with a pretty townscape. Do not miss the old *Apotheke* (apothecary's shop) from 1523 nor the St Nikolausbrunnen (fountain) from 1610. The parish church of St Nikolaus has a late-Gothic choir, a seventeenth-century nave and stained glass from 1524.

This charming little health resort with its modest but more than adequate range of accommodation makes an ideal base for those who prefer to be away from the main tourist centres yet to have easy access to a very attractive countryside. A popular short ramble is that to the pilgrimage chapel of the Neun Linden (nine lime trees). Beyond Elzach, the river Elz may be followed north-eastwards into the steep, twisty but very pretty Prechtal.

In the village of Oberprechtal, about 8km (5 miles) from Elzach, the road divides and the river makes a sharp turn southwards. The left fork descends steeply to reach the Gutachtal between Gutach and Hornberg in about 8km (5 miles). The right fork (signposted Triberg) follows the river and climbs steadily for some 14km ($8^3/_4$ miles) to **Schonach** (population 4,600), a *Luftkurort* only 4km ($2^1/_2$ miles) from Triberg.

This is a summer holiday town and a winter sports centre with 100km (62 miles) of ski touring routes marked out. There is a baroque parish church but also an unfortunate tendency to follow the bad example of nearby Schönwald, with new building construction marring the hitherto unspoiled countryside. There is still a fine view from the Wilhelmshöhe but even this is not as beautiful as it used to be. Triberg was visited in Chapter 2 so steps must now be retraced to Bleibach. Turning left here on leaving the Simonswäldertal, one is almost immediately in yet another Gutach, a pretty little village lying mostly a little aside from the main road which arrives at Waldkirch in another 3km (2 miles).

Waldkirch (population 19,000) is a *Kneippkurort* which developed from a Benedictine nunnery founded in AD916 and received its town charter in 1300. The suburb of Kollnau just to the north is even older, having originally been an Alemannic settlement. Waldkirch now includes many outlying areas so the town itself is not as big as the population figure might suggest. It is served by a branch railway line from Freiburg.

There is too much high-rise development and industrial intrusion for this to be an immediately attractive town, despite its *Kur* status, but it has a fine position at the foot of the 1,243m (4,077ft) high Kandel. There are a number of interesting buildings, not the least of these being the town church (1732-4). This is a masterpiece of baroque architecture from the hand of Peter Thumb, of whom more will be said later. One of the original bells, cast in Strasbourg in 1763, is displayed outside the church. The rococo banqueting hall of the priory and the beautiful *Marktplatz* are both worth seeing.

The prosperity of the town was founded on the preparation of semi-precious stones and the construction of musical instruments; the name Waldkirch can still be seen on some splendid fairground organs. There is an important clinic above the town on the lower slopes of the Kandel where people with heart and circulatory conditions are treated. In the town itself there is a small but interesting zoo, while a stiffish climb takes one up to the inevitable ruined castle, the Kastelburg, for fine views over the town and valley.

The ruins were purchased by the town in 1971 and are now cared for by the fire brigade which organises cheerful folk events up there from time to time. It is a feature of Black Forest life — indeed of West Germany in general — that the voluntary fire brigades play an active part in the social and cultural life of the community. Though the outlook from the Kastelburg is not what one normally regards as typical Black Forest scenery, it is one of the many joys of the Black Forest that a few kilometres can make all the difference to the surroundings. That is certainly the case in Waldkirch; the beautiful Simonswäldertal lies only a short distance to the north, but it is to the magnificent Kandel east of the town that the Waldkirchers mostly look for their recreation. Twelve kilometres ($7^1/_2$ miles) of steep, winding road climb the 1,000m (3,280ft) from the town to the summit, but it is only necessary to go a short part of this distance to be among the pinewoods and have access to the numerous footpaths which criss-cross the slopes. At every bend the motorist may catch a tantalizing view back over the valley, but the driver will find little opportunity to relax as he or she negotiates the numerous Z-bends and will need frequent stops if not to feel utterly frustrated.

The long-distance footpath *Kandelhöhenweg*, which started away in the north at Oberkirch, passes close to Waldkirch before making the steep ascent to the summit. It is possible to join the path for this section, thereafter returning to Waldkirch by bus. A less strenuous alternative, of course, would be to do this in the reverse direction. Once the path is located it can be readily followed along the *Schwarzwaldverein* trail, marked by a white letter 'K' in a red diamond, and no detailed description of the route is necessary here.

A pretty but little-known, pear-shaped area lies north of Waldkirch, bounded on the south-east by the Elztal and B294 and on the west by the *Badische Weinstrasse* (B3) which converge at the south end near Denzlingen. The north end is enclosed by the Kinzig valley road B33 and its branch from Biberach down into Lahr, the B415. The area measures some 25km (16 miles) from north to south and almost as much from east to west; at the centre is **Schweighausen**, mentioned briefly in Chapter 1 in the course of an excursion from Ettenheim. The five roads which converge at Schweighausen all have to climb to reach the village which stands close to the 726m (1,732ft) Schillingerberg. The area can conveniently be explored by taking each of these roads in turn.

From Lahr, the B415 follows the Schuttertal past Kuhbach, which has already been mentioned, and at Reichenbach the main road is left to follow the valley south to **Seelbach**, a *Luftkurort* of 4,500 inhabitants reached in 7km (4 miles) from Lahr. The B415 is picturesque as it continues eastwards towards Biberach, climbing first to the Schönberg pass at 370m (1,215ft) before dropping gently down into

Places of Interest In and Around Furtwangen, Simonswald and The Elz Valley

Furtwangen
Deutsches Uhrenmuseum
In town centre
Comprehensive collection of timepieces and mechanical instruments. Film shows.

Brend
1,149m (3,770ft) summit, 6km (4 miles) north-west of town. Observation tower and outstanding views. Martinskapelle and source of river Breg.

Hexenlochmühle
10km (6¹/₄ miles) south-west through Neukirch.
Unique mill with two waterwheels. Shop for clocks and other gifts.

Urach
Village Church
Prominent 'onion' tower and beautiful interior.

Vöhrenbach
Parish Church (Thirteenth-century)
Notable Gothic Madonna.

Zur-Sieben-Frauen-Kapelle
Gruesome reminders of witch hunts.

Simonswald
Obersimonswald Church
Contains a famous painting, *The Seven Holy Sleepers*.

Altsimonswald Church
Artistic sixteenth-century wooden sculptures.

Märchenwald
Fairytale wood at Untersimonswald.

Elzach
Apotheke (1523)
Apothecary's shop

Nikolausbrunnen (1610)
Fountain

St Nikolaus' Church
Late-Gothic choir, seventeenth-century nave, stained glass from 1524.

Bleibach
Old Charnel House Chapel
'Dance of Death' frieze (1733)

Parish Church (sixteenth-century)

Waldkirch
Kastelburg
Castle ruin with fine views.

Baroque Church (1732-4)
In town centre
A masterpiece by the architect Peter Thumb.

Zoo
Close to town centre
Small but interesting collection well laid out.

Kandel
1,243m (4,077ft) summit, 12km (7¹/₂ miles) south-east on road to St Peter
Splendid views.
Hang gliding.

Mosaic of St Christopher, Glottertal church

the Kinzig valley. Near the summit is the ruined Burg Hohengeroldseck built in the twelfth century to protect the pass. It is well-worth the climb up to the castle for the splendid view. Needless to say, there is a hostelry at the pass; the Löwen (lion) which is one of several claiming to be the oldest *Gasthaus* in Germany.

Near Seelbach, in the side valley called Litschental, is a real rarity among Black Forest craft workshops — the Geroldsecker Waffenschmiede or armourer's workshop. The smithy has been in the possession of the Fehrenbach family for many centuries and the present smith works in the same traditional way as his predecessors of 700 years ago. The smithy was always in the service of the Counts of Geroldseck (hence the name) and provided them with their swords and halberds.

After the Burg Hohengeroldseck fortress was overthrown by the French in 1689, the Fehrenbachs took a vow never to manufacture weapons of war again. The business continued with the making and repair of domestic and agricultural implements but twentieth-century economics made the livelihood ever more precarious. Some years ago, Ludwig Fehrenbach, master smith, decided to break the vow of his forefathers and resume manufacture of weapons by the same methods and to the same patterns as 300 years earlier. Although quite usable weapons, today they are not produced for warlike purposes but for ceremonial occasions, museums and private collectors.

The products of this little workshop, each bearing the family's symbol of a clover leaf, are now to be found all over Germany and Switzerland. Indeed, so great is the demand, that a younger Fehrenbach has already been installed in the smithy to carry on the great tradition. Visitors are welcomed on Saturday and Sunday afternoons when the three waterwheels which provide the power are set in motion. At 6.5m (21ft), the main wheel is the second largest in Germany.

Before leaving the Seelbach area, it is worth visiting the ruins of Burg Dautenstein, often destroyed and rebuilt, with its three fine corner towers. Southwards from Seelbach, the observant traveller will notice that many of the farmhouses are built of a reddish sandstone, a material widely available in this area, as can be seen from the ruins of Burg Hohengeroldseck.

Continuing up the Schuttertal, the *Luftkurort* of that name (population 3,400) is reached in another 5km (3 miles) and it seems quite appropriate in this idyllic valley that the modest mountain to the east is called the Himmelsberg (Heavenly Mountain). Then go on to Dörlinbach, an outlying part of Schuttertal, and follow the road as it climbs up out of the valley to Schweighausen. The several resorts in the Schuttertal are by no means prime tourist centres but they each have *Gasthöfe* and a certain amount of other accommodation for the visitor.

The second road to be followed is that which leaves Steinach, with its famous hostelry in the Kinzigtal, and passes through Welschensteinach to reach Mühlsbach on the eastern flank of the Himmelsberg in about 7km (4 miles). The road is picturesque throughout and it becomes quite twisty after Mühlsbach as it climbs towards Schweighausen. The Welschensteinach area is particularly lovely in spring, when the many fruit trees blossom. The valley is also notable for its many well-preserved, traditional houses.

Just south of Elzach, a little road climbs north-westwards out of the Elztal, passing in turn through the villages of Unterbiederbach, Biederbach and Oberbiederbach, past which there is a camp site. The previously mentioned road is joined just 4km (2$^1/_2$ miles) before Schweighausen. The road in the opposite direction, from Ettenheim on the *Weinstrasse*, has already been referred to in Chapter 1. Herbolzheim and Kenzingen, also on the *Weinstrasse*, are starting points for tourists making their way into the area through the quiet Bleiche valley. There are numerous parking places in the valley, enabling nature-lovers to leave their vehicles and ramble in the pleasant countryside.

From Emmendingen and Denzlingen on the *Weinstrasse*, and from Bleibach in the Elz valley, three roads straggle gradually northwards, to merge and run together into the scattered holiday resort of **Freiamt** (population 3,900). It is only another 8km (5 miles) from here to Schweighausen. Freiamt is a good centre for the visitor seeking a peaceful holiday in pleasant surroundings with, perhaps, an emphasis on outdoor pursuits. The village occupies a sunny position on the south-west slopes of the Hünersedel which, at 746m (2,447ft), is the highest mountain in this area. It is readily ascended on foot or by car and from the heights there are good views into the Elz valley to the east and the Rhine plain and valley to the west.

There is a good network of footpaths all round and these can be used for getting to a number of places of interest in the vicinity. Two kilometres (1$^1/_4$ miles) west of Freiamt, **Ottoschwanden** has a church

Places of Interest In and Around Schweighausen, Glottertal, St Peter and St Märgen

Seelbach

Burg Hohengeroldseck
(Twelfth-century)
Impressive castle ruin 4km
(2$^1/_2$ miles) north-west. near B415
Panoramic views. Ancient
Gasthaus 'Löwen'.

Geroldsecker Waffenschmiede
Old armourer's workshop in
Litschental near Seelbach.
Huge waterwheel.

Burg Dautenstein
Above Seelbach
Another castle ruin.

Ettenheimmünster

Impressive former *Kloster* church.

Ottoschwanden

Church with Romanesque and
Gothic elements.

Tennenbach

Chapel of former Cistercian *Kloster*
and graves from 1812-5 wars of
liberation.

Glottertal

Village Church
Huge mosaic picture of St
Christopher outside and a fine
carved triptych within.

Schwarzwaldklinik
Location of the television series of
the same name.

St Peter

Baroque Church (1717-19)
Another imposing edifice by
architect Peter Thumb.
Organ concerts in summer.

Former Kloster
Magnificant rococo library also by
Peter Thumb.
Conducted tours of whole
complex.

Lindenberg
2km (1$^1/_4$ miles) from village
Charming pilgrimage church.

Zweribach Waterfalls
7km (4$^1/_2$ miles) north-east of St
Peter via Schmittenbachstrasse
Nature conservation area.
(Also accessible on foot from St
Märgen)

Sägendobel
4km (2$^1/_2$ miles) north on road to
Kandel
Roadside display of models
operated by water power.
Chapel with wood carvings by local
artist.

St Märgen

Rankmühle
1km ($^1/_2$ mile) from village on field
road
Picturesque old water mill.

Klosterkirche (1723)
Baroque pilgrimage church.

House with fruit trees near Welschensteinach

with a sacral choir and there are Romanesque and Gothic elements in the building itself. It is not a long walk to the Bleichtal, through which the road climbs from Kenzingen, and here there is another historic smithy.

In the village of **Tennenbach** — still part of Freiamt — the chapel of a former Cistercian *Kloster* may be inspected together with soldiers' graves from the 1812-5 wars of liberation. Back in the centre, the *Kurhaus* provides for the unsophisticated entertainment of the guest. There is a sauna at the *Hallenbad* and massage facilities are available.

A modern dual carriageway runs from Waldkirch to Freiburg and 7km (4 miles) from Waldkirch is the entrance to the Glottertal. This name not only refers to the valley but also the twin villages of Unter-und Oberglottertal. First though, at the mouth of the valley, is the little town of **Denzlingen**, through which the river Glotterbach flows on its way to the nearby Rhine. The town, with a population of some 9,000, lies in the 'V' formed by the convergence of roads B3 and B294 coming in from the north and is thus spared the worst of the heavy traffic. It does, however, lie on the route of the long-distance path Rhein-Kaiserstuhl-Schwarzwald which starts at Breisach and runs some 114km (70 miles) eastwards to Donaueschingen.

There is an early Gothic church in the town and the waymarks of the named path (red diamond on yellow background) could be followed northwards up to the little wood called Mauracher Hölzle where there is a good view up into the Glottertal. The route then turns east to the Mauracher Hof, a rural inn, and from here the ruins of St Severius (or Severin) Chapel may be visited for an extensive view over the Rhine valley and towards the steeply rising Black Forest hills to the east. The town's indoor and outdoor swimming pools will be found near here. Return to the town centre by any of the quite pleasant streets running downhill.

The Glottertal has no railway but a somewhat infrequent bus service operates from Freiburg. There is significant fruit and wine production here and the sunny, south-facing slopes of the valley are clothed with vineyards. The vines even grow at an altitude of 500m (1,640ft) — higher than anywhere else in Germany and evidence of the sheltered situation on this flank of the Kandel.

There is a splendid timber house in **Unterglottertal** which is the hotel and restaurant 'Engel' (Angel), venison dishes are a speciality on the menu here. In fact, this is only one of several very fine hostelries encountered along this road, most of them in historic buildings.

In **Oberglottertal** there is a heated swimming pool with the usual large and well-kept grassed area around it for sunbathing and games. There is also a new *Hallenbad* at the sports centre, which is available during the months when the *Freibad* is closed, usually about mid-September to mid-May. The exterior of the village church has a large and colourful mosaic depicting St Christopher, the patron saint of travellers, and inside is a fine carved triptych (a carving on three panels with sides able to fold over the centre). Traditional dress is still worn by some of the villagers for going to church on Sundays. Oberglottertal's scattered farmhouses can be seen all around on the slopes of the Kandel and other mountains. As one leaves the village, there are large sawmills serving the forests which crowd into this end of the valley.

Because of its favourable climate, the Glottertal was one of the first areas settled by the Alemannians and it has long been the haunt of the discerning holidaymaker. **Glottertal** is a health resort and it is recorded that as early as 1500, intrepid travellers were coming here to enjoy the healing properties of the Glotterbad. By 1880, about a hundred visitors were coming annually; the local information office now records around 200,000 bed-nights each year. This is the location of the *Schwarzwaldklinik* (Black Forest Clinic) made known to the world through the German television soap opera of that name.

The visiting angler may fish in the river Glotter from April to September. Day tickets are obtainable from the tourist office which also has bicycles for hire. Here, as in most other resorts, the visitor, upon paying the *Kurtaxe*, is provided with a card which entitles him or her to free use of certain amenities in the area, as well as reduced admission charge to swimming pools, museums and so on. Fortunately, the growth of tourism in recent years has not been allowed to spoil this lovely place.

After leaving Glottertal, the road climbs quite steeply to the resort of **St Peter**, which is dominated by the twin towers of the fine baroque church designed, once again, by Peter Thumb. Thumb, who lived from 1681 to 1766, was the most significant member of a family of German master-builders and architects from the Vorarlberg. The church in St Peter must surely be one of the loveliest in the whole Black Forest and, having recently received a thorough renovation, the interior makes a bright and colourful impression. It is attached to the former *Kloster*, now used as a school for those entering the priesthood.

The *Kloster* was moved to this site in 1091 by Duke Bertold II of Zähringen and was granted many privileges by the rulers. At that time, this area was in the Austrian border region and the *Kloster* suffered a great deal from the various border incidents, with fire and looting being responsible for the loss of many medieval art treasures. The church was the funerary church of the Zähringen dynasty, eight members of which are buried here. The very fine organ is one of those used regularly for the Black Forest cycle of organ recitals which takes place each year.

A guided tour of the church and *Kloster* complex includes a visit to the remarkable rococo style library which cannot otherwise be seen. It is noted for an interesting ceiling painting by B. Gambs (1751). There is no charge and no gratuities are accepted, but one is invited to make a contribution to charity.

It is the custom in suitable weather, for the congregation to linger before and after Mass, in the square in front of the church where they exchange news and gossip with their friends and relatives. This sometimes provides an opportunity to see the wearing of *Tracht*, the traditional dress; many girls wear the colourful festal costumes to their first communion and on the occasions of other special church services such as those for the ordination of the new priests from the seminary. The outstanding feature of the St Peter *Tracht* is the *Schäppel* or head-dress, with its many coloured glass pearls and silver ornaments which glitter in the sunshine. Many hours of toilsome handwork are required for the construction of these 'crowns' which then become a valued possession. In many places, especially where the blight of

Baroque interior of church in St Peter

St Peter with the twin towers of its church

St Märgen church

The Rankmühle, an old water mill near St Märgen

modern tourism is most marked, the wearing of *Tracht*, particularly the head-dress, has virtually died out but this is by no means the case here.

The farmhouses belonging to St Peter are scattered widely over the surrounding slopes and many of them have self-catering flats to let. There are ample facilities in the village including a *Freibad* and a modern *Hallenbad*. Regular folk evenings, slide shows and other entertainments are provided during the summer months. There is also winter activity here, for the surrounding hills are sufficiently high to ensure that there is usually suitable snow for skiing. As well as the open slopes, there are marked paths through the woods for skiers.

Like St Peter, St Märgen depends on the bus service from Freiburg for its public transport. St Märgen is a mere 8km (5 miles) from St Peter and the road continues to climb through a series of bends with wide views over the countryside to the south. There are lay-bys at the most suitable points for viewing or photography. As the twin towers of St Peter disappear behind, those of the former *Klosterkirche* of St Märgen come into view ahead. There are some fine old farmhouses to be seen, the finest being, perhaps, the Luxhof with its own small chapel and a pond constructed to provide a supply of water for fire-fighting. Both of these features are typical of the farms in this area and the little chapels are nearly always beautifully kept and worth a peep inside.

St Märgen is a health resort on a smallish scale and, like all the other resorts in this area, has a wealth of holiday accommodation, largely in private houses or in self-catering flats. As with St Peter, there are no ugly modern developments to offend the eye. The church has been undergoing renovation both inside and out during recent years but is still something of a disappointment after the splendours of St Peter. There is skiing here in winter with a ski shop in the village. Although St Märgen is one of the better-known holiday locations, the newcomer can easily find the peace and beauty which he or she is seeking. An open-air pool and an ingenious children's play area contribute to the popularity of the resort for family holidays.

St Märgen is one of the places in which traditional Black Forest dress may be seen on the days of certain religious celebrations. The *St Märgener Rosstag* or *'Tag des Schwarzwälder Pferde'* (Day of the Black Forest Horse) takes place every third year on the 10 September and is associated with *Maria Geburt*, the church festival which traditionally celebrates the birth of the Virgin Mary. The ceremonial blessing of the horses takes place in the morning and in the afternoon, horses, riders and carriages assemble for a colourful procession with, of course, musical accompaniment provided by local bands.

St Peter and St Märgen, each with a population of about 2,000, lie at altitudes of 720m (2,362ft) and 887m (2,910ft) respectively, although the surrounding hills are much higher. There is a lot of dairy-farming in this area and, in addition to the pinewoods, there are pleasant upland pastures to vary the scenery. Both places are excellent walking centres. A walk up from St Peter to the peaceful pilgrimage church on the Lindenberg gives one a salutary reminder of the horrors of the Nazi regime. Here, on a plaque in the church, one finds the names of some of the many priests who died in Hitler's concentration camps or within a few days of their 'release'.

The field path to the Lindenberg passes wayside 'Stations of the Cross'. Such series of monuments are widespread in one form or another and the Black Forest is also rich in individual wayside shrines. These vary from a simple cross erected in memory of a beloved member of the family to a small chapel with a miniature altar and perhaps one or two bench seats.

An interesting marked 13km (8 mile) walk (black spot on yellow ground) leads from St Märgen to the Zweribach waterfalls. Signs to the Rankmühle are followed from the village and lead to a picturesque old water mill, no longer in use, in less than 1km ($\frac{1}{2}$ mile). After this, the path climbs steadily through the Rankwald to the highest point of the walk, where, at a height of 1,029m (3,375ft), there is the tiny but beautiful Kapfenkapelle, which has an interesting story. A certain Josef Hummel loved to walk up and enjoy the view from the Kapfenberg but in 1848 he suffered a stroke and thereafter could only walk with difficulty, using a stick or a crutch. He vowed that if God restored him sufficiently for him to go once again to the mountain unaided, he would have a chapel built there in gratitude. He was able to do this in 1850 and his chapel stood until 1973, when it was burned down. Two years later, a local resident had it rebuilt and this is the lovely wooden building seen today. Josef Hummel's view is still there as one looks down the valley from the front of the chapel.

Continuing through the woods, one soon crosses a tiny stream, the Hirschbach, and turns right to the Geschwanderdobelhütte and the start of the nature conservation area known as Zweribach. (The hut is occasionally open for refreshments.) Almost hidden in the trees near a small spring is a memorial to freedom fighters of the 1930s. The path follows the edge of the reserve in a north-westerly direction for about 1.5km ($^3/_4$ mile) and then plunges abruptly down into the heart of the reserve towards the waterfalls.

The Zweribach reserve is known as a *Bannwald*, an area which is left entirely to nature without the aid of man to clear fallen trees, maintain paths and so on, the aim being to discover how the landscape will develop without human intervention. For this reason, the paths here are not of the normal standard and great care is needed to negotiate the steep slopes; stout footwear is essential. The main waterfall can be quite spectacular but the visitor is warned against following the example of one local who stepped back to admire it and plunged to his death on the rocks below. The nature-lover will find much of interest in this small area, which is eventually left to follow an alternative route back to St Märgen.

Four kilometres (2$^1/_2$ miles) up the Schmittenbachstrasse north-east of St Peter, there is a parking place known as Potsdamer Platz which makes a good base for a day's ramble, which covers 18km (11 miles) including the summit of the Kandel. Since the starting point is already at about 1,000m (3,280ft), the climb is not too strenuous. About 1km ($^1/_2$ mile) along the surfaced road from the car park, one reaches a farm called Gschwinghof. Here a left fork leads to a field track marked 'Kandel' and identified by the blue diamond on white ground of a *Schwarzwaldverein* connecting route. The track climbs gently, first northerly and then westerly until, about 4km (2$^1/_2$ miles) from Gschwinghof, the main St Peter to Waldkirch road is crossed at a bus stop and small car park called Linie. The woodland path is now parallel to the road and after passing a hut called Schwärhütte at 1,064m (3,490ft), the remaining distance of 2km (1 mile) involves a stiffish climb to the summit viewing platform at 1,243m (4,077ft).

Part of the summit is marked off to protect the rare sub-alpine plants and this area should not be entered. Late summer visitors should look for the remarkable low-growing silver thistle in pasture-land and on sunny banks. The flower is of the everlasting type and is not often found below the 1,000m (3,280ft) line. In any case, it soon disappears, as the local women collect it for winter floral arrange-ments. In summer the Kandel is ideal for rambling at quite high level through the woods round the summit, and in winter it is a paradise

*Woodcarving of
preacher in St Märgen*

for skiers. Not only are there good walks and good views in every
direction, but there is good food here too. As the rest days of the two
hotels, the Berghotel Kandel and the Kandelhof, do not coincide, one
need never go hungry.

For the return to the starting point, the *Kandelhöhenweg* (white 'K'
on red diamond) can be followed from the summit to descend fairly
steeply for 5km (3 miles) to the sleepy little village of Sägendobel
760m, (2,493ft) lying just off the main road. The bubbling Glotterbach
runs down through the valley to power the small sawmills, and there
are two inns. It is worth going into the little chapel, constructed in the
basement of the old school house, to admire the beautiful wood
carvings made by a local craftsman. After crossing the main road to
continue the walk, one ought to stop for a few moments, especially
if accompanied by children, to see the little water-driven models
which are found on the side of the road further from the village. The

clever builder has included a roundabout, men sawing and chopping wood, and even a woman tolling the church bell.

Unless one wishes to follow the 'K' route back into St Peter itself, turn left from the models and walk beside the road towards the Kandel for a short distance. Turn right into a small road marked, somewhat inadequately, by blue and red arrows and a sign to Eckjörghof, a farm which is soon passed on the right. After about 1.5km (³/₄ mile) of fairly stiff climb, one should see a red triangle sign indicating the path back to Potsdamer Platz. Always proceed in a generally easterly direction; a tendency to follow more obvious tracks going north must be resisted as these lead down into the upper part of the Glotterbachtal and would add some 4km (2¹/₂ miles) as well as an unnecessary climb.

Apart from the longish walks described, there is ample opportunity for shorter excursions in an area which has countless small car parks beside the roads or at the edge of the woods. The list of walks exhibited in St Märgen includes this as yet another place from which to ramble to the Hexenlochmühle.

South of St Märgen, the road runs through fairly sparsely populated but beautiful country and soon joins the B500, the so-called *Panoramastrasse*, to Breitnau, a scattered resort in a wide valley beneath the 1,125m (3,692ft) high Rossberg. At several places, lay-bys allow the motorist to pull off the road to admire the view. With so many variations, it is difficult to say just what constitutes 'typical' Black Forest scenery but this area, with its many traditional farmhouses, lush meadows and forested slopes, must surely approach it.

The farms in the vicinity are noted for their length of ownership by the same family. There is a simple explanation for this; instead of the eldest son inheriting the property, here it is the youngest son who does so and accepts the responsibility of caring for his other brothers and sisters as well as for aged parents. The arrangement is often difficult in practice but it ensures that the properties remain undivided and explains the widely spaced scattering of the farm houses over the landscape.

Each farm has a name, often derived from a name in Christian history. Thus Thomalihof, Barthleshof and Simonshof have fairly obvious origins. Nazihof is not so immediately evident. Needless to say, it has nothing to do with Hitler's ill-famed political party but means, in fact, the farm of Ignatius. There are several farms having this name; one of them is close to the main road at Breitnau while a mile or so further north there is a Nazishäusle (the little house of Ignatius). These great old farmhouses are ideal for farm holidays (*Ferien auf dem Bauernhof*) and many of them have holiday flats or rooms to let.

There are several *Gasthäuser* on the main road, although the village centre of **Breitnau** (population 1,900) lies just to the west of it. One of those south of the village is called 'Zur Ravennaschlucht' and it not only makes a good stop for a drink or a meal but is a place from which to commence a walk to the famous Ravennaschlucht (gorge) itself. There are other hostelries in the village and there is a *W-Parkplatz* right in the centre, a starting place for a number of round walks.

A typical one of 6km (3³/₄ miles) starts in a south-westerly direc- tion (waymark; blue spot) towards the rim of the Höllental (Hell valley). After about 2km (1¹/₄ miles) this track crosses the east-west long-distance path, from Freiburg to Lake Constance, which is marked by a red/white diamond on a yellow ground. Turn east along this latter route for a good 2km (1¹/₄ miles) until it crosses the little river Ravenna, about to plunge down into the lower *Schlucht* (gorge). One can also add about 4km (2¹/₂ miles) for the worthwhile side excursion (waymark; green spot) down into the gorge and back (more about this in Chapter 4). On returning to the original route, continue into the upper gorge, stick with the green spot route going northwards back to the starting point in Breitnau, reached in another 2km (1¹/₄ miles).

The visitor will find many old water mills in this area — several are encountered in the course of the walk just described — but unfortunately most of them are more or less derelict and they are steadily disappearing altogether. In the past, every big farm had its own mill but the internal combustion engine has changed all that. However, funds are available for the restoration of a few mills that are already over 150 years old. Some of these were real works of art and the mill builder was just as important as the miller himself. Water power in the mills was principally used for grinding corn and sawing timber. The message for the visitor is clear; if a water mill is found which is in presentable condition, take the opportunity of examining and photographing it — it may be gone by the next time one passes this way. Breitnau is much concerned with winter activities and has an extensive network of ski-touring routes. Breitnau is under the administration of Hinterzarten, a few kilometres further south, described in the next chapter.

Walking on the Kandel

Return northwards along the B500, and one will come to **Thurner**. Here the road from St Märgen comes in and there is the principal *Langlauf* (cross-country skiing) centre in the area. The Thurnerwirtshaus, at 1,036m (3,398ft), has fifty-five beds, an indoor pool and a sauna but it is closed from 15 November to 15 December. Although this comfortable hotel is eminently suitable for the winter visitor, it is fine at all other seasons too and specially welcomes family holidaymakers in the summer months. There is also a certain amount of more simple accommodation here including some self-catering.

The B500 now continues north-eastwards in the direction of Furtwangen and, in a few kilometres, bypasses the village of Waldau where the valleys Jostal and Langenordnachtal come in from the direction of Neustadt. In another 4km (2¹/₂ miles), take a right turning signed 'Donaueschingen' leading down into the Urachtal and, after a few minutes, notice the remarkably big church in the village of **Urach**. Its red onion tower is a prominent feature on the skyline and there is an unusual barrel vault roof inside, with every panel painted most beautifully. The pulpit is also a splendid creation and the visitor should certainly take the opportunity of stopping to

Interior of church with painted, barrel vault roof, Urach

inspect this fine church with its surrounding fortified wall.

Continue down the valley to Hammereisenbach where several roads come together. Turn north here to follow the river Breg — a tributary of the Danube — upstream in the direction of Vöhrenbach. The minor road leading into the Linachtal goes off to the left after about 2km (1¹/₄ miles). This is another place for those who want to relax in rural surroundings of great charm and there is a large *Stausee* (man-made lake) with recreational facilities.

Vöhrenbach is an *Erholungsort* of about 3,900 inhabitants. It was founded in 1244 and is now an important centre for the production of Black Forest clocks. There is a Gothic Madonna in the thirteenth-century church which should be seen. One of the more gruesome tales of medieval witch-hunting is commemorated in the 'Zur-Sieben-Frauen-Kapelle' where there is a picture showing the burning of seven young women. They had protested their innocence but, as witches, they were sentenced to death on a funeral pyre. All seven uttered curses which were later fulfilled. The youngest threw a bunch of seven keys to the ground and prophesied that as a sign of her innocence a spring would burst forth at the spot. This did, in fact, happen and even today many people visit the spring with its reputedly healing water.

A road runs westwards from Vöhrenbach to Furtwangen (visited earlier in this chapter) but the route to be followed now turns towards the north-west and reaches the *Luftkurort* and winter sports centre of **Unterkirnach** after about 8km (5 miles). For a small place, there is a lot of accommodation and there is the *Gartenhallenbad*, an all-weather pool with solarium. Unterkirnach is the mid-point on a walk from Villingen to be described a little later. However, do not turn towards that city at this stage but continue for another 8-10km (5-6 miles) in the same direction to **Königsfeld**, a health resort of 5,400 inhabitants.

The famous doctor and organist Albert Schweitzer had a house in Königsfeld from 1923 until 1957. In a letter written from Lambarene, in March 1965, he declared 'I think back to Königsfeld so often. There I could walk in the woods, had friends and those friends still think of me.' Not surprisingly, a huge medical complex here is known as the Albert-Schweitzer-Klinik. This, like other public buildings such as the new high school and the *Haus des Kurgastes* (the social centre for visitors) has been designed to blend harmoniously with the countryside.

The town is comparatively new; it only started in 1806 as a settlement for the Brüdergemeine Herrnhut, a religious fraternity from Saxony. Permission had earlier been obtained from the lord of the land, one Friedrich based in Stuttgart, with the proviso that the place should be named Friedrichsfeld. However, through the political manipulations of Napoleon, Friedrich was made a king (*König*) soon afterwards and the order went out that the name was to be changed to Königsfeld. The brothers were at first rather put out that the new king should play fast and loose with the name of their community but soon came up with the solution that the name should be interpreted as meaning '*our* King's field' — in other words, named after their heavenly king.

They quickly built essential accommodation for their life in this new area and this was followed by the ecclesiastical buildings. The first house outside the religious community was built in 1807 as an inn for those visiting the brothers and is now an hotel called Herrn-huter Haus. Many years were to pass before it was realised that the gentle surrounding countryside would be ideal for people able to take only modest exercise for health reasons and thus a very pleasant health resort came into being. Now there is a good range of hotel and pension accommodation and a modest selection of visitor facilities although it appears that most of the guests are those coming for health reasons.

The Baar

Where the spectacular hills and valleys of the central Black Forest give way to a more gentle upland, is the area known as *die Baar*, a land of broad horizons lying at an altitude of between 700 and 800m (2,300 and 2,625ft). This has been regarded as fine arable land for centuries and the grain grown here found ready markets in Switzerland and Italy. Evidence of this international trade is to be found in Löffingen where the Mailänder Tor (the Milan gate) still stands. The Baar has no geographical boundaries laid down but Löffingen, Donaueschingen, Villingen-Schwenningen and Geisingen, for example, are all within it.

The landscape does not make the same immediate impact on the senses as do the mountains and valleys of most of the Black Forest. Nevertheless, the visitor is soon likely to consider it an area of considerable charm and there is certainly no lack of accommodation and facilities in general for his or her benefit. The bigger centres already mentioned and many of the smaller towns and villages are of considerable interest; they are all the more pleasant for being a little aside from the more popular tourist routes.

Villingen is 13km (8 miles) due south of Königsfeld and is the more historic twin town which united with Schwenningen in 1972 to form a city with a combined population of about 80,000. Villingen was one of the towns founded by Duke Bertold III of Zähringen (see Chapter 4). Much of the original encircling wall and most of the gate towers are still in existence. The old town centre is one of the best preserved in Germany, thanks largely to the stoutness of the wall which withstood attacks during the peasant revolt in 1525 and, 100 years later, the onslaughts of the Swedes allied with the forces of Württemberg. Bombardments by the French under Marshalls Villars and Tallard in 1703-4 also failed to breach the defences.

Riettor, Villingen

The present Liebfrauenmünster was built to replace the earlier building which was destroyed by fire in 1721. Some parts of the old are incorporated and some of the original furnishings survived, notably the stone pulpit (around 1500-10) with its fine sculptured decoration and the fourteenth-century Nägelein crucifix on the altar of the Cross. The Romanesque double portal on the south side should not be overlooked. The late-Gothic *altes Rathaus*, with its Renaissance extension, houses a museum with exhibits on early and prehistory, applied arts, sculpture and painting.

The Franziskaner-Museum has collections on folklore and finds from the Celtic period with a special section on the dating of archaeological finds. The *Heimatmuseum* concentrates on the development of clock- and watch-making over the past 400 years and has a collection of some 1,500 timepieces. The former Franciscan monastery, founded in 1268, is worth seeing with its church, cloisters and

Romanesque minster portal, Villingen

chapel — there are concerts in the cloisters during the summer months. Villingen is famed for its *Fasnet* celebrations and large crowds assemble to see the parades of the 'fools' in their historic costumes and grotesque wooden masks, some of which may be seen at other times in the museums.

Schwenningen was previously a farming community but has now developed into a modern industrial town in which clock-making is an important activity. Indeed, the Kienzle factory is one of the biggest clock-making centres in Germany and the firm's museum has a valuable collection of timepieces. The former Benedictine monastery, which has an eighteenth-century church and buildings, is worth inspecting.

The prospective visitor should not fear the industrial aspect of these twin towns. There is ample open space and about half the total area is taken up by parks, gardens and woods. There are indoor and outdoor swimming pools and a golf course. Plenty of accommodation is available in and around the towns and the area is a good one for farm holidays. There is also a youth hostel and many restaurants which are noted for the variety of local dishes on offer. At the nearby Schwenninger Moos, a favourite goal for ramblers, is the source of the river Neckar which flows northwards out of the forest on its way to Heidelberg and the Rhine. Other modest excursions are to the Lorettokapelle (1705) and to the Magdalenenbergle, a little hill where graves from the Hallstatt period have been found.

The valley of the Brigach may be followed for a splendid walk to St Georgen, about 16km (10 miles) upstream. Another valley walk is westwards through the Kirnachtal. The route follows the road towards Furtwangen at first but when this turns south-east at Unterkirnach, go straight ahead following the river and a minor road to Oberkirnach. It is worth making the modest ascent of the Kesselberg 1,000m (3,280ft) for a lovely view back down the valley. The distance from Villingen to Oberkirnach is about 11km (7 miles).

An easy walk of 16km (10 miles) in the other direction takes one to Bad Dürrheim. The *Ostweg*, Pforzheim to Schaffhausen (black/red diamond on white ground) passes through Villingen and east of the town centre it crosses the railway and the B33. Identify and follow this long-distance path. East of the railway, turn south and for a short distance share the route with the Baden-Württemberg cycleway. The cycle route continues eastwards and the walker turns to the left to go roughly north through woodland for about 450m (492yd), passing near the *Aussichtsturm* (look out tower) at the Wannenhohe.

Turn east here through open country and, after less than 2km (1 mile), enter woods on the outskirts of Schwenningen. Notice the especially fine trees in the open country and in the woods where there is a *Waldlehrpfad* and a *Wildgehege*. Follow the waymarks as the route turns south and as it curves in an anti-clockwise direction round he town and across the railway into the *Naturschutzgebiet* (nature conservation area) of the Schwenninger Moos. Here the source of the river Neckar may be visited. The path then crosses the B27 after which, in about 250m (270yd), fork right into a path leading directly to the centre of Bad Dürrheim.

For the return, pick up a walking route near the church in the main street and follow it westwards, at first through little streets, until it passes over the B27 (a dual carriageway here) and turns right to cross the B33. Then turn left, roughly parallel with the main road and, after 1.5km (1 mile), cross the railway and enter a small wood. On emerging from the wood, cross the Zollhäusleweg — which is the cycleway — and walk due north and dead straight for exactly 1km

($^1/_2$ mile). Then make a right-angle turn to the left (west) and after another 1km ($^1/_2$ mile) rejoin the outward route for return to Villingen station or town. The motorist can, of course, travel direct between the two places along the B33.

All the usual amenities of a holiday and health resort are at hand in **Bad Dürrheim** which suffers the cumbersome designation *Sole-Heilbad und Heilklimatischer Kurort*, reflecting its possession of the only saline baths in the Black Forest with a salt content of up to 6%. The visitor should visit the 'Narrenschopf' museum which is housed in an old mushroom-shaped salt store. All the different forms of Alemannic and Swabian carnival lore are displayed here.

The B27 between Bad Dürrheim and Donaueschingen is a fast dual carriageway so this is a journey of no more than a few minutes. **Donaueschingen** is a pleasant town of around 18,000 inhabitants, lying on the *Grüne Strasse* (green road) which runs from Breisach on the Rhine to Lake Constance. This is where the rivers Breg and Brigach unite to form the Donau (Danube). The twin-towered parish church of John the Baptist and St John was built between 1724-47 and has an imposing façade as well as a richly decorated interior. The style is Bohemian baroque; the only surviving example of this in the whole of Germany. The most significant relic here is a Madonna dating from around 1525.

The straightforward baroque layout of the *Schloss*, built about 1723, was drastically altered by rebuilding at the end of the nineteenth century and lost most of its architectural significance because of this. In the courtyard one finds the so-called *Donauquelle* (Danube spring) with an allegorical group of figures in marble by A. Weinbrenner. However, it is in the interior of the *Schloss* and the nearby Karlsbau that one finds a splendid collection of works of art from the Renaissance and baroque periods. The gallery of paintings has many old German masters, including works by Holbein the Elder and Matthias Grünewald. The court library, where the poet Joseph Victor von Scheffel was librarian from 1857 to 1859, houses a fine collection of valuable books.

The Romans came to this area as early as 15BC when the Emperor Tiberius set up a fortress at nearby Hüfingen where he thought he had discovered the source of the Danube. Three centuries later, the Alemannic tribes started to drive the Romans out, but it was not until AD889 that the settlement in the middle of the Baar is recorded with a name — *Esginga* — the forerunner of Donaueschingen.

Places of Interest In The Baar

Villingen
Towers and walls
Well-preserved medieval fortifications.

Liebfrauenmünster
(eighteenth-century)
Gracious church replacing former building destroyed in 1721.
Fourteenth-century crucifix.

Altes Rathaus
Late-Gothic and Renaissance building now housing museum.

Franziskaner Museum
Folklore and finds from Celtic period.

Heimatmuseum
Clock- and watch-making history.

Schwenningen
Former Benedictine Monastery
Interesting complex includes eighteenth-century church.

Schwenninger Moos
2.5km (1$^1/_2$ miles) to the south
Source of river Neckar.

Bad Dürrheim
Sole-Heilbad
Only saline baths in Black Forest.

Narrenschopf Museum
Display of Alemannic and Swabian carnival artefacts.

Donaueschingen
Church of John the Baptist and St John (1724-47)
Richly decorated church in Bohemian baroque.

Schloss (1723)
Baroque with later rebuilding. Situated in splendid parkland.

Donauquelle
At the Schloss
Traditional source of the Danube.

Karlsbau
Art gallery with large Renaissance and baroque collection.

Entenburg (1471)
At Pforen, 5km (3 miles) to the south-east. Moated castle with four round corner towers.

Hüfingen
Well-preserved medieval town centre with fourteenth-century fortified tower.

Roman bath

Parish Church
Enlarged in 1553, restored in 1910.

St Leonhard's Kapelle (1476)

Stadtwald
Fine woodland noted for orchids.

Bräunlingen
Mühlentor
One of the original Gothic town gates.

St Remigius-Kapelle
Known as the mother church of the Baar.

Löffingen
Mailänder Tor
Attractive old town gate.

Rathaus
The former Kornhaus
(corn exchange).

Heimatmuseum
Includes finds from Alemannic burial place.

Witterschneekreuz
1km ($^1/_2$ mile) north-west
Pilgrimage church (1894-7) with wooden chapel (1846-7).

Wildpark
2km (1 mile) north-west
Spacious family leisure centre.

Former Benedictine Nunnery
(founded in 1125)
At Friedenweiler, 8km (5 miles) to the north-west
Incorporates splendid church (1725-31) by Peter Thumb.

Donaueschingen Schloss

*Traditional source
of the Danube,
Donaueschingen*

It has long been a town which supported culture and the arts, mainly due to the earlier influence of the princes of Fürstenberg for whom the *Schloss* was built. Mozart, Liszt and Kreutzer were among the notable musicians called upon to appear at the court. Today, the autumn music festival called the Donaueschinger Musiktage attracts lovers and performers of contemporary music from all over the world.

Every September another great international event brings visitors in their thousands for a feast of riding, coach-driving, dressage and so on. Seven hundred or more horses from all over Europe congregate in the Schlosspark which provides a splendid setting for the various events. Five kilometres (3 miles) south-east of the town, at **Pfohren**, stands the moated, cube-shaped castle of Entenburg with four massive round corner towers. It was built by the Counts of Fürstenberg in 1471.

The little town of **Hüfingen** (population 6,000) lies about 3km (2 miles) to the south and has a well-preserved medieval centre. Historically, it was a place of residence of the Fürstenberg and Schellenberg dynasties. There is quite a lot to see here, including the old Roman bath and a fortified tower from the fourteenth century. The parish church was enlarged in 1553 and thoroughly restored in 1910. St Leonhard's Kapelle (1476) is also worth a little of the visitor's time. The *Stadtwald* (town forest) is of particular interest and is sometimes called the orchid paradise because of the number and variety of the plants which grow there.

Another floral event is on Fronleichnamstag (Corpus Christi), the Thursday after Trinity Sunday, when the main street of the town is covered with a carpet of flowers. The citizens also collect millions of wild flowers and use them to create clever ornamental designs and religious motifs in front of their houses to adorn the route of the traditional procession. The custom originated about 150 years ago when a local sculptor, Franz Xaver Reich, brought the idea back from a journey he made to Italy.

Bräunlingen, just 3km (2 miles) to the west, is another historic little town. Like Hüfingen, its history goes back to a Roman settlement on the site. However, it shares with Villingen — and several other towns in the area — a more 'modern' history which is associated with the activities of the Dukes of Zähringen in the twelfth century. One of the original Gothic town gates, the Mühlentor, still stands as a reminder of that period. There are a number of carefully restored medieval houses in the old town centre.

St Remigius-Kapelle is the parish church and is known as the mother church of the Baar. It is well-worth seeing and has a fine late-Gothic carved altar. Bräunlingen is a good centre for less strenuous walking and there is a pleasant excursion westwards along the stream called Brändbach to the Kirnbergsee, about 6km (4 miles) from the town. The stream has been dammed to create this charming little lake with its camp site and bathing place. (There is a car parking charge.)

The *Grüne Strasse* (B31) runs westwards from Hüfingen and, after 5km (3 miles), passes through Döggingen where there is a *W-Parkplatz* which is a good starting place for the descent into the Wutachschlucht. This is a remarkable gorge but something for a later chapter. **Löffingen** is reached in 12km ($7^1/_2$ miles) and is one of the Baar towns the visitor should certainly endeavour to visit. It is an old market town and in earlier years was much involved in the grain trade. Indeed, the old *Kornhaus* is now the *Rathaus* and is a building well-worth seeing. The *Heimatmuseum* has a varied collection which includes finds from an old Alemannic burial place.

If one follows the signs 'Wildpark' from the town centre, the unusual pilgrimage church known as Witterschneekreuz soon comes into view. The story begins in the winter of 1740. A traveller reached the hill then known as Witarsne in a snowstorm and did not know which way to turn. He prayed for Divine guidance, soon heard the church bells of Löffingen and a wood-cutter came by and took him into the town. As a sign of gratitude, he had a cross erected at the spot where he heard the bells and, as the story spread, the local people made it a place of pilgrimage.

A little chapel was erected in 1792 and in 1846-7 this was replaced by the present 'old' wooden chapel. The years from 1894-7 saw the construction of the present pilgrimage church in neo-Romanesque style under the direction of the town priest, Stephan Wehrle. The old chapel has been kept and renovated to contain the many votive tablets and pictures which have accumulated over the years. The 'new' church has numerous items of beauty and interest.

The heated *Freibad* is passed a little further on, before one reaches the extensive *Wildpark* with its enclosures for bears, wolves, wild boar, deer and other creatures. This is a good place for families, with many amusements for the children and a summer *bob-bahn*. There is a wide range of accommodation in Löffingen and its satellite villages

Witterschneekreuz pilgrimage church with its painted ceiling, Löffingen

Friedenweiler

as well as every facility for activity holidays including tennis courts, riding stables, a *Hallenbad* and heated *Freibäder*. There is also ample scope for skiing in the winter. A road running north-west from Löffingen leads, in about 8km (5 miles), to Friedenweiler. Mid-way between the two is the attractive village of **Rötenbach**, another access point to the Wutachschlucht.

Friedenweiler is a Kneippkurort where, once again, the *Kur* treatments are in accordance with the principles of Sebastian Kneipp. The small, heated *Freibad* adjoins a lake with boats for hire and one may swim there too, if desired. Here, in the pretty Kloster-bachtal, provision is also made for winter sports. The former Bene-dictine nunnery founded in 1125 is worth seeing, together with its church which was built between 1725 and 1731 by the renowned Peter Thumb. Friedenweiler is a quiet and dignified resort yet it is within very easy reach of more sophisticated centres such as Titisee or Donaueschingen. The western part of the B31 in the direction of Freiburg will be explored in the next chapter.

4
FREIBURG AND THE HELL VALLEY

Freiburg, the Black Forest capital, is a busy city today with some 180,000 inhabitants but it does not have a particularly long history. Duke Bertold III of Zähringen had been held prisoner in Cologne; he got to know that old Roman city well and was much impressed by its prosperity, which was based largely on international trade. He realised that his own part of Europe was backward in terms of commerce and, after his release in 1118, he called for the establishment of a brand new trading city to take advantage of the growing cross-border traffic. He invited businessmen and workers from Cologne to assist him in the project. The Bertolds had come west from Swabia in the tenth century and established a family seat in a castle above the village of Zähringen, now a northern suburb of Freiburg, whose name they adopted as the family title. They were ambitious and despite the fact that they were by no means big landowners, they became one of the most powerful families in this part of Europe before the line died out in 1218.

Bertold III chose a level, 'green fields' area between the Black Forest mountains and the Rhine where he started the building of his new market town from scratch, complete with its imposing minster. It was walled, of course, and the streets were laid out with geometrical precision. The settlement was christened Freiburg, the word *frei* (free) having subtle political connotations. Each new settler was given exactly the same start; a plot of land measuring 50ft by 100ft (16.2 x 32.4m) to build his house and establish his business on. Most of the plots filled the distance between two of the narrow streets and the living quarters were built at the sunny end with the workshops, etc at the shady end.

The minster was built diagonally across its square in order to maintain the tradition of having the high altar at the east end. Only two years after Bertold's first call for support, the town had become a reality and was granted all the appropriate rights to regularise its existence. With the successful founding of his completely new town, Bertold then looked for similar opportunities elsewhere and, in the Black Forest area, he was responsible for Offenburg, across the Rhine from Strasbourg, and for Villingen and Rottweil on the eastern side. Another Freiburg (Fribourg) was established in Switzerland and he was also the founder of Bern, now the Swiss capital.

Freiburg is the cultural and economic centre of the southern part of the Forest and, like other German towns, it always seems to have much more importance as a transport and business centre than a town of similar size in England would. It is a calling point for inter-city trains on the main route to Basel, and also an interchange station for a number of branch lines, in particular that running to the east, serving many important towns and eventually reaching Munich.

The city of Freiburg has a considerable tramway network and is the terminus for a number of bus routes which serve outlying areas not reached by the railway. Some of the main shopping streets are pedestrian zones, although in several cases the tramcars still pass through them. The attractive open channels which carry streams through some of the streets are the remnants of a sewage system from the thirteenth century but now, needless to say, the water is sparkling and clean. One cannot claim to be a genuine Freiburger unless one has at some time inadvertently stepped into one of these channels! There are many cafés and other eating places, some with tables on the pavement, and a number of attractive high-class stores, especially in the Kaiser-Josef-Strasse, with its cool arcades.

Freiburg is dominated by the 116m (381ft) high tower of the minster. The filigree-like spire which surmounts the more solid tower is an architectural marvel and one can only wonder at the skill of the artisans who created this masterpiece in the year 1330. The Freiburg minster is the only German cathedral which achieved its final form in the Middle Ages, the year of completion being recorded as 1513. As in many old cathedrals, there is nearly always work going on, with scaffolding erected and sections closed off. There will be some excitement when all the work of restoration and cleaning is finished and the whole building is revealed in all its glory. As it is, there is much to be seen and wondered at, whether it be the sun or

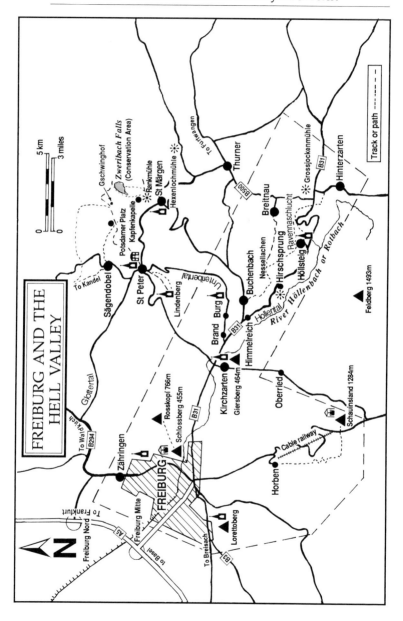

moon shining through the lacy stonework of the tower, the view from the tower watchman's room or that from the belfry itself. Be warned, however, that Germany's oldest bell, the 5-ton 'Hosanna', cast in 1258, has been sounding loud and clear over the countryside for more than 700 years and its thunderous peal will not be halted because tourists are present.

There are some rather fine medieval towers and several other old buildings, all of which have been lovingly restored since the grievous bombing inflicted on the city in 1944, when the greater part of the old town was destroyed. Thanks to the existence of detailed plans and photographs, the restoration work here, as in many other German towns, has made it possible to reproduce the architecture of earlier centuries in every minute detail. The university, founded in 1457, is one of the oldest in Germany, and has 18,000 students. Other educational establishments include the State High School for Music. Two principal museums, a fine theatre and numerous churches ensure that there is plenty for the visitor to see and do in the city.

The Augustinermuseum contains not only the town collection of paintings, tapestries and folk art but also the Diocesan Museum of objects of sacred art. There is a separate ethnological department in the Adelshauser Kloster. The study of nature in its several forms is the speciality of the Museum für Naturkunde. The Protestant Ludwigskirche is a good example of modern church architecture and was built on a new site to replace the older church of the same name destroyed in World War II. The modern synagogue stands in the city centre and was built a few years ago to replace the former Jewish place of worship which was destroyed during the Nazi regime.

The forested hills extend into the city limits, which also enclose a considerable acreage of vineyards. In an easy half-hour walk from the city streets, one can reach the excellent vantage point of the Schlossberg 455m (1,492ft) for wonderful views over the city and countryside and then wander on to the Rosskopf which, at 766m (2,513ft), is the highest point in the immediate vicinity. The Friedrichsturm there is a 100-year-old observation tower which provides extensive vistas in every direction. The Schlossberg can also be reached without effort in a few minutes by means of the *Gondelbahn*, the small cabin cable cars which carry one up swiftly from the town.

The Schauinsland 1,284m (4,215ft) is the mountain which the Freiburgers regard as their own. The summit area can be reached readily by road or by cable car from the lower terminus of the *Schauinslandbahn* at 490m (1,608ft) near Horben in the Günterstal, Horben being served by tram from the city. Literally translated, Schauinsland means 'look into the countryside' and one can certainly do that admirably from the top. However, the name is comparatively new; earlier the mountain was called Erzkasten, Erz meaning ore and Kasten meaning coffer. It was rightly regarded as Freiburg's treasure chest in the days when silver was mined there, an industry which was at its peak in the fourteenth and fifteenth centuries. The remains of entrances to the underground workings are still to be found here and there. There is a window in the Freiburg minster depicting scenes of the mining activity which was of considerable financial advantage to the minster itself.

The Schauinsland can be included in a day's ramble from the city, in the course of which one should also see the Lorettokapelle, which dates from 1657. It actually consists of three small chapels under one roof; the centre one was erected to commemorate the freeing of the city from the armies of France following a fierce battle in 1644 in which the Bavarian Field Marshal, Mercy, used the strategically important Lorettoberg to the disadvantage of the French. There was much interest at the time in the pilgrimage chapel Loreto at Ancona in Italy and it was resolved to make the new chapel in Freiburg an exact replica of this. It is the centre chapel seen today, the two smaller side chapels were added at a later date. It was presumably only after construction of the chapel that the hill became known as the Lorettoberg, from which, incidentally, the sandstone for building the minster was quarried.

In winter there are excellent skiing facilities on the Schauinsland and some of the numerous ski-lifts are floodlit. There are countless rambling opportunities in summer and even if one has not walked all the way up from Freiburg, an enjoyable stroll can be made round the summit area, starting either from the upper cable car station at 1,200m (3,940ft) or from one of the many car parks. The cable railway has been in continuous operation since it was built in 1930. There is an observation tower at the summit which raises the vantage point to 1,302m (4,267ft) — this is included in the route of many of the marked walks.

One of these, covering 9$\frac{1}{2}$km (6 miles), starts from the upper cable car station and climbs to the summit, returning by a parallel path to the saddle near the station, this section will take about 1 hour.

The path leads along the edge of and then through the woods before heading west to the *Gasthof* at Giesshübel at 1,071m (3,513ft). Turning north with several good viewpoints on the left, there then follows a steep zig-zag descent through Kaltwasser to the Lehhof and on to a junction of several paths and a good all-round vantage point at Eduardshöhe. Here there is a choice of routes, but the shortest goes almost directly north, passes the inn at Buckhof in about 1.5km (1 mile) and in about the same distance again, about 200m (220yd) before the church, reaches a turning to the right. This leads back to the lower cable car station, the descent from the upper station having taken about 2¹/₂ hours.

There is a registered health resort known as Schauinsland, officially an outlying suburb of Oberried in the Bruggatal. This includes the summit of the mountain and there are quite a number of hotels scattered about the area as well as a ski-school and the usual supporting facilities.

At around 1,000m (3,280ft) on the south-east slopes of the Schauinsland, at Hofsgrund, is an old farmhouse called Schniederlihof, which was occupied by Walfried Lorenz until his death in 1966. Five years later, the nearly 400-year old building was acquired by the local authority with the object of preserving this rare example of a typical house of the period. The building was set in order and fitted out to form a small museum showing the rural life of the area, including the mining activity already mentioned. A brief visit will certainly open the visitor's eyes to the interesting history of the Schauinsland area.

Leaving Freiburg in an easterly direction along the B31 road — the so-called *Grüne Strasse* (green road) — the suburbs are soon left behind and one is heading for the Höllental (Hell valley). This is a busy road and it is infinitely more pleasurable to make the journey by train, stopping off here and there for exploration. **Kirchzarten**, aside from the main road, is a bustling little town, a useful and reasonable shopping centre for the self-caterer. There is a good choice of inns and restaurants and the information centre will gladly provide details of a wide range of attractions and activities in the vicinity.

The parish church is a late-Gothic building (1508-10) with some Romanesque influence; it is dedicated to St Gallus and has Renaissance and baroque furnishings, etc. It has, among other things, a rather fine coloured triptych. Of interest in the town are the Talvogtei

(1621) — a horseshoe plan building which was the valley office of the Freiburg councillors — an old tithe barn and a smithy which is open to visitors on Tuesday and Thursday afternoons from June to September.

A pleasant, short walk from the town takes one to the little baroque pilgrimage chapel of St Laurentius (1737) on the Giersberg where there are also two *Naturlehrpfade* as well as a 'keep fit' circuit. There is a pleasant little café in the old chapel house (closed Wednesday evenings and Thursdays) providing

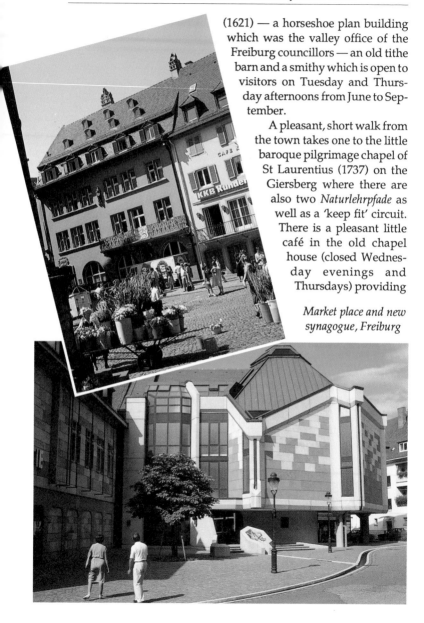

Market place and new synagogue, Freiburg

Cable car on the Schauinsland

an opportunity for rest and refreshment.

Kirchzarten's heated, open-air pool is called the *Schwimmbad* and is, in fact, a complex of four separate pools catering for every taste and degree of proficiency. There is the usual extensive sunbathing area, children's play park and so on. The adjoining well-appointed camp site has 500 pitches for caravans or tents. It is one of those used by the Eurocamp organisation and is popular with British and Dutch campers. Kirchzarten is a useful base for the traveller by train who does not wish to stay in Freiburg but wishes to have easy access to both the city and the countryside to the east. It is also a good base for the motorist wishing to explore the Feldberg and other mountains lying to the south-east of Freiburg.

Back on the main road beyond Kirchzarten, one comes almost immediately to a left turning signposted to Burg and Unteribental. About 2km ($1\frac{1}{4}$ miles) along this road is the beautiful, modern *Vaterunserkapelle* (Lord's Prayer Chapel) in which the Lord's Prayer is written as a frieze right round the inside of the circular building. Items of interest in this little church include a handmade copy of an ancient book of music in plainsong with text in Latin.

About 1km ($^1/_2$ mile) further on, at the village of Unteribental, a woodland nature trail passes close to the *Rathaus* where information ✳ is available. Incidentally, *Lehrpfad or Naturlehrpfad* is a nature trail and *Waldlehrpfad*, as in this case, is one which is concerned with trees in particular. Another type of trail which is found in many places and especially near holiday centres is the *Trimm Dich* (keep fit) path. This is laid out in the woods with a series of sixteen or twenty stations, at each of which there is simple equipment and a pictorial sign indicating the exercises which should be undertaken there. The signs are then followed to the next station, walking or jogging as instructed.

Returning to road B31, one soon passes a *Gasthaus* called Himmelreich (Kingdom of Heaven). Behind this is the railway station of the same name, a name which is surprising, since one is now on the threshold of Hell valley — the Höllental. The origin of the name Höllental is not clear, but it is probably related to the history of disasters which befell travellers passing this way in earlier times. If they managed to survive sudden rock falls and unexpected flash floods of the little river Rotbach, also called Höllenbach, they were likely to be attacked by brigands lurking in the crags above the road.

Only in 1770 was a passable track made through the narrow ravine which was the route of the little river. The 'road' was provided to facilitate the journey of Marie-Antoinette from her Austrian homeland to Paris for her marriage to Louis XVI. Today's motorist may have his own ideas about the name of the valley after he has negotiated it. In fact, no surfaced road was built through the valley until 1857 and the railway did not follow until 30 years later.

Robert Gerwig, who had built the *Schwarzwaldbahn* described in 🚆 Chapter 2, was also the engineer responsible for the *Höllentalbahn*, the first section of which, between Freiburg and Neustadt, was opened in 1887. The line was extended to Donaueschingen in 1901. In avoiding the huge curves of the *Schwarzwaldbahn*, it was necessary to accept a maximum gradient of 55% between Höllsteig and Hinterzarten necessitating, until 1938, expensive cog-wheel operation. The costs were defrayed by imposing on passengers a special *Bergzuschlag* (mountain supplement). The line between Freiburg and Neustadt was electrified in 1939 using single phase AC current at 50Hz, 20,000 volts — the first railway use of the so-called industrial frequency in Germany. However, in 1960 the supply was converted to 16,000 volts DC to conform with the rest of the West German railway network.

After Himmelreich, the valley quickly narrows until there is barely space for the river and road, while the railway is squeezed up on to the northern slope and has to dive in and out of short tunnels to pass the steep cliffs. Above are the ruins of the Falkenstein, hideout of the robber knights in earlier times, while one of the many summit crosses to be found throughout the Black Forest can also be seen here.

The busy, winding road must be negotiated with care but in one place the near-vertical walls have left sufficient space for a small car park on the roadside where one must park diagonally. It is worth getting out for a few moments to view the bronze stag which stands proudly on a rock high above the road. This is the Hirschsprung (Stag's Leap) and the story tells of a fine stag pursued by huntsmen, which made a spectacular leap from one side of the valley to the other in order to escape. There is a footpath from the car park through a tunnel and then along the river, partly on wooden walkways, until a wider part of the valley is reached near Hirschsprung station, some 600m (657yd) further on. Unfortunately, it is impossible to reach the actual position of the bronze stag easily from either direction and the climbing of the steep cliffs is prohibited.

Despite the widening of the valley, the railway continues to twist and turn, sometimes in a tunnel or on a viaduct, in order to climb 450m (1,476ft) before reaching Hinterzarten, less than 30km (18$\frac{1}{2}$ miles) from Freiburg. The longest viaduct is that over the Ravennaschlucht (Ravenna gorge); 40m (131ft) high and 224m (735ft) long, it was built in its present form with south Black Forest granite in 1926. The railway traveller has no more than a fleeting glimpse of the gorge but the motorist can turn aside at Höllsteig on to the old road.

Near the junction, he or she will find the St Oswalds-Kapelle, a little chapel built in 1148; there are frescos inside dating from the fourteenth to sixteenth centuries. To view the interior, obtain a key from the Hofgut (Gasthaus) Sternen. Park on the old road and enjoy a pleasant walk through this picturesque ravine. The path makes its steep way up beside the little river, sometimes on walkways or over bridges until, after climbing a steep wooden stairway, the great Ravenna waterfall is reached. One can go further on to the small waterfall and to the Grossjockenmühle (1883), an old Black Forest water mill which, although disused, is still in good order.

Incidentally, the Gasthaus 'Sternen' is an old coaching inn — as was Gasthaus Himmelreich — which provided for the frequent changes of horses necessary to negotiate this steepest part of the

Kirchzarten

*St Laurentius'
chapel,
Kirchzarten*

An early music book in the Lord's Prayer chapel, Unteribental

House and wayside shrine, Unteribental

valley in the days before motorised transport. Marie Antoinette is said to have stopped at the 'Sternen' on her fateful journey in 1770 and Goethe was certainly a guest here in 1779. The present modern 'Sternen' building was only completed in the mid-1980s and is at least the third hostelry of the same name. The previous one, built in 1859, still stands and provides additional accommodation.

In order to continue up the valley, one returns to the modernised main road, but before doing so, a visit to the nearby glass-blowing works and shop may provide an interesting gift or souvenir. It was a marvellous engineering achievement to lift the B31 road out of the Höllental to the comparatively level upland where Hinterzarten lies. While low gears will be much in use, the modern motorist is unlikely to endure the agonies of earlier travellers faced with the gradients and twists of the old road, which may be appreciated by going to the end of that road past the 'Sternen'.

With an indigenous population of only 2,200, **Hinterzarten** caters for many times this number in the course of a year. It is not only a health resort but also a winter sports centre which has developed in a quite pleasing way over the years, with several first-class hotels and a great variety of more modest accommodation. Hinterzarten is justifiably proud of its gastronomy and two of the hotels are often recommended in this respect. The 'Park-Hotel Adler' has been in the ownership of the same family since 1446 while the 'Weisse Rössle' is referred to in records as far back as 1347. There is a *Hallenbad* in the 'Adler' which, upon payment, is available to non-residents. The Kur-Zentrum makes provision for the visitor with pleasant reading rooms, a television room, games rooms, restaurant and a cinema/concert hall.

The modern Catholic church has been skilfully grafted on to the onion-domed tower of an earlier building. There is a Pietà from the school of Tilman Riemenschneider (1440-1531), the master-carver of the Middle Ages. This is an unusual find in this area for most of Riemenschneider's work is to be found far away in Würzburg and the Tauber valley. In its turn, the Protestant congregation has also built a modern church of unusual design. There is a signboard in the centre of the village giving directions for a vast selection of walks. Few resorts can have more walks available and it is, therefore, particularly well-suited to the visitor who has arrived by train.

The fit walker can obtain what is almost a bird's eye view of the Höllental by walking along the ridge on the north side. The 14km (9 mile) walk starts at Himmelreich station, where there is space for parking. Leaving the station, one goes north for about 250m (280yd) to the road eastwards to Buchenbach. The path, whose sign is a red and white diamond on a yellow ground, runs beside the road for 1.5km (1 mile), and then leads into the Pfaffendobelweg just opposite the church in Buchenbach which, incidentally, is worth a brief visit. The little road is followed until after the last of the houses. Soon after passing an attractive *Waldspielplatz* (playground), leave the road and take a footpath on the right to climb fairly steeply to the Pfaffeneck 748m (2,454ft), where several paths meet, already 300m (984ft) above the starting point in Himmelreich. Pauses for breath during this climb allow one to admire the view back towards Buchenbach in the valley below.

At Pfaffeneck, the route-marking is joined for a while by the blue diamond on white ground of one of the long-distance connecting paths. Continue to climb until, at about 1,000m (3,280ft) the viewpoint of Nessellachen with its nearby *Gasthof* 'Sonne' (closed on Fridays) is reached. A path (red spot on white) to the right leads down towards the valley and is an alternative route back to Himmelreich. Nessellachen is a good spot for a break and perhaps some refreshment; this is the half-way point of the tour, reached after about 2 hours' walking. Continuing in an easterly direction, the red and white diamond soon takes leave of the blue diamond as the path swings to the right to head directly for Hinterzarten.

The altitude remains around the 900-1,000m (2,950-3,280ft) mark and there is a continually changing panorama as the path gradually edges closer to the Höllental with its road, river and railway far below. Several distinctive rocky outcrops clinging to the steep valley walls are passed, and 6-7km (4-5 miles) from Nessellachen, the Ravenna river is crossed. From here one can take a side excursion into the Ravennaschlucht. After this, the route turns southwards towards the main road, which is crossed on the outskirts of Hinterzarten. Carry on through the resort to the station for a train back to Himmelreich or Freiburg. A further 3 hours should be allowed for the walk from Nessellachen.

Climbing by railway or road into Hinterzarten, the Höllental is left behind and the landscape assumes quite different characteristics, with rivers no longer flowing westwards but south and east into the area which will be described in Chapter 6.

Places of Interest
In and Around Freiburg

Freiburg
The Minster
116m (380ft) high spire can be
climbed for a bird's eye view of the
old town.
5-tonne 'Hosanna' bell.
Numerous important relics.

Augustinermuseum
In town centre.
Paintings, tapestries, folk and
sacred art.

Museum für Naturkunde
In town centre
Natural history.

(Several other smaller museums
on various topics in the city).

Ludwigskirche
In town centre.
Highly commended modern church
architecture.

Synagogue
In town centre
Modern centre of Jewish worship.

Schlossberg
456m (1,495ft) hill on eastern edge
of city
Views of the minster and old town.

Rosskopf
East of city, 3km (2 miles) from
Schlossberg
766m (2,512ft) high with observation tower.

Lorettoberg
Just south of city
A modest hill with interesting
Lorettokapelle.

Schauinsland
12km (7$^1/_2$ miles) south of city.
7km (4$^1/_2$ miles) to lower cable car
station in Gunterstal.
Freiburg's own mountain. 1,284m

(4,215ft) high with observation
tower.

Kirchzarten
Parish church (1508-10) with
painted triptych

Talvogtei (1621)
Former valley office of Freiburg
councillors.

Kienzle-Schmiede
Old smithy with two waterwheels.

St Laurentius' Kapelle (1737)
On the Giersberg, 1.5km (1 mile)
to the south-east
Baroque pilgrimage chapel.

Unteribental
Vaterunserkapelle
Modern church with theme of the
Lord's Prayer.

Höllental
Hirschsprung
Bronze stag on rocky outcrop
commemorates legendary leap by
hunted animal.

Ravennaschlucht
Deep gorge spanned by 224m
(245yds) long railway viaduct.

Waterfalls and water mill
The Grossjockenmühle is an old
water mill which is disused but
worth seeing.

*Glass-blowing workshop and gift
shop*
Interesting gifts and souvenirs

Gasthaus 'Sternen'
Visited by Marie-Antoinette in 1770
and by Goethe in 1779.

St Oswalds-Kapelle (1148)
Chapel with frescos from fourteenth
to sixteenth centuries.

Grossjockenmühle,
Ravennaschlucht

Street-side café in Hinterzarten

5

MOUNTAINS OF THE SOUTH-WEST

This area contains nearly all the highest mountains of the southern Black Forest and lies between the *Badische Weinstrasse* and the Wiesental, through which road B317 runs in a north-easterly direction from Basel to Neustadt. Almost every road is green-edged on the map, meaning, according to the legend, 'Stretches with particularly beautiful landscapes'. It is impossible, in the space available, to give a comprehensive survey of every place of beauty or interest, but those mentioned are typical of very many more in this concentration of natural splendours. There are no large towns, but almost every town and village is dedicated to the needs of the holidaymaker, in this, the most popular part of the Forest.

Here, in a compact group, we find mountains such as the Feldberg 1,493m (4,895ft), the Seebuck 1,450m (4,754ft), the Stübenwasen 1,388m (4,549ft), the Belchen 1,414m (4,636ft) and the Blauen 1,165m (3,823ft). Just to the north is the Schauinsland, mentioned in the previous chapter, and a little to the east, are the Hochkopf 1,263m (4,147ft) and the Hochgescheid 1,205m (3,956ft). These are some of the giants which serious walkers feel they must conquer, but there are many, many more, less known and less visited summits which offer an equal challenge and pleasure.

There is little access to this area by train because, with the exception of the Feldberg/Seebuck group, the nearest stations are too distant to be of value without road transport. However, the Feldberg/Seebuck area can, given some determination, be reached on foot from Bärental station on the Schluchsee branch line. Steep hills, deep valleys, serpentine curves and many small villages are the significant features here. So, instead of towns, it is more appropriate to describe a few of the mountains and valleys, and to mention, in passing, some of the little resorts encountered on the way.

Its superior height is almost the only attraction of the climb to the summit of the Feldberg, for it is the most unlovely of all the Black Forest mountains. If one can ignore the clutter of functional buildings associated with the television/radio transmitter, the weather station and various military installations, there are magnificent panoramic views in all directions, perhaps the most spectacular being that over the Feldsee towards the Bärental. In the middle of the last century, the intrepid tourist determined to reach the summit of the Feldberg had to obtain the services of a guide in Freiburg.

Today the picture is very different; in summer and winter alike, thousands of visitors make their way to the top without supervision or guidance. As there is also road access for most of the way, the treeless summit plateau is almost always busy during favourable weather. Germany's first ski-club was founded here in 1892, the polar explorer Nansen being one of its original members. The Feldberg, the most popular winter sports centre in the Black Forest, is especially busy during winter weekends. A large number of designated walks, both local and of longer distance, include the climb to the summit of the Feldberg in their itinerary.

In common with other Black Forest summits, the Feldberg area is especially popular in late autumn and early winter when there is the best chance of a clear and pure atmosphere. These are the seasons beloved by the photographer, who will often be able to obtain clear pictures of the surrounding mountains and, perhaps, southwards to the Alps. Sunrise and sunset can produce quite splendid effects on the heights while the valleys below may well be shrouded in mist and not get a glimpse of the sun all day. This can have the unusual effect of making it several degrees warmer on the mountains above the mist than it is in the valleys.

Once the snow comes, the winter walker must beware of the *Schneewächten*, the overhanging walls of snow driven by the wind, which can sometimes break free unexpectedly and bury anyone unfortunate enough to be below. This hazard is said to be particularly noticeable in the Zastler area.

The 'Feldbergerhof', a first-class hotel with 145 beds, is at an altitude of 1,279m (4,199ft), making it one of the highest hotels in the

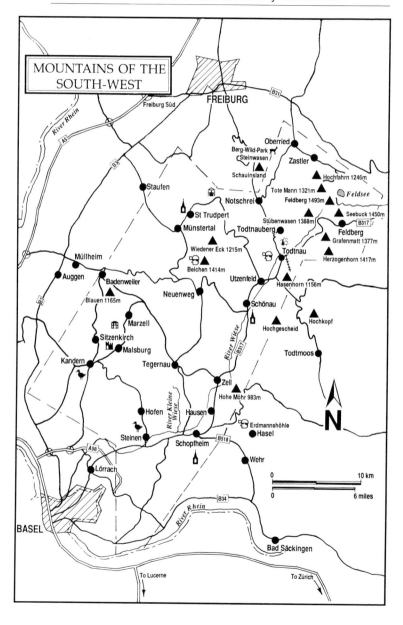

Black Forest. It is nearer the Seebuck than the Feldberg and is reached by the principal access road into the area off the B317 Basel to Neustadt main road on the south side of the group.

The little town of **Todtnau**, to the south-west of the Feldberg massif, is an ideal centre for exploring the surrounding mountains and valleys. Again there is a history of disastrous fires; hence there are no very old buildings, but the town is quite attractive and a recognised health resort. For the walker it would be difficult to find a place with more possibilities for expeditions on foot — *Wander-möglichkeiten* as the Germans would say.

About 4km (2¹/₂ miles) north of Todtnau is the separate part of the resort called **Todtnauberg**; between the two is a spectacular

The summit of the Feldberg and one of the mountain's panoramic views

100m (328ft) high waterfall. There are swimming pools in both places and Todtnauberg has several hotel *Hallenbäder* as well, some of these being available to the general public. Pleasantly free of through traffic, this is one of the most popular Black Forest resorts. Near the main street in Todtnau is the lower station of a chair lift for an effortless journey to the Hasenhorn 1,156m (3,794ft) behind the town, while within easy distance of Todtnauberg there are seven ski-lifts for the winter visitor, several of them flood-lit.

Many consider the Belchen to be the most beautiful of all the Black Forest mountains. The views in every direction from the summit are as grand as those from the Feldberg. A good road goes right to the top, but there is ample parking space and the unfortunate clutter of the Feldberg is absent — even the inevitable hotel is not intrusive. The walker may make the ascent by a variety of routes, each of which has its own attractions and devotees. Several pleasant *Gasthäuser* and cafés along the way provide sustenance for the quite energetic climb.

One, perhaps less obvious, route to the summit of the Belchen is from Neuenweg which lies directly to the south of the mountain. Start at the Taubenbrunnen (fountain) in the middle of the village. Leave the filling station on the left and after 100m (110yd) turn sharp left in a westerly direction. A steep, curving path soon brings one to the last houses of the village and, in 15 minutes, to the open ridge. Before reaching a main road, go to the right (north) between two telegraph poles and continue on a broad forest track which climbs gently.

In rather less than 1 hour from the start, one reaches a five-way junction of paths and from here the red diamond of the *Westweg* is followed towards the summit. Look back after 15 minutes or so for a splendid view down the valley. Now the way becomes steep as it goes through the rocky corries of the Hohe Kelch. There are some viewpoints which provide opportunities to interrupt the romantic climb. Near a seat there is a sign to the Felsenkranz, the ridge viewpoint which should on no account be missed.

Now the red diamond is followed along a shady woodland path and a sign to the right, 'Belchenhaus', will soon be seen. However, continue forward on the path which now becomes smaller, reaching the summit at 1,414m (4,636ft) in half an hour for an unforgettable panoramic view all round. It is splendid at any season but the best time of all is in October when the autumn colours are at their best and the air is clear enough for a view of the Alps.

From the summit, walk down to the Belchenhaus (hotel) and then, at the turning place for the car park, look for a sign reading 'Neuenweg, Wanderheim 3.5km'. A blue diamond leads down the steep path with rocky outcrops and fine views, back to the starting point. Stout walking footwear is necessary for this ramble which involves a distance of 13km (8 miles) and includes a total climb of some 700m (2,300ft).

As with the Feldberg, many walking tours include the Belchen climb, while for those who make the ascent by car, there is a well-marked path round the summit which can be encircled in about 1 hour. The Belchen is a favourite spot with hang gliding enthusiasts, who take to the air from just below the summit car park.

Todtnau and the little holiday town of **Schönau** are popular starting points for routes to the Belchen. The church at Schönau, although only built in 1890, is worth a visit, on account of the late-Gothic carved altar. The church is known as the minster of the Wiesental. The popularity of Schönau is reflected in the fact that despite the 600 beds available for visitors, accommodation there always seems to be that bit more difficult to obtain than at most other resorts in the Forest.

At the northern end of this area, only 3 or 4km (2-2$^1/_2$ miles) from Kirchzarten, the little resort of **Oberried** is an excellent centre for exploring not only the Schauinsland, but several other mountains, notably the Hochfahrn 1,264m (4,150ft) and the Tote Mann (Dead Man) 1,321m (4,329ft), which form part of the Feldberg group. Most of the 900m (2,950ft) ascent from Oberried to the Tote Mann can easily be made by the motorist.

Leaving the village through the hamlet of Zastler, the sharp right turn into the Stollenbachstrasse is reached in about 5km (3 miles). This road climbs steeply with many Z-bends for about 4km (2$^1/_2$ miles) and ends at the Stollenbacher Hütte, a traditional *Gasthof* at about 1,100m (3,610ft). The extensive parking area here is virtually deserted in summer but thronged with crowds during the winter sports season. The nursery slopes with a short ski-lift lie just behind the *Gasthof* and twin ski-lifts climb in the opposite direction almost to the summit of the Tote Mann.

There is a most enjoyable 5km (3 mile) summer walk which starts from the car park and includes the summit. A small, surfaced road leads to some cattle sheds, about 400m (437yd) away and then it

*Waterfall,
Todtnau*

*Stations of the Cross,
Schönau*

Hang gliding on the Belchen

becomes a farm track swinging round to the left, eastwards, to cross under the ski-lift cables and past some pastures, continuing through woods until a fine viewpoint is reached about 1.5km (1 mile) from the start. The waymarking from the *Hütte*, a red cross on yellow ground, is followed along a right-hand fork at the view point, curving steadily right, through plantations of young fir trees, until the way divides at the foot of a fenced meadow. The red cross now takes the left fork south-eastwards towards the Feldberg, but the summit of the Tote Mann lies due south from here and one must go into the meadow through the fence openings provided and climb steeply up the grassy slope to reach the top in about 600m (650yd). The Feldberg and its buildings are clearly visible about 3km (2 miles) away, and many other summits are identifiable.

For a short time the path is in a *Naturschutzgebiet* (nature reserve), but this is soon left as either of two paths, with red spot on white marking, is followed westwards, gradually curving round to the north to reach a junction of six or seven paths in 1.5km (1 mile). The red spot marking goes away to the left but the Stollenbacher Hütte is now clearly visible some 800m (875yd) away on the right, down a well-trodden path.

Back in Oberried, the rather strange church occupies a prominent position. The *Bauernhaus* (farmhouse) museum of Schniederlihof has already been mentioned but if the weather is good the visitor may prefer to visit the Berg-Wild-Park (mountain wildlife park) which is also on the slopes of the Schauinsland at Steinwasen, 5km (3 miles) south of Oberried. A selection of creatures can be found in their natural habitats in an area of 40 hectares (99 acres) of forests, rocky cliffs and a lake. Deer, ibex, chamois, marmots and wild pigs are among the species to be seen from the well-kept paths which surmount the steep slopes. The young of many of these have been brought together in a *'Kindergarten'* as they can rarely be seen otherwise. This is, of course, a special attraction for children, and there are also two 750m (820yd) long summer 'toboggan' runs to round off the visit.

It is, perhaps, unfair to single out a few mountains for particular mention, as they represent only a very small proportion of the many delightful summits in a small area. There is always an attraction in the highest peaks — if, indeed, Black Forest mountains can be said to have 'peaks' — but many of the lesser ones can be just as rewarding, perhaps even more so because they are less visited. Nearly all of them can be climbed without much difficulty if suitable footwear is worn. The acquisition of good maps, such as the 'Atlasco' Schwarzwald Wanderkarte series, which come complete with a large selection of suggested walks and details of the signs to be followed, is strongly recommended.

The mountains mentioned, together with numerous other summits, are included in a rather strenuous 11-day ramble which is organised, on the same lines as those previously described, by the Kurverwaltung Titisee-Neustadt under the title *Rund um den Feldberg* (Round about the Feldberg). Again, if the whole tour is too much, separate sections can be booked to suit individual wishes.

Before leaving this area the visitor should explore at least two of the main valleys. The lovely Münstertal takes its name from a small town which was destroyed in 1346 and never rebuilt. It must have been an attractive place with its walls and towers, but today every trace has disappeared. The valley leads from the comparatively flat lands of the Rhine in the west, right into the heart of the mountains described earlier, with the Belchen prominent ahead as one travels eastwards. The main town, Staufen, is where the valley really starts and here again are the vineyards which line the *Badische Weinstrasse*.

Going up the valley beside the tiny river Neumagen, one soon enters the health resort called **Münstertal** which has a good selection of accommodation. Opposite the Untermünstertal station there is another 'Löwen', a beautiful old *Gasthof*. This valley of the Untermünstertal now swings south to run along the west flank of the Belchen. A left turn leads into the Obermünstertal, which is dominated by the buildings of the Kloster St Trudpert.

Around AD600, the Irish missionary Trudpert ventured over the Rhine into this valley in order to convert the inhabitants to Christianity. He was murdered by fanatical heathens and the natives pursued their pagan way of life until the Benedictine monks founded their monastery about AD800 and named it after Trudpert. The present baroque buildings are obviously not the original ones; the settlement has been destroyed by fire no fewer than three times in its 1,000 years' history.

The present church was another brainchild of Peter Thumb, who was able to incorporate parts of the former Gothic church in his plans. Today, organ and orchestral concerts are held in the church and it is a popular place for wedding ceremonies. The *Kloster* itself, now the mother-house of the Sisters of the Holy Joseph, is not open to the public. The St Trudpert chapel behind the church is worth a visit. The oldest *Gasthof* in the whole Münstertal, the 'Spielweg', is to be found in this part of the valley at the end of the resort. It has an interesting history and a reputation for good food, but is closed on Mondays and until 3pm on Tuesdays.

The Untermünstertal has a former silver mine which has been turned into the museum 'Teufelsgrund'; there are tours underground and its relics date from the eleventh century. One of the side galleries in the mine has been set aside as an *Asthmatherapiestation* for it has been found that the air in the mine is beneficial to sufferers of that complaint. There is another specialised museum in Obermünstertal, the Bienenkundemuseum which deals with every aspect of bees and bee-keeping. There is a total of 200km (124 miles) of well-marked paths at various altitudes round the resort. In addition, there are three *W-Parkplätze* on the main road through the Obermünstertal, including one at St Trudpert, with a total of eight suggested walks.

The river Wiese enters Switzerland briefly before joining the Rhine at Basel. The first town on the German side of the border is Lörrach, which has been mentioned earlier. Only 4km (2^1/$_2$ miles)

Protestant church,
Geschwend

Gasthaus Linde, Münstertal

Some Places of Interest In The South-West

Todtnau
Todtnauer Wasserfall
1.5km (1 mile) north of town
Spectacular waterfall 100m (328ft)
high.

Schönau
Parish Church (1890)
Known as the minster of the
Wiesental. Late-Gothic carved
altar.

Oberried
Bauernhausmuseum 'Schniederli-hof'
At Hofsgrund, Schauinsland, 7km
(4¹/₂ miles) south-west
Small but interesting collection of
local relics in a traditional farm-house.

Berg-Wild-Park Steinwasen
5km (3 miles) south
Mountain wildlife park with deer,
chamois, wild pigs, etc. Summer
'toboggan' runs.

Münstertal
Kloster St Trudpert
Benedictine monastery founded
about AD800. Church by Peter
Thumb, with St Trudpert chapel
behind the church.

Gasthof 'Spielweg'
Oldest hostelry in the valley with
an interesting history.

Besuchsbergwerk 'Teufelsgrund'
Former silver mine now a
museum. Tours underground.

Bienenkundemuseum
Located in street called Spielweg.
Specialist museum about bees and
bee-keeping.

Kandern
Station
Terminus for historic steam train
from Basel.

Stork Sanctuary
In Holzen, 3km (2 miles) to the
south-west

Sausenburg
4km (2¹/₂ miles) to the north-east
Castle ruin with fine views.

Schloss Bürgeln (1762)
5km (3 miles) to the north
Beautiful palace known as the
Pearl of the Markgräflerland.

Blauen
1165m (3,823ft) mountain with
outstanding panorama reached
from Marzell, 8km (5 miles) north-east of Kandern.

Steinen-Hofen
Vogelpark Wiesental
4km (2¹/₂ miles) north of Steinen
More than 300 species of native
and foreign birds in natural
surroundings.
Tropical house.

Schopfheim
'Hans Sachs' Gasthof
Historic inn located in the castle.

St Michael's Church (1492)
Well-preserved frescos.

Erdmannshöhle
Hasel, 6km (4 miles) to the east
Spectacular subterranean caverns.

Hausen
Memorial to poet Johann Peter
Hebel, in front of church.

Feldberg
Feldsee
Lake with cliffs of geological
interest.

Bismarck memorial tower
Located on the Seebuck 1,450m
(4,754ft).
Fine viewpoint.

from the *Autobahn* near Lörrach, there is the group of villages which make up the resort of **Steinen**, the focal point being the pleasant little town of Steinen itself (population 4,000). It is little more than a stone's throw from France in the west and Switzerland in the south and it is hardly surprising, therefore, to find that the local dialect is shared with the residents of the nearby corners of those countries.

Various parts of the resort lie between 335m (1,100ft) and 1,000m (3,280ft) in altitude and between them contain most of the ingredients for a successful family holiday. There is a large, heated swimming pool, indoor and outdoor tennis courts and a sports centre. One hundred kilometres (62 miles) of well-kept footpaths provide for the walker and the long-distance path from Pforzheim passes through on its way to its destination in Basel. The Wiesental Bird Park (*Vogelpark*) at **Hofen**, a few kilometres north of Steinen, is a fairly recent development but it is already attracting international attention as a superb example of wildlife conservation. The exotic plants and birds in the tropical house are particularly worth seeing.

A pretty but rather twisty road runs north-westwards from Hofen to the important town of **Kandern**. This is a holiday centre with about 6,500 inhabitants, lying on the route of the long-distance *Westweg* from Pforzheim to Basel with the ruins of Sausenburg castle (1230) nearby. Kandern is known as the *Brezel- und Töpferstadt*, reflecting the fame of its *Brezeln* (pretzels) and its pottery and ceramic ware. By 1813, the crisp *Brezeln* were famous all over Germany and it is recorded that thirteen bakers were employed in their production. Pottery goes back to 1564 when the suitability of a local clay for this purpose was discovered. The modest shopping centre provides adequately for those occupying the abundant self-catering accommodation in the area.

The poet Johann Peter Hebel made the name of Kandern known when he related the story of a ghost on the Kandern road. It seems the apparition was liable to appear to all those who had sat too long over the wine in the *Gasthaus*. Today's motorist probably has better grounds for moderation in his enjoyment of the local wine. Johann August Sutter, the pioneer and so-called emperor of California, was a famous son of Kandern. Each September, a local festival called the Kanderner Pferdemarkt (horse market) is now the occasion for a variety of riding and associated events.

The town is surrounded by a network of well-marked paths which make it easy to organise rambles to various places of interest in the vicinity. The terrain is fairly easy so that stout walking shoes will suffice rather than the boots usually desirable in more mountainous areas. Footpath No 2 can be followed for about 1.5km (1 mile) southwards from the town to the bizarre Wolfsschlucht (wolf ravine) which is in a small *Naturschutzgebiet*. The path then continues in the same direction for a further 2km (1¹/₄ miles) to the photogenic village of **Holzen**, which has a stork sanctuary on its outskirts; there is also a stork's nest on the church roof.

Northwards from Kandern, local path No 1 (it is also the *Westweg* — red diamond on white ground) may be followed to the Sausenburg ruins, a distance of about 4km or 2¹/₂ miles. This is a long, steady climb for one has to overcome an altitude difference of more than 300m (985ft) in this fairly short distance. However, the splendid view on reaching the Sausenburg at 665m (2,185ft), high above the village of Sitzenkirch, makes it well worthwhile. The Sausenburg once belonged to the Zähringen dynasty and later to the Margraves of Hachberg-Sausenberg, but it was unoccupied by the time it was reduced to ruins by French artillery in 1678.

Shortly after the Sausenburg, the *Westweg* and path 1 separate; follow the latter westwards to Schloss Bürgeln, about another 3km (2 miles). Where the paths divide, there is a car park reached via Sitzenkirch, from which the Sausenburg may be reached in about 1km (¹/₂ mile), nearly all on level ground. The fine palace of Bürgeln is known as the Pearl of the Markgräflerland and it occupies a lovely vantage point looking south from this spur of the Blauen, the summit of which at 1,165m (3,823ft) lies about 4km (2¹/₂ miles) to the north above Badenweiler.

Schloss Bürgeln was built by J.K. Bagnato in 1762 and until Secularisation in 1803, it was the residence of the prior of St Blasien monastery. There are guided tours of the palace and there is a *Gaststätte* here so this would make a good place for a break and refreshment before resuming the circular walk along path 1 back to Kandern, a distance of some 5km (3 miles) through fields and woods. The whole walk covers 12km (7¹/₂ miles). It should be noted that it is impossible to see even the exterior of the *Schloss* unless one pays for and participates in the guided tours.

Kandern has an excellent heated *Freibad* with an extensive *Liegewiese* (grassy area for sunbathing) and a small restaurant. Table tennis is available and there is also a small bowling alley. In the summer months, a museum railway, the *Kandertalbahn*, operates

St Trudpert church, Münstertal

Picturesque café, Schopfheim

steam passenger trains between Kandern and Haltingen on the outskirts of Basel.

About 4 to 8km (2-5 miles) north-east of Kandern there is another holiday area known as **Malsburg-Marzell**, made up of these two places and several smaller ones strung out along the valley of the river Kander. Marzell, at the northern end, is the starting point for two routes to the summit of the Blauen involving a round distance of 9-12km ($5^1/_2$-$7^1/_2$ miles) with a climb of about 460m (1,500ft) and a descent of the same order to get back to the starting place. Those desiring to do so can, however, get close to the summit by car and ample parking space is available.

For the visitor seeking a holiday amidst beautiful scenery but without too many of the trappings of modern tourism, this valley would appear to be ideal. Both Kandern and Malsburg-Marzell are on the Atlasco Wanderkarte, sheet No 257, which not only has the large-scale map (1:30,000) but also numerous easily followed suggestions for walks in the area.

The beautiful Eggenertal (Eggen valley) runs northwards from Sitzenkirch for about 12km ($7^1/_2$ miles) to Müllheim in the Rhine valley, with lesser roads running off westwards towards Auggen and Schliengen. The routes include the villages of Obereggenen, Niedereggenen and Feldberg — a different place from that associated with the Black Forest's highest mountain, of course. The valley is famous for its fruit trees which consist principally of the various varieties of cherry. A drive through here in May, when thousands of trees are in blossom, provides a sight to remember. By August the harvest is in full swing and the heavily laden branches droop down to the roads and footpaths, tempting the rambler to refreshment along the way.

About 1.5km (1 mile) from Sitzenkirch, the road ascends to a miniature pass at St Johannis Breitehof at 482m (1,582ft) before the descent into the valley proper. At this highest point there is a car park which gives access to the circular walk already described, taking in Schloss Bürgeln and Kandern. The name comes from that of a tiny chapel which once stood here, dedicated to St Johannis, the patron saint of Bürgeln. The Breitehof farmhouse was built in 1826 by the forbears of the present owners.

Going on up the Wiesental from Steinen, one comes, in about 7km (4 miles), to **Schopfheim**, where a certain amount of the old has been rescued from the scourge of modernisation. Places of interest here include the historic inn, the 'Hans Sachs', which is to be found in the castle, and St Michael's Gothic church which dates from 1492. There are well-preserved frescos inside which date from about the time the church was built.

A gallery of paintings can be found in the *Rathaus* (1820), a building in pure Classical style, and in the so-called *Hirtenhaus* (shepherd's house) there is a historical museum. Three *W-Parkplätze* are to be found in or near the town, each with one marked walk. A diversion can be made from Schopfheim into the idyllic Kleine (small) Wiesental with its fine farmhouses and country inns. The Kleine Wiese is a tributary of the main stream and there are splendid views if it is followed to its source near the Höhen-Restaurant Haldenhof.

The various hostelries in the Kleine Wiesental pride themselves on their cuisine and offer many local specialities prepared in accordance with time-honoured recipes. They have published a *Gastronomieführer* (gastronomic guide) to the valley which may be obtained from the *Verkehrsamt* in Steinen. Another worthwhile excursion from Schopfheim takes one 6km (4 miles) eastwards to Hasel for a visit to the spectacular subterranean caverns known as the Erdmannshöhle.

The main road bypasses Hausen, the home of the dialect poet Johann Peter Hebel (1760-1826), to whom there is a memorial in front of the church. Ten kilometres ($6^1/_4$ miles) from Schopfheim, the little town of **Zell** (another!), though busy with weaving and spinning industry, lies in typical Black Forest countryside and is a good starting point for walks in the locality. By travelling a few more kilometres up the valley to Mambach, all traces of industry are left behind, and one is in completely beautiful surroundings again.

After Wembach, which is a village a little aside from the main road but with a number of spacious and comfortable Black Forest farmhouses, is Schönau, at the foot of the Belchen. Further up the valley is Geschwend, from where a twisty road runs eastwards towards Bernau and the Albtal. Continuing in this direction, the traveller arrives once again in Todtnau, attractive both as a centre for exploring the highest mountains and for many more modest excursions.

Past Todtnau, road B317 is still accompanied for a while by the river Wiese. There is a path for the walker called the Feldbergpfad which runs parallel to the road and river, all three being hemmed into the steep-sided valley by the mountains on either side. These are dominated to the north by the Stübenwasen and the Feldberg itself. There are several parking places giving access to the paths in the valley bottom, but it is not until about 6km (4 miles) from Todtnau that there is an opportunity to take to the hills. Then suddenly, at the foot of the Seebuck, one is in the resort called **Feldberg** and among a veritable network of ski-lifts going up to the slopes of the Ahornbühl and Grafenmatt to the south and to the Seebuck north of the road.

A hotel and several *Gasthöfe* close to some of the ski-lifts provide for the traveller, and a little further on is the main access road to the Feldberg mountain. (One of the many youth hostels in the area is here.) The summer walker will find countless opportunities for exploring the heights or going round the lake, the Feldsee, with its near vertical rocky cliffs on three sides. Close to the summit of the Seebuck is the Bismarck memorial tower which has a fine viewpoint. Here one is in the large *Naturschutzgebiet* which protects the whole of the Feldberg area.

Bärental and its railway station are reached in another 6km (4 miles) while road B317 combines with B500 to continue north-eastwards to Titisee and the area to be described in the next chapter.

6

THE SOUTH-EASTERN CORNER

The Hinterland

Like all the other parts of the Black Forest, this is an area of great natural beauty, but here most of the big mountains are left behind and the rivers are insignificant, even compared with the modest ones further north. The rivers here flow southwards and, while they still join the Rhine, they do so in that stretch which forms the border with Switzerland.

Again, it is an area of villages and small towns, apart from a few larger centres, mostly close to the Rhine, such as Bad Säckingen and Waldshut. In general, the area is less well-known than those already described, but it does contain, at its northern extremity, the very popular holiday centres around the Titisee and the Schluchsee.

The village of **Titisee** has only a small resident population of about 2,000. On a summer weekend one could be forgiven for thinking that it might be nearer 20,000, for the lake, beaches and streets will be crowded with sun- and water-lovers. Titisee is, without doubt, the modern tourist mecca of the Forest and if one is on a coach tour which includes an overnight stop in the Forest, it is likely to be here. There is a great deal of first-class accommodation and large camping and caravan sites, as well as a youth hostel at the south end of the lake.

In an area not very well endowed with lakes, it is understandable that the 2km ($1^1/_4$ miles) stretch of water from which the village takes its name is a huge attraction and it is not surprising that water

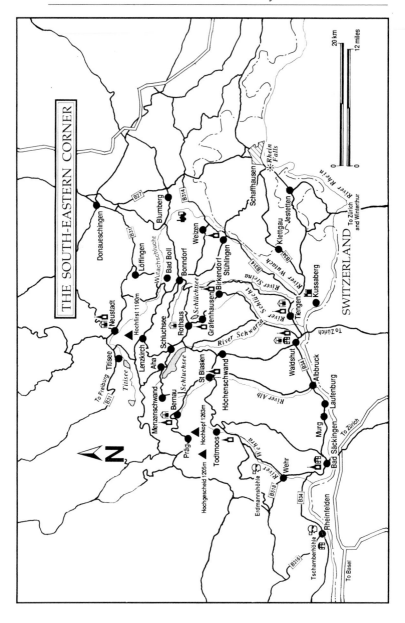

activities of every kind occupy the major part of the day for many holidaymakers. The village has souvenir shops, boutiques and cafés and is very much a tourist centre. Leaving aside the commercial aspects, it is a good walking centre and is crossed by several long-distance paths, including those from Pforzheim to Basel and from Freiburg to Bodensee.

An excellent and not too strenuous walk of 13km (8 miles) starts in Titisee and takes in the summit of the Hochfirst. Leave the busy resort near the Hotel Seehof — a fine traditional building — and follow the red diamond waymarks along the south-eastern shore of the lake. A short distance past a camp site at the end of the lake, turn back sharply to the left and follow the path steeply uphill and under the railway to the busy main road which must be crossed with care. Go a few paces to the left to pick up the path on the other side of the road (sign 'Saig-Hochfirst') and continue uphill to a road junction and car park at Rotes Kreuz, about 1 hour from the start of the walk. (This would be an alternative starting point if it has not been possible to find parking space in Titisee.)

Follow the waymarks (blue beetle) along the edge of and just inside the wood to the Saiger Höhe and the hotel of the same name, passing the Café Alpenblick a little later on the right and skirting the village of Saig itself. Before reaching the Waldhotel at the foot of the Hochfirst, notice the red/white diamond on yellow ground waymark coming in on the left from Titisee. This should now be followed for the best route to the summit at 1,190m (3,908ft) where there are wonderful panoramic views if one has the energy to climb the observation tower.

For the descent, follow the woodland path (blue bird waymark) and rejoin the outward route near the Waldhotel. Now follow the red/white waymark past the hotel and into the path already mentioned which is marked 'Titisee 2km'. Continue downhill on a broad track and pass under the road and the railway to get back to the starting point. Rest and refreshment can be found at Hotel Saiger Höhe, Café Alpenblick, on the Hochfirst (*Ruhetag* Friday) and at the Waldhotel. Ordinary stout walking shoes will be adequate for this walk which is almost entirely on well-kept paths or tracks.

Titisee is one of the constituents of the combined resort of **Titisee-Neustadt**, the latter being the much larger place with a population of some 8,500 and having the status of *Kreisstadt* (administrative centre of a district). The resort is listed as a *Heilklimatische Kurort* and

Neustadt has the additional designation of *Kneippkurort*, reflecting its adoption of the medical treatment pioneered by Sebastian Kneipp. **Neustadt** has considerable possibilities as a centre for touring by road or rail and the town itself is a pleasant place to return to after a day of exploration. The mighty neo-Gothic church has a number of features of interest and there is a small folk museum which contains items of local significance, including a clock-maker's workshop. The area offers good skiing facilities in winter although there is only one short ski-lift in the immediate vicinity of the town.

As the main road B31 now bypasses the town, one is not unduly disturbed by heavy traffic. However, parking can be quite a problem in this important centre, despite the four car parks provided. There is a surrounding network of footpaths, many of them linking with the neighbouring resorts of Titisee, Hinterzarten, Saig and Lenzkirch. Some 3km (2 miles) south-west of the town is the Hochfirst 1,190m (3,595ft) with a *Gasthof* and a *W-Parkplatz*. A short marked walk includes several good viewing points, but this could be a base for walks of any desired length. As already described, some of the path markings in this area are in pictorial form — birds, animals, butterflies, etc, instead of the more usual geometrical designs.

An interesting excursion from Neustadt is that north-westwards into the sparsely populated, rural Jostal through which the little river Josbach runs. This is another area in which there were once many water mills, some of which can still be seen. Another feature of the Jostal and the several little side valleys leading from it is the considerable number of wayside shrines, often in the form of a crucifix and sometimes with a tiny chapel nearby. These *Bildstöcke*, as they are called, were erected for various reasons. Sometimes it was in thanks to the Almighty for deliverance from illness or the saving of a threatened harvest, sometimes in memory of a deceased member of a family and quite often as a place of worship to be resorted to when the winter snows made travel to the church impracticable.

About 2km (1¼ miles) from the point at which the valley road leaves the main road, at Hölzlebruck, between Neustadt and Titisee, one comes to the first westward running side valley, signposted to Schildwende. The *W-Parkplatz* 'Jostal' is at the junction. The tiny Klaus-Kapelle will be seen nearby; this is a chapel looked after by the residents of the two nearest farms.

Outside the chapel, there is a fine example of a cross which was erected in memory of a 37-year-old soldier who was killed in Alsace in World War I. The details are inscribed in the stone from which the cross is made. The figure of Christ is made of wood and has a gilded loin-cloth. The car may be left here for a 12km (7½ mile) walk in which a number of *Bildstöcke* may be seen, as well as some fine farmhouses.

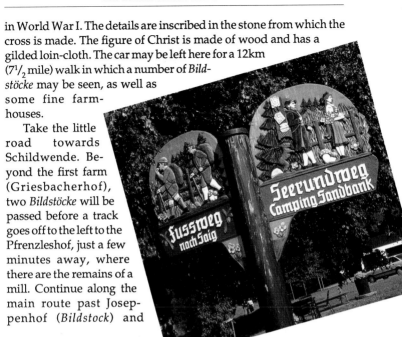

Take the little road towards Schildwende. Beyond the first farm (Griesbacherhof), two *Bildstöcke* will be passed before a track goes off to the left to the Pfrenzleshof, just a few minutes away, where there are the remains of a mill. Continue along the main route past Joseppenhof (*Bildstock*) and

Wooden signpost at Titisee

Boating on the Titisee

Knöpfleshof (mill) and then climb steadily to Fürsatzhöhe at 1,071m (3,513ft). Here, 3.5km (2$^1/_4$ miles) from the starting point, there is a junction of several little roads and footpaths. The long-distance *Westweg* crosses here, as does a cross-country ski route from Thurner on the *Panoramastrasse*; there is also a *Gasthaus* nearby.

Turn northwards following the *Westweg* and, after about 300m (330yd), note a short path going right to a viewpoint. Shortly after this, the *Westweg* is joined by another path (red spot) coming in from the left and the two run together along the ridge for about 1km ($^1/_2$ mile) when the *Westweg* goes off to the left (west) while the red spot continues to mark the path being followed.

Four kilometres (2$^1/_2$ miles) from Fürsatzhöhe, this comes down to a little road at Danielenhof where there is a mill and a *Bildstock*. Turn right and continue for about 500m (545yd) to the group of buildings around the Rainhof and the Josenhof where the main Jostal valley road is regained. Here there are three *Bildstöcke* as well as a *Gasthaus*. Turn right and follow the valley road south-eastwards back to the starting point which is reached in 4km (2$^1/_2$ miles) from the Josenhof. Walk along the field edges to avoid walking on the road. There is yet another *Gasthaus* at about the midway point.

An alternative walk of about the same length from the W-*Parkplatz* is the 'Jostal Rundwanderweg' which is illustrated on the sign there. However, the route does not always follow footpaths shown on the *Wanderkarte* for the area and the quite adequate signs have to be relied upon.

At many of the farms a smaller dwelling house will be seen. This is the *Liebgedinghaus*, a little home for the old people and an indication of the youngest son caring for the other family members, as was mentioned earlier. Another very pleasant valley, the Langenordnachtal, runs northwards from Hölzlebruck for about 7km (4 miles) to a *Gasthaus* called Schneehof near which there are two ski-lifts. There are several other *Gasthäuser* on the way but, unfortunately, there is no very obvious footpath along the valley bottom, although the road is bisected by numerous paths running between the ridges on either side. The skier can, however, follow the *Langlauf* track parallel with the road.

The train traveller has to change at Titisee to reach the Schluchsee which is the biggest lake in the Forest, more than 7km (4 miles) long, and has three holiday resorts, namely Aha, Schluchsee and Seebrugg. There is a station at each of these; Seebrugg, at the south end of the lake is also the end of the branch line. The so-called *Dreiseenbahn* (Three Lakes Railway) from Titisee to Schluchsee was only opened in 1934. The three lakes are the Titisee, the idyllic Windgfällweiher and the Schluchsee. Although comparatively short (21km, 13 miles) and without the major engineering features of the *Höllentalbahn*, this little line has the distinction of serving the highest station on West Germany's public railway network at Bärental, 937m (3,074ft) above sea level.

The lake occupies a splendid position among woods and meadows and is popular for its excellent bathing. Steamers ply between the resorts and many sailing events contribute to the general interest. Windsurfing is probably the activity most practised on the Schluchsee today. Keen fishermen retire to the more peaceful west bank, where, it is said, a good catch can be assured.

The new **Schluchsee** *Kurhaus* is open from 8am until 10pm and the complex includes a restaurant and a concert hall, the latter also being used for ballroom dancing and tea dances. There are also TV rooms and bowling alleys. Schluchsee is one of the resorts which organises a baby-sitting service. There are several camp sites around the lake and there is a modern *Feriendorf* (holiday village) but, in general, it seems to have escaped the excessive commercialism which tends to spoil Titisee.

The Schluchsee seen today is a man-made lake and its principal purpose is to provide a head of water for the hydro-electric power stations at Schwarzabruck and Waldshut. There are considerable variations in the water level of the lake because, at periods of peak demand, the power stations use more water than can be replaced quickly by natural means. As a result, old roads and bridges long since lost beneath the waves sometimes come into view, particularly opposite the Auerhahn *Gasthof*. At night, when electricity in the Federal network is cheap, water is pumped back from the Rhine to restore the proper level in the lake.

A mere 7km (4 miles) south of Seebrugg along the B500, is the *Luftkurort* of **Häusern** on a saddle between the valleys of the rivers Alb and Schwarza. In addition to a *Naturfreundehaus* with twenty-eight beds, there are nearly a thousand beds available here in all other categories. The usual resort facilities are at hand including a heated *Freibad* and a *Hallenbad*. Good food is a byword and gourmets are liable to make for the Schwarzwaldhotel 'Adler', with its many local specialities.

'Village in the sky' is the title sometimes given to **Höchenschwand** which is just a couple of kilometres away. It is Germany's highest *Kurort*, lying on a plateau at over 1,000m (3,300ft) and has the reputation of often having a clear sky when the valleys below are filled with cloud or autumn mist. The 'spa' season lasts all year and summer and winter visitors are equally well-catered for. Facilities for the latter include a ski-school — at this altitude snow can almost be guaranteed. Much of the accommodation is in hotels, several of which have their own indoor pools. Road B500 continues south to Waldshut on the banks of the Rhine, 17km (11 miles) away.

The Schlüchttal is the first of two important valleys running northwards from near Waldshut. The river Schlücht joins the Rhine just east of the town, immediately after its confluence with the Wutach. The Schlücht has its birth a mere 19km (12 miles) away in the Schlüchtsee and it is a typical, but rather reticent, small Black Forest watercourse, often hidden by rocks or undergrowth. In the Middle Ages, the valley road was an important trade route from the south, and there are various ruined hideouts that were used by robbers who preyed upon the travellers.

Another river, the Schwarza, has its source in the Schluchsee, some 15km (9$^1/_2$ miles) to the north-west, and flows through a pretty valley to join the Schlücht just north of Witznau. The Schlüchttal itself becomes even more narrow and enclosed, with steep rocky walls and three picturesque old water-mills on its way north towards Grafenhausen. Here the road leaves the river, which is now worming its way along the boggy valley floor. The wise motorist will leave his or her vehicle for a while and follow the nature trail round the tiny Schlüchtsee and to Rothaus where the little museum 'Hüsli', in an original Black Forest house, is a gem.

The history of 'Hüsli' (little house) is quite interesting. It was built by Frau Helene Siegfried who, in earlier times, had been an extremely attractive and popular concert singer in Berlin. She used to come to the Black Forest to recuperate between concert engagements and finally decided to build a retirement home for herself here. The house, with its great shingled roof, reflects her own tastes and requirements. She was a great collector of all sorts of objects from the old Black Forest farmhouses and in 1958 she decided to make over the house and its contents to be used as a museum after her death. She died in her hundredth year on 28 June 1966 and her wishes were honoured, the house being opened as a museum in 1968.

Working sawmill waterwheel in Jostal

The old-fashioned bathing place on the little Schlüchtsee is particularly attractive. **Grafenhausen** and **Rothaus** make a combined resort which caters for family holidays, with accommodation in well-equipped houses, and there is a fine baroque church dating from 1624. In 1985, the resort was the state winner in a competition *Ferien für die Familie* which highlighted places noted for their friendly and realistic approach to family holidays. There is much good upland walking at around 1,000m (3,280ft) in the district and as this is also the altitude of the resort, no serious climbing is involved. No fewer than six *W-Parkplätze* offer a selection of fourteen round walks, having pictorial waymarkings in this area.

One should explore the Schlücht's companion river before leaving the area. In contrast with the short Schlücht, the Wutach is one of the longest rivers which can be followed, as it half-encircles a huge area of the south-east corner of the Forest. It actually originates in the Feldsee at the foot of the Feldberg and flows eastwards into the Titisee, 5 or 6km (3 or 4 miles) away. Over this short distance, the river is known as the Seebach, but it emerges at the other end of the Titisee as the Gutach, which should not be confused with either of the Gutachs further north. This continues in an easterly direction, flows through Neustadt and then, 10km ($6^1/_4$ miles) further on, is joined by the Haslach and now assumes its third and final name, the Wutach.

Having already visited the areas crossed by the westernmost sections of the stream, it is from this point that the journey downriver is started. It continues to meander eastwards for a while, flowing through a sparsely populated landscape, twisting and turning as it is ever more hemmed in by the valley. There may be a glimpse of the ruins of Burg Stallegg far above and, a little later, those of Boll close to the valley edge near the small resort of Bad Boll.

This is one of the starting points for an excursion which no Black Forest visitor should miss. The **Wutachschlucht** (gorge) is one of the most spectacular natural features, not only of the Black Forest, but of all central Europe and has been compared with some of the grand gorges in the Alps. Steep walls, primitive forest and water foaming over the rocky river bottom make this a memorable experience. The flora and fauna of the Schlucht are exceptional, particularly the orchids and the butterflies, many hundreds of varieties of the latter having been identified in the area. However, the path through the Wutachschlucht is not for the timid, especially in bad weather. In places the walkway projects from the overhanging cliffs and although handrails are provided for safety, there can well be cause for apprehension, particularly as one will probably have to return by the same route.

At Rümmelesteg, part of the river disappears abruptly from view under a rocky cliff and reappears a kilometre later. The similar Gauchachschlucht then empties its waters into the Wutach and one reaches the old Wutachmühle 15 minutes later. There are parking places at Bad Boll and at Wutachmühle but there is no public transport between them.

If one goes into the **Gauchachschlucht**, there is a further series of natural beauties and it is, perhaps, worthwhile wandering up this valley to the Burgmühle (about 30 minutes away) and past the remains of the Birnmühle and the Lochmühle. These old water mills were continually affected by violent flooding of the river and were finally destroyed by it in 1895. Just above the Lochmühle there is a little chapel in memory of that catastrophe, and a plaque tells the story.

The section described is the most popular part of this remarkable area — it has been a *Naturschutzgebiet* (conservation area) since 1939 and has been named the Ludwig-Neumann-Weg after a president of the *Schwarzwaldverein*. A more extensive tour may be started at Rötenbach off the B31 between Neustadt and Löffingen, where a quarry provides a suitable parking place at the beginning of the Rötenbachklamm or -schlucht (ravine). One climbs down through the ravine to reach the Wutach and this is a good appetiser for the spectacular scenery to come.

The route, which includes that already described, is some 40km (25 miles) in total so requires more than a single day's walk for most people. However, there are opportunities for overnight stops here and there or the really well-organised might return to their own base and complete the expedition another time. This longer route would finish at Döggingen back on the B31. The visitor should obtain a large-scale map of the area and, if he or she can read German, the excellent guide *Wanderführer durch die Wutach und Gauchachschlucht* by Fritz Hockenjos. Needless to say, maps and guides are readily available in the area.

For those unable to arrange a linear walk through the gorges, a circular route which embraces much of the best scenery covers 13km (8 miles) and takes about 3 hours. Park at the Wutachmühle *W-Parkplatz* and follow the road uphill in the direction of Mundelfingen for about 300m (330yd) and then go left following the signs through a field path to the nearby wood. Reach the Wutach river bank, go upstream and one will arrive, after about 15 minutes, at the point where the Gauchach joins. The Wutach is spanned here by the roofed Canada/Deutschland footbridge. Now follow signs (blue diamond) beside the Gauchach up to the Burgmühle, which can be reached in 15 minutes or so. Beyond the mill, the ravine is certainly very lovely but the subsequent detour via Unadingen is not recommended. It is better to be satisfied with a further 5 minutes' walk up the valley, over a wooden bridge and then past overhanging cliffs where great care is needed. From here, one can return to the *Naturfreundehaus* at Burgmühle and make the short, sharp climb westwards to open country.

After a good 20 minutes, the big farm Neuenburg is reached with its Café Burgstüble. Turn left (south) here, leaving the surfaced access road and go straight ahead to the wood; follow the blue diamond signs to go westwards to the cemetery at the approach to the village of Bachheim and go on into the village if desired. (Time from the Burgmühle, about 45 minutes). From the cemetery, turn back south-eastwards at the sign 'Zur Wutachschlucht'. Pass a *W-Parkplatz* and follow the unmistakable route until reaching a choice of direction near a spring. If time permits (allow half an hour), a short side excursion to the right (west) takes one to Rümmelesteg where part of the Wutach goes underground. Return to the junction and now follow the red/white signs downstream.

After about 15 minutes, take the right fork at another junction and soon cross to the right bank of the Wutach over a little bridge. Now follow the rocky path through the ravine, noting the point at which the hidden stream rejoins the main river and leave the valley near the confluence with the Gauchach by crossing the Canada bridge and climbing back to the starting point which is reached in about $1^{1}/_{2}$ hours from Bachheim. Refreshments can be found at the Wutachmühle, the Naturfreundehaus Burgmühle, the Café Burgstüble and in Bachheim. Footwear with a good grip is necessary for this walk.

Visitors wishing to spend some time exploring these various river valleys should consider the little town of **Bonndorf** with its satellite villages as a convenient base. It is centrally situated and only about 3km (2 miles) from the Wutachschlucht at Boll. Bonndorf is a *Luftkurort* offering 760 beds in a variety of accommodation including

Windsurfing on the Schluchsee

A quiet corner of the Schluchsee

a youth hostel. There is a heated *Freibad* and a *Hallenbad*, together with all the usual amenities associated with a popular holiday resort. The sixteenth-century *Schloss* houses the *Kreismuseum* and also a *Narrenstuben*, for Bonndorf is another place in which *Fasnet* is celebrated. The *Schloss* is also the venue for popular concerts during the summer months. The parish church is worth seeing as an example of nineteenth-century architecture.

Back at the Wutachmühle, the river now crosses agricultural country and, before it reaches Blumberg, turns to the south for its destination in the Rhine. We are told, however, that many thousands of years ago it continued eastwards to join the Danube. The Swiss border is approached in another 7 or 8km (4 or 5 miles) but the Wutach remains German. The natural obstacles are now left behind, and ahead, in the distance, is Schloss Hohenlupfen near the little border town of **Stühlingen**. The *Klosterkirche* here is all that remains of the former Kapuzinerkloster of 1738. It has a baroque choir screen and the painting, *Madonna of Loretto*. The parish church in the lower town has a fine high altar from 1787. In the picturesque upper town there is a fine *Marktplatz* and chapel buildings from the seventeenth and eighteenth centuries.

Between Blumberg and Weizen, 4km (2^1/$_2$ miles) to the north of Stühlingen, there is a great attraction for railway enthusiasts in the steam-operated 'museum' railway which runs between these places. Motive power is provided by a former Deutsche Bundesbahn class 93 tank locomotive (originally Austrian and built at Linz in 1931) and a type T3 built by Borsig in Berlin in 1901. However, the line is important as much for its civil engineering interest as for the traction.

Built in the years 1887-90 as a strategic line for the state of Baden, with the possibility of access to the Gotthard, it was soon overshadowed in economic importance by the line through the Rhine valley to Basel but was nevertheless maintained for military reasons, regardless of cost. This aspect ceased to be of significance after 1945 and the line, by now part of Deutsche Bundesbahn, was taken out of use in 1955. At the behest of NATO, it was restored during the years 1962-4 and finally closed, as far as Deutsche Bundesbahn was concerned, on May Day in 1976. An agreement between the town of Blumberg and the Federal Railway enabled it to be reopened the following year as a museum.

The section of preserved line is almost 26km (16 miles) long, although the straight line distance between the termini is no more than 9.6km (6 miles). The line has to climb 231m (757ft) in this short distance; it has numerous horseshoe curves and the only spiral tunnel in Germany, 1,700m (1,860yd) long and rising 15.5m (50ft). Because of these features the line is nicknamed 'Sauschwänzlesbahn' (the pig's tail railway). There are four other tunnels on the line as well as three major viaducts and a bridge over the Wutach. A variety of historic passenger vehicles provides up to 500 seats on each train, as well as a buffet car. The station at Blumberg is at Zollhaus on road B27 from Donaueschingen. Passenger services operate between mid-May and mid-October, but not daily, and intending visitors are well-advised to write to Blumberg in advance for the current timetable.

Another pretty road leads south-east from Grafenhausen to **Birkendorf**, which is 5km (3 miles) away, lying at 786m (2,579ft) between the Steina and Schlücht valleys. This pleasant climatic health resort has won many new friends in recent years — people who enjoy the upland climate, the broad views of the countryside and, above all, the friendly village outlook and good lodgings. There is plenty of fine walking with easy gradients and from time to time there are conducted rambles. There is a *Freibad* in the woods, heated to 24 °C (75 °F), with a nearby nature trail, and an indoor pool at the hotel 'Sonnenhof'.

North-east of Birkendorf in the Steinatal are the noted Roggenbach-Schlösser which are two neighbouring ruins, visible from the road and easily reached. First, on a steep slope, comes the single-towered Burg Steinegg which was owned in the twelfth century by the Herren von Steinegg, the lords of the manor. Nearby, Burg Roggenbach — sometimes known as Weissenburg — has two mighty square towers. Its twelfth-century owners were the Herren von Roggenbach who were in the service of the dukes of Zähringen. In the fifteenth century, the abbot of St Blasien had the castle destroyed as a result of a quarrel about ownership. It was successfully rebuilt only to suffer, with its neighbour, irreparable damage in the Peasants' Revolt of 1524-5.

Continuing southwards from Birkendorf, the road drops down towards Uhlingen which is reached in about 4km (2½ miles). Ten kilometres (6¼ miles) further at Witznau, the road joins one which has come south through the Schwarzatal. Ruined castles come thick and fast in this part of the world; two or three kilometres before Witznau the remains of Allmut will have been passed and now, in quick succession, follow Schörringen, Isnegg and Gutenberg, Isnegg

Sixteenth-century Schloss, *Bonndorf*

Museum railway, in the Wutachtal

in particular, being worth a brief halt.

Seven kilometres (4 miles) west of Waldshut, the river Alb also adds its waters to the Rhine. It has followed a quite direct course from its several sources in the Feldberg area, making its way through the Albtal, which is interesting throughout its 35km (22 miles) length. (There is, of course, another river Alb in the north.) The sparsely populated valley through which this runs is ideal walking country. From this southern end, the first 6km (4 miles) are in a narrow, rocky gorge which has some impressive views. The road climbs up the valley on the steep flanks and a stop at the Gasthaus Hohenfels allows one to visit the nearby viewpoint. The road continues to climb through numerous curves and tunnels and it is only after Tiefenstein that the valley begins to broaden.

The landscape gradually assumes a more friendly countenance, farmhouses begin to appear on the slopes, and there are several comfortable *Gasthäuser* along the way to cater for the traveller. Before **St Blasien**, the Alb-Stausee is reached, a 1½km (1 mile) long reservoir of particular beauty. It stretches to the outskirts of the village where the imposing dome of the *Klosterkirche* — said to be the fourth largest dome in the world — attracts immediate attention.

The history of the *Kloster* goes back at least a thousand years and includes many tales of disaster and destruction. The present building was erected between 1772 and 1783 to the design of the Frenchman, Pierre Michel d'Ixnard. The Benedictine monks here have been noted for their interest in cultural affairs and have made significant contributions to German cultural history. Secularisation after 1803 brought the life and culture of the monastery to an end and, in 1807, the monks withdrew to Austria where, in the Kloster St Paul in Lavanttal (Kärnten), they continue the traditions of St Blasien to this day.

Following the departure of the monks, the monastery buildings were used at first as a small-arms factory and later as a spinning mill. A fire in 1874 destroyed much of the former *Kloster* buildings and the choir and dome of the church. The dome was rebuilt in 1875 and the monks' choir restored and refurbished to become the parish church. Further renovations have taken place in the twentieth century and during the 1980s the interior was repainted in gleaming white to recapture the early Classical style of the building.

The visitor entering the church, which dominates the village, will be surprised and impressed by the mighty scale of the interior. The *Kloster* buildings have been used since 1933 as a seminary for members of the order of Jesuits. In charming contrast to the huge Catholic church, the Protestant place of worship is completely timber-built in traditional Black Forest style.

A glance at the map will reveal that St Blasien is another ideal centre for exploration of the surrounding countryside. There is a good selection of accommodation, mostly of a fairly modest type. At the north end of the village, there is a sports centre with a swimming pool and tennis courts. Several car parks give easy access to a variety of walks and a *Trimm Dich* path. There is also a *Wildgehege* (enclosure for deer, etc) nearby.

The river divides about 3km (2 miles) further up the valley to become the Bernauer Alb to the left, and the Menzenschwander Alb to the right. A little further on, the road also divides, to Bernau and to Menzenschwand. Just past the junction on the Bernau road, one of the three car parks is a *W-Parkplatz* with two round walks marked.

Some 8km (5 miles) from St Blasien, there is the quiet resort of **Bernau**, which lies in a sunny, alpine-like valley, and has a good range of facilities for visitors and plenty of accommodation in hotels and *Gasthöfe* with quite modest prices. The Restaurant and Pension 'Bernauer Hof' (1622) has changed little in over three hundred years and should be visited for its homely atmosphere as well as its food. There is a *Hallenbad* here and a camp site.

Bernau is the home of many wood-carvers and turners. The famous Black Forest artist, Hans Thoma, was born here in 1839 and there is an exhibition of his work with memorabilia in Bernau-Innerlehen *Rathaus*. He was responsible for two large paintings in the parish church. The modern *Kurhaus* and a *Hallenbad* are also in Innerlehen. There is a museum of rural history in the Resenhof in Bernau.

A variety of walks start from the resort but they can be quite strenuous, for Bernau lies only a few kilometres from the southern outposts of the Feldberg group, notably the 1,417m (4,646ft) high Herzogenhorn. Once out of the valley, the walker will spend much of his time at around 1,200m (4,000ft). The motorist will find no lack of parking places in the vicinity. The *W-Parkplatz* Rotes Kreuz (red cross) at 1,090m (3,575ft) about 3km (2 miles) along the Todtmoos road has two marked walks. With the aid of a map, one can readily devise numerous other longer or shorter routes.

One such walk, of 7$^1/_2$km (4$^1/_2$ miles), is southwards from the car park, where there is a good view back towards Bernau, on to the tiny settlement of Rütte with its *Gasthof,* in about 1.5km (1 mile). Go right here without crossing the main road along a path (red cross on white) to the few houses at Prestenberg, with another viewpoint. Following the same sign, resume the southerly direction to cross the main road and turn north almost immediately into a path to the right (red rectangle on white) to head directly towards the summit of the Hochkopf at 1,263m (4,147ft). There is a very good all-round observation point with a tower here but one need not go right up; by turning away north-eastwards before the final ascent, it is possible to walk back to the car park in about 3km (2 miles). If one goes to the summit, a slightly longer return route is followed which makes the total distance 9km (5$^1/_2$ miles).

The main road through Bernau gradually assumes a westerly direction and arrives at a parking place by an old quarry in 2 or 3 kilometres which is close to the point where the *Westweg* long-distance path crosses the road. The path climbs southwards in a series of very steep, zig-zag curves to reach the summit of the Blössling at 1,309m (4,290ft) in a straight line distance of 1km ($^1/_2$ mile) but at least double this along the path. There is an altitude difference of 336m (1,103ft) from the road to the summit so it is a rather stiff climb, but the outlook from two viewpoints at the top makes it worthwhile.

The road now descends gently for about 4km (2$^1/_2$ miles) to **Präg**. This is without doubt one of the prettiest villages in this part of the Forest. It has been known as the *Gletscherdorf* (glacier village) because the valley in which it lies was formed in the Ice Age by the convergence of seven glaciers. Today, protected by the surrounding 650-750m (2,000-2,500ft) hills, it enjoys a mild climate and the valley is particularly attractive in autumn as the changing colours of the trees gradually spread down from the heights to the valley floor. There are splendid views from the nearby Spitzenberg 1,143m (3,751ft) and the Hochkopf 1,263m (4,147ft) — especially from the latter with its wooden viewing tower. It is little wonder that Präg has long been a favourite haunt of artists and photographers.

An extremely twisty road climbs southwards out of Präg; there are numerous parking places giving access to viewpoints with wonderful vistas back into the valley. The resort of Todtmoos is reached in about 8km (5 miles). Another pretty but less winding road leaves Präg in the direction of Todtnau, about 9km (5$^3/_4$ miles) away.

Menzenschwand lies northwards along the other branch of the

*Street scene in
St Blasien*

*St Blasien's Klosterkirche
and the dome's interior*

Bernau church

Alb, about 6km (4 miles) from St Blasien, the youth hostel being among the first buildings at the entrance to the village. Although having much the same characteristics and surroundings as Bernau, this resort is squeezed into a much narrower valley. To escape from the valley bottom, the walker has a fairly stiff climb, in any direction. However, a short walk at the north end of the village leads to a waterfall. Trout-fishing is possible in the vicinity, there is a children's play area and over 100km (62 miles) of marked paths are available to the visitor. There are concerts or brass band performances nearly every week in the newly built *Kurhaus*, forming part of the variety of cultural and social events which take place.

Winter visitors are very well-catered for with convenient ski-lifts — of which there are seven in the area — and a terrain which is suitable for both downhill and cross-country skiing. There are courses for advanced skiers and for beginners, including one for 3-5 year-olds. The authoritative magazine *Euroski* commented that Menzenschwand is an ideal place for families who like to do some uncomplicated skiing together. There is a good choice of hotels and *Gasthäuser* in Menzenschwand but many of them close for the whole or second half of November and do not reopen until mid-December, as do those in St Blasien and Bernau.

The Wehra is another of those southward-flowing rivers which feed the Rhine, which it reaches near Bad Säckingen. **Wehr** is some 5km (3 miles) from its mouth and is the main town of the valley, with textile and paper-making industry down-river. There are some places of interest in and around the little town, including the spectacular subterranean caverns at Hasel 4km ($2^1/_2$ miles) to the north. However, Wehr is not a major tourist centre and the visitor is more likely to press on north-eastwards up the valley.

The walker could leave the north end of the town and follow the Wehratalweg (Wehra valley way), past the Wehrabecken, a Stausee or man-made lake created by the damming of the river, and continue through the almost uninhabited valley for the 12km ($7^1/_2$ miles) or so to Todtmoos-Au, where the situation changes quite dramatically. The river alters its character from a meandering meadow waterway to acquire all the features of a high Black Forest valley river. Here is the health resort of **Todtmoos** (population 2,400), a *Luftkurort* at the foot of the Hochkopf with its summit observation tower giving fine views in every direction.

Todtmoos is one of the foremost spas and a centre for holidays and winter sports with many favourable opportunities for *Langlauf*. The facilities here are well-suited to the younger generation. There are well-equipped playing areas for children and the 'Aqua-Treff' open-air swimming pool has a novel arrangement of water spouts and fountains. Excellent trout-fishing may be had in the vicinity.

Bypassed by the main road, the peaceful little town has a large range of entertainments and recreation for both the active and the less active visitor. Nobody should miss a visit to the significant baroque pilgrimage church of Maria Himmelfahrt which was built in 1627. Todtmoos has been a place of pilgrimage since the fourteenth century and the Gnadenbild (miraculous image) in the church stems from that time.

Wood-carving and hand-weaving workshops can be found in the numerous outlying settlements and it is possible to purchase their products. There are many hotels, pensions and *Gasthäuser*, most of them of a fairly modest size but there are, nevertheless more than four thousand beds available. Apart from the two weeks before and after Christmas, the late/early season runs from the beginning of October until the end of May; those who take their holidays during this time can take advantage of the lower rates. (Here again, closure for several weeks prior to mid-December is fairly usual.)

THE RHINE, SCHAFFHAUSEN TO BASEL

In the travels made so far, the numerous pleasant towns and villages strung out along the southern fringe of the Black Forest and facing Switzerland across the Rhine have been rather neglected. It is some 80km (50 miles) from the border near Schaffhausen to Basel and the planned *Autobahn 98* will bring merciful relief to a number of towns through which the present main road (B34) passes.

Jestetten is the most easterly of the places along this fringe — a large village of 4,300 inhabitants in pretty surroundings and a mere stone's throw from the Swiss border. Indeed, it lies in an enclave and is almost completely surrounded by Switzerland, the narrow neck at the west end being the only direct connection with the rest of Germany. The village is only about 8km (5 miles) from Schaffhausen itself and even closer to the famous Rhine falls which provide an essential excursion for visitors to this area.

To visit the falls, one can go across country on quiet paths or tracks — about 5km (3 miles); or leave Jestetten by car in the direction of Schaffhausen, cross the border and signs to the falls (Rheinfälle)

Places of Interest In The South-Eastern Hinterland

Neustadt
Heimatstuben
Folk museum with worthwhile collection reflecting Black Forest life-style.
Clock-maker's workshop.

Parish Church
Mighty neo-Gothic building with features of interest.

Schlüchtsee
Small lake encircled by attractive nature trail.

Rothaus
Heimatmuseum 'Hüsli'
Folk art of the Black Forest.

Grafenhausen
Baroque Church (1624)

Wutachschlucht
Spectacular gorge noted for its flora and fauna.
Must be explored on foot.

Gauchachschlucht
Similar to above but additional interest with old water mills.
Include in Wutachschlucht excursion or start from Wutachmühle.

Stühlingen
Klosterkirche (1738)
Baroque choir screen and interesting painting.

Blumberg-Weizen
Museumsbahn Wutachtal
Steam-operated railway with many outstanding engineering features.
Length of line 26km (16 miles).

St Blasien
Klosterkirche (1783)
The immense dome of the church is said to be the fourth largest in the world.

Bernau
Restaurant and Pension 'Bernauer Hof'
Built in 1622 and little-changed since then. Homely atmosphere and good food.

Rathaus
Memorabilia and exhibition of the work of artist Hans Thoma.

Parish Church
Two large paintings by Hans Thoma.

Wehr
Erdmannshöhle
4km (2$^{1}/_{2}$ miles) to the north
Spectacular subterranean caverns.

Todtmoos
Aqua-Treff
Modern open-air leisure pool with water spouts and fountains.

Church of Maria Himmelfahrt
(1627). Baroque pilgrimage church.

will soon be seen. An enormous amount of car parking space is available and at busy times one may be faced with a walk of 20 minutes or so back to the falls. This is no disadvantage since the route is beside the river, with its ever increasing turbulence and noise, until the actual falls are reached. No simple waterfall this, with a sheer drop but also rather a large area of 'rapids' over which the whole volume of the Rhine pours continually westwards in an awe-inspiring spectacle.

This may be observed in comfort from the promenade on the north side but to experience the real impact of this impressive natural phenomenon, the visitor should make the short boat trip out to a steep rock which stands as an island in the middle of the torrent. After disembarking at the foot of the rock, a narrow stairway is climbed to the top for a magnificent view of the turbulent waters.

Going west and emerging from the 'neck' of the Jestetten enclave, one soon reaches **Klettgau**, a place with just under 6,000 inhabitants, lying at an altitude of 400-700m (1,300-2,300ft) and much involved in the wine industry. As at Jestetten, there is not much tourist development but information about accommodation can be provided by the *Gemeindeverwaltung*. **Küssaberg** lies off the main road towards the river so through traffic is not a problem here. Seven small communities go to make up this resort of 4,600 inhabitants. Between them there is a considerable amount of accommodation in *Gasthöfe*, pensions, private houses and holiday flats. Indoor and outdoor tennis courts are available and there are opportunities for fishing. A bridge across the Rhine leads one to the modern Swiss resort of Zurzach with its thermal springs. There are promenades on both banks of the river with a total length of 16km (10 miles). The remains of three bridges, the earliest of which dates from Roman times, can be seen at **Rheinheim**, one of the constituent communities of Küssaberg. Important finds in this area indicate that this was the site of the earliest Roman settlement on the north bank of the Rhine. The ruined castle of Küssaburg stands nearby on high ground which provides good views over the Rhine towards the Swiss Alps. The rail traveller reaches Küssaberg by bus from the station at Waldshut-Tiengen.

Tiengen and Waldshut, already mentioned briefly, are 8km (5 miles) apart but are administered as one place with a joint population of 22,000. Both parts have interesting medieval town centres and a wide range of facilities for the holidaymaker. Two open-air pools and a *Hallenbad* are to be found, together with tennis, riding, bowling, fishing and other recreational activities. The remains of **Tiengen's** old town wall and one of the towers are of interest; the Storchenturm (stork tower) is the emblem of the town and there are examples of *Sgraffito-Häuser* where the decoration is provided by scratching in the outer layers of plaster, which often reveals other colours beneath. The baroque church of 1751 is yet another of the great works of Peter Thumb. It contains a number of interesting relics and, having recently been thoroughly restored and redecorated inside and out, it will now be seen for some years as the architect intended.

The pre-Lenten *Fasnet* celebrations here have a very long history, having first been authorised in 1503. On the first Sunday in July there is a great Trachtenfest — a festival of traditional costumes and customs — known as the Schwyzertag, which is a merry celebration of amity between the peoples on either side of the Rhine. The visitor can identify all the buildings, etc of interest in Tiengen's Altstadt from the neat plaques which have been provided by a thoughtful town council. The town has a fine *Naturkundemuseum* (natural history museum) with an excellent review of the nature of the landscape and examples of the semi-precious stones to be found in the Wutach and Gauchach valleys.

Waldshut's strategic position beside the Rhine has meant a history of frequent upheavel and changes of sovereignty but all this is long past and today the ancient walls enclose a haven of peace. The visitor is presented with a colourful and photogenic picture of tranquillity. A visit to the Friedhofskapelle may be of interest for it has a high altar which is based on the holy sepulchre in Jerusalem.

The parish church will be found in the north-east of the old town. The Gothic choir was incorporated when it was rebuilt in 1804. The interior is mainly neo-Classical and the decoration is nearly all in marble with altars by J.F. Vollmer. In the Hauptstrasse there are numerous examples of the house architecture of the sixteenth to eighteenth centuries as well as late-Gothic town towers.

The *Rathaus* in Kaiserstrasse is a baroque building completed about 1770 and the *Heimatmuseum* in the same street is housed in a sixteenth-century building and includes prehistoric exhibits. Within a kilometre (¹/₂ mile) or so of the town on the north side, there are no less than four strategically located parking places, one of which provides for easy access to the viewing tower on the Haitzenhöhe at 456m (1,496ft).

On the third Sunday in August, Waldshut celebrates the end of its siege by the Swiss in 1468, in a festival known as the Kilbi or Chilbi. Nowadays, the Swiss enjoy the merry-making to the full and come, not with their armies but with their traditional flag-throwers and yodellers to join in the fun. Along the river bank there is a 3km (2 mile) promenade which can provide a pleasant stroll, perhaps for those who have indulged a little too much in one of the many excellent eating places in the town. Either Waldshut or Tiengen, both with a wealth of accommodation in all categories, would provide good bases for the exploration of the river valleys mentioned earlier in this chapter as well as for rambles close to the river Rhine.

Continuing westwards, one soon reaches **Albbruck**, where the ✳ river Alb enters the Rhine. This lovely old place has been a winner in the 'Most beautiful old town in West Germany' competition which is sufficient recommendation in itself. Like many other resorts, it is made up of a number of small settlements, some of them as much as 8km (5 miles) from the centre of the old town which is also quite small itself. Here again there is a good choice of accommodation although there is only one hotel which is in Albbruck proper. The *Gasthöfe*, farms, private houses and self-catering flats supply adequate alternatives. There is a railway station in Albbruck and bus connections to the outlying villages. The 48km (30 mile) long *Hochrhein-Querweg* (Upper Rhine Way) ends here while a footbridge across the Rhine has its further end in Switzerland, making it easy for the walker to extend his explorations into that country.

Next comes **Laufenburg**; this little town has its counterpart of the same name across the river in Switzerland, the two being connected by a road bridge. In fact, it is worth crossing the river to visit the Altstadt in the Swiss town.

The medieval town north of the river has many of the characteristics of Waldshut and Albbruck, with nooks and crannies, twisty lanes, steps and fountains. Facilities for visitors include a heated open-air pool and there is an hotel and a range of more modest accommodation. Bus connections are provided from the station to the outlying parts of the resort. The barriers which separate the Swiss and German communities are officially removed once each year to allow the people on both sides of the river to celebrate their Fasnacht together. This they have done for hundreds of years, for prior to 1803 they were one community, undivided by today's political boundary. This is another place where the fools in their masks reign supreme in

*The Rhine Falls,
near Schaffhausen*

the pre-Lenten events. The fantastic masks of the participants in the fool's procession are matched only by the equally fantastic life-size cardboard figures depicting the *Salmenfischer* of yesteryear.

Unfortunately, the salmon once found in large numbers in this stretch of the Rhine have long since disappeared, along with other river-life which once provided a livelihood for many riverside dwellers. During the carnival period, the narrow streets of the town are decorated with flags and garlands and there is no musical instrument, however large or small, which does not make its contribution to the general cacophony in the streets.

Yet another pleasant little town is to be found 3km (2 miles) further on. This is **Murg** (population 6,300) and it has its own tiny river of the same name running into the Rhine through a romantic little valley with waterfalls and a ruined castle. This Murg is usually known as Murg/Baden to distinguish it from its more northerly

Sgraffitohaus
in Tiengen

Pavement cafés in Tiengen

namesake. It has a heated swimming pool and a modest selection of amenities including riding, fishing and bowling. However, the amount of accommodation for guests is somewhat limited.

Bad Säckingen is on one of the main routes to and from Switzerland. With a population of 14,800, it is of greater importance than the other little towns lying to the east. Being a spa, the accommodation of visitors is organised on a large scale and facilities for the treatment of those here for medical reasons are of a high standard in the several *Kur* establishments. Those visiting Bad Säckingen for pleasure are not overlooked and there are many amenities including a heated outdoor pool, a *Hallenbad* in one of the hotels and, rather unusually, a nine-hole golf course.

In the romantic old part of the town, one finds the baroque Fridolinsmünster which is worth seeing. It has lavish rococo decoration which was added by J.M. Feuchtmayer after a fire in 1751. Despite later additions, the church is essentially Gothic from the fourteenth century with a fifteenth-century nave and sixteenth-century towers. The fire of 1751 was not the only one to afflict the building and it has quite a long history of renovation and alteration.

A church on this site was first started in connection with a mission founded by the Alemannic apostle Fridolin on a Rhine island in AD522. Notable features of the interior furnishings in the present building are the high altar by J.P. Pfeiffer (1721), the choir stalls of 1682 and the church treasure which includes the shrine of St Fridolin (1764) in Augsburg silver. Remains of the old nunnery building can be seen around the church square.

Literary fame came to Bad Säckingen as a result of Victor von Scheffel's verse epic *The Trumpeter of Säckingen*. This tells of a romance played out in Schloss Schonau when a young trumpeter, Franz Werner Kirchhofer, came down from the forest to woo Margareta, the daughter of the Schlossherr — the lord of the manor. It was in 1853 in Capri that von Scheffel completed his great poem but it might well have been forgotten had not an opera composer, Victor Nessler, chanced upon it and written a splendid melody for the trumpeter's farewell. Since then, the little palace of Schonau has been more commonly known as the Trompeterschloss and this background has resulted in Bad Säckingen becoming known as the *Trompeterhauptstadt* (trumpet capital), with an active musical life based upon this instrument. Details of festivals planned should be obtained from the Verkehrsamt, am Bahnhof, 7880 Bad Säckingen.

The little palace dates from 1500 and is built on the site of an earlier Romanesque building. It now houses the *Heimatmuseum*, known as the Hochrheinmuseum (Upper Rhine Museum). This specialises in early and prehistory but also has an interesting collection of watches and trumpets, together with memorabilia of Victor von Scheffel, whose house may be seen in the town. Near the minster, a historic wooden bridge — the longest of its kind in Europe — provides a picturesque means for the pedestrian to cross the Rhine into Switzerland. Boat trips on the Upper Rhine can also be started here. Bad Säckingen is only 33km (20$^1/_2$ miles) from Basel and, like the other places mentioned, is served by the railway line running from that city to Schaffhausen.

Past Oflingen, where the Wehra joins the Rhine, is **Schwörstadt**, an old settlement beside the river on a former Roman road. The palace of the former barons of Schonau is on the river bank but the most significant sight hereabouts is the 3,000-year-old so-called *Heidenstein* (heathen's stone, part of a megalithic grave).

Mid-way between Bad Säckingen and Basel, is **Rheinfelden** which is another town with a Swiss namesake across the river. Rheinfelden is a *Kreisstadt* and, with 29,000 inhabitants, some of whom live in the outlying villages, it is by far the biggest town along this east-west route. There is also a great deal of very obvious industrial activity. The palace-like main building of Schloss Beuggen, once a headquarters of the Knights of St John (1246), was refurbished by J.K. Bagnato between 1752 and 1757. The ceiling painting in the church depicts the life of St Elisabeth. The bizarre 500m (546yd) long Tschamberhöhle (caves) nearby are worth a visit.

Although not primarily a tourist centre, there is plenty of accommodation in hotels and *Gasthöfe*. There are many facilities for recreational pursuits, including swimming (heated outdoor pool and *Hallenbad*), tennis, riding, fishing and gliding. If all this is not enough, a walk over to the Swiss spa town on the south bank will provide yet more diversions of various kinds.

It will be seen that this area bordering the Rhine is more populous than most of the other parts described but this should not be allowed to deter the prospective visitor. The environment is quite different from that found anywhere else in this corner of Germany and there is plenty to see and do, even if one cannot catalogue a series of outstanding ancient monuments for inspection. The warm, south-facing slopes have a number of vineyards but fruit-growing is also

Places of Interest Along The Rhine From Schaffhausen to Basel

Jestetten
Rhein Falls
Near Schaffhausen
Dramatic waterfall and rapids.

Küssaberg
Küssaburg
Ruined castle with extensive views towards Alps.

Remains of Bridges
At Rheinheim
Remains of three Rhine bridges including one from the Roman period.

Tiengen
Baroque Church (1751)
Another church by the architect Peter Thumb. Painted interior well-worth seeing.

Naturkundemuseum
Natural history museum with special reference to the Wutachtal.

Waldshut
Parish Church
Neo-Classical interior with marble decoration.

Rathaus (1770)
In Kaiserstrasse. Baroque building.

Heimatmuseum
Housed in sixteenth-century building
Collection includes prehistoric exhibits.

Albbruck
One-time winner of 'Most beautiful old town in West Germany' competition.

Laufenburg
Picturesque riverside town with namesake across bridge in Switzerland. Altstadt in Swiss town is worth seeing.

Bad Säckingen
Fridolinsmünster
Huge baroque church with rococo decoration added in 1751. Notable interior furnishings.

Schloss Schönau
Known as the Trompeterschloss due to Viktor von Scheffel's verse epic *The Trumpeter of Säckingen*. Now houses the Hochrheinmuseum (Upper Rhine Museum).

Historic Covered Wooden Bridge
Crosses the Rhine to Switzerland. Longest such bridge in Europe.

Schwörstadt
Heidenstein
Part of megalithic grave. Three thousand years old.

Rheinfelden
Schloss Beuggen (1246)
Once a headquarters of the Knights of St John Refurbished in rococo style 1752-7.

Tschamberhöhle
500m (1,640ft) long caves

Rhine bridge at Laufenburg

Schloss Schönau (Trompeterschloss), Bad Säckingen

important here and walking up through the orchards can be very pleasant, particularly during blossom time. The sights of Lörrach and Inzlingen, in the area closer to Basel, have already been referred to in Chapter 1.

This south-eastern corner of the Black Forest contains the greatest variety of scenery and the greatest scope for varied activities. The surface has barely been scratched and every visitor will uncover some new delight to add to what has been written. That is the joy of any holiday in a new environment, but if this and the preceding chapters have aroused some interest and given an indication of what may be found, the purpose of this book will have been achieved.

USEFUL INFORMATION
FOR VISITORS

Note: The postcode for German addresses appears immediately before the name of the town, eg 7800 Freiburg. To telephone to Germany from Great Britain, dial 010-49- then omit the first 'O' of the telephone number.

ACCOMMODATION

Accommodation is available in the Black Forest in hotels, inns, pensions, private houses, farm-houses, holiday flats or houses, youth hostels and camp sites.

Accommodation lists for the principal resorts can be obtained from the German National Tourist Offices (GNTO) overseas, but these often exclude private houses, farms, holiday flats and camp sites. More detailed lists may be obtained from the local tourist information office (*Verkehrsamt*). The following glossary lists the terms most frequently encountered when seeking or booking accom-modation:

Aufenthaltsraum — Lounge; sitting-room
Bad — Bath
Bankkontonummer — Bank account number
Bauernhof — Farm
Doppelzimmer (Dz) — Double room
Dusche — Shower
Einzelhof — Isolated farm, i.e. not in a village
Einzelzimmer (Ez) — Single room
Endreinigung — Cleaning after departure of visitor from self-catering accommodation
Feriendorf — Holiday village, usually with specially built bungalows
Ferienhaus — Holiday house
Ferienwohnung — Holiday flat
Fernseher — Television
Frühstück — Breakfast
Gasthaus — Restaurant, inn or tavern
Gasthof — Hotel or inn
Halbpension (HP) — Half board
Hotel-garni — Hotel which does not serve meals (except breakfast)

Kinderermässigung — Reductions
for children
Mehrbettzimmer (Mz) — Family
room
Nebenkosten — Extras
Pension — Boarding house; board
and lodging
Postleitzahl — Postcode
Ruhige Lage — Peaceful situation
Strom — Electricity
Übernachtung mit Frühstück (UmF)
— Bed and breakfast
Vollpension (VP) — Full board
Vor- und Nachsaison (VN) —
Outside the main holiday season
Wasser — Water
Wirtshaus — Inn or public house
Zentralheizung — Central Heating
Zimmer — Room/s
Zimmer frei/besetzt — Vacancies/
No vacancies
Zimmer zu Vermieten — Room/s to
let

Holiday Villages
In addition to self-catering
accommodation (lists from local
tourist information offices), there
are many holiday villages, some of
these being run by religious or
other charitable bodies. Brief
details of some of these villages are
given below.

Bad Liebenzell
Schwarzwald-Ferienpark-
Verwaltungs GmbH
Postfach 1164
7263 Bad Liebenzell
☎ 07052-875

Bernau
Kurverwaltung
Postfach 20
7821 Bernau
☎ 07675-316
Houses for (up to) 6 persons.

Enzklösterle
Familienerholungswerk der
Diözese Rottenburg-Stuttgart e.V.
Heusteigstrasse 86A
7000 Stuttgart. ☎ 0711-603077
Feldberg
Feriendorf Neumatte
7821 Feldberg/Schwarzwald 4
☎ 07655-562

Grafenhausen-Rothaus
Familienferienhöfe e.V.
Postfach 1362
7012 Fellbach (Stuttgart)
☎ 0711-586771 (☎ in Grafenhausen,
07748-302)

Kappelrodeck
Verein für Familienerholung in
Deutschland e.V.
Kurt-Schuhmacher-Strasse 23
6000 Frankfurt am Main 1
☎ 0611-2165229

Lenzkirch
Ferien Touristik im Hoch-
schwarzwald
7825 Lenzkirch
☎ 07653-821

Lossburg-Wittendorf
Sonnenrain-Schwarzwälder-
Ferienhaus GmbH
7298 Lossburg-Wittendorf
☎ 07462-2172

Neuhausen-Schellbronn
Ferienpark-Schwarzwald
7831 Neuhausen-Schellbronn
☎ 07234-8515

Sasbachwalden
Gaishöll Wohn- und Ferienpark
Sasbachwalden
Gaishöllpark 7
7595 Sasbachwalden
☎ 07841-5775 or 5773

Schluchsee-Faulenfürst
Eva Woelk
7826 Schluchsee-Faulenfürst
☎ 07656-319

Schramberg-Sulgen
Address as for Enzklösterle

Todtnau
Deutsches Erholungswerk e.V.
Schlüterstrasse 26
2000 Hamburg 13
☎ 040-456208

Waldachtal-Oberwaldach
Feriendorf Waldachtal
7244 Waldachtal-Oberwaldach
☎ 07445-1022

Youth Hostels and Similar Accommodation
A complete list of hostels in Germany can be obtained in exchange for eight International Reply Coupons sent to Deutsches Jugendherbergswerk, Weinweg 43, 7500 Karlsruhe 1, West Germany. ☎ 0721-615066-7. Details can also be obtained from YHA Travel Bureau, 14 Southampton Street, London, WC2 or American Youth Hostels Inc, 1332 'I' Street NW, Washington DC, 20005. ☎ (202) 783 61 61
Hostels in Germany can be recognised by the familiar green triangle and the letters DJH (Deutsche Jugendherberge).
The *Schwarzwaldverein* operates many *Wanderheime* (ramblers' hostels) along its waymarked routes. Information about these and also about maps and guides, can be obtained from Schwarzwaldverein, Hauptgeschäftsstelle, Rathausgasse 33, 7800 Freiburg. ☎ 0761-22794

Hostel-type accommodation is also provided by the tourist association *Die Naturfreunde* (Friends of nature) which has more than forty establishments (*Naturfreundehäuser*) in the Black Forest. Admission is not restricted to members of the association. Information is available from Touristenverein 'Die Naturfreunde', Landesleitung Baden, Schützenstrasse 12, 7500 Karlsruhe.

BANKS AND POST OFFICES

The unit of currency in Germany is the Deutsche Mark (DM). 100 Pfennige (Pfg) = 1DM
Typical hours of opening of the bank (*die Bank*) and the post office (*die Post* or *das Postamt*) are 9am-12noon and 2-4pm (except Saturday) but banks may close all day on Saturday. In small towns or villages, both may operate part-time or may be mobile offices calling at fixed times.
All banks exchange travellers' cheques. If the cheques are in Deutschmarks, the full face value will be given but if they are in foreign currency, the bank will make a charge, usually 2 per cent.
Eurocheques, obtained from one's own bank together with a cheque card, are used exactly as ordinary domestic cheques and must be made out in the local currency. They may be used for paying bills and making purchases but filling stations make an additional charge, usually 50pfg.
Credit cards such as Access,

Visa, American Express, etc are not as widely accepted in Germany as they are in other countries but they are becoming more widespread in the major tourist centres and in most filling stations on main roads.

Bank of England notes and US dollars may be exchanged but not Scottish bank notes. Some main post offices can also undertake currency transactions.

BUILDINGS AND GARDENS OPEN TO THE PUBLIC

It is not possible to list all the many buildings open to the public. Many of the museums are housed in historic buildings and there are virtually hundreds of ruined castles, many of which have no charge for admission. All the spas and many other resorts have libraries, reading rooms, games rooms etc. which the visitor may use.

Gardens are also mainly associated with the resorts and are often beautifully laid out with fairly formal areas. Many have a restaurant or café and facilities for outdoor games such as garden chess, mini-golf and table tennis. There is usually no charge for admission to such gardens, often known as the *Kurpark*.

CHURCHES

The following churches mentioned in this book are particularly worth seeing.

Alpirsbach
Klosterkirche (1125).
In town centre.

Baden-Baden
Autobahnkirche. On A5 at Baden-Baden Raststätte

Breisach
Minster. In town centre.

Donaueschingen
Catholic parish church of John the Baptist and St John (1724-47).

Ettlingen
Schlosskapelle (former palace chapel).
No longer used for religious purposes. In town centre.

Freiburg
Minster. In city centre.
Ludwigskirche. In city centre.
Lorettokapelle. On a hill just south of city.
Synagogue. In city centre.

Freudenstadt
Stadtkirche. At corner of the market square.

Friedenweiler
Baroque church
6km (4 miles) north-west of Löffingen.

Grafenhausen
Baroque church (1624). In village.

Hirsau
St Aurelius Church (1071).
In village.

Kappelwindeck
Baroque church (1765). 3km (2 miles) south-east of Bühl.

Kentheim
Ninth-century church. 3km
(2 miles) south of Calw.

Löffingen
Witterschneekreuz (Nineteenth-
century). 1km ($^1/_2$ mile) north-
west.

Münstertal
Klosterkirche and St Trudpert
chapel. 9km ($5^1/_2$ miles) east of
Staufen in Obermünstertal.

Nagold
Eighth-century Remigiuskapelle.
South of town near bypass (road
B28).

Niederrotweil
Late-Gothic church of St Michael.
In village.

Rottweil
Heiligkreuzmünster (fifteenth-
century). In town centre.
Kapellenkirche (fourteenth-
century). In town centre.

St Blasien
Klosterkirche (1783). In village.

St Peter
Baroque church (1717-19). In
village.

St Ulrich
Baroque church. 4km ($2^1/_2$ miles)
south-east of Bollschweil.

Schenkenzell
Kloster Wittichen (church of
nunnery founded 1324). 8km
(5 miles) north of Schenkenzell.

Schwarzach
Former Benedictine Klosterkirche

(1220). 9km ($5^1/_2$ miles) north-west
of Bühl.

Stühlingen
Klosterkirche (1738). In town.

Sulzburg
Synagogue (1823). In village.
Church of St Cyriak (1510)

Tiengen
Baroque church (1751). In town
centre.

Unteribental
Vaterunserkapelle. 3km (2 miles)
north-east of Kirchzarten through
Burg.

Urach
Fortified village church

Waldkirch
Baroque church (1732-4). In town
centre.

LOCAL EVENTS AND FESTIVALS

Every resort has a programme of
activities available from the local
information office. Freiburg issues
a visitors' newspaper, the
Freiburger Gäste- Blatt. It has a
wealth of information and
suggestions for excursions,
theatres and concerts. A free
weekly news sheet, the *Wochenber-
icht*, is for the city itself.

In the resorts, the programme
includes *Heimatabende* (folk
evenings with traditional music
and dancing), open-air concerts,
slide shows of the district and conducted walks.

Seasonal events include

Silvesterabend (New Year's Eve) with bonfires and fireworks. There is also *Karneval* or *Fasnet*, the time of the festivities which precede Lent with dances, folk evenings and processions in which many of the participants wear grotesque masks. National *Wandertage* (rambling days) usually take place on the first or second Sunday of September and local assembly points are well-publicised in the weeks beforehand. Horse shows are also likely to be held in the early autumn.

The various religious festivals are celebrated enthusiastically throughout the Black Forest and often provide the visitor with an opportunity to see traditional dress.

MINES AND CAVES

Many parts of the Black Forest are riddled with old mine workings, some of which have been opened up as tourist attractions and, with the caves listed, allow for safe, conducted underground excursions.

Erdmannshöhle
7861 Hasel
4km (2¹/₂ miles) north of Wehr, 6km (4 miles) east of Schopfheim
Open April to November, afternoons. Stalactite caves, 2,150m (7,050ft) accessible.

Besuchsbergwerk Teufelsgrund
Mulden, 7816 Münstertal
☎ 07636-1450
Open April to mid-June and mid-September to end-October, Tuesday, Thursday, Saturday and

Sunday, mid-June to mid-September, Tuesday to Sunday and November to mid-January, Saturday and Sunday only 2-6pm.

Historisches Silberbergwerk
Hella-Glückstollen, 7265 Neubulach, 8km (5 miles) south of Calw
☎ 07053-5791 (Kurverwaltung)
Open October, Monday to Friday 10am-12noon, 2-4pm, Saturday and Sunday 9.30am-5pm. Old silver mine. Also mining and mineral museum open on Sunday 10am-12noon, 2-4pm

Frischglück
Besuchsbergwerk, 7540 Neuenbürg
☎ 07082-7970 (Verkehrsamt)
Open April to October, Saturday and Sunday 9am-6pm. Groups by prior arrangement also on Wednesday, Thursday and Friday.

Tschamberhöhle
7888 Rheinfelden
Visit by prior arrangement by telephoning 07623-5482
500m (1,640ft) long cave.

Landesbergbaumuseum Baden-Württemberg
Hauptstrasse 58, 7811 Sulzburg
☎ 07634-702
Open daily except Monday 2-5pm. State mining museum.

Besuchsbergwerk Finstergrund
7861 Wieden
4km (2¹/₂ miles) west of Todtnau
☎ 07673-505
Open April to October, Wednesday, Saturday, Sunday and holidays, 10am-5pm.

MOTORING

At the filling station (*Tankstelle*)
Unleaded (*bleifrei*) petrol is now
the norm in West Germany. There
are two grades, 'Benzin' (normal)
and 'Super' while a third grade,
'Super-Plus', is gradually being introduced. Leaded petrol is also
available everywhere.

Vehicle Lights
Left-dipping headlights must be
adjusted to dip to the right. Cars
may not be driven on sidelights
and headlights must be used, even
during daylight hours, if visibility
is impaired by fog, snow, rain, etc.
Rear fog lights may be used if
visibility is less than 50m (160ft)
but not in built-up areas.

Documentation
There are no special requirements
for private cars. The vehicle
Registration Document should be
carried and although not obligatory, the possession of an insurance 'Green Card' may well help
to avoid complications in the event
of an accident.

On the Road
General speed restrictions are
50km per hour (31mph) in built-up
areas; 100kph (62mph) on ordinary
roads outside built-up areas;
130kph (81mph) (recommended)
on *Autobahnen*. These speeds are
not indicated by signs but
variations from them are shown in
km per hour. The rectangular
yellow sign bearing the place name
denotes the entrance to a built-up
area and the similar sign with a
diagonal stripe indicates the exit

from this. Place names on a green
sign do not constitute a speed
restriction.

Other than on minor roads in
rural areas, priority is always
indicated on signs approaching a
junction. Traffic on a *Bundesstrasse*
(state main road) always has
priority. *Bundesstrassen* are
recognised by a small rectangular
yellow plate bearing the road
number. Priority is shown
elsewhere by a yellow square with
white border set on its corner
while the same sign with diagonal
black line indicates the end of
priority. Standard 'Give Way' or
'Stop' signs will be found on
converging roads.

Parking is forbidden on main
roads or those with fast moving
traffic, on or near tram lines, near
bus or tram stops, traffic lights,
taxi ranks and intersections. It is
also forbidden to park on the
'wrong' side of the road, except in
one-way streets.

The German police are very
strict on tyre condition and a
vehicle found with less than 2mm
tread depth over the whole surface
will not be allowed to proceed
until the tyres have been replaced.

Warning triangles are compul-
sory and must be placed 100m
(109yd) behind a broken down
vehicle. (200m (219yd) on an
Autobahn).

The German equivalent of the
Automobile Association is ADAC
(*Allgemeiner Deutscher Automobil-
Club*) and AA members will be
given advice or assistance should
the need arise. ADAC operates a
road patrol service similar to that
of the AA and the yellow patrol

vehicles will be recognised by the word *Strassenwacht* on the front. The organisation has branch offices in the Black Forest towns of Baden-Baden, Freiburg, Lörrach, Offenburg, Pforzheim and Villingen-Schwenningen.

Motorway telephones are clearly indicated and may be used by the motorist in distress to communicate with the police who will, if appropriate, inform the ADAC patrol. Emergency telephones are now gradually being installed on other main roads.

Traffic signs, in general, conform to international standards but the meanings of the following signs should be memorised:

Ausfahrt — Exit from motorway or dual carriageway
Bankett nicht befahrbar — Soft verges
Einbahnstrasse — Nothing to do with the railway (*Eisenbahn*) but a one-way street
Einordnen — Get in lane
Freie Fahrt — End of restrictions, usually after passing roadworks
Gegenverkehr — Oncoming traffic
Glatteisgefahr — Danger of icy road
Langsam fahren — Drive slowly
Rollsplit — Loose chippings
Umleitung (on yellow arrow) — Not the way to the next village but a traffic diversion
Links/Rechts fahren — Drive on the left/right

MUSEUMS AND ART GALLERIES

This alphabetical list by town excludes museums which have very limited or irregular opening hours.

Achern
Sensen und Heimatmuseum
Berlinerstrasse 31, 7590 Achern
☎ 07841-5659
Open February to December, Sunday 2-6pm.
Groups any day by prior arrangement.

Bad Dürrheim
Narrenschopf
Luisenpark, 7737 Bad Dürrheim
☎ 07726-64281
Open weekdays 2-6pm and Sunday 10am-12noon, 2-5pm.
Displays relating to Alemannian *Fasnet*

Baden-Baden
Römische Badruinen
Römerplatz, 7570 Baden-Baden.
☎ 07221-275920
Open April to October, daily, 10am-12 noon and 1.30-4pm.

Brahms Museum
Maximilianstrasse 85, 7570 Baden-Baden
☎ 07221-71171
Open Monday, Wednesday and Friday 3-5pm and Sunday 10am-1pm.

Staatliche Kunsthalle
Lichtentaler Allee 8a
7570 Baden-Baden.
☎ 07221-25390
Open daily except Monday 10am-6pm (8pm Wed).

Cistercian Abbey Museum
Kloster Lichtental
Hauptstrasse 40, 7570 Baden-Baden.
☎ 07221-72332
Open Monday to Saturday 9am-12noon and 2-5pm and Sunday (except first in month) 3-5pm.

Stadtmuseum
Küferstrasse 3, 7570 Baden-Baden
☎ 07221-278488
Open daily except Monday 10am-
12.30pm and 2-5pm.
Free museum prospectus available.

Stadtgeschichtliche Sammlungen
Schloss-strasse 22, 7570 Baden-
Baden
☎ 07221-278381
Open March to December, daily
except Monday 10am-12.30pm and
2.30-6pm. Collections relating to
town history.

Bad Herrenalb
Spielzeugmuseum
Klosterstrasse 2
7506 Bad Herrenalb
☎ 07083-4144
Open June to September, daily
except Monday, 10am-12noon and
2.30-5.30pm. In other months only
Saturday and Sunday afternoons.
Collection of toys.

Bad Krozingen
Dampfmaschinen-Museum
7812 Bad Krozingen
☎ 07633-2002
Information from Kurverwaltung.
Steam engines and machinery.

*Sammlung Historische Tasten-
instrumente*
Schloss, 7812 Bad Krozingen
☎ 07633-3700
At present only open after concerts
in the Schloss. Admission free.
Old Keyboard instruments.

Bad Säckingen
Hochrheinmuseum
Schloss, 7880 Bad Säckingen
☎ 07761-51311
Open Tuesday, Thursday and
Sunday 3-5pm.

Heimatmuseum and displays
covering pre- and early history,
timepieces; European trumpet
collection.

Baiersbronn
Galerie Root
Im Postgebäude, 7292 Baiersbronn-
Mitteltal
☎ 07442-6706
Open Tuesday to Friday, 9am-
12noon and 3-6pm, Saturday 9am-
12noon. At other times by prior
arrangement.

Bernau
Holzschnefler- und Bauernmuseum
Resenhof, 7821 Bernau/Oberlehen
☎ 07675-895 or 896
Open May to October, Tuesday to
Sunday 2-5pm, also July and
August, Tuesday to Saturday
10am-12noon, November to April,
Wednesday and Sunday 2-4pm.
Museum prospectus available.

Hans Thoma Gemälde-Museum
Im Rathaus, 7821 Bernau-
Innerlehen
☎ 07675-895 or 896
Open Tuesday to Friday 9am-
12noon, 2-6pm (5pm November to
April), Saturday, Sunday and
Holidays, 10.30am-12noon, 2-6pm
(5pm November to April).
More than eighty original
examples of the artist's work.
Memorabilia. Prospectus available.
Hans Thoma's birthplace at
Oberlehen 24 may also be visited
by arrangement free of charge.
☎ 07675-207

Bonndorf
Kreismuseum Schloss also *Schloss-
Narrenstuben*
Schloss-strasse, 7823 Bonndorf.

☎ 07703-7978
Open Tuesday, Thursday,
Saturday and Sunday 10am-
12noon and 2-5pm.
Admission free.
Changing exhibition and carnival
masks etc. Museum prospectus
available.

Calw
Heimatmuseum
Bischofstrasse 48, 7260 Calw.
☎ 07051-167260
Open May to October, Monday to
Saturday 2-4pm and Sunday 10am
12 noon.
Admission free.

Donaueschingen
Die Fürstenberg-Sammlungen
Karlplatz 7, 7710 Donaueschingen.
☎ 0771-86563
Open all year except November,
daily, except Monday, 9am-12noon
and 1.30-5pm.
Art Collection.
Museum prospectus available.

Elzach
Heimatkundliche Sammlungen
Hauptstrasse 39
7807 Elzach
☎ 07682-515
Open daily 10am-12noon.
Admission free.
Regional and folk art collection.

Ettlingen
Städtische Sammlungen
(Albgau- und Albickermuseum)
Markplatz 2, 7505 Ettlingen
☎ 07243-101273
Open daily except Monday 10am-
5pm. Children and students
admission free.
Town art and local history

collection, East Asian exhibition,
mechanical musical instruments.
Karl Albicker and Karl Hofer
galleries.

Freiburg
Augustinermuseum
Salzstrasse 32, 7800 Freiburg
☎ 0761-2163300
Open daily except Monday 10am-
5pm (8pm Wednesday).
Admission free.

Museum für Naturkunde
Gerberau 32, 7800 Freiburg
☎ 0761-2163325
Open daily except Monday
9.30am-5pm. Admission free.

Museum für Ur-und Frühgeschichte
Colombischlösschen, 7800
Freiburg
☎ 0761-2163310
Open daily, except 24 and
31 December, 9am-7pm.
Admission free.
Pre- and early history.

Museum für Völkerkunde
Adelhauserstrasse 33, 7800
Freiburg
☎ 0761-2163324
Open daily, except Monday,
9.30am-5pm. Admission free.
Ethnology.

Kleines Stuckmuseum
Liebigstrasse 11, 7800 Freiburg
☎ 0761-500555
Open Monday to Friday 1-6pm,
Saturday and Sunday by arrange-
ment. Admission free.
Stucco.

Zinnfigurenklause
Im Schwabentor, 7800 Freiburg
☎ 0761-24321
Open June to August, Tuesday to

Saturday, 10am-12noon, 3-6pm,
Sunday 10am-1pm. May, September and October, Saturday only.
Admission free.
'Tin' soldiers and other figures.

Museum für Neue Kunst
Marienstrasse 10a, 7800 Freiburg
☎ 0761-2163673
Open daily except Monday, 10am-5pm, (8pm Wednesday). Admission free.
Modern art.

Furtwangen
Deutsches Uhrenmuseum
7743 Furtwangen.
☎ 07723-656227
Open April to November daily
9am-5pm, December to March,
Monday to Friday 10am-12 noon
and 2-4pm.
Museum prospectus available.

Gengenbach
Narrenmuseum
Im Niggelturm, Hauptstrasse, 7614
Gengenbach
☎ 07803-5749
Open April to October, Saturday
2.30-5.30pm, Sunday 10am-12noon, 2.30-5.30pm.
Exhibition on the *Fasnet* 'fools'.

Gutach
Schwarzwälder Freilichtmuseum
Vogtsbauernhof, 7611 Gutach
☎ 07831-230
Open April to October, daily
8.30am-6pm.
Museum prospectus available.

Haslach
*Schwarzwälder Trachtenmuseum
(Heimatmuseum)*
Klosterstrasse 1, 7612 Haslach
☎ 07832-8080

Open April to October weekdays
except Monday 9am-5pm and
Sunday 10am-5pm.
Museum prospectus available in
English. Ticket also admits to next
below.

Hansjakobmuseum
Freihof, Hansjakobstrasse 13, 7612
Haslach
☎ 07832-8233
Open Wednesday 10am-12noon
and 3-5pm, Friday 10am-12noon.

Herrischried
Heimatmuseum Klausenhof
Grossherrischried,
7881 Herrischried
☎ 07764-6191
Open June to September, Tuesday,
Wednesday and Saturday, 2-5pm,
Sunday 1-6pm. Old Hotzenwald
house, reputed to be the oldest
dwelling place in the Black Forest.

Karlsruhe
There are numerous museums and
art galleries in Karlsruhe. Details
from Verkehrsverein, 7500
Karlsruhe. ☎ 0721-35530

Kenzingen
Oberrheinische Narrenschau
Verbande Oberrheinischer
Narrenzünfte
Alte Schulstrasse 20,
7832 Kenzingen
☎ 07644-501/5 (Rathaus)
Open May to October, Tuesday,
Thursday and Saturday, 2-5pm,
Sunday and holidays 10am-12noon, 2-5pm; November to
April, Sunday and holidays 2-5pm.
Groups on weekdays by prior
arrangement.
Principal exhibition of fools'
costumes etc.

Lahr

Museum im Stadtpark
Kaiserstrasse 101, 7630 Lahr
Open Wednesday 3-5pm (2-4pm in winter), Sunday 10am-12noon, 2-5pm. Admission free.

Geroldseckermuseum
Im Storchenturm, 7630 Lahr
Open May to October, Wednesday and Saturday 4-6pm, Sunday 11am-12noon, 4-6pm. Admission free. (Telephone contact for both above is the Verkehrsbüro, Lahr, 07821-282216)

Lenzkirch

Zunft und Heimatstube
Im Kurhaus, 7825 Lenzkirch
☎ 07653-68439
Open Monday to Friday, 8am-12noon, 1-5pm. Admission free.
Guilds and folk museum.

Lörrach

Museum am Burghof
Basler Strasse 143, 7850 Lörrach.
☎ 07621-415613
Open Wednesday 2.30-5.30pm and 7.30-9.30pm, Saturday 2.30-5.30pm, Sunday 10am-12 noon and 2.30-5.30pm. Admission free.
Museum prospectus available.

Lossburg

Schwarzwaldmuseum
Hauptstrasse, 7298 Lossburg.
☎ 07446-18345 (Kurverwaltung)
Open mid-May to end-September, Sunday and Monday 10.30am-12 noon, Wednesday 4-6pm.

Marxzell

Fahrzeugmuseum
7501 Marxzell (near Bad Herrenalb)
☎ 07248-6262

Open daily April to September, 10am-6pm, October to March, 2-6pm.
Transport including early rail vehicles.

Müllheim

Markgräfler Wein- und Heimatmuseum
Wilhelmstrasse, 7840 Müllheim.
☎ 07631-87201
Open April to October, Thursday 3-6pm, Sunday 10am-12noon. Groups on other days by prior arrangement.
Museum prospectus available.

Münstertal

Bienenkundemuseum
Spielweg, 7816, Münstertal.
☎ 07636-881
Open Wednesday, Saturday and Sunday 2-5pm.

Waldmuseum
Wasen 47, 7816 Untermünstertal
☎ 07636-70730
Open June to October, Wednesday, Saturday and Sunday 2-5pm.
Forestry.

Neuenburg

Stadtgeschichtliche Sammlungen
Altes Rathaus am Franziskaner-platz, 7844 Neuenburg
☎ 07631-7711 (Bürgermeisteramt)
Open Monday to Friday, 8.30am-12.30pm, also Wednesday 2-7pm. Admission free.
Collections relating to town history.

Neustadt

Heimatstuben
Scheurlenstrasse 31, 7820 Neustadt.
☎ 07651-1055

Open mid-May to September,
Monday to Friday 2-5pm, Saturday
10am-12 noon; October to mid-
May, Thursday 2-5pm, Sunday
10am-12noon.

Oberried

Bauernhausmuseum Schniederlihof
Hofsgrund, Schauinsland, 7801
Oberried.
☎ 07602-448
Open July and August, daily
10am-6pm, May, June, September
and October, Saturday 2-6pm and
Sunday 10am-6pm.

Pforzheim

Reuchlinmuseum (Schmuckmuseum)
Jahnstrasse 42, 7530 Pforzheim.
☎ 07231-392329
Open Tuesday to Saturday, 10am-
5pm (8pm Wed), Sunday 10am-
1pm and 3-5pm. Admission free.
Museum prospectus available in
English.
Jewellery etc.

Rastatt

Freiheitsmuseum
Herrenstrasse, 7550 Rastatt.
(In Schloss.)
☎ 07222-39475
Open daily except Monday 10am-
12 noon and 2-5pm. Admission
free.

Wehrgeschichtliches Museum
Herrenstrasse, 7550 Rastatt.
(In Schloss.)
☎ 07222-34244
Open daily except Monday 10am-
12noon and 2-5pm. Admission
free.

Heimatmuseum
Herrenstrasse 11, 7550 Rastatt.

(Opposite Schloss.)
☎ 07222-385332
Open Wednesday, Friday and
Sunday 10am-12noon and 3-5pm.
Admission free.

Schloss Favorite
Rastatt-Förch, 7550 Rastatt.
☎ 07222-41207
5km (3 miles) south-east of Rastatt.
Open March to November, daily
except Monday 9-11am and 2-5pm
(4pm in October and November).
Conducted tours. Additional
admission charge for porcelain
exhibition.

Rothaus

Heimatmuseum 'Hüsli'
7821 Rothaus.
☎ 07748-212
Open Tuesday to Saturday 9am-
12noon and 2-6pm, Sunday and
holidays 2-6pm. Closed November
to mid-December.

Rottweil

Städtisches Museum
Hauptstrasse 20, 7210 Rottweil.
☎ 0741-494256
Open Monday to Thursday and
Saturday 9am-12noon and 2-5pm,
Friday 9am-12noon, Sunday 10am-
12noon. Admission and prospec-
tus free.
Folk museum and Roman
collection.

Kunstsammlung Lorenzkapelle
Lorenzgasse, 7210 Rottweil.
☎ 0741-494298
Open weekdays except Monday
10am-12noon and 2-5pm, Sunday
2-5pm. Admission free on first
Sunday in month.
Art collection.

Römerbad
beim Stadtfriedhof
Königsstrasse, 7210 Rottweil
Always open. Admission free.
Outdoor remains of Roman baths.

St Georgen
Heimat und Phonomuseum
Im Rathaus, 7742 St Georgen
☎ 07724-8794
Open Monday to Friday 9am-
12.30pm, 1.30-5pm also May to
September Saturday 10am-12noon.
Admission free.
Complete history of the
'gramophone'.

Sasbach
Turenne Museum
Schwarzwaldstrasse 3, 7591
Sasbach/Obersasbach
☎ 07841-21020
Open Monday, Tuesday, Thurs-
day, Friday 9am-12noon, 2-5pm,
Saturday and Sunday 2-5pm.
Admission free.

Schliengen
Schloss Bürgeln
Obereggenen, 7846 Schliengen
☎ 07626-237
10km (6 miles) west of Schliengen
Open March to November,
Monday, Wednesday and Sunday.
Conducted tours (obligatory) at
11am, 2, 3, 4 and 5pm.
Fine palace dating from 1726.

Schiltach
Flösserstube
Schuttesäge, 7622 Schiltach
☎ 07836-648 (Verkehrsamt)
Open May to September daily
10am-12noon. Admission free.
Recollections of timber floatage on
Black Forest rivers.

Schramberg
Stadtmuseum
im Schloss, 7230 Schramberg.
☎ 07422-29268
Open Tuesday to Friday 10am-
12noon (except mid-September to
end April) and 2-6pm; Saturday
and Sunday 10am-12 noon and
2-5pm. Admission free.
Timepieces, stoneware, castle
histories etc.

Seelbach
Geroldsecker Waffenschmiede
7633 Seelbach
☎ 07823-1066
Open March to October Saturday
and Sunday 1-5pm.
Traditional armourer's smithy.

Triberg
Schwarzwaldmuseum
Wallfahrtsstrasse 4, 7740 Triberg
☎ 07722-4434
Open mid-May to October daily
8am-6pm, November to mid-May
9am-12noon, 2-5pm.

Villingen-Schwenningen
Museum Altes Rathaus
Villingen,
7730 Villingen-Schwenningen
☎ 07721-82408
Open daily except Monday 10am-
12noon, also Thursday 3-5pm.

Heimatmuseum und Uhrenmuseum
Kronenstrasse 16, Schwenningen,
7730 Villingen-Schwenningen
☎ 07720-398282
Open Monday to Friday 10am-
12noon and 2-5pm, also first and
third Sunday in month 2-5pm.
Prospectus available.
Folk and clock museum.

Franziskaner Museum
Rietstrasse 39, Villingen,
7730 Villingen-Schwenningen.
☎ 07721-82408
Open Thursday, Saturday and
Sunday 10am-12noon, Tuesday to
Friday 3-5pm.
Museum prospectus available.

Vogtsburg
Kaiserstühler Weinbaumuseum
Achkarren, 7818 Vogtsburg/
Kaiserstuhl
8km (5 miles) north-east of
Breisach
☎ 07662-81234
Open April to November, Monday
to Friday 2-5pm, Saturday and
Sunday 10.30am-4pm.
Viticulture.

Waldkirch
Elztäler Heimatmuseum
Kirchplatz 14, 7808 Waldkirch
☎ 07861-206104
Open April to October, Tuesday,
Wednesday, Thursday, Saturday
3-5pm, Sunday 10am-1pm.
Admission free.
Folk museum of the Elz valley.

Wolfach
Glasmuseum Dorotheenhütte
Glashüttenweg 4, 7620 Wolfach
☎ 07834-751
Open weekdays 8am (9.30am
Saturday)-3.30pm, also Sunday
May to October 9.30am-3.30pm.

Heimatmuseum
Grosser Schlosshof, 7620 Wolfach
☎ 07834-1433
Open May to September, Tuesday,
Thursday and Saturday 2-5pm,
Sunday 10am-12noon, 2-5pm. Rest
of year Thursday 2-5pm and first

Sunday of each month 10am-
12noon, 2-5pm.

NATURE CONSERVATION AREAS

Feldberg
Includes the whole Feldberg area;
8km (5 miles) north-south and
10km (6^1/$_4$ miles) east-west.

Freudenstadt
Parkwald on fringes of town. The
biggest reserve in Germany.

Hinterzarten
Hochmoor. Adjacent to village.
Bistenwald. 2-3km (1-2 miles) west
of village.
Kesslermoos. 1.5km (^{3}/$_4$ mile)
south of village.

Kaltenbronn
15km (9^1/$_2$ miles) south-east of
Wildbad.

Lenzkirch
Ursee. 3km (1^1/$_2$ miles) west of
town.

Menzenschwand
Scheibenlechtenmoos. 2km (1 mile)
west of village.

Neuenbürg
Schlossberg above the town.

Pfalzgrafenweiler (Kälterbronn)
Conservation area 'Hohe Tannen'.

Rottweil
Eschachtal and Neckarburg. 6-8km
(4-5 miles) north of town.

Schlüchtsee
In the Schlüchttal near Grafenhausen.

Schwarzwaldhochstrasse
Area bordering the Black Forest High Road B500.

Wutachtal and Wutachschlucht
6-20km (4-12 miles) south-east of Neustadt.

Zweribach
8km (5 miles) by road from St Peter or on foot from St Märgen.

NATURE TRAILS AND 'KEEP FIT' PATHS

The signs to look for are *Naturlehrpfad, Waldlehrpfad* or even *Weinlehrpfad* for the nature trails and *Trimm Dich* or *Sportpfad* for those with exercise instructions and equipment.

Biberach (*Waldlehrpad*)
Starts from *W-Parkplatz* 1km (¹/₂ mile) east of station. To Zell am Harmersbach and back, 6km (4 miles).

Ehrenkirchen (*Wald- und Weinlehrpfad*)
On the *Badische Weinstrasse* 15km (9¹/₂ miles) south of Freiburg. Starts 1km (¹/₂ mile) away in Kirchhofen.

Enzklösterle (*Waldlehrpfad*)
At the edge of the village; red-deer park.

Kirchzarten (*Trimm Dich* and two *Naturlehrpfade*)

On the Giersberg close to the town.

Lossburg (*Waldlehrpfad*)
Starts 0.8km (¹/₂ mile) from village on Schömberg road. 2km (1 mile) to Rodt. (*Waldsportpfad*) Starts 1km (¹/₂ mile) from village near Schömberg road. Eighteen exercise stations.

Nagold (*Waldlehrpfad*)
Starts from *W-Parkplatz* at the Schlossberg. 3.5km (2¹/₂ miles).

Pforzheim (*Naturpfad*)
Starts on the southern edge of the town at Kupferhammer. Restaurant and car park.

Rottweil (*Naturlehrpfad*)
In suburb Göllsdorf east of railway about 3km (1¹/₂ miles) from town centre.

St Blasien (*Trimm Dich*)
Close to and north-east of village. Car park nearby.

Schlüchtsee (*Naturlehrpfad*)
From Grafenhausen around the little lake to Rothaus, about 3km (2 miles).

PLEASURE PARKS

Wild und Freizeit Park
7827 Löffingen.
☎ 07654-606
10km (6¹/₄ miles) east of Neustadt north of road B31.
Open Easter to November daily 9am-6pm. Modest admission charge, extra for some rides. Large free car park.

Freizeit und Familienpark
Europapark Rust, 7631 Rust.
☎ 07822-770
12km (7$^1/_2$ miles) south-west of
Lahr.
Open daily April to mid-October,
9am-6pm (later in summer).
Prospectus available.

SPORTS AND LEISURE ACTIVITIES

Boating and Sailing
Rowing boats and pedalos are
available at Titisee, Schluchsee and
many of the smaller lakes.

Bowling
Indoor bowling alleys are popular
and are usually in a *Gasthaus*. The
signs *Kegeln* or *Kegelbahn* will be
found outside.

Cycling and Cycle Hire
From April to October, cycles can
be hired from most railway stations
which can provide details of recommended tours, and cyclists
arriving by train pay only half the
hire charge.

Fishing
Most local information offices have
details of locations and facilities. A
seven-day package holiday is
available in Bad Herrenalb from
April to September. Details are in
the brochure 'Hobby Holidays'
from the GNTOs.

Riding and Pony-Trekking
Numerous stables and riding
schools offer facilities for the
visitor, many of them being listed
in *Urlaub auf dem Bauernhof*, the

handbook for farm holidays
available from the GNTOs.

Tennis
Seven-day tennis package holidays
are available at Hinterzarten and
Schluchsee, where coaching can be
in English. Details are in the
brochure 'Hobby Holidays' from
the GNTOs.

STEAM AND OTHER RAILWAYS

**Achern-Kappelrodeck-
Ottenhöfen
(Achertalbahn)**
Deutsche Gesellschaft für Eisen-
bahngeschichte e.V. Postfach 1627,
7100 Heilbronn.
☎ 07131-160391
Local address: Betriebsleitung
Ottenhöfen der Südwestdeutschen
Eisenbahnen AG, Bahnhof, 7593
Ottenhöfen.
☎ 07842-2231.
Operates steam passenger trains
on alternate Sundays, May to
October. Three trains in each
direction between 10am and 6pm.
Times in *DB-Kursbuch*, table 715.

**Blumberg-Weizen
(Museumsbahn Wutachtal)**
Stadt Blumberg, Verkehrsamt, 7712
Blumberg 1.
☎ 07702-5127 (8am-12noon only)
Operates May to early October.
Steam passenger trains Friday,
Saturday, Sunday and holiday
afternoons, also Wednesday and
Sunday mornings and afternoons
in peak holiday period. Actual
times and dates in *DB Kursbuch*,
table 736 and in Swiss *Kursbuch*.

Children under 4 free, 4-14 years and in school groups half-fare.

Emmendingen
Museumsbahnhof, Kollmarsreuter Strasse, 7830 Emmendingen (Postal/telephone inquiries to first address under Achertalbahn.) Small collection of historic railway vehicles.

Ettlingen-Bad Herrenalb (Albtalbahn)
Albtal-Verkehrsgesellschaft (AVG), 7505 Ettlingen.
☎ 07243-18115
Operates steam passenger trains May to October, usually two weekends per month. Sundays only May, June, September, October; Saturdays and Sundays July and August. Special 'Nikolaus' service first two weekends in December. Prospectus and current timetable on request. Times and dates also in *DB Kursbuch*, table 711.

Kaiserstuhl
A leisurely journey in the *Rebenbummler* steam train through the vineyards from Riegel to Breisach. Usually operates one Sunday each month June to October with morning departure Riegel to Breisach and afternoon return. Times and dates in *DB Kursbuch*, table 723. A 2-hour Rhine cruise may be taken during the stopover at Breisach. Children under 6 free, 6-12 years half-fare. Reductions for groups of ten or more. Information from Eisenbahnfreunde Breisgau e.V., Escholzstrasse 40, 7800 Freiburg.
☎ 0761-272688

Kandern-Haltingen (Basel)
Eurovapor, Gartenstrasse 7, 7842 Kandern
Historic steam train 'Chanderli' operates on certain Sundays May to October. Journey time 40 minutes. Refreshments on train. Museum. Prospectus and timetable on request. Times and dates also in *DB Kursbuch*, table 731. Connections between Haltingen and Basel Badische Bahnhof, journey time 6 minutes.

Wildbad
Funicular railway to Sommerberg 836m (2,743ft). Operates daily at frequent intervals.

USEFUL ADDRESSES

Aral Aktiengesellschaft
4630 Bochum, West Germany
(For motoring maps.)

Belgian National Tourist Office
38 Dover Street, London W1X 3RB

DER Travel Service
18 Conduit Street,
London W1R 9TD
(Package tours and travel.)

German National Tourist Office
Nightingale House, 65 Curzon Street, London W1Y 7PE
(General information, hotel lists.)

German National Tourist Office
444 South Flower Street, Suite 2230
Los Angeles, CA 90017, USA

German National Tourist Office
2 Fundy, PO Box 417
Place Bonaventure
Montreal, H5A 1B8, Canada

German National Tourist Office
747 Third Avenue, 33rd Floor
New York, NY 10017, USA

Landesfremdenverkehrsverband
Baden-Württemberg, Esslinger
Strasse 8, 7000 Stuttgart, West
Germany.
(General information about whole
of Baden-Württemberg.)

Netherlands National Tourist
Office, Savory & Moore House
143 New Bond Street, London,
W1Y 0QS.

North Sea Ferries
King George Dock, Hedon Road,
Hull, HU9 5QA.
(Services: Hull to Rotterdam and
Zeebrugge.)

Olau-Line Ferries
Sheerness, Kent, ME12 1SN
(Services: Sheerness to Vlissingen
(Flushing).)

P & O Ferries
Dover, Kent, CT16 3BR
(Services: Felixstowe to Zeebrugge
and cross-channel.)

Sally Viking Line
Ferry Terminal, Ramsgate
Harbour, Ramsgate, Kent, CT11
8RP
(Services: Ramsgate to Dunkirk.)

Sealink UK Ltd, PO Box 29,
Victoria Station, London, SW1V
1JX.
(Services: Harwich to Hook of
Holland and cross-channel.)

Fremdenverkehrsverband (FVV),
Bertoldstrasse 45, 7800 Freiburg,
West Germany

(Detailed information about Black
Forest.)

WALKING

Walking without baggage

A walking tour of between 4 and
11 days can be made without
having to carry one's baggage by
taking part in one of the organised
walks which go from hotel to hotel
in stages, luggage being conveyed
forward as the tour progresses.
The stages provide for 4 to 6 hours
walking each day, the maximum
distance covered is about 24km
(15 miles). Information about the
five tours mentioned in this book
can be obtained as follows. Firm
bookings for the tours should also
be sent to these addresses.

1 'Fröhliche Weinwanderung'
(Merry wine ramble — Chapter 1)
'Ortenauer Weinseminar',
Gärtnerstrasse 6
7600 Offenburg
☎ 0781-82253

2 'Auf Spätzlespfaden'
(On dumpling trails — Chapter 2)
Herrenalber Reiseburo, Im
Stadthaus,
7506 Bad Herrenalb.
☎ 07083-553

3 'Auf der Fährte des Rothirsches'
(On the track of the red-deer —
Chapter 2)
Kurverwaltung, Postfach 440,
7290 Freudenstadt.
☎ 07441-6074

4 'Auf dem Weg der Uhrenträger'
(In the steps of the clock carrier —
Chapter 2)
Kurverwaltung

7740 Triberg im Schwarzwald
☎ 07722-81230/31

5'Rund um den Feldberg'
(Round about the Feldberg —
Chapter 5)
Kurverwaltung,
7820 Titisee-Neustadt
☎ 07651-5566/7321

Long-distance paths
These paths are waymarked as
follows:
Markings for paths running
generally north to south are on a
white ground. Those for the east-
west *Querwege* are on a yellow
ground.
     Paths leading to a long-
distance route are marked with a
blue diamond on a white ground.
     Paths connecting two long-
distance routes are marked with a
blue diamond with a white vertical
stripe on a white ground.

Westweg (over 275km, 171 miles)
Between Pforzheim and Basel. Red
diamond on white ground.

Mittelweg (over 230km, 143 miles)
Between Pforzheim and Waldshut.
Red diamond with vertical white
stripe on a white ground.

Ostweg (over 237km, 147 miles)
Between Pforzheim and Schaffhausen. Black and red diamond on
a white ground.

Kandelhöhenweg
(110km, 68 miles)
Between Oberkirch and Freiburg.
Red diamond with white K on a
white ground.

Schwarzwald-Jura-Bodensee-Weg
(109km, 67 miles)
Between St Georgen and
Radolfzell. Blue and yellow
diamond on a white ground.

**Querweg-Schwarzwald-Kaiser-
stuhl Rhein** (110km, 68 miles)
Between Donaueschingen and
Breisach. Red diamond on a
yellow ground.

Hochrhein - Querweg
(49km, 30 miles)
Between Rheinfelden and
Albbruck. Blue and white diamond
on a yellow ground.

Hotzenwald - Querweg
(45km, 28 miles)
Between Schopfheim and
Waldshut. Black and white
diamond on a yellow ground.

Querweg (92km, 57 miles)
Between Lahr and Rottweil. Blue
and red diamond on a yellow
ground.

Querweg (51km, 32 miles)
Between Gengenbach and
Alpirsbach. Blue diamond on a
yellow ground.

Ortenauer Weinpfad
(100km, 62 miles)
Between Baden-Baden and
Offenburg. Red diamond with blue
grapes on a white ground.

Querweg Freiburg - Bodensee
(177km, 110 miles)
Between Freiburg and Konstanz.
Red and white diamond on a
yellow ground.

WINE TASTING AND SALES

All along the *Badische Weinstrasse*, one can visit wine cellars and tastings (*Weinproben*) and buy the wine direct from the producer. The following are places fairly near Freiburg where such visits and purchases may be made.

Zentralkellerei,
Badische Winzergenossenschaft
e.G.
7814 Breisach
☎ 07667-820
On the Kaiserstuhl 25km
(16 miles) from Freiburg via road
B31.
Cellars usually open for inspection but visitors are requested to telephone in advance.

Winzergenossenschaft
7801 Ebringen.
☎ 07664-6350
7km (4 miles) south of Freiburg on road B3.
Open Monday to Friday 8am-12noon and 1.30-5.30pm, Saturday 9am-12noon.

Winzergenossenschaft
Wolfenweiler
7801 Schallstadt-Wolfenweiler
☎ 07664-7013
7km (4 miles) south of Freiburg on road B3.
Open Monday to Friday 8am-12noon and 1-5pm, Saturday 9am-12noon.

Winzergenossenschaft
Pfaffenweiler,
7801 Pfaffenweiler
☎ 07664-7081
9km (5$^1/_2$ miles) south of Freiburg

via road B3. Open Monday to Friday 8am-12 noon and 1-5.30pm, Saturday 9am-12noon.

Winzergenossenschaft Ehrenstetten EG
7801 Ehrenkirchen
☎ 07633-5428
15km (9$^1/_2$ miles) south of Freiburg via road B3.
Open Monday to Friday 8am-12noon and 1-5pm, Saturday 9am-12noon.

Winzergenossenschaft
Kirchhofen e.G
7801 Ehrenkirchen 1
☎ 07633-7027
16km (10 miles) south of Freiburg via road B3.
Open Monday to Friday 8am-12noon and 1.30-5pm, Saturday 9am-12noon.

Winzergenossenschaft Ballrechten-Dottingen
7801 Ballrechten-Dottingen
☎ 07634-8233
25km (16 miles) south of Freiburg via road B3 to Heitersheim.
Open Monday to Friday 8am-12noon and 1-5pm, Saturday 8am-12noon.

Winzergenossenschaft Laufen e.G
Weinstrasse 48, 7811 Sulzburg 2/
Laufen
☎ 07634-8262
27km (17 miles) south of Freiburg via road B3 to Heitersheim.
Open Monday to Friday 8am-12noon and 1.30-5pm, Saturday 9am-12noon.

Winzergenossenschaft
7841 Auggen
☎ 07631-4045

33km (21 miles) south of Freiburg on road B3.
Open Monday to Friday 8am-12noon and 1.30-5.30pm, Saturday 8am-12noon.

Weingut Fritz Blankenhorn
7846 Schliengen
☎ 07635-1092
36km (23 miles) south of Freiburg on road B3.
Tasting room open daily until 6pm (4pm Saturday).

ZOOS AND WILDLIFE PARKS

The many forest enclosures (*Gehege*) for wild boar or deer are usually accessible at all times without charge. The list given is by no means exhaustive and, as exact locations are changed from time to time, the visitor is advised to check with the local tourist information office before setting out.

Baiersbronn
Deer parks 3.5km (2 miles) south-west in Sankenbachtal, 4.5km (3 miles) north in Klosterreichenbach, 9km ($5^1/_2$ miles) north in Schöne-grund and 24km (15 miles) north-west in Langenbach.

Enzklösterle
Red-deer park.

Kaltenbronn
Deer park. 15km ($9^1/_2$ miles) south-east of Wildbad.

Löffingen
Wild und Freizeit Park. 10km (6 miles) east of Neustadt on road B31.
For details see under Pleasure Parks.

Oberried
Berg-Wild-Park Steinwasen, 7801 Oberried.
☎ 07671-451
5km (3 miles) south of village.
Open daily. Admission charge.
Free car park.

Rottweil
Red-deer park at Eckhof in Aschachtal about 6km (4 miles) from town centre.

Steinen
Vogelpark Wiesental, 7853 Steinen-Hofen.
4km ($2^1/_2$ miles) north of Steinen.
☎ 07627-7420
Open 15 March to 15 November daily, 9am-6pm.
Admission charge.
Free car park.

Waldkirch
Zoo. Near town centre.
Open daily. Admission charge.

INDEX

Critical acclaim for *Habibi*

"Readers will be engaged by the character, the romance, the foreshadowed danger. Poetically imaged and leavened with humor, the story renders layered and complex history understandable through character and incident. *Habibi* succeeds in making the hope for peace compelling, personal and concrete."—*School Library Journal*

"[B]reaks new ground in YA fiction."
—Hazel Rochman, *Booklist*

"This is the work of a poet, not a polemicist. The very title, an Arabic form of endearment that has been adopted into everyday Hebrew, bespeaks a vision of a gentler world in which kisses are more common than gunshots."
—*Houston Chronicle*

"Nye's prose keeps both feet on the ground, barefoot, while her eyes are fixed on the angels."—*Aramco World*

ALA Best Book for Young Adults
ALA Notable Children's Book
Jane Addams Book Award
New York Public Library Book for the Teen Age
American Bookseller "Pick of the Lists"
Judy Lopez Memorial Award for Children's Literature
Texas Institute of Letters Best Book
for Young Readers

HABIBI

Naomi Shihab Nye

SIMON PULSE

SIMON PULSE
An imprint of Simon & Schuster Children's Publishing Division
1230 Avenue of the Americas, New York, NY 10020
Copyright © 1997 by Naomi Shihab Nye

Designed by Heather Wood
The text of this book was set in American Garamond.

Manufactured in the United States of America
First paperback edition June 1999

28   30   29   27

The Library of Congress has cataloged the hardcover edition as follows:
Habibi: a novel / by Naomi Shihab Nye   p. cm.
Summary: When fourteen-year-old Liyana Abboud, her younger brother, and her parents move from St. Louis to a new home between Jerusalem and the Palestinian village where her father was born, they face many changes and must deal with the tensions between Jews and Palestinians.
ISBN-13: 978-0-689-80149-5 (hc.)   ISBN-10: 0-689-80149-1 (hc.)
[1. Family life—Fiction. 2. Jerusalem—Fiction.
3. Emigration and immigration—Fiction. 4. Jewish-Arab relations—Fiction.]
I. Title. PZ7.N976Hab 1997 [Fic]—dc21 97-10943 CIP AC
ISBN-13: 978-0-689-82523-1 (pbk.)   ISBN-10: 0-689-82523-4 (pbk.)

"Damascus Gate" by Yehuda Amichai appears in *Selected Poetry of Yehuda Amichai*, Translated by Chana Bloch and Stephen Mitchell (Harper & Row, 1986)

"Homing Pigeons" by Mahmoud Darwish was translated by Lena Jayyusi and W. S. Merwin and appears in *Anthology of Modern Palestinian Literature*, Edited by Salma Khadra Jayyusi (Columbia University Press, 1992)

Thanks to Kevin Henkes and Andrea Carlisle for their friendship and advice, to Madison Nye for his technological expertise, to Anton Shammas for his inspiration, to Madhatters Tea, San Antonio, to Sarah Thomson and Susan Rich, and especially to my editor, Virginia Duncan, who knows both when to drink Vietnamese iced coffee and when to crack the whip.

For my father, Aziz
and my mother, Miriam
who have loved us so well

For Adlai, my brother

For Grace and Hillary Nye

For my Armenian friends in the Old City of Jerusalem

And for all the Arabs and Jews
who would rather be cousins than enemies

For you

Habibi

I forget how this street looked
a month ago, but I can remember it,
say, from the Time of the Crusades.

(Pardon me, you dropped this. Is it yours?
This stone? Not *that* one, that one fell
nine hundred years ago.)

From "Damascus Gate," by Yehuda Amichai

Where do you take me, my love, away from my
    parents
from my trees, from my little bed, and from my
    boredom,
from my mirrors, from my moon, from the closet
    of my life…from my shyness?

From "Homing Pigeons" by Mahmoud Darwish

Is a Jew a Palestinian? Is a Palestinian a Jew?
Where does one begin to answer such a question?
I will say this: we are cut from the same rock,
breathe the scent of the same lemons & olives,
anchor our troubles with the same stones,
carefully placed. We are *challah* & *hummus*, eaten
together to make a meal.

Anndee Hochman

$\mathcal{K}$ISS

The secret kiss grew larger and larger.

Liyana Abboud had just tasted her first kiss when her parents announced they were leaving the country. They were having a "family meeting" at the Country Time Diner in St. Louis, the place Liyana and her brother Rafik felt embarrassed in because their father usually returned his dinner for not being hot enough.

Of course no one knew about the kiss, which Liyana was carrying in a secret pouch right under her skin.

Dr. Kamal Abboud, whom they called Poppy, jumped right in. "What do you think about moving to Jerusalem and starting new lives?" His face cracked into its most contagious smile. He was handsome and lean, with rumpled black hair and dark eyes. Liyana's best friend, Claire, always said he looked more like a movie star than any of the other dads.

Liyana's mother, Susan, filled in the gaps, as usual. She had long brown hair, which she usually wore pulled back in a straight ponytail, hazel eyes, and a calm way of talking. "Our family has reached a crossroads. You"—she opened her hand toward Liyana—"are going into high school next year. You"—she pointed at Rafik—"are going into middle school. Once you get into your new schools, you will feel less like moving across the ocean. This is the best time we can think of to make the big change."

The kiss started burning a hole up through Liyana's smooth left cheek where it had begun. The blaze spread over to her lips where the kiss had ended. She could imagine her lips igniting over the menu.

"Wow!" Rafik said. He combed both his hands backward through his curly black hair, the way he always did when he was excited.

"Liyana, what are you looking at?" Poppy asked.

She hadn't smiled back yet. Her eyes were fixed on the floral wreath hanging over the cash register and her mouth tried to shape the words, "Maybe it's a bad idea," but nothing came out. She felt the same way she did after the car accident on an icy road last winter, when she'd noticed the Magic Marker stain on the seat instead of the blood coming out of her elbow. Stunned into observation.

Leave the country?

Of course it was a rumor Liyana had been hearing all her life. Someday her family would leave the United States, the country her mother and she and her brother had been born in, and move overseas to the mixed-up country her father had been born in. It was only fair. He wanted to show it to them. He wanted them to know both sides of their history and become the fully rounded human beings they were destined to be.

"You know," Poppy said, "I never planned to be an immigrant forever. I never thought I'd become a citizen. I planned to return home after medical school. I didn't know"—and here Rafik picked up the familiar refrain with him, like the chorus to "America the Beautiful"—*"I'd fall in love and stay for so many years."* Rafik covered his heart with his hand and closed his eyes. Poppy laughed.

Poppy wanted Liyana and Rafik to know Sitti, their grandmother. He would transfer to Al-Makassad Hospital in Jerusalem—he'd been in touch with them by mail and fax. Liyana and Rafik would have doubled lives. When Liyana was younger, she used to think this sounded like fun. That was long before last night's kiss.

⁓

The biggest surprise about the kiss was it didn't come from Phillip, the person on Liyana's right at the movie theater, who *might* have kissed her because they'd been good friends for years and she had a crush on him, but from Jackson, on her left.

Jackson was in her social studies class. Liyana liked the way he smelled—like Poppy's old bottle of English Leather. They'd traded notes about Mali and Ethiopia, and she complimented him on his enormous vocabulary. Sometimes they stood together in the lunch line, discussing the dazzling enchiladas, and they ate together, but not every day.

Jackson had leaned over to ask what the actress in the movie had just said and the next thing Liyana knew, his lips were nuzzling her cheek. They moved to her mouth and held there for a moment, pressing lightly.

Liyana had no idea what happened at the end of the movie. It was a swirling blue blur, like an underwater scene. Afterward, her friends crowded toward the exit doors, laughing. Jackson tripped over someone's empty popcorn tub on the floor. Liyana liked that he picked it up and threw it away. It said something about him. But they didn't talk much at Claire's pizza party, and all they said when Poppy picked Liyana up later was, "See you at school," as if nothing had happened.

Still, there was something different between them now. A little glimmer. His lips were so warm. Liyana had never imagined lips being warm.

––––––––

And now she was leaving the country. The waitress refilled Poppy's tea.

"What will we do with our things?" mumbled Liyana. The piano; the blue bicycles; the boxes of tangle-haired dolls Liyana hadn't played with in years, though she refused to give them away; the mountains of books; the blackboard on an easel where she and Rafik left each other notes. It stood in the hallway between their rooms.

Did you take my red marker? Big trouble, buddy!
Red marker seized by Klingon intruders!

Who would they be if they had to start all over again? Liyana started thinking of the word "immigrant" in a different way at that moment and her skin prickled. Now *she* would be the immigrant.

Poppy curled his finger at the waitress. "Honey," he said to her. "My potato is positively icy inside."

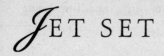

JET SET

Some days were long sentences
flowing into one another.

They flew to New York in steamy June, left their seventeen suitcases and Liyana's violin stored at the airport, and spent one day lugging stuffed backpacks around to the Empire State Building and riding up to the inside of the Statue of Liberty's head. Poppy was retracing his steps. He wanted them to see exactly what he had seen when he first came to the United States.

"When Miss Liberty appeared through the fog holding up her hand in the harbor, I felt she was an old girlfriend welcoming me. I'd seen so many pictures of her."

"It's not just a hand, Poppy, it's a *torch*," Rafik said. His mother flashed him a quieting look. She wanted Poppy to keep telling stories.

Poppy recalled, "When I saw a sign for hot dogs, I thought they were made of dog meat. It scared me. I thought the big shiny trash cans were mailboxes."

Nineteen years after his first arrival, they ate

giant pretzels from a cart on the street. The big grains of salt on the pretzel skin tasted delicious. They bumped into disoriented families on summer vacations. They ate double scoops of Rocky Road ice cream.

"After this, you'll call ice cream *booza*," Poppy said. "And it won't have marshmallows, either. I don't think they've crossed the ocean yet."

"They'd get wet," said Rafik. Liyana rolled her eyes.

Liyana felt exhilarated by the skyscrapers. Their glittering lines lifted her out of her worry. She wished she could ride every sleek elevator up and down, punching buttons, seeing who got on and off. Some days you remembered the world was full of wonderful people you hadn't met yet. She bought seven postcards with different pictures—the Brooklyn Bridge, Washington Square, the fish market—imagining which one she might send to Jackson.

By the time they returned to the airport at sundown for their night flight overseas, a storm was swirling somewhere over the dark Atlantic. They heard rumors about it from passengers at the gate. Ominous booms of distant thunder made Liyana feel edgy inside. *Yippity loosebugs,* she thought. Their flight was running two hours late. Liyana kept her eyes on the other people waiting to fly. She wanted to see if they looked nervous.

But they only looked sleepy. A yawning lady with a flowered scarf tied under her chin lugged a food basket jammed with Jell-O boxes, paper napkins, and coffee filters. Didn't they have those things in the Middle East? Another lady rolled up her husband's raincoat and made her little children lie down on the floor with their heads on it. No one looked nervous at all.

When Rafik unzipped his backpack and pulled out a giant sack of Cornnuts, Liyana went to sit at the other side of the gate. She couldn't stand to sit next to somebody crunching. She scribbled in her notebook. *One Indian lady in a purple sari crying. The size of good-bye.*

CLOVER CHAIN

Some days I am brave,
but other days I almost disappear.

Before the Abboud family left St. Louis, there were many times Liyana thought she would rather be anyone else on their block, someone who planned to stick around in the neighborhood doing dull things like going to Mannino's grocery store and staring at watermelons and jars of peanut butter stacked up. She would rather *not* have to change her life.

She knew the bush with red berries that were probably poison. She knew which bus number to take downtown. Often the Abboud family drove around on slow Sunday evenings with their car windows wide open to "smell the air." That's what Poppy said people did in Jerusalem.

St. Louis air smelled of tar and doughnuts, old boards washed up out of the muddy river, red bricks, and licorice. Leafy greens of bushes and trees ran together outside their car. How could Liyana give all this up? She knew what grass smelled like, a rich brew of dirt and green roots, right after rain.

And her fingers knew exactly the best way to twist skinny green clover stems together to make a long chain to stretch across the street to stop cars. She would stand on one side and Rafik would stand on the other, holding his end for as long as he could pay attention.

Of course the cars could have driven right through the chain if they tried. Most drivers would laugh and motion for Liyana and Rafik to pull the chain back. But one day right after they started telling people they were moving overseas, a man in a red pickup truck slammed on his brakes, shook his fist from the window, and shouted that he'd tell the police and make them pay a fine.

"We are children!" Liyana called out. He glared at her then. They dropped the chain and he drove away.

"Could he really do that?" Rafik asked.

"Let's go in," Liyana said. "I don't want to play."

BLIP

Being little was a skin that fit.

It had seemed to Liyana that Poppy was walking differently during the weeks before they left. His stride had a new lift in it. He made lots of overseas phone calls. Mrs. Abboud would watch him and raise ten fingers like a coach or a referee when she thought he should get off.

But he also kept falling into silent spells. At the dinner table he forgot to remove the blue denim baseball cap he wore for yard work. He wasn't combing his hair as carefully as usual. When he read a newspaper story about demonstrations in Jerusalem, he rolled the newspaper into a tube and slapped it against his arm.

"What's up?" Liyana asked him as he poured gasoline into the lawn mower for the last time. He jumped. "Are you worried we're making a mistake?"

"No," he said. "I was just thinking about…how I like doing this."

She caught him staring at odd things—the hinge on the pantry cabinet, the medicine chest in the bathroom. When she asked what he was doing, he said, "Remembering."

Liyana, too, had been trying to memorize at least one small detail about each house on their street. The blue cottage with the crooked chimney, the green two-story only half painted. Did the painters break their arms? Did they lose their enthusiasm for that color? The brick house with the pink vine wrapped around its forehead in the summers. Liyana might never see the cherry trees or tulip beds or gray pebbles or cracked sidewalks again.

When she was younger, before she went to middle school and her arms seemed to grow longer in the night, she knew the easy latitude and longitude of her world. Now she was moving away to a land she knew little of, except the skillet of olive oil with crumbles of garlic and pine nuts browning on the stove. Liyana's mother stood over the skillet with the spatula poised, like a scientist. Poppy would pass through the house lifting his nose to the air, saying, "There it is, there's my country."

Well, where was hers? Was she on the verge of finding out? Sometimes Liyana felt she had passed her own country already and it was an age, not a place.

She wrote it down in her notebook.

An age, not a place.

What did it mean, exactly?

Liyana loved thinking of first lines for stories or poems or movies.

Since fourth grade, she'd kept a running list of them and liked to reread it to see if she could get the stories to go further in her head.

The secret kiss grew larger and larger.

No one had dialed her number for a dozen years.

If she had known her cousin's secret, would she have teased her at dinner?

Sometimes she took her lists of lines to Mrs. Lindenwood, her old fourth-grade teacher who loved creative writing, and Mrs. Lindenwood would put stars by the ones she liked best. Or Liyana would read them to Poppy in the yard after they'd washed the dinner dishes, as he sat drinking a cup of Arabic coffee in his favorite green metal chair with the scalloped back. On one of their last evenings in St. Louis, Poppy said, "Tell *me* her cousin's secret!"

Liyana hadn't read him the one about the kiss.

"Sometimes you remind me of Sitti, my mother," he told her.

"Why?" Liyana had a little picture of Sitti in her wallet, standing in a long dress in the archway entrance to her house.

"Making something out of nothing. It's her

favorite thing to do. She gets a whole story out of—a button. Or a rock."

Liyana was quiet. She flicked at a mosquito, thinking how people considered other people. Did other people think *she* was strange? Sitti was eighty and Poppy said her mother had lived to be ninety-nine. What if it ran in the family?

Liyana and Poppy sat silently in the backyard while their gray cat, Sami, leaped down from the top of the wooden fence to bury his nose in the grass. Sami was going to live at their aunt's house, but Rafik and Liyana worried she might forget to feed him. They had discussed giving him tranquilizers and stowing him away in a backpack.

Liyana asked Poppy, "Do you remember that Emily Dickinson poem I liked a lot in second grade that starts, 'I'm nobody, who are you?'"

"Sort of. But I never thought you were nobody."

"I'm even more nobody now than I was then."

"Oh *habibti,* don't say that! You're everything you need to be!"

"Poppy, remember when you told us your twentieth birthday was the most important landmark day of your life? I do *not* think it will be a very good day in mine."

"That's okay. You're only fourteen. You have a lot of time. And I only meant it was the landmark day of my life till *then*. I've had *lots* of better land-marks since. Like the days you and Rafik were born! And every day after! Twenty was just a lit-tle—blip—now that I look back on it."

Liyana wrote down what he said. *"A little blip—now that I look back on it."* She closed her notebook as Sami ran toward them with a lizard in his mouth.

*E*STATE SALE

Their family was half and half,
like a carton of rich milk.

Liyana and Rafik had tucked three apology notes into mailboxes in their neighborhood. Sorry to Mrs. Moore for borrowing her daisies more than once. Sorry to Lucy Hummer for calling her a witch after Rafik's ball skipped into her yard and she kept it a week before pitching it back. Sorry to Frank for leaving a sign on the windshield of his antique station wagon without wheels that said HUNK OF JUNK.

Their mother was having problems with her own mother, Peachy Helen, Liyana and Rafik's other grandmother, who lived by Forest Park in a high-rise apartment. Peachy wore flowery dresses and high spots of blush on her cheeks and she couldn't *stand* it that they were leaving. She was addicted to their after-school phone calls. She was used to dropping in at a moment's notice. She stayed with Liyana and Rafik when their parents went out of town. She and Liyana often ate lunch together on Saturdays at fancy ladies' tearooms.

They chose custard pies off the gleaming dessert cart.

After she heard they were moving, Peachy Helen kept crying. She even hung up on Liyana so she wouldn't hear her cry. This cast a dim glow on Liyana's mother, who suddenly had trouble finishing sentences and meals. She would leap up from the table, thinking of more things she needed to do.

Liyana and Rafik lettered poster-board signs for the Estate Sale while their mother gathered stacks of yellowed newspapers from the corners, throwing them into recycling bins. "I would hardly call this an estate," she said dubiously. But the woman at the newspaper who copied down their ad had been adamant—a "Garage Sale" meant you carried things outside and an "Estate Sale" meant you sold the whole household from the inside out.

Harpsichord music blared from Liyana's cassette player. Liyana said, "Estate Sale sounds disgraceful to me, as if we're planning to display stained baby clothes and sticky ketchup bottles! I hate it!"

She worried, What if Jackson came? What if he saw the dumbo Pretty Princess game with half its jewels missing in the bargain bin? What if her girlfriends pawed through her threadbare socks,

Nancy Drew mysteries, and frayed hair ribbons, casting them aside and choosing none?

Her mother arranged sale items on long folding tables they'd rented and urged Liyana and Rafik to get their suitcases organized, all at once. Liyana packed a pink diary with a key, the Scrabble game, and a troll with rhinestone eyes, collecting other childhood treasures—the Mexican china tea set, the stuffed monkeys—to leave boxed up in Peachy Helen's already-stuffed closets and in a friend's barn. She arranged a small box of odd treasures—stones, butterfly wings, a carved wooden toad—to give to Claire.

Liyana sorted through perfect spelling tests and crackly finger paintings from a box under her bed. She folded the red velvet embroidered dress that her faraway relatives had stitched for her long ago. It had arrived in the mail wrapped in heavy paper, with twine knotted around it. Now she was going to meet the fingers that knotted the thread. She polished her violin, placing it tenderly back in its case with the white cloth over its neck. She considered whether to take an extra cake of rosin along with new strings. There was so much to think about when you moved.

Rafik tried to throw his old report cards away, but their mother caught him. Who even *cared* about the minuses on his old conduct grades by now? If the cards went into the barn boxes, mice might chew them up. The *E*'s and *S*'s could turn into dust.

Rafik agonized at length over his beloved Matchbox car collection. He lined fire trucks and emergency vehicles on one side of his bed and vans and trucks with movable doors on the other side. Poppy had said he could take ten or twenty. Rafik felt nauseated trying to decide which ones he'd have to abandon. Liyana, passing his room with another cardboard box in her arms, found him poking race cars into his socks.

"So let me pick for you," she offered. He shook his head, knowing she had a strange preference for milk trucks and tractors. Liyana left him alone and pitched the box onto her bed.

———

Poppy poked his head through Liyana's doorway. "You won't need those shorts," he said. "No one wears shorts over there."

"That's not true! I've seen pictures of Jerusalem and some people are definitely wearing shorts."

"They're tourists. Maybe they're pilgrims. We're going to be spending time in older places where shorts won't be *appropriate*. Believe me, Arab women don't wear shorts." He walked away.

Lately Poppy kept bringing up Arab women and it made Liyana mad. "I'm not a woman or a full Arab, either one!" She slammed her bedroom door, knowing what would happen next. Poppy would enter, stand with hands on his hips, and say, "Would you like to tell me something?"

Liyana muttered, "I'm just a half-half, woman-girl, Arab-American, a mixed breed like those wild characters that ride up on ponies in the cowboy movies Rafik likes to watch. The half-breeds are always villains or rescuers, never anybody normal in between."

She rolled six socks into balls and found some old birthday cards tucked beneath them. Then she had to read the cards.

Poppy knocked on her door.

Liyana opened it and threw her arms around him. "I'm sorry, dear Poppy. What if I don't take my very short shorts? What if I only take the baggy checkered old-man shorts that come down to my knees?"

He shrugged, hugging her back. "Maybe you can wear them when we visit the Dead Sea." That was the sea so full of salt, you could sit upright in it as if it were a chair.

Liyana gave her short shorts to Sandee Lane, her friend down the block who kept saying how great it was that they were going to live in

"Jesus's hometown." Liyana didn't think of it that way. She thought of it as her *dad's* hometown.

<hr>

"Where did all these people *come from?*" Rafik whispered during the Estate Sale.

He and Liyana sat behind a bush next to their house in the thinnest, softest grass watching customers travel up the sidewalk. They must have driven in from other neighborhoods. Thankfully, no one looked familiar.

One woman carried out their dented metal mixing bowl. A man pulled Poppy's lovely green wheelbarrow behind him. Liyana covered her eyes. "Oh! I'll miss that wheelbarrow."

She thought of all the things she *couldn't* pack, imagining the slim green locker she would have had at high school next year if she weren't moving to the other side of the ocean. She thought of Lonnie and Kelly and Barbara, her friends, just starting to streak their lips with pale lipstick for special events. She and Claire didn't, because they thought it was dumb. "Lucky you!" Claire had said. "You'll miss the tryouts for youth symphony next season."

"Lucky you!" Lonnie had said. "There are really cute guys in Jerusalem. I've seen them on CNN."

"Lucky nothing." Liyana had said private

good-byes to the third step outside the school cafeteria where she ate when the weather was nice and the chute at the library where she'd poured her books since she was five and the fragrant pine needles on the trees between their house and the Ferraris'. Liyana and her friends used to make forts on the ground inside those branches.

Liyana and Rafik had never yet found out what animal lived in the hole by the back sidewalk. It wasn't a mole—moles made big mounds in the middle of the yard. How could they leave when it still hadn't come out?

Rafik poked her, whispering, "I am NOT BELIEVING this! Look at that! Someone just bought my Dracula Halloween costume, the ugliest costume on earth! I was *sure* it wouldn't sell!"

***

That evening their house looked stripped. A few large pieces of furniture people would pick up the next day wore red tags with names and phone numbers on them. The piano was going to live with MERTON at 555–3232.

Their mother played Mozart the night before the piano left. Liyana noticed she wasn't keeping her ponytail pulled back neatly in its silver clip as she usually did. Loose strands of hair cluttered the sides of her elegant face.

"Amazing," she called out to Liyana in her bare room, "that Mozart could write this when he was six and I have trouble playing it when I'm forty."

Liyana could play one line better than her mother could. She got up from bed to show her and was startled to see tears gleaming on Mom's cheeks. She placed her hands alongside on the keyboard.

"Your hands are more like your father's," her mother always said.

Liyana's hands and feet peeled in the spring-time like Poppy's did, an inherited genetic trait. She didn't sweat, either.

"Why couldn't you have kept the piano?" Liyana said. "You could have stored it somewhere. Couldn't Peachy Helen have fit it into her apartment?"

There were only a few things Liyana's mother was attached to.

"Clean slate," Mom said, as if they were talking in code, and Liyana said, "Huh?"

"We are starting over." Her mother's voice was so thin and wavery, it scared her.

She was usually so upbeat about things. Liyana and Rafik teased her about being the general of the Optimist's Army. *Positive thoughts, ho! Forward march!* Liyana thought her words turned up at the ends, like elf shoes. "Look for the Silver Lining" was her mother's favorite song. She made Liyana and Rafik memorize it. Their mother wouldn't even let them say things like "bad weather." She wouldn't look at a newspaper till afternoon because she didn't want bad news setting the tone for the day. Peachy Helen, on the other hand, crouched over the newspaper on her kitchen table, moaning over kidnappings, hijackings, and hurricanes as if each one were personal. "I can't stop thinking about Sarah's mother," Peachy said once.

"Who's Sarah?"

"The girl who drowned in Colorado."

This was some poor person Peachy and the Abbouds had never *met*.

Liyana's mother placed her American hand over Liyana's half-half one on the keyboard. "Go to bed. You're going to need all the sleep you can get."

On their last night in St. Louis, the neighborhood gave the Abboud family a going-away party in their front yard. The FOR SALE sign on the house had a red SOLD slapped across it. Liyana licked custard from a cream puff and stared at their familiar, rumpled neighbors in their summer clothes. They'd be around all summer and Liyana's family would not. She eavesdropped on everybody—eavesdropping was her specialty. Talk about camp and favorite teachers and the opening of the neighborhood swimming pool made her feel wistful.

She tried to remember the exact sensation of Jackson's kiss, but it was dissolving in her mind. She wished she had thought to invite him to this. But he might not have come, and that would have been worse. Claire dropped a small velvet ring box into Liyana's hand at the last minute and ran home crying. A tightly folded note tucked under a silver friendship ring said, "I will never *ever* forget you."

CIVILIZED

I vote for the cat sleeping in the sun.

When the weary passengers finally boarded the giant jet at Kennedy Airport and it lifted off the runway, her mother clutched Liyana's wrist hard. "Oh my," she whispered. She closed her eyes.

Liyana pressed her face to the window and looked down. Every little light of New York City was a period at the end of a sentence. A dusty silver sheen in the sky capped the city as it shrank behind them. The airplane dipped and shivered. Liyana had only flown short flights to Kansas City and Chicago before. She had never flown across an ocean.

After they reached their transatlantic altitude, Poppy took pillows and fuzzy blue blankets down from the overhead bins. Flight attendants moved up the aisles handing out bedtime cups of water. Rafik already had his head tipped off to one side, eyes shuttered, and mouth slightly open. Liyana couldn't believe it. He could sleep anywhere, even with his life changing in the middle of a stormy sky. Liyana couldn't imagine sleeping now. She pressed the button over her seat so a sharp circle of light fell onto her lap. She wrote in her note-book, *"Do overnight pilots drink coffee? Do they take turns napping? A new chapter begins in the dark."*

Even her teachers back home had been nicer to her when they knew she was leaving. "Why don't you tell us about where you're going?" Mr. Hathaway, her history teacher, had said the last week of school. He had never liked Liyana since the day she let Claire, who sat behind her, French-braid her hair in class. "Of course we all *know* about Jerusalem—it's such a big part of religious history and constantly in the news—but why do you think people have had so much trouble acting *civilized* over there?"

Civilized was his favorite word. Once when Mr. Hathaway said people were and animals weren't, Liyana raised her hand.

"Just—look at the front page of any newspaper," she said nervously. It was harder to speak with a whole class staring at you. "Look at the words—for what people do: *attack, assault, molest, devastate, infiltrate.*"

He raised one eyebrow.

Liyana continued, "And that's just one page!"

When he invited her to write an essay about

Jerusalem for extra credit and read it to the class, she gulped. "It's a pretty big story." Crazy words came into her mind. *Yakkity boondocks. Flippery fidgets.*

"Interview your father…make some informal notes," Mr. Hathaway said. "Just use your own information—no encyclopedias for this! It may be your last chance for extra credit, you know."

JERUSALEM: A BIT OF THE STORY

When my father was growing up inside the Old City of Jerusalem—that's the ancient part of town inside the stone wall—he and the kids on his street liked to trade desserts after dinner.

My father would take his square of Arabic hareesa, a delicious cream-of-wheat cake with an almond balanced in the center, outside on a plate. His Jewish friend Avi from next door brought slices of date rolls. And a Greek girl named Anna would bring a plate of honey puffs or butter cookies. Everybody liked everyone else's dessert better than their own. So they'd trade back and forth. Sometimes they traded two ways at once.

Everybody was mixed together. My father says nobody talked or thought much about being Arabs or Jews or anything, they just ate, slept, studied, got in trouble at school, wore shoes with holes in the bottoms, hiked to Bethlehem on the weekends, and "heard the donkeys' feet grow fewer in the stone streets as the world filled up with cars." That's a direct quote.

But then, my father says, "the pot on the stove boiled over." That's a direct quote, too. After the British weren't in control anymore, the Jews wanted control and the Arabs wanted control. Everybody said Jerusalem and Palestine was theirs. Too many other countries, especially the United States, got involved with money, guns, and bossing around. Life became terrible for the regular people. A Jewish politician named Golda Meir said the Palestinian people never existed even though there were hundreds of thousands of them living all around her.

My father used to wish the politicians making big decisions would trade desserts. It might have helped. He would stand on his flat roof staring off to the horizon, thinking things must be better somewhere else. Even when he was younger, he asked himself, "Isn't it dumb to want only to be next to people who are just like you?"

Rifles blasted. Stone houses were blown up. They were old houses, too, the kind you think should stand forever. My father's best Arab friend of his whole childhood was killed next to him on a bench when they were both just sitting there. He won't talk about it. My mother told me. My father remembers church bells ringing before that moment. Because of this, church bells have always made him nervous.

Everyone in my father's family prayed for the

troubles to be solved. Probably the Jewish and Greek families were doing exactly the same thing. They held candlelight vigils in the streets. They carried large pictures of loved ones who had died. Everybody prayed that Jerusalem would have peace.

One night, when gunfire exploded near their house, Sitti, my grandmother, cried out to my father and his brothers, "Help! What should we do?"

My father said, "I don't know about you, but I'm covering my head."

And he did.

He says he just wasn't interested in fighting. He was applying for scholarships so he could get out of that mess. Sometimes he still feels guilty, like he ran away when there was trouble, but other times he's glad he left when he did. He always hoped to go back someday.

During those bad troubles, my father's family traveled north to a small village to stay with relatives. Sitti was too scared to stay home. Weeks later, they returned to Jerusalem to find their house "occupied"—filled with other people—Jewish soldiers with guns. Later the "Occupied Territories" indicated Palestinian lands that were seized by Israelis, so "occupied" became a nasty word.

My father's family went back to the village and moved into a big old house there, but they lost all the things inside their Jerusalem house. They lost their furniture and their dishes and their blankets and never got anything back. The Jewish soldiers with guns wouldn't let them. The bank wouldn't give them their money either. So it was really hard.

I don't understand how these things happen, personally. I'm just telling you what my father told me.

Other Palestinians ended up crowded together in refugee camps, which still exist today. They lived in little shacks, thinking they would be there only a short time. Unfortunately that wasn't true.

My father got his scholarship to study medicine in the United States and his family was not happy. They didn't want him to leave. He promised he would come back someday. It was hard for him to watch the evening news all these years. Sometimes the Middle East segments show people he knows. In medical school, he specialized in the care of old people because young people were too mixed up. Maybe he should have become a vet.

Then he met my mother, an American, which is why he stayed over here so long. Stories of the American Indians made my father very sad. He knew how they felt.

Only recently he grew hopeful about Jerusalem and his country again. Things started changing for the better. Palestinians had public voices again. Of course they never stopped having private voices. That's something you can't take away from people. My father says, wouldn't you think the Jews, because of the tragedies they went through in Europe themselves, would have remembered this? Some did. But they weren't always the powerful ones.

The Arabs and Jews shook hands again, at the White House and in lots of other places, too. Many of them had never stopped doing it, secretly. Of course some people believed in the peace process more than others. Can you imagine why anyone would not? I can't.

That's when my father began planning for us to move back. He wants us to know our relatives. He wants to be in his old country as it turns into a better country. If it doesn't work out, we can always return to the United States.

I think of it as an adventure. I will miss all of you, especially Mr. Hathaway's pop quizzes and Clayton's fascinating monologues about mummies. If I become one, I hope you all will be fortunate enough to dig me up.

P.S. to Mr. Hathaway—that last part was just a joke.

Liyana Abboud

$\mathcal{P}$ALS

*Are dreams thinner at
thirty-three thousand feet?*

When their plane landed at Tel Aviv, Poppy was talking so fast, Liyana couldn't pay close attention to details. Normally she liked to notice trees first—their leaves and shapes—when she arrived in a new place. Then she'd focus on plants, signs, and, gradually, people. Liyana believed in working up to people. But Poppy leaned across the aisle jabbering so fast, she could barely notice the color of the sky.

"When we go through the checkpoint for passports, let me do the talking, okay? We don't let them stamp our passports here. They stamp a little piece of paper instead. And don't leave anything on the plane. Look around! Did you check under the seats? We'll go to the hotel first and rest awhile, then we'll call the village. My family will come in to see us. They won't expect us to travel all the way out to visit them today. Make sure you have everything. Did you get those pistachios? What about that book Rafik was reading?"

"Poppy's nervous," her mother whispered to

Liyana. "He hasn't been here in five years."

He was making Liyana nervous, too. *Jitterbug bazooka.* He didn't like it when she said foolish words lined up, like *mousetrap taffy-puller.* That's what she did inside her head when she got nervous. Poppy hadn't told his family their exact arrival time on purpose. "They don't need to come to the airport and make a big scene," he said.

Powder-puff peanut. She'd be good. She wouldn't talk at Customs. She wouldn't say, *Yes I'm carrying my worst American habits in the zipper pouch of my suitcase and I plan to let them loose in your streets. There's a kiss in there, too! I'll never tell.*

Right away, the Israeli agents singled Liyana's family out and made them stand off to the side in a troublemaker line with two men who looked like international zombies. Other travelers—sleek Spaniards, Irish nuns—zoomed right through. The women soldiers at the gate seemed meaner than the men. They all wore dull khaki uniforms. Big guns swung on straps across their backs.

Poppy had said this singling-out treatment often happened to Palestinians, even Palestinian-Americans, but one of Poppy's Palestinian friends had had a better arrival recently, when an Israeli customs agent actually said to him, "Welcome home." Poppy said it depended on what good or bad thing had just happened in the news.

Five years before, when Poppy had traveled here with his friend Mustafa, a Palestinian-American psychiatrist, the customs officer held them up so long at the gate, checking every corner of their suitcases and interrogating them so severely, that Mustafa leaned over, kissed the officer on the cheek, and said, "Let's just be friends, okay?" The Israeli man had been so stunned to be kissed that he waved them both through. And the two of them laughed all the way to Jerusalem.

Today the guard chose his words carefully. "Why are you planning to *stay* here?" Poppy had written "indefinitely" on the length of their visit when he filled out the papers on the plane. The papers were so boring. Liyana thought of more interesting questions they might ask. *What's the best word you ever made in Scrabble?*

She heard her father explain, in an unusually high-pitched tone, "I happen to be *from here,* and I am moving back. I have a job waiting for me at the hospital. I am introducing my family to my country and to their relatives. If you will notice, I have taken care of all the necessary paperwork at the embassy in the United States." He jingled some coins in his pocket. Liyana worried for him. He only jingled coins when he was upset.

The airport guards checked through their suitcases and backpacks extremely carefully. They lifted each item high in the air and stared at it. They wheeled the empty bags away on a cart to be x-rayed. They placed things back in a jumble. Liyana's flowered raggedy underpants fell to the floor and she scooped them up, embarrassed. The guards did not care for her violin. They looked inside its sound hole and shook it, hard. They jabbered fast in Hebrew.

Rafik tried to set his watch by a giant clock on the wall. He said, too loudly, "This airport seems ugly," and their mother shushed him. It was true. The walls were totally gray. There were no welcome posters, no murals, no candy stands. Three other stern-looking guards moved in closer to Liyana's family. Did they think they were going to start a riot or something? The guards looked ready to jump on them. Liyana felt a knot tightening in her stomach.

Maybe one reason their father wanted them to be quiet is they had trouble calling this country "Israel" to begin with. Why? Because Poppy had always, forever and ever, called it Palestine. Why wouldn't he? That's what he called it as a little boy. It was "Palestine" for the first years of his life and that's how most Arabs still referred to it to this day. Maybe he was afraid his family would slip.

In the airplane, somewhere over the Mediterranean, Liyana had whispered to Rafik, "Too bad the country namers couldn't have made some awful combo word from the beginning, like *Is-Pal* or *Pal-Is,* to make everybody happy."

Rafik said, "Huh?"

"But hardly anybody there has been pals yet."

"Are you going crazy?"

"And Pal-Is sounds like palace—but they don't even have a king. Do you think they would have been better off with kings?"

Later when the guard at the customs gate pointed at Rafik and asked Liyana weirdly, "Is this your brother?" as if he might be a stranger she'd just picked up in the air, she was moved to say, "He *is* my *pal,*" and they both started giggling, which made Poppy glare at them worriedly.

The guard sighed. He couldn't find any reason to detain them further. He shoved the passports back at Poppy. "You may go on."

WELCOME

*She opened her mouth
and a siren came out.*

At the hotel in Jerusalem, Liyana sat on the lumpy couch staring at her blue passport. *Given name, nationality, date of birth...* she turned herself upside down. She had braided her dark brown hair the day she got the picture taken. Now she wished she hadn't. One braid was fatter than the other. She thought her large eyes looked too hopeful, like the eyes of a dog.

Rafik bounded into the room with two glasses of freshly squeezed lemonade in his hands. His long, checkered shirttail was hanging out of his pants. "You should see it down there!" he babbled excitedly. "There's a real live sheep tied up right outside the back door of this hotel! I touched its head and it went *baaa-aaa!* Then I saw mysterious carving in a stone on the floor by the restaurant! It looks like a code! Was this place here when Jesus was?"

"Goofball!" Liyana said. They downed their lemonades in three great gulps each.

Poppy kept talking a mile a minute as they

waited for Sitti and the family to appear. He unpacked his travel kit and sprayed on fresh cologne. He combed his thick hair back from his forehead and stared into a mirror, probably for the first time in weeks. Then he turned to them and placed his hands together.

"Remember, Sitti comes from a different world. She's very—earthy. She doesn't wear anything but old-fashioned long clothes and she never did. She may seem strange to you. You won't understand her. I'll translate whatever you need, since she knows absolutely nothing in English—"

Liyana interrupted—"As little as we know in Arabic?"—and her mother hushed her.

Poppy continued without blinking, "They'll want us to come out to the village tonight to eat, but look, it's a twenty-eight-mile drive one way and it's four P.M. already. I'll say you're tired from the long flight. All right? If we go to the village, a hundred people will be pouring into the house to see us. It's too much for tonight. Is everyone okay?"

Liyana said, "We used to be okay, till you started making us so nervous!" She whispered to Rafik, "Does he think they won't like us? Does he think we won't like them?"

Rafik lay on the bed, sighing happily. He said, "Have you felt these pillows? They're the deepest pillows in the world!"

Liyana lay down on the next bed. Her head sank into the soft feathers and she said, "You're right." Then she got up again and changed from her blue corduroy pants to her pleated black skirt. She was thinking how amazing it was that people could get on an airplane and step off again in a different universe.

After Poppy had peeked out the window twenty times at taxis veering by with honking horns and squealing tires and their mother had combed and recombed her hair, applying a new dash of perky red lipstick, everyone finally arrived. Their babbling echoes filled the lobby before they got on the elevator. Poppy stepped outside the door to greet them.

Then a huge crowd of relatives burst into the room, bustling, hugging, pinching cheeks, and jabbering loudly. They were smoky smelling, not like cigarette smoke but the deeper smoke of a campfire that goes into clothes and stays there after the fire's out.

Indeed, they were not like any relatives Liyana had ever met before. In the United States their extended family (except for Peachy Helen, who always acted cozy) held back from them politely as if they might have a cold. Uncle Leo had never hugged Liyana yet. He shook her hand like an insurance man. Aunt Margaret spoke formally to children, about general subjects. *Are you enjoying the summer? Do you have nice friends?*

But this bustling group of aunts and uncles swirled in circles as Sitti, their grandmother, threw her strong arms around each one of them in succession, squeezing so tightly that Liyana lost her breath. "She's blessing you," Poppy whispered.

Liyana had an impulse to stand very close to Poppy, for protection, and also for translation, so he could keep her posted on what was being said. Tears poured down Sitti's rugged cheeks. Suddenly she threw her head back, rolled her tongue high up in her mouth, and began trilling wildly. Liyana had never heard anything like it. Aunt Saba and Aunt Amal began clapping a rhythmic beat. Mom looked startled. Rafik raised his eyebrows.

Poppy shook his head, waving both hands in Sitti's face to quiet her down. "That's her traditional cry," he explained. "She uses it as an announcement at weddings and—funerals."

"Which one is *this*?" Liyana asked.

Poppy spoke rapidly to Sitti in Arabic, but she didn't stop right away. She trilled and trilled and trilled. She shimmied her arms in the air like a Pentecostal preacher. The backs of her hands were tattooed with the dark blue shapes of flying birds.

Liyana said, "Poppy! You never told us she had tattoos!"

Poppy said, "I didn't want you to get any ideas."

"I'm considering an eagle, myself," Rafik said.

Sitti pulled Poppy's face close to hers again and again to kiss him on both cheeks. Liyana liked that. Two kisses seemed better than one.

Liyana was being kissed by so many people whose exact identity was unknown to her, though Poppy tried to clarify names of aunts, cousins, and wives of cousins, to help his family out. Even he had trouble. He gave two different names for the same woman and everyone laughed. Liyana kept nodding and trying to kiss people back, even when she missed their cheeks. She kissed Aunt Lena on the scarf and felt silly. Still, after all that flying, the enthusiastic welcome was nice. At least Liyana knew they had landed in the proper hemisphere.

The women's long dresses were made of thick fabrics, purple, gold, and navy blue, and stitched brightly with fabulous, complicated embroidery. Aunt Lena had rich lines of multicolored rainbow thread wrapped around her wrists. All the women wore gold bangle bracelets. The older ones had long white scarves draped and knotted firmly over their hair. The younger ones had bare heads, which made Liyana feel relieved.

They wore plastic, slip-on shoes in pastel colors. The modern shoes seemed strange with their old-fashioned clothes. Aunt Saba touched Liyana's blue-and-yellow Swiss children's watch that had little people's heads on the ends of its hands. She put her face down to stare at it and laughed. The women even touched Liyana's earlobes. She wore no gold earrings, as they did. But Liyana didn't mind. She didn't feel like a "specimen." She liked their curiosity. The men wore dull gray or black suits, white shirts, and striped ties, more like men anywhere. Liyana wondered how men ever got such boring uniforms, anyway. Sometimes she looked at encyclopedia pages showing "native dress" styles from around the world. Elsewhere, in Zambia maybe, or Timbuktu, the men knew how to dress. In the older days, Arab men wore long, flowing robes and cloaks with golden edges, but suits had sneaked into their closets now. Poppy had told Liyana she would like the men's elegant clothing in Saudi Arabia and the United Arab Emirates better.

Two of the older uncles, Zaki and Daoud, wore black-and-white-checkered *kaffiyehs* on their heads, which made them look more interesting. Liyana liked their weather-beaten brown faces immediately. Rafik was tugging at her elbow. He whispered, "Does that mean his name is *Daoud Abboud?*"

Liyana said, "I think he's married to one of our aunts. He must have a different last name. But let's not find out what it is right now, okay? My head is spinning!"

Poppy translated what Aunt Amal said, about how scary it had been for them to pass the Israeli checkpoint when they entered Jerusalem. Her face looked alarmed. All four taxis filled with family members had been stopped. They'd been asked to show special permits they had secured two days ago. The Israeli soldier shouted at them and they got scared. He had a gun. He threw Uncle Daoud's pass on the ground because it was slightly bent and made him get out of the car to pick it up. When he was done looking at the passes, Sitti thought he said, "Go away," but he meant, "Go on."

Liyana noticed her mother's face turning worried as Poppy translated. Her mother fingered the edge of Sitti's sleeve. "What?" Liyana asked her. "What are you thinking of?"

"I thought things were supposed to be much better now."

"That's not what they're telling me," Poppy said. "They say the rules change every two days. And they almost never come into the city anymore."

Rafik said, "I think the same person just kissed me for the tenth time."

Poppy rubbed his hands together. "We should go downstairs to get some tea or coffee." Liyana knew he was trying to lighten the atmosphere, but a huge babble broke loose. "They aren't used to hotels," he explained.

In fact, today was the first time *in her life* Sitti had ever ridden in an elevator. Always before, in any building with more than one floor, she insisted on taking the stairs. Sitti said little boxes were for dead people. She didn't want to enter the elevator today, either, and they had to push her.

Liyana noticed the women of the family eyeing her mother closely. She was an inch taller than Poppy, and her skin two shades lighter. Liyana and Rafik had inherited Poppy's olive skin. *Did they think her mother was pretty?* They seemed to like her mother's long hair. They all had long hair, too, braided, or knotted in buns. Liyana guessed the ones with scarves had long, hidden hair. Everyone must have wondered about a woman who could have kept a man from living in his own country till now. They must have had mixed feelings.

Liyana's mother kept smiling widely at them, placing her hands on top of theirs like in that game for babies where the bottom hand keeps getting pulled out. Beyond the window, cars and trucks of Jerusalem swerved and honked, screeching their brakes and wailing up to the curb. Rafik, peeking out the window at her side, said, "Have you noticed how many old Mercedes Benzes there are here?" Her brain swirled with names, *Lena, Saba, Leila,* ending in *a,* like her own. Would she ever get them straight?

Suddenly, just as everyone headed out the door for a tea party, Rafik vomited on the floor.

Mrs. Abboud rushed toward the bathroom for tissues, which were so small and thin that she threw them up in the air when she returned. What about bath towels? Awful. "Liyana," she hissed. "Move! Help!" Poppy broke the momentary frozen spell by waving his hands to urge everyone out into the hall. Whenever he saw anyone vomit, he felt nauseated himself.

Rafik stumbled toward the bathroom. Liyana followed, saying, "Are you sick?"

He said, "No, dope-dope, that's how we say hello in my language. What do you think?"

Their mother buzzed the hotel desk to ask for a mop, but the clerk brought a broom instead. Then he ran for wet rags. Liyana sat with Rafik on the edge of the bathtub, considering aloud details of the last three meals they had eaten, to his horror. "Could it have been the cucumber on the plane? The little scrap of tomato in your sandwich?"

"Could you please please please keep your mouth shut?"

When he didn't throw up again, but began smiling weakly and making jokes, their mother produced antinausea tablets from her medicine bag, told Rafik please to rest and take it easy, asked Liyana to stay with him, and went downstairs to join the family.

Liyana lay on the other twin bed, idly reciting, "One potato, two potato, three potato, four…"

Rafik said, "Did anyone ever tell you you're mean?"

$\mathcal{F}$IRST THINGS LAST

*Her own first things
kept lasting longest in her brain.*

Rafik fell asleep on top of his white bedspread immediately, so Liyana shut her eyes on her bed, too, and plummeted into a frozen scene. She dreamed she was standing at the top of the steepest hill in Forest Park, St. Louis, in front of the art museum, on a fresh morning of new snow. No one else was out yet.

She held her wooden sled by its rope, trying to decide whether to jump onto it and swoop down the slope, but it was hard to do when your sled's runners would be the first to mark the surface. Better to watch someone else doing it first—otherwise you weren't sure how fast you would go.

The horse statue was iced like a cookie. Bare trees poked their bony arms into the sky. At the bottom of the hill, the frozen lake glistened in the light. Liyana wore a nubby brown coat that hadn't fit her in years. She'd kept it in the back of her closet till recently and felt sad, after the estate sale, that it was gone forever. She wore her turquoise mittens with a long cord connecting them, running up her sleeves and across her back to keep them together.

How old was she in this dream, three? She was biting her lip hard, the way she used to do to make a decision.

Although she'd thought she was alone in the snow, someone pushed her abruptly from behind and she plopped onto the sled, shrieking, flailing down the slope on her stomach. Who did that, Rafik? But Rafik would still have been a baby then. The sled was soaring. It became a rocket ship, a dizzy runaway. She couldn't steer for a minute. The rope flew out behind her. What if she crashed into the lake? What if the ice broke? She screamed and closed her eyes. When she opened them, Rafik was leaning over her in real life, in Jerusalem, saying worriedly, "Are you okay? Or are you going bonkers, too?"

"What do you mean, 'too'?" Liyana's tongue felt thick after her brief, busy nap. "Who else has gone bonkers? Do you know what I dreamed? Remember that hill in front of the museum?"

Rafik's main interest was, who had pushed her? Had the horse statue reared up completely off its base and given her a kick?

He yawned. Then he said, "I'm surprised I still feel exactly like myself, you know what I mean? I thought when I got to the other side of the world, I might feel like somebody different."

$\mathcal{T}$O THE VILLAGE

Think of all the towns and cities
we've never seen or imagined.

Despite Rafik's questionable health, the family talked Poppy into traveling out to the village that very first night. They were insistent with him at the tea party downstairs. *Dinner is ready. You* must *come. The lamb is killed in your honor.*

Everything was decided, mysteriously, without anyone really saying yes or no. They crowded downstairs in a flurry to hail a whole herd of taxis and head north. Sitti rode in the car with the Abbouds, jammed up body to body with Poppy in the front seat beside the driver. Sitti muttered and patted him. It was the first time Liyana had ever pictured Poppy as the *son,* with his own mother bossing him around. Liyana, Rafik, and their mother crowded together in back.

The taxi veered wildly around a corner, then chugged slowly north on the road from Jerusalem to Ramallah. Poppy pointed out landmarks to them. *There's the garden where we had a party when I graduated from high school. Red lanterns were strung from ropes. There's the shop of the shoemaker Abdul Rahman—he's been inside hammering soles since I was born.*

Liyana's eyes swirled with stone buildings, TV antennas, metal grillwork over windows instead of screens, flapping white sheets strung from clotheslines right on the flat roofs of houses, signs in Arabic, Hebrew, and English, and lumbering buses. Rafik had gone to sleep again with his head back against the seat. Liyana felt like poking him to wake him up.

"It's not how I pictured it. What about you?" her mother said.

Liyana answered softly, "Nothing is ever as I picture it."

Had she thought Jerusalem would have a halo? She certainly didn't think about—diesel exhaust. They passed the military checkpoint surrounded by striped orange sawhorses. In the bustling Arab town of Ramallah, everyone walked around carrying large mesh shopping bags. A man with a tray of round flat breads stacked sky-high grinned at Liyana through the car window when their eyes met.

Then the taxi headed into the rural West Bank of orchards and tiny villages, each with its own minaret and perched houses. Liyana said, "It's gorgeous here!" and breathed deeply. She was also thinking, "It's strange," but she was looking for the silver lining. The dusky green of olive trees planted in terraced rows up hillsides, walls of carefully stacked stones, old wells with real wooden buckets.... Ancient men wearing white head-dresses leaned on canes talking in slow time as the train of taxis, driving faster now, flew by into another dimension.

When the cars climbed the steep hill into the village, children popped out of front doors to look at them, as if cars didn't drive up there very often. Rafik sat bolt upright and Liyana said, "We're on the moon." Every house was made of golden or white chunky stone.

The moment they piled out of their seats, they were surrounded by relatives kissing their cheeks again. Liyana's face was starting to feel rubbed *raw*. A bearded man in a long cloak, whom Poppy introduced as Tayeb the Elder, shot a gun off into the air like a military salute. Poppy begged him to stop. What if the bullets came down on their heads?

Inside Sitti's arched main room, they sat on flowery gingham mattresses arranged in a circle on the floor. Liyana sat between Rafik and a shy girl cousin named Dina who kept smiling at her. An old picture of Poppy before he came to the United States hung high and crookedly on one wall. Liyana wanted to take a broom handle and straighten it.

"We're here!" Poppy kept announcing in English, then Arabic, like some kind of television host, and everyone would cheer. And a strange cloud passed through Liyana—they were *here,* but no one really knew her here, no one knew what she liked, or who her friends had been, or how funny she could be if she had any idea what was going on. She would have to start from scratch.

Poppy and Mom—whom everyone had started calling Soo-Sun, in a way that made her common American name sound almost Chinese—began distributing presents to everybody. They passed out boxes of heart-shaped soaps, fuzzy slippers, creamy pink lotions, fancy hand towels, men's shiny ties, and chocolates, which surprised Liyana, since they'd barely eaten chocolate in their own house. Mom had scurried around St. Louis buying these things before they left.

Everyone looked very hopeful. After they received their gifts, they compared them. Liyana produced ten pairs of earrings she'd bought for a dollar each for her girl cousins. Dina, amazingly, had tears in her eyes as she selected her pair. Rafik offered up—reluctantly, Liyana thought—a few packages of small cars to the boys.

Then the whole gigantic family sat around forever, visiting, waiting for dinner to appear. What Liyana would discover was this was positively everyone's favorite thing to do here—*sit in a circle and talk talk talk*. Poppy had told her they liked to talk about—everyone else. They watched each other with their hundred deep eyes. When Cousin Fayed and his family poked their heads through the door, or Cousin Fowzi and Aunt Muna entered with welcomes and a basket of oranges, everyone stood up, hugged, kissed, exclaimed, patted, and went through the entire cycle again.

"I think I'm getting hypnotized," Rafik said.

Then Aunt Saba, which Poppy said meant "morning," appeared carrying a large brass tray filled with steaming glasses of musky-smelling tea—*maramia*—an herb good for the stomach. Rafik drank five glasses. Back home he could drink a whole bottle of cranberry juice by himself at one sitting.

The grocer showed up, and the postmaster, and the principal of the village school, and the neighbor, Abu Mahmoud, who grew famous green beans, and all of their wives and babies and teenagers and cats.

But the extra visitors left just as a huge tray of dinner appeared, hunks of baked lamb surrounded by rice and pine nuts. The remaining family members gathered around to dig into it with their forks. Poppy asked if his family could have individual plates since they weren't used to eating communally.

Aunt Amal brought out four plates of different sizes and colors. Liyana's was blue, with a crack. Her aunt looked worried, as if she might not like it. Liyana ate a mound of rice and onions and sizzled pine nuts, but steered clear of the lamb.

Sitti kept urging Liyana, through Poppy, "Eat the lamb." She said Liyana *needed* it. Poppy told her Liyana was a very light eater, a big lie of course, but convenient for the moment. Rafik was drinking soupy yogurt, one of his two thousand favorite food items. "I'm recovering," he whispered to Liyana. "I'm feeling better now. Who is that guy and why does he keep waving at me with his ball?"

Rafik and their animated cousin Muhammad stepped into Sitti's courtyard to play catch in the glow from a single bright bulb, but Liyana felt too tired, suddenly, to follow them. Sitti asked Poppy some questions about Liyana—Liyana could tell because they both stared at her as they talked. Now and then her name cropped up in their Arabic like a little window. But she couldn't see through it. She thought she could close her eyes and sleep for two days. Even her watch felt heavy on her arm. It was 10 P.M. She hadn't taken it off since they left Missouri—how many time zones had they crossed by now?

Liyana tried to be polite to everyone by smiling

and tipping her head over to one side so they couldn't tell if she were saying no or yes. How long would it take till they knew one true thing about her?

Voices in the village streets bounced off stone walls. They rose into the night sky like kites, billowed, and disappeared. A *muezzin* gave the last call to prayer of the day over a loudspeaker from the nearby mosque and all the relatives rose up in unison and turned their backs on Liyana's family. They unrolled small blue prayer rugs from a shelf, then knelt, stood, and knelt again, touching foreheads to the ground, saying their prayers in low voices. They didn't mind that Liyana's family was sitting there staring at them. When they were done, they rolled up the rugs and returned to sit in the circle.

"Poppy," Liyana whispered, touching his hand. "Did you ever pray the way they pray?"

"Always—in my heart."

Sitti told Poppy she was going to make a pilgrimage to Mecca this year for sure, especially if he would give her money to ride the bus. Tayeb the Elder asked for money to install a shower in his new bathroom and Uncle Hamza said he could really use a stove and suddenly everyone was asking for things, voices tangling together as Poppy translated. He looked more and more uncomfortable.

Soon he turned toward their mother, saying, "When the talk gets to money, we get rolling," and he stood up.

He said they were so exhausted their heads were falling off. They needed to return to Jerusalem to their hotel immediately. Some angry grumbling erupted because the older relatives thought they should be sleeping in the village with their family, not in a hotel. Liyana felt the weight of centuries pressing her into a small ball. A yawn rose up in her so large she could not hold it back.

Sitti stood beside Liyana. They were exactly the same height. Sitti took both Liyana's hands in her own. She said, through Poppy, "I hope you will come back tomorrow and stay for many many days." Sitti said they would teach her how to sew and pick lentils and marinate olives and carry water from the spring on her head and speak Arabic. Poppy said, "She'll also teach you how to give a weather report by standing on the roof and licking one finger and holding it up in the wind." Everyone laughed when he translated this. Was it a joke? Were they making fun of her?

Sitti moved her hands around when she spoke, letting them weave and dance in the air. She lifted the tip of Liyana's braid to look at it. She kissed her twice on each cheek. And she pressed Liyana's face into her smoky scarf.

Outside, the sky felt deep and dark as if a large soft blanket had been thrown over the hills and valleys. They stood for a long moment with their suddenly huge family staring off across shadowy fields and orchards, smelling the turned soil and the sweet night breeze. A donkey hee-hawed somewhere, the sound echoed, and a car motor cut off so the silence seemed deep as the sea. Poppy took a deep breath. "Home," he said, and nodded at Liyana. He had his arm around her.

MANGER

*She did not want her head
to be filled with large wishes and worries.*

The Abbouds began looking for a house near Jerusalem and everything was either too big, too expensive, too little, too crumbling, too noisy, or too strange. One elegant house faced a billboard advertising "The Museum of Jewish Hatred." Poppy told the realtor soberly that he was sorry, but he couldn't bear to look out his window at that depressing sign.

Waves of sadness swept over Liyana unexpectedly every time they entered a house that *might* become theirs and left it again. She thought of their neat white house with green shutters in St. Louis. She thought of their wooden screen door banging on its hinge. They kept passing the road sign TO BETHLEHEM and Liyana found herself singing, "O Little Town of Bethlehem" and "Away in a Manger" till Rafik covered his ears.

Each night, she added to her sack of dirty laundry at the hotel, refolding any clothes she could stand to wear another day in a stack on top of her open suitcase. Poppy asked, "Didn't you bring *anything* but that black T-shirt?" Only one of her suitcases had been sprung open so far. She wanted to be surprised later to find more familiar clothes and treasures waiting in her bags.

Rafik, however, had opened every case he brought and was living in a heap of toys and treasures, a neon battery-powered yo-yo, a skunk puppet, and a harmonica. He even had the group picture of his last year's school class standing up on his bedside table.

Liyana wished Uncle Zaki, Poppy's elder brother, had not asked "for her hand" for his son on their second trip to the village. Poppy got so furious, he actually hissed, and translated his answer for them later. "We do not embrace such archaic customs, and furthermore, does she look ready to be married? She is fourteen years old." In the village everyone seemed to be staring at her now as if she were an exotic animal in a zoo. She felt awkward around her relatives, as if they had more in mind for her than she could ever have dreamed.

She wished she had not heard that an Arab boy who was found kissing a girl in the alley behind her house got beaten up by the girl's brothers. What was wrong with kissing? Everybody else kissed *constantly* over here—but on both cheeks, not on the mouth. Had people reverted to the

Stone Age just because everything in Jerusalem was *made* of stone?

Poppy sat Liyana down on the hotel room couch, which they were growing quite familiar with.

"You are missing the point," he said, "if you imagine you can measure one country's customs by another's. Public kissing—I mean, kissing on the mouth, like romantic kissing—is *not okay* here. It is simply not done. Anyway, it is not *supposed* to be done."

"Not by anyone?" she asked. "Not by Greeks or Jews or Armenians, or only not by Arabs?"

With her luck she had been born into the only nonkissing culture, just when it started feeling like a valuable activity.

"I cannot speak for Greeks and Jews and Armenians. I used to trade desserts with them, but I cannot speak for them regarding kissing. Somehow I do not think they are as strict about kissing as the Arabs are. Probably to their benefit. Of course anyone can kiss once they are married."

Poppy looked suddenly alarmed. "Is there someone you want to kiss?"

"Oh sure, I just arrived nine days ago and I've already staked him out."

"Liyana, you must be patient. Cultural differences aren't learned or understood immediately. Most importantly, you must abide by the guidelines where you are living. This is common sense. It will protect you. You know that phrase you always hated—*When in Rome, do as the Romans do?* You must remember, *you are not in the United States.*"

As if he had to remind her.

When she went to bed that night, she pressed her face into the puffy cotton pillow. It smelled very different from the pillows in their St. Louis house, which smelled more like fresh air, like a good loose breeze. This pillow smelled like long lonely years full of bleach.

———

The next day Liyana's family rented the whole upstairs apartment of a large white stone house out in the countryside, halfway between Jerusalem and the town of Ramallah. A bus stopped right in front.

Surrounded by stony fields, the house had a good flat roof they'd be able to read their books on, if they spread out blankets. Poppy pointed out the old refugee camp down the smaller road behind the house—it had been one of the first ones from 1948. From the roof it looked like a colorful village of small buildings crowded close together. "Believe me," Poppy said, "it looks better from a distance. Camps are difficult places." Beyond it sat the abandoned Jerusalem airport—a few streaks of gray runway and a small tower. "It's fast asleep," Poppy said sadly.

Each wide-open empty bedroom in the house had a whole wall of built-in wooden cupboards and closets and a private sunporch. Finally they'd be able to unpack.

Their new landlord, Abu Janan, which meant the Father of Janan, looked like the Prophet of Gloom, with a huge stomach too big for his pants. He told them they probably wouldn't be able to get a telephone hookup for at least a year, since he just got his after requesting it forever.

Poppy said, "Well, I'll work on it immediately since I'm a doctor and require one. Also" (he winked at Liyana), "don't teenagers need to have telephones?" As if she had anyone to call.

"Where is Janan?" she asked.

"Who?" Poppy said.

"The person this man is the father of."

"In Chicago. Grown up."

Too bad. She'd thought she might have a built-in friend.

From the immaculate bare kitchen of their new flat, Rafik and Liyana could hear squawking rising from the backyard. They went downstairs and stepped outside to find a pen of plump black chickens pecking heartily in straw. A short cottage held their laying nests.

"We're living at a manger after all," Rafik whispered. "You want to sneak down sometimes and give them treats?"

"What is a treat to a chicken?"

"Cantaloupe seeds and the middles of squash."

"How do *you* know?"

Rafik shrugged. "I have many secrets. We could let them out someday!" The yard was surrounded by a wall so they wouldn't be able to go far.

Liyana felt a pleasant mischief lay its cool hand on her head again.

Rafik said, "Did you see that landlord of ours? He could use some exercise! If he chases them, he'll get some!"

Liyana mused. "Shouldn't we wait at least a week? Let's establish ourselves as law-abiding lodgers first."

"Then?"

A bus kicked up dust on the road after letting off a crowd of passengers. Their new neighbors who didn't yet know they existed.

"Then we have fun."

INTERIOR DECORATORS

*My father once said he'd like to paint
every board of our house a different color.*

Rafik tacked up bright travel posters from Poppy's travel-agency friend on the freshly painted white walls of his room. He posted "New York" and "Portugal," though he'd never been there, and "The Doors of Jerusalem" and "TEXAS USA," the place he hoped to go someday.

Liyana said, "Did you get any for me?"

Rafik said she could have "Lufthansa" but she didn't want it. She'd never even flown on that airline.

In St. Louis, Liyana's room had been painted a deep, delicious color called "Raisin." Her walls looked like an art gallery arranged with block prints and dreamy watercolors by her friends. She had a bulletin board with silly pictures taken at people's birthday parties and dried flowers and pages ripped from magazines that were too nice to throw away. The gleaming, golden eyes of a cat stared right at her in bed. She had a framed pastel portrait her mother had sketched of her when she was two and fell asleep on the blue rug in the living room. Liyana loved it very much and would have brought it to Jerusalem, but she worried the glass in the frame might break. She didn't bring Peachy's needlepoint alphabet or her personal portrait of Peter Pan, either.

Liyana thought she'd try living with blank walls for a month or two.

It was just an experiment.

JERUSALEM ABOVE MY HIGHEST JOY

The city was a cake made of layers of time.

"I'm not going," Liyana told Poppy.

They were talking about Sitti's invitation to come out to the village so she could "teach her things" on weekends.

"Why doesn't she want to teach Rafik things, too?"

"Because she's a woman and she knows womanly things."

"She can keep them."

Poppy sighed, "Fifty years from now you will deeply regret this moment." He turned and stalked down the hallway toward his own bedroom. That's what he always said. *Fifty years from now I'm going to be very busy,* Liyana thought.

A few days before, Poppy had actually thumbed through a Bible looking for a quote he liked from the Psalms: "If I forget thee, O Jerusalem, may my right hand forget its cunning. May my tongue cleave to the roof of my mouth, if I do not set Jerusalem above my highest joy."

It made Liyana mad when he read it to her. Was there an underlying meaning? Was he saying she wasn't acting happy enough to be here? She wasn't in the mood to go shopping day after day to replenish their household supplies. She didn't even act excited about their new white Toyota, which smelled like fresh carpet and roses inside. "We could drive to Damascus or Aleppo!" Poppy said, standing back proudly to admire his purchase. "Well, we might have trouble getting across the border...."

Mostly they would just be driving back and forth from Jerusalem to Ramallah to their house, which sat so neatly in between.

Every morning at breakfast, when Poppy greeted Rafik and Liyana with his characteristic, "Good *morning!* And how are *you* today?" she felt like answering in a gloomier way. *I'm fair. I'm floundering. I'm lonesome.* Liyana begged Poppy to pass by their new post office box often to see if she had received any letters from home. *What was wrong with Claire?* She imagined Poppy watched her from the corner of his eye.

The Abbouds spent an entire exhausting weekend sightseeing nonstop around Jerusalem morning till night. Poppy wanted them to "get the lay of the land."

He led them up winding alleyways and down ancient stairs to the Church of the Holy Sepulcher he'd been telling them about for years. The priests here were famous for arguing to get the best altars for their own services. Poppy had done his homework on the wall outside the door when he was a boy and once saw two priests have a fistfight, rolling in the dust.

The dim Chapel of Calvary held a mournful mural of Jesus lying arms outspread and dead on the cross after it was taken down and laid on the ground. Mary Magdalene pressed her head to his feet. Mrs. Abboud cried when she saw it. At the Garden of Gethsemane, she cried again. Jerusalem was not exactly fun and games. Liyana's mother held a tissue to her eyes. "I'm just feeling very *moved* today, thinking of all Jesus went through—it's so haunting to stand on these same spots."

"There's always controversy, you know—which spot is the exact one," Poppy said.

"It's close enough for me," she said.

They walked along the crowded Via Dolorosa, where Jesus carried the cross and stopped at every station, so Mrs. Abboud could read aloud from her guidebook. German pilgrims, Italians humming hymns, and Japanese travelers wearing small purple caps converged on the same narrow pathways.

At the Wailing Wall, Jews in *yarmulkes* were tucking tiny notes and prayers into cracks between stones. Rafik wanted to know how long the notes stayed there. The most famous mosque of Jerusalem, the Dome of the Rock, gleamed golden against the sky.

The Abbouds trudged around the outside of the Old City while Poppy gave them a lesson in the gates—Damascus Gate, Herod's Gate, Jaffa Gate, the New Gate, the Lion's Gate (also known as St. Stephen's Gate), and—their favorite—the Dung Gate. Rafik and Liyana debated how the Dung Gate might have gotten its name.

They stopped at a hundred miniature stores with crooked floors so Poppy could greet the owners, kiss-kiss on both cheeks, introduce the family, and be offered coffee or tea, though he kept saying no. He said they had too many places to go to sit down anywhere.

"Everybody is a cousin of somebody and Poppy knows them all," Liyana sighed to Rafik.

"Yep," said Rafik, "but will you remember a single person you've seen? Good luck!"

Liyana knew she would remember sensitive-looking Bassam, who ran a spice shop, because he had a poster of the Hindu elephant-headed god Ganesha on the wall of his shop and that seemed a little—unusual—here.

Liyana and Rafik wanted to buy something from every food stand, but Poppy begged them to wait till their "very large and special lunch." As he greeted some ancient melon vendors who had known their grandfather, Liyana's eyes fell on a young man, who appeared to be a dwarf, weighing bananas on an old-fashioned hanging scale. He stood on a tall wooden crate behind his cart. His bananas were stubby and short themselves, more like exclamation points than parentheses.

He wore an orange stocking cap though the weather was warm. His tiny blue jeans must have been made for a boy. And his face looked as stony as the streets of the city—chiseled and sharply defined. He didn't smile even when he had three customers lined up. He just nodded and weighed their bananas. Liyana kept staring at him, the way she always picked one person in any crowd to stare at. She said to Rafik, "See that banana man? I'll remember *him*. On the day I see him smile, I'll buy a banana." Maybe he was sad because he was short, or he had wanted to do something else in his life.

"Where are the camels, anyway?" Rafik asked

Poppy. "I was hoping for camels." Poppy said they might see a few out in the desert toward Jericho, so immediately they begged him to take them there instead.

Liyana groaned, "Our feet are killing us. Also we're expiring from hunger. Isn't history better in small doses?"

"My precious children!" Poppy exclaimed.

They ate lunch in a famous underground Arabic restaurant, full of Oriental rugs, called *The Philadelphia.* Poppy gripped a waiter's wrist and introduced him around the table. "This young man's father," he said, "was the smartest student in my high school chemistry class!" Liyana noticed another handsome young waiter watching her as he rolled silverware into white linen napkins and stacked them in a mound. Did he wink? She thought he winked.

The owner, a nice man about Poppy's age, brought them steaming bowls of aromatic lentil soup, saying once they tasted it, they would keep coming back for more. The table filled up with olives, purple marinated turnips, plates of *baba ghanouj* and *hummus,* and hot flat breads, even before the real lunch came.

Liyana was feeling better by the minute. "With so much holiness bumping up against other holiness, doesn't it seem *strange* Jerusalem would have had so much fighting?" she said. Liyana was thinking of her teacher Mr. Hathaway back home, remembering the skeptical way he lifted one eyebrow any time she spoke.

"Think about dinner tables," her mother said.

"Huh?"

"How many fights there are in families, every day. People in families love each other, or want to love each other, but they fight anyway. With strangers you don't care so much. Think about it."

"Yeah," said Rafik, "if you didn't love someone, why would you even *bother* to fight with him?"

Poppy patted him. "My son, more a philosopher every day!"

"Do you think the Arabs and Jews secretly love one another?" Liyana asked.

"I think," Poppy said, "they are bonded for life. Whether they like it or not. Like that kind of glue that won't let go."

Two strong rays of light entered the subterranean restaurant through high-up windows along the street. One sunbeam fell directly onto the octagonal center design of a blue Oriental rug and the other lit up the red head of a very old lady. Poppy whispered, "See her hair? She dyes it with henna."

"That's what I'll do after I get my eagle tattoo," Rafik whispered.

"Being here with you all, I feel my heart has come back into my body." Poppy lifted a teacup and smiled.

Still, Liyana noticed Poppy didn't take them over to western Jewish Jerusalem for any kind of tour. He said he "didn't know it" and they might have to get a tour bus for that. The handsome waiter slipped a plate of *baklava* onto their table for dessert. They hadn't even ordered it.

THE PRINCIPAL WEARS A HAT POINTING TO THE MOON

Air was grinning around them.

Rafik was going to attend the Friends Girls School in Ramallah, even though he was a boy. The school accepted a few boys, too. It had been started by Quakers long ago and had a sunny campus with pots of geraniums lining the front steps.

Liyana's mother seemed happy because the schoolyard where Rafik would spend his recesses was surrounded by a high stone wall. She'd recently started talking about "safety" in a way that made Liyana jumpy. Liyana never thought about safety unless someone else brought it up. She didn't *want* to think about it, either. She wanted to live in an unlocked world.

Poppy and Mom did some research regarding Liyana's high school education and decided she might do best at an Armenian school called St. Tarkmanchatz deep in the Armenian district of the Old City.

The students there were trilingual, speaking

Arabic, Armenian, and English, three languages with completely different alphabets.

"Are the classes like a three-channel television set? What will I do when they're on the other channels? Will they think I'm a dunce for speaking only English?" Liyana asked Poppy. She was worried.

Liyana and Poppy went into town for the interview with the headmaster. They entered a huge iron door that led into the Armenian sector of the Old City and wandered the curling streets as if they were in a maze. The streets were unevenly paved and Liyana kept tripping. Poppy paused to gaze around them, saying, "I haven't been on these streets since I was a boy."

An old man sold roasted peanuts on a corner. When Poppy asked him in Arabic for the school, he pointed to an ancient building right ahead of them. The sign over the school's door was in Armenian—they could only read 1929.

Inside the main office sat a priest in a long burgundy robe wearing a giant pointed hat, or crown. Liyana wasn't sure what you would call the burgundy triangle sitting straight up on top of his head. Headgear? She tried not to stare at it.

He rose to shake hands, then waved them to sit on two rickety wooden chairs, speaking to Liyana in a careful, formal voice. "Do you know much about the Armenians?"

"I know they have a long and troubled history, like everyone else over here," Liyana said, equally carefully. "I know there was a terrible massacre of Armenian people, but I couldn't say the exact year. I'm sorry it happened."

"And you know that's why many in our community came to live in exile so far from our original homeland?"

She nodded. She was afraid he might ask her to say the Armenian alphabet or something, which she certainly didn't know.

A fan spun and a water cooler clicked. All the books on his shelf were in Armenian.

Then something wonderful occurred to Liyana.

"I love William Saroyan."

"Who?"

When she said, "The great Armenian-American writer who lived and wrote in California," he said, "Oh yes, oh yes!"

When Liyana was in seventh grade, her class had a story by Saroyan in their textbook. She looked up more of his works at the library and read "The Pomegranate Trees" out loud to Poppy. They laughed so hard, Poppy couldn't catch his breath. He lay down on the floor laughing, absolutely overcome. Later he said the wacky conversations in the story reminded him of his own family.

Liyana leaned toward the priest, suddenly

inspired. "I feel very close to what I know of Armenian culture through Saroyan's stories and look forward to learning even more."

That's when the air in the room changed. The priest leaned forward, too. His hat slipped a little. "So you are interested in our culture?"

"Absolutely."

Above their heads invisible angels started clapping.

The priest enrolled her, though she wasn't even one-fourth or one-eighth Armenian. He said she would be the only "outsider," a term that made her father flinch. Poppy spoke heartily, "Let's believe together in a world where no one is inside or outside, yes?" The priest didn't answer, but Liyana felt proud of Poppy for saying it.

Shaking hands again, the priest noticed the plain silver ring, her gift from Claire, on Liyana's finger and said, "I'm sorry, but you will note when you read our handbook that rings are not allowed in our school."

"Why is that?" Liyana asked.

"Distraction."

Poppy gave her side a meaningful poke that translated, "Ask no more."

Walking back through the narrow, winding streets to find their car, Poppy said, "Great idea you had, bringing up Saroyan."

Liyana said, "Distraction? If I were wearing a giant cosmic cone on my head, would I have room to talk?"

VERY VERY DISTANT RELATIVES

*"Genetics" means we have
the same little bowties in our blood.*

The beginning of school felt awkward for Liyana.
She told her parents she didn't want to make any
judgments till a month had passed. Liyana said to
Rafik, "I would like to go to school with the donkeys in the field. To stand all day in the free air
with an open mouth. No bells ringing."

Rafik shrugged and said, "Too bad for you.
Maybe you'll like it soon." He said his school was
a "piece of cake."

One day when Liyana returned from school by
public bus, a lady she'd never seen before was sitting in their living room on the low couch. She
rocked back and forth in her long, blue village
dress, humming to herself.

Liyana nodded at her and went off to find her
mother, who was in the bedroom digging through
a box.

"Who's that lady in the living room?"

"I don't know. She showed up this morning and hasn't left. She doesn't speak a word of English. I kept hoping Poppy would come home for lunch today and help me out."

"Did you call him?" (Poppy had worked some magic with the phone company and gotten their phone installed within a week after all.)

"I did. He talked to her at length, but when I got back on, he said he hadn't the foggiest idea. She claimed to be his relative."

"So she's been sitting in there all day?"

"All day. I tried to feed her, but she waved the food away. I think she's shy."

"What are you looking for?"

"A packet of old pictures, the only ones Poppy has, to see if she might look through them and recognize people. Maybe that could give us a clue."

They found the pictures in a puffy envelope and the lady nodded for every one of them.

When Rafik came home after soccer practice, he said, "Who's that?"

"She's the sister of the Lost Pharoah," Liyana told him.

"Who's the Lost Pharoah?"

⁓

Rafik lit a stick of incense and wandered back and forth in the hall as if conducting a ritual. When

Poppy finally appeared, he sat with the woman and they talked a long time. She kept gesturing with her hands, but she didn't look upset.

In the kitchen Liyana washed spinach. Rafik had recently started cutting up onions, which their mother said was a great help to her. "That really irritates me," Liyana muttered, "that he does *one little thing* and you act so grateful. I do things every day!"

Poppy stepped in, shaking his head. "The woman's a mystery," he said. "I think she's a cousin of a cousin of a cousin who died before I was born and no one ever remembered to tell me about him. She lives in that little village on the lip of the mountain before you get to Nablus. I've hardly spent any time there, so I don't know any of the people she keeps mentioning."

"What does she want?"

"She wants me to buy her a dress."

"What?"

"It's an old custom. When someone returns from America, they buy every woman relative a bolt of cloth, for making a new dress. I guess it's to signify the success the traveler has had in America."

Liyana thought about the ten thousand relatives she'd met already.

"Everyone? Buy *everyone* dresses? Wouldn't that be impossible?"

"Of course. Especially if you had to buy them for people you'd never heard of before."

"So what are you going to do?"

"I'm going to drive her as far as Ramallah, where the fabric store is, and—I'll think of something. She can take the bus to her village from there."

━━◆━━

They were breathing the rich scent of grilled onions and keeping dinner warm in the oven by the time he returned. "Well?" they all spoke at once.

He grinned. "I took her to the fabric store, all right. I told her to go ahead and get out. She thought I was going to park the car and come back and pick out a huge piece of red velvet for her. But instead I drove around the block and came straight home."

Rafik said, "You *dumped* her?"

Poppy shrugged. "The old customs have to be changed somehow, you know? Little by little. I told her I thought it was a stupid custom while we were still sitting here—but she was relentless. So—as easily as she appeared in our house, I disappeared. She'll get over it."

"Won't she be mad at you?"

"Have I ever seen her before? Do I live my life

being scared of the anger of people I don't even know? I am related to Hassan who is related to Hani who is related to Naimeh who is related to Fatwa who is related to this glass of water who is related to the river Jordan who is related to John the Baptist—come on!"

ℛEMEMBER ME

I'm the snip of red thread caught on a twig.

Maybe the hardest thing about moving overseas was being in a place where no one but your own family had any memory of you. It was like putting yourself back together with little pieces.

At home in St. Louis even the man at the grocery store remembered the day a very young Liyana poked a ripe peach too hard and her finger went inside it. She shrieked and the neighborhood ladies buying vegetables laughed. Forever after when she came into his store, the grocer would say, "Be careful with my plums! Don't get too close to my melons!"

It was a little thing, of course, but it helped her be *somebody.*

In Jerusalem she was just a blur going by in the streets. The half-American with the Arab eyes in the navy blue Armenian school uniform. Who?

ℙAST AND PRESENT ROLLED INTO ONE

*Water came from the earth
and stories sprang from the stones.*

Sitti kept Liyana's bed in the village ready, the pillow puffed. She pointed it out each time the Abbouds arrived for their regular weekend visit, but Liyana turned her face away. Why was it such a *big deal?* Sitti stroked her face saying, *"Ya Habibi, Habibti,"* cackling like a giddy munchkin.

But one Saturday morning, Liyana felt ready, as if a compass had swung round inside her and held. "I'll stay at the village," she said. She told Poppy and her mother that they could return on Sunday night and pick her up.

They'd be there all Saturday afternoon themselves, as usual, which relieved Liyana. If Poppy were with her, he could *explain*—who was who, what was what. It was all a guessing game without him.

Liyana put her backpack in Sitti's corner. She had brought a collection of poems in case she had time to read, and her writing notebook, and her small troll with rhinestone eyes. Sitti might like it. She could already tell Sitti got excited over very little things.

Rafik had disappeared with Muhammad again. Aunt Amal arrived to take Liyana's mother out to the orchards and show her the almonds and olives ripening on the branches. They carried baskets for picking herbs—oregano and mint, sumac and thyme.

Sitti motioned Liyana and Poppy toward the mounded oven called the *taboon,* large enough to step into, beside her house. She showed Liyana how to slap bread dough into flat rounds and fling them onto a hot black stone to cook. When her long dress flapped dangerously close to the flames, Liyana stooped to pull it back, but Poppy said, "She knows what she's doing." Their other relatives had modern electric bread ovens now, but Sitti refused to touch them. She remained devoted to the old ways of doing things.

She pitched Liyana another ball of dough, inviting her to try it. Liyana copied her motions, kneading, slapping, and swinging the dough high in the air as she'd seen pizza makers do in Italian restaurants back home. Sitti's loaves were perfectly round, but Liyana's bread looked like Australia. Sitti helped her shape and reroll.

By the time the hot breads were placed on a white cotton towel on the table to cool, Poppy had fallen asleep on top of Sitti's bed like a boy. Sitti leaned over him for a minute, as if she were examining her baby closely. Then she whispered to Liyana and gestured that they should leave him alone. Liyana was thinking, *So much for my translator.*

But it turned out she didn't need him so badly after all. Sitti lifted a tall clay jug onto her head and motioned Liyana to hike with her down the dirt road. They charged off into the breeze. Sitti kept glancing at Liyana's face as if to check on her. *Was she happy? Did she like this?* Sitti waved her arm at the expansive view across the valleys and hills. She blew a kiss to the air, which helped Liyana take a deeper breath herself. Liyana could skip if she wanted to. She could twirl in a circle with her arms out to feel dizzy.

No one watched them or acted formal. Liyana felt as invisible and happy as she used to feel coasting on her bike.

They passed the telephone operator's house and he waved at them through the open door. He had a switchboard in front of him with wires and holes, just like the switchboards in old American movies. They passed a few lone houses sitting off by themselves under gnarled trees. They passed a cemetery and Sitti turned her face away. Liyana noticed there were no words on any of the white gravestones.

Then they came to the spring, where water

gathered in a shining pool by the roadside. Sitti filled her hand and let Liyana drink from it. She'd never drunk from anybody else's hand before. The water tasted crisp. Then Sitti filled the jug slowly from a pipe jutting out of a ledge. Poppy had said the women still preferred this fresh "earth water" to the water that came from faucets. Sitti placed a thick cloth pad on her head and heaved the full jug back up there, to carry back to the house. Once the jug was in place, she balanced it without using her hands. She motioned to Liyana. *Did Liyana want to try carrying it?* Liyana jumped back. She couldn't even carry a peach on her head!

After delivering the water home and snapping green beans into a big pot to steam with a cinnamon stick, Sitti took Liyana to meet a neighbor who was stringing orange beads on nylon thread. The woman opened a cupboard to show Liyana dozens of lovely necklaces hanging on nails. She urged her to choose one. Liyana didn't wear necklaces herself, but selected a turquoise one strung with antique Palestinian coins. She could hide the necklace till her mother's birthday. The woman kept song sparrows in small wicker cages and gave Liyana two fat olive oil soaps to take home to her mother, too. She hugged Liyana good-bye.

Later Liyana realized how many things they had all communicated without trading any words.

Toward evening, when Rafik had returned sweaty from playing with his cousins in the fields and their mother had returned sunburned, happily stocked with a year's worth of herbs and some miniature embroideries to practice on, and Poppy had awakened from his second nap, they sat together on floor cushions by Sitti's bed cracking almonds into a wooden bowl. Liyana leaned against Sitti's shoulder so she could reach the bowl.

Sitti kept Poppy busy translating. She related her dreams as if they were news reports, staring into Liyana's face as Poppy spoke. "The other night I dreamed that a relative named Salim who died long ago came and asked me to accompany him to Mecca. I was so afraid. I want to go to Mecca, but not with somebody dead. I thought he would take me with him to the next world and make *me* die."

But then?

"When I woke up I saw that ugly cat sitting in my window, so I knew I was still alive."

Sitti popped two almonds into Rafik's mouth when he laughed and then she left the room to arrange the green beans and stuffed squash they were having for dinner on big trays.

Poppy leaned toward his family and said, "You'll notice Sitti's stories don't always hang together. She has no logical sense of cause and effect. Anyway, in this part of the world, the past and present are often rolled into one."

All the uncles were away at another village that day for a big meeting about land problems. The aunts had gone to Bethlehem to help a distant cousin prepare for her wedding. Liyana liked having fewer people around.

Poppy said he was afraid to buy Sitti a bus ticket for the pilgrimage to Mecca, because he really did think she might die soon afterward.

Why?

Sitti was back in the room by now, listening to them talk English and nodding her head. She said the squash would be cool enough to eat as soon as two birds crossed in the sky. Poppy didn't even blink. He just kept talking.

"Sometimes when a person looks forward to something for such a long time, it keeps them alive. Then when they accomplish it—*boom*." He studied such subjects. He said the old people he'd been seeing in the hospital here were incredibly "durable" for their advanced ages. "Lots of them are waiting for a true, independent Palestine, too. They're not going to give up when they're this close."

Sitti collected the almond shells in her skirt and went outside.

Liyana kept considering what Poppy said

about hopes being accomplished.

"Like you coming back to Jerusalem, Poppy?"

"I hope not."

⸻

At the last minute Liyana begged Rafik to spend the night in the village with her. He wouldn't care that he didn't have a toothbrush or change of clothes. "Listen," she hissed, "if I'm going to be out here pretending I understand what's going on, at least you could be with me." He agreed. He was really having fun here. The boys didn't do as many chores as the girls did, which irritated Liyana again. She felt like ordering them to go chop wood or mulch the trees.

Their parents left them after the big delicious dinner and two rounds of hot tea with mint and sugar. Sitti said she could read their fortunes in the tea leaves in the sugary bottoms of their cups. The tea leaves had their own alphabets and conveyed messages once the tea was gone.

Liyana felt so tired and chilly she wished she could curl up like a mouse in a hole. The minute the sun went down, the temperature in the stone rooms plummeted.

Rafik and Liyana looked hard at one another as the sound of their parents' car disappeared down the mountain. They were sleeping in the same room with Sitti, who took many minutes to unroll her gigantic pouchy belt, which doubled as a pocket. She emptied it of coins, a few crumpled money bills, a giant key, some loose buttons, and a pink comb, lining her treasures on a table. She wore her white pajamas under her clothes so she wasn't shy at all to slip her dress off right in front of them. Liyana took her own pajamas into the bathroom to change.

They slept on three skinny beds in a row, like in a dormitory. Sometimes Aunt Saba or Aunt Lena slept here, too. Sitti's bed had a big dent in the metal headboard. Poppy had asked her about it and she said the Israeli soldiers did it one day when they were in a bad mood.

Sitti muttered to herself after the lights were out.

"What is she saying?" Rafik whispered.

"You think I know?"

"Do you think she's praying?"

"No. It sounds more like a conversation."

"With who?"

"Did you know she believes in angels and dreams?"

Long silence.

He was fading, his voice slower.

"I hope—she doesn't dream—we're monsters."

MAD

What good is a mouth
if it won't open when you need it to?

Sometimes people carried anger around for years, in a secret box inside their bodies, and it grew tighter like a hardening knot. The problem with it getting tighter and smaller was that the people did, too, hiding it. Liyana had seen this happen, even in elementary school. Somebody wasn't fair to someone, and the hurt person just held it in. By the end of the year they had nearly disappeared.

But other people responded differently. They let their anger grow so large it ate them up—even their voices and laughter. And still they couldn't get rid of it. They forgot where it had come from. They tried to shake the anger loose, but no one liked them by now.

Liyana wondered if the person who could let it out, the same size it was to begin with, was luckiest.

In Jerusalem so much old anger floated around, echoed from fading graffiti, seeped out of cracks. Sometimes it bumped into new anger in the streets. The air felt stacked with weeping and raging and praying to God by all the different names.

———

One afternoon, Liyana walked over to Bassam's spice shop to buy coriander for her mother. She needed a purpose to start feeling at home. So she'd actually begged her mother for an errand. Bassam smiled to see Liyana again.

His shop was a flurry of good smells—jars, barrels, small mountains of spicy scent. Bassam weighed whatever you wanted on an antique scale that looked as if it came straight from the Bible. He put weights on one side of the scale and a large spoonful of coriander on the other. Then he poured it through a paper cone into a brown bag and folded the top over twice. He said, "So how are you doing over here? Are you finding your way?"

He gave her some fresh cardamom seeds still in their pods as a present.

She pointed at his elephant-god poster. "I read about Ganesha," she said.

He brightened and said, "He's my friend!"

They were talking about the Armenian sector and the best music stations on the radio when a Jewish man in a *yarmulke* walking by the shop addressed Liyana loudly in Hebrew.

Of course she didn't understand him. She

didn't even realize he was talking to *her*. But Bassam motioned to her to turn.

"What?" she said, and the man switched over to English.

"Why you bother with this animal?" he said, pointing to Bassam. "Be careful. Don't trust animals. Go to better stores in our part of town," so she knew he thought she was Jewish.

He probably didn't care that Bassam spoke very good English.

Liyana's legs started shaking. Her mouth opened wide and puffed out nothing. She felt feverish. She could have fainted on the ground.

The man said one more thing. "Be smart." Then he turned and walked away. Satisfied.

Later Liyana wished she had chased him through the streets and hit him with her little spice bag. She could have swung it into his face till coriander clouded up his eyes.

Bassam didn't say a word. He turned away and busied himself brushing spice crumbs off his table.

All the way home the words she hadn't said kept crying out inside her. "I'm an animal, too! Oh, I'm so proud to be an animal, too!"

She couldn't tell Poppy. She felt she had betrayed him.

What, she wondered, would Sitti have said?

Sitti might have howled like a coyote.

ℛAFIK'S WISHES

He wished for a whole basket of
yellow pomelo fruits,
sweeter than grapefruits,
to eat by himself.

A German archaeologist was coming over for dinner. Rafik, starving as usual, flitted around their rooms saying, "I wish she'd hurry up. I wish I wish I wish."

"Bro, you're always wishing," Liyana said. She was reading about the old kings and queens of England for her history class. Now *there* was an unhappy group.

Rafik wished he could do his homework sitting straight up in the salt of the Dead Sea. He wished he could dig a hole so deep, he'd find a lost city. Or a scroll.

He wished someone would lower him into a well. When Poppy was a boy, he'd been lowered into a village well on ropes because his aunts and uncles wanted to know what was down there.

Inside the musty hole, Poppy discovered secret shelves and shallow corridors dug into its sides above the water level. He shone his light on ancient clay jars. Maybe they'd been lined up there from biblical times.

Poppy lifted out a deep blue vessel with a wide round mouth and a clay stopper. Small dried-up carob seeds rattled around inside.

Dozens of village people came by to see it that night. "How many jars are down there?" they asked him.

"Hundreds."

They had a town meeting about it. What should they do?

Poppy kept shivering inside. What if he had seen bones? Skeletons and skulls?

And why did the ancestors hide their jars inside a well, anyway? Maybe the jars were filled with precious oils back then. Maybe the well was a secret hiding place in case of invasion.

The villagers decided not to tell anybody. If they told, no telling what would happen—already the countryside teemed with jeeps and foreigners and curious expeditions.

Poppy said he could never look at a well in the same way again. He went back to his own family house in Jerusalem and started wondering what might be buried inside the *walls*.

All this made Rafik want to *discover* something.

"It's part of your heritage," Poppy told him. "Dig, dig, dig."

Finally the archaeologist appeared, smelling faintly of perspiration, and they dove into their cucumber-mint soup. She wore a khaki shirt and a gold neck-lace charm shaped like a shovel. She told about the project she'd been digging on for ten years, in the desert near Jericho. "It takes *patience*," she said, looking at Liyana as if she didn't have any. How did she know?

Rafik asked her if he could apply for a job.

She didn't laugh. She said he could come out on a holiday sometime and she'd find tasks for him to do. He could carry buckets or sift through shards. He could be an apprentice. Then Liyana started getting interested, too.

"Just today," the archaeologist said, "we uncov-ered a rich cache of pottery chips painted blue."

Liyana and Rafik stared at Poppy meaning-fully.

Later, when the adults had a boring discussion about what was wrong with the world these days, Rafik wished they'd be quiet. He preferred talk-ing about *bones*. He'd told Liyana that whenever adults started talking about "the world," the air grew heavy. Liyana was impressed with him some-times. She agreed.

They wandered outside onto the balcony, just the two of them, and sat close together in the evening breeze facing west. Even though the Mediterranean loomed far out of sight, beyond hills, neighborhoods and coastal towns, Liyana imagined she could feel sea breezes brushing her face. Sometimes it seemed they were coming from another world.

"Do you like it here?" she asked Rafik.

To her greatest surprise, he answered, "Yes."

He hoped they would stay here forever.

He liked it so much more than he had expected to.

He didn't even miss playing baseball in the back lot anymore. Soccer was better. And he *certainly* didn't miss his piano lessons.

For the first time, Liyana felt totally alone.

$\mathcal{F}$RIENDS

How long does a friend take?

One afternoon Rafik was working on definitions for his English vocabulary list and asked Liyana, "When does a person go from being an *acquaintance* to a friend? Where is the line?"

Liyana said, "Hmmmm. The line. Well, do you have any what-you-would-call-friends here yet?"

He thought about it. "Sure. Well, maybe. This guy Ismael in my class is my friend already. I might have more than that. Don't you?"

Liyana said, "Hmmmmmm." He hated when she was in this mood.

Rafik persisted. "Could becoming a friend take just a few minutes? So someone would be your *acquaintance* very briefly? Or could you skip that step and go straight to friend? And can it go the other way, too? Like, can you be friends first, then become only acquaintances later? If you don't see each other anymore?"

Liyana wanted to think her friends back home would always be her friends. She said, "I think friendships are—irrevocable. Once you're friends you can't turn back."

"What's *irrevocable?* Another vocabulary word?"

Something bad was happening today. A chain of Israeli military tanks lumbered up the road. Liyana stared out the window glumly. "It looks ugly out there."

The silver-lining theory made her think they should do something to change the mood in the air. It wasn't hard to convince Rafik to drop his pencil. Having seen Imm Janan, their landlord's wife, take the bus toward Ramallah thirty minutes before, they went downstairs to their stony, grassless backyard and unhinged the door to the chicken coop for the first time. The chickens stepped out, at first tentatively, then wildly, as if they'd been loosed from prison. They flapped their wings up and down. The happy hens scrabbled in the dirt for bugs and worms. Were there worms here, like back home? Did the whole world have worms?

Liyana stooped to see a chicken gobble a plump green caterpillar. It wasn't long, thin, or brownish like an earthworm. Rafik interrupted her reverie by screaming, "It's leaving! One of the hens has flown away!"

The hens were so fat, Liyana felt astonished

they could fly. But one had indeed just taken off, over the whitewashed wall. Rafik and Liyana left the others, unlatched the gate, and went running after the vagrant.

Down the road, past the looming cedar trees that looked as if they might once have circled a cemetery, the chicken did a mixed fly-flap-and-skid routine. She bounced onto the earth, taking off again so quickly, they couldn't catch up with her. Rafik waved his arms as he ran. Liyana tried to keep up. "What will we do? She's too fast!"

They lost sight of her at the gate to the refugee camp. Liyana thought she had gone inside. "Oh no!" she wailed. "What if someone catches her and eats her?"

But Rafik thought she had passed the camp and was heading down through low bushes and scraggly trees toward the runways at the abandoned airport. "She thinks she's a jet plane!" he yelled. "She's taking off!"

Breathless, they ran around the perimeter of the airport, now strung with barbed-wire fences and signs that said NO ENTRY in English, Arabic, and Hebrew. "Do you see her in there?" Liyana called. But they saw only cracked pavement and dust.

Would the chicken come home automatically at nightfall, like a homing pigeon or one of those movie dogs that walked a thousand miles by secret radar?

"What if the *other* chickens have flown over the fence by now and Imm Janan has returned and the soldiers are circling our yard?" Liyana asked.

Rafik said what Poppy always said. "You're a dramatist."

But then something great happened. Walking back toward home past the refugee camp, Liyana stared over the clutter of wires, posts, and sawhorses that made up its jagged boundary, and there, among clotheslines and ramshackle dwellings, she spotted one tall redheaded boy with their chicken cradled in his arms. He was petting it, his head down close to its face.

"Hey!" Liyana called. "Hello! *Marhaba!*"

The boy looked up and grinned. He called out something in Arabic that Liyana and Rafik couldn't understand. Then he walked out the front gate of the camp and said, shyly, "Hello? He is—your bird?"

"*She,*" Rafik said. "She is—girl bird." Liyana couldn't imagine being technical at a moment like this. She felt so relieved to see the wayward chicken again that she put her hand out enthusiastically to shake the boy's free hand.

"*Ana Liyana,*" she said, using the Arabic phrase for "I am Liyana" that pleased her, since it echoed so neatly.

The boy said, "*Ana Khaled.*"

Rafik said, "*Ana Rafik.*"

"You speak—Arabic?" Khaled asked.

Rafik answered, "Not yet. You speak English?"

Khaled said, "Maybe."

Liyana and Rafik laughed. Rafik asked, "What's *maybe* in Arabic?"

"*Yimkin.*"

A younger girl with puffy red curls similar to Khaled's ran up to them. She wore a loose pair of pants that looked like bloomers, and a pink T-shirt with Donald Duck on it. Khaled said, "This—Nadine. My—brother."

"No—your sister!" said Rafik.

The chicken was trying hard to get away again. One taste of freedom had inspired it. Khaled seemed happy to hand it to Liyana.

"You—tourist?"

"No," Liyana said. "We live in that house." She pointed up the road. "Can you come over sometime and visit us?"

Khaled looked at his sister, who looked hopeful. "You are—*Araby*?"

This gave Liyana a chance to say her favorite new Arabic phrase. "*Nos-nos.*" Which meant, half-half. Somehow it sounded better in Arabic.

Khaled and Nadine liked this a lot. They walked up the road with them, reaching over to pet the chicken as they went.

At the back gate to the house, they all shook

hands and laughed again. Nadine and Khaled pointed at the other chickens flapping around the yard and said, *"Alham'dul-Allah!"* which meant, Praise be to God!, and which Arab people used for nearly everything.

"Come back!" Rafik said to them. "Come over soon!"

After Liyana and Rafik had caught the rest of the chickens with great difficulty and latched them inside their pen, they dissolved in a flurry of giggles just as Imm Janan stepped off the bus out front with her loaded shopping bags. Liyana said to Rafik, "Khaled and Nadine. They're nice. Now you tell me. Are they acquaintances or friends?"

INVISIBLE

Her mountain of notebooks hid
under four folded black sweaters.

Since his childhood, Poppy had been wishing for a hat that would make him invisible.

Where would he go if he had one? Where would he travel?

"I would travel in and out of the rooms where big decisions are made," he said very seriously. "I would listen to things people say when they think no outsider is listening. When they make decisions that will affect other people. I would be their conscience, tugging at them quietly. And there would have been peace in Jerusalem long ago."

Rafik said, "I would be like Superman. I would fight crime and evil forces and no one would even see me."

"It's a hat," Liyana told him. "It's not wings."

Their mother got all dreamy when Poppy said, "*You* put the hat on now—where will you go?" She would sit at the feet of great musicians and opera singers as they practiced. She would soak up their trills and scales, their perfect pitches. Or she would ride around in Mother Teresa's pocket. She would shadow great saints and learn how to do selfless things for the world.

"Mom," Liyana said. "You're doing that already."

"No," she said, smiling. "I'm only doing it for you. I could do more."

What would Liyana do? She'd pop that invisible hat on her head, go to the airport, and get on a plane headed back to the United States. She would sit in First Class. She would curl up on somebody's food tray with the real silverware and the china plates.

Rafik said, "Let's hope the hat has shrinking powers, too, and makes you tiny, the size of a salt shaker. Otherwise that tray's going to *tip*."

Later Liyana would float around their old neighborhood, invisible as tree pollen, and see if anyone mentioned her.

Maybe she was completely forgotten.

She would drift in through Mrs. Mannino's window and hang suspended over the kitchen sink while she washed dishes. Liyana still remembered what Mrs. Mannino's coffee cups looked like, white with painted shafts of wheat tied together. She and Claire and Kelly Mannino drank spiced cider out of them.

She would fly into Peachy Helen's bedroom

where Peachy was buttoning her satiny housecoat, and whisper, "Lavender's blue, dilly-dilly, lavender's green." She'd click her invisible fingers, reciting rhymes Peachy taught her when she was very little. "Jack be nimble, Jack be quick, Jack jump over the candlestick." Where was Jack now? Was his candle all burned out?

$\mathcal{N}$O MORE MEAT

*I will speak the language of animals
and wipe their blood from my teeth.*

One day, when Poppy had taken the bus to work so
Mrs. Abboud could pick up Rafik after soccer practice, Liyana rode along and they stopped first at a
butcher shop to buy chicken for dinner. It was the
first time Liyana had entered one here. She followed
her mother into the stinky store crowded with
stacked shelves of crooked stick and wire cages.

The chickens in the cages were alive and
cramped, jabbering, in their boxy prisons. They
were not headless body parts on Styrofoam plates
wrapped neatly in anonymous plastic in a refriger-
ated grocery compartment. They were not thighs,
drumsticks, and breasts.

Downy feathers from their soft chests stuck
between the bars of the cages. Liyana pulled a
feather free and smoothed her finger over it. The
chickens were breathing, chattering, humming.
They were *looking at her. At each other.* And lifting
their wings.

Her mother took a deep breath and said,

"Wahad, min-fadlack." One, please. Poppy had taught her the necessary phrases to get through a day. She seemed to be avoiding eye contact with the chickens herself. The butcher would let you pick your own chicken if you wanted to, but Liyana's mother didn't.

Turning her back on the scene, Mom stared into the street as the butcher plunged his hand into a cage toward one very upset white chicken. Liyana didn't want to see any of it either, but she couldn't stop looking. He grabbed it roughly by its legs and it screamed. Then he swung it abruptly, upside down, so it went into shock and dangled limply a moment before he plopped it onto his bloody counter, grabbed the big knife, and slashed off its head.

Liyana couldn't help herself. "No!" She waved her arm as if to slap him.

Her mother gripped her shoulder. "Oh, stop."

Liyana's eyes filled up.

She had eaten chicken hundreds of times, but she had never witnessed this scene before. She thought, *It happens over and over and over.*

The chicken's body trembled and writhed after the head was severed, then fell still. The butcher turned to plunge the body into a steaming pot, then deftly stripped the feathers off, wrapping the body in white paper.

Did Liyana just imagine the other chickens grew much   quieter for a moment? That a sheen of horror hung in the air? Each time a new person stepped into the shop, the chickens must worry.

My turn.

People might say chickens couldn't worry, but something sensitive in their bodies must know.

At that moment, full of the rotten stench of the shop, Liyana's poor mother handing her money over to the butcher, not liking it either but saying *"Shookran,"* in a tight voice, Liyana became a vegetarian.

Her mother cooked the chicken's body with tarragon leaves that had traveled in a plastic bag all the way from St. Louis. She served the chicken's body over rice. Liyana took only rice.

"Why aren't you eating any?" Poppy asked.

Rafik shouted, "Liyana's on a diet! Someone told her she has pudgy cheeks!"

Liyana held her fork straight up like a scepter. "It's dead," she announced loudly. "And it didn't want to die."

RAFIK'S ESSAY ABOUT LIYANA

My sister is a very unusual person and I don't think she would mind to hear me call her that. She loves to read and walks around talking to herself. Or she can stay quiet for a really long time staring at something like an egg.

She has a very primitive hairdo and wears mostly the same three shirts and blue jeans or one skirt over and over. She says she will never cut her hair or wear makeup in her life and if I paid her one hundred dollars she wouldn't paint her fingernails red. Actually she looks younger than she is, which is almost fifteen.

She doesn't need lots of things to make her happy. In fact, money is one of her least favorite subjects. She says one thing she fears about growing older is that she will have to think about money and she doesn't want to. I told her I would be her banker. Personally I like to think a lot about cars, what features they offer and what they cost, but my sister will only talk about where they GO. She doesn't want to know anything else. I'm also better on the computer than she is, but we don't have one over here yet. Our father sold it when we moved. My sister does not want to know any of the fancy programs, she only wants to know HOW TO TYPE.

My sister and I don't fight much, but sometimes she gets mad at me like when we were still in St. Louis and I found this list she made called "Against Growing Up" that included things like "They forget what it felt like to see a rabbit for the first time" and "They are always busy and sticking to schedules." I stuck it on the refrigerator with a magnet where both our parents read it. They thought she meant them.

I probably shouldn't even talk about it now.

Rafik Abboud

TWENTY-NINTH DAY OF SCHOOL

> *I wish I could press my mind*
> *as flat and smooth as I press my shirt.*

"People talk about their first day of school or their last day, but they never talk about their twenty-ninth day," Liyana said to Rafik. They were sitting on the short wall in the backyard cracking pumpkin seeds between their teeth, tossing shells into the lilies.

Liyana had been counting. Her twenty-nine-day Armenian friends acted very kind to her. They seemed genuinely glad she was among them, as if grateful for a newcomer to liven things up. They liked it when she mimicked popular songs from the radio in the schoolyard. Liyana had never been shy to sing in front of people. Why was singing any more embarrassing than talking was?

She'd learned they were supposed to stand formally when a teacher entered the classroom. She tried clicking her heels together, like Dorothy in *The Wizard of Oz*. She learned that Armenian boys are dashing and have a mischievous glint in their eyes. A boy named Kevork said, "We heard Americans are wild. Are you wild?"

By the twenty-ninth day, Liyana's papers had proper headings, and her navy blue uniform had lost its bright gleam, its sharp pleat. She kept her silver ring in her pocket and slipped it on every day as she left school. On the twenty-ninth day, she forgot to remove it in the morning and the "directress" snapped at her as the girls stood in line for their "daily checkup."

On the twenty-ninth morning, the teacher called roll by last names only: Hagobian, Melosian, Tembeckjian, Yazarian, Zakarian. Liyana was last—*Abboud*—even though alphabetically she should have been first. She was the P.S. in the roll book. Her new friends added "ian" to her name to tease her.

On the twenty-ninth morning, her class discussed the isosceles triangle as if it had just been invented. Babgen Bannayan got in trouble for not bringing in his history research on the Colossus of Rhodes for the third day in a row.

Mr. Bedrosian, the English teacher (though he liked his students to call him a "professor" as if they were in college), wore his gray suit, the only suit he seemed to have besides his black one. Small threads dangled from the hem and the buttons. He could use some mending. He spoke about William Blake and John Keats with *veneration* in his voice, though Liyana wished he would pick somebody a little more modern to talk about soon. Liyana wondered if he lived alone.

On the twenty-ninth day a funeral procession passed slowly beneath the open classroom windows. The students heard the low voices of the mourners growing louder and louder as they approached. Liyana didn't realize what the sound was at first since she'd never heard it before. Everyone in the classroom was silently reading. She stood to look out the windows and stared right down into the face of the first dead person she'd ever seen.

A woman's petite body wrapped in white was being carried in an open coffin high above the heads of the mourners. Her head looked small, precise, with pale wavy hair and closed eyes in purplish skin. Liyana felt magnetized. Had the dead woman studied geometry? Did she have a happy life?

Mr. Bedrosian said, "You will please take your seat, Miss Abboud."

By the twenty-ninth day, Liyana knew exactly where to go for lunch, either out into the sunny walled courtyard to buy sesame bread from the vendor with the huge tray on his head—she ate it with hard-boiled eggs and cheese and apples—or home with her new friends to eat their mothers' folded spinach pies. Here, in the slowest country on earth, the students had a whole hour-and-a-half lunch break.

Or Liyana could stroll by herself into the streets of old Jerusalem beyond the Armenian Quarter to walk among the shops. She pretended she lived in a different time. She squinted her eyes. She liked the *falafel* sandwiches at a place called Abu Musa's Falafel House.

On the twenty-ninth day, Liyana gave directions to French tourists. She carried an old lady's giant sack of onions up some steep and crooked steps.

On the twenty-ninth day she did something slightly bad. She didn't come back into school the minute the bell rang after their long lunch. She couldn't stop thinking about the dead woman. Had she died suddenly? There certainly were a lot of people in her funeral march.

Liyana lay on a low wall outside the school, her head swimming in a pool of sun, body hidden by a tangled vine from anyone who might approach. She thought, *How close this peaceful wall is every day while we are trapped inside.*

Voices from the classrooms reached across the hedge. Her Arabic teacher on the kindergarten floor hit a short stick on the back of a chair for rhythm, teaching the little ones another useless sentence. *Please hand me the bellows for my fire.* "And who has a bellows anymore?" Liyana wanted to shout. How many bellows would they ever have to ask for?

Liyana wanted to say useful things: *Tree, stump, soup, cloud.* She wanted to say, *No way! Let's get out of here!*

On the twenty-ninth day, she nodded an apology when she entered late. She could still feel the quiet leaves unfurling inside her mouth.

The kindergarten students stared at her in wonder when she appeared daily for fifty minutes after lunch and stuffed herself into one of their miniature wooden desks. All the little faces turned in her direction. She felt like a giant lost from her homeland. They wore white pinafores. Their cheeks were glowing and peachy. They must have thought she was a very slow learner.

Sometimes, when it was her turn to answer and she stayed silent, they whispered hints to help her. She couldn't even tell them how grateful she was. The teacher, who reeked of sour ash, rapped the tiny backs of his students' hands when they made a mistake. Their rosy faces puffed up with tears. He didn't hit Liyana, even after the twenty-ninth day's tardiness, though she made more mistakes than they did. Did he fear she'd knock him over backward? Well, she would.

Liyana had already started drafting a letter to the editor for the daily English/Arabic newspaper in Jerusalem, pronouncing such behavior primitive and unacceptable. Would the school expel her if it got printed?

On the twenty-ninth day of school Liyana decided she could forget about Jackson if Atom, the boy who sat across the aisle from her in regular class, smiled at her a little more.

WHAT YOU CAN BUY IN JERUSALEM

I keep my eye on
the mother-of-pearl dove earrings
in the shop window,
waiting for them to fly away.

You can buy gray Arabic notebooks with soft covers just the right size for folding once and sticking in your pocket. Liyana's class used them at school and she'd started using them for her own writings. She liked how the place for a "title" was on what English speakers would call the back. She even started writing in one back to front.

You can buy miniature Christmas cards that say "Flowers from the Holy Land" and include a flattened burst of wildflowers. The blue flowers turn out best, pressed.

Postcards show the Old City behind its golden wall and the inside of the Dome of the Rock through a fish-eye lens and the giant water jug at the Kfar Kana Church and the craggy olive trees in the Garden of Gethsemane and the mosaic floor of Hisham's

Palace. Liyana found some dusty black-and-white postcards at the American Colony Hotel gift shop that said "Palestine" instead of Israel and she bought them, too. They showed camels, steep cliffs, the skinny Jordan River, donkeys, and Bedouins in tents. A crooked sign on the stationery store said, SPECIAL BIG GOODIES SALE GOING FAST AND NOW.

You can buy glass vases handblown in Hebron and olive-wood rosaries and creamy white mother-of-pearl star pins and shiny brocade from big bolts of cloth at Bilal's Tailor Shop. You'd almost never see anyone in the United States wearing clothes made of such cloth unless it was a high-society person or a Barbie doll.

Liyana liked to finger the rich brocade. Bilal gave her scraps from the ends of bolts. She had red and purple, gold and silver. She was learning to sew small pillows at home. She made one for her troll. Poppy had gone to school with Bilal's father long ago, so Bilal told Liyana she could have his shop when she got older. He said he wasn't planning to get married or have any children.

Why not?

Because I'm too ugly.

He wasn't ugly.

Liyana stared at him when he wasn't looking.

You can buy millions of little decorated cups, with tiny saucers, for Arabic coffee and tea.

You can buy painted Palestinian plates and roasted chickpeas and olive oil soap made in Nablus with a red camel on the package and saffron, that spice that costs a lot of money in American grocery stores, very cheaply. You can also buy vials of holy oil and fancy jars of water from the River Jordan (stamped: **For External Use Only**, so you don't get carried away and drink it) that has a Certificate of Authenticity in Arabic, German, and English on the side of the box. It also says the Bishop of Jerusalem of the Arab Episcopal Church authorizes it. Liyana thought you were supposed to dab it on your temples if you were having an extremely hard day.

You can buy sweets and treats, gooey, sticky, honey-dipped, date-stuffed fabulous Arabic desserts on giant round silver trays. Some have layers of sweetened, toasted shredded wheat. Some are packed with white cheese or walnuts or pistachio nuts. The bakery shops have little low stools and low tables out in front of them. Liyana liked *katayef* best—a small, folded-over pancake stuffed with cinnamon and nuts and soaked in syrup. She took home three half-moons of *katayef* in a white cardboard box.

If you asked the price of anything, the shop-keeper would say, *"For you...."* and pretend he was giving you a great deal, but you knew he would say that for anybody.

$\mathscr{D}$ ISPLAY

Is the whole world really looking?

Liyana combed her long wet hair out on the open front balcony of their house where the breeze smelled sweet as olive oil. Up the road, white sheets ballooned like parachutes from neighbors' rooftop clotheslines. She wondered if Jackson had kissed another girl in the same movie theater by now. She tried to remember the way his crisp shirt collar stood up against his neck. She wondered if Claire had a new best friend. Her recent letter, on a blue air-letter sheet, didn't say so. Far off, Liyana could see a girl with red hair running at the refugee camp, carrying something large in her arms. Was it Nadine? Then Poppy called her back inside.

"Please," he said urgently. "Don't be so public about it. You're making a *display*. Comb your hair in the bathroom. Comb it in your own bedroom! Don't do it out there where all the taxis and shepherds can see you."

Sometimes he sounded as if she were breaking his heart.

Liyana's father still talked about shepherds as if they were everywhere. Now and then an ancient shepherd in a dusty brown cloak would pass Sitti's house up in the village, tapping a wooden cane against the stones. He didn't even turn his head to notice Liyana and Rafik staring at him from the doorway. All he cared about were his goats and sheep with painted red or blue bottoms so he could find them if they got mixed up with other animals. Maybe his own dusty memories followed him up the path.

But Poppy acted as if their modern apartment on the Ramallah road was still surrounded by shepherds. Poppy saw what *used* to be there.

Maybe, Liyana thought, he's afraid a shepherd will fall in love with me and come ask for my hand. I will never *ever* give my hand away. Even the phrase disgusted her.

Sometimes she heard her father say, "We are *Americans,*" to his relatives—when she walked the village streets alone just for exercise, pretending she was giving Jackson a tour, or when she flipped the round dial on Sitti's radio, or when she slouched in the corner of Sitti's room with a book in front of her face.

Americans?

Even Poppy, who was always an Arab before?

Of course there was never any question about

their mother being an American, but Rafik and Liyana walked a blurry line.

Liyana tipped from one side to the other.

The minute Poppy told her to stop combing her hair on the balcony, she toppled onto the American side, thinking, *If I were at home on a beach I could run up and down the sand with just a bathing suit on and no one would even notice me. I could wear my short shorts that I didn't bring and hold a boy's hand in the street without causing an earthquake. I could comb my wet hair in public for a hundred dumb years.*

$\mathcal{L}$IT UP

*She turned a corner
and everything changed.*

"You keep getting me in trouble," Liyana's friend Sylvie sighed on one of their lunchtime walks from school to the *falafel* stand. That morning Liyana had urged Sylvie to defy the "directress" who ordered her to remove a tortoise-shell clip from her hair. Liyana whispered, "This is getting ridiculous! Say no!" and Sylvie peeped, "No" in a thin voice that caused her to get a detention note. She would have to stay after school.

Sylvie pointed to the Armenian man with giant keys dangling from his belt who locked the door of the Armenian Quarter every night at 10 P.M. He opened it again at 6 A.M.

Sylvie said, "Last week, I was running up the street fast from a movie at the British Library. This man saw me coming, but the time on the clock was 10:01 and he locked the door right before I reached it. He would not let me come in! I had to walk to the house of my aunt in the new city to sleep—a long walk in the dark! My mother was so mad. She said I can't go to movies anymore."

Liyana marched up to the man and asked, "Why do you need to keep that door locked, anyway? No one *else's* neighborhood is locked."

He stared at her as if she were a thief digging for secrets. "Security," he said gruffly, and turned away. She hated that word. Now Sylvie was embarrassed and walking back to school early without her. Maybe it was an excuse. She still had some leftover homework to do.

Just outside the Quarter's huge door, on the path to Jaffa Gate, sat the Sandrouni family's famous ceramics shop. Poppy had pointed it out to Liyana as a landmark. The Sandrounis painted beautiful tiles, lamps, and bowls with blue interiors, and scenes of Jerusalem—domes, towers, and pointy trees.

Liyana, feeling suddenly bereft without her friend, saw a crowd of tourists heading in there, so she turned and followed them, as if she were part of their group. No one noticed her.

The tourists began buying like crazy. They pointed and flipped credit cards, speaking a language Liyana couldn't identify—Danish? Dutch?

Liyana's eyes fell upon a small, shapely green lamp, exactly the color of the green grass she missed back home in the United States—who ever thought about grass when you had it? Who ever thought about missing a *color*? The lamp would be perfect for reading in bed.

Then she looked at the price tag. She couldn't understand it because the writing was so fancy, like calligraphy. She motioned to a boy standing behind the counter with his arms folded, near the reams of tissue paper and stacks of cardboard boxes. He raised his eyebrows and walked over to her.

He smelled like cinnamon. Liyana thought he might be one or two years older than she was.

"Excuse me, how much does this cost? Can you read it?"

He stared at her school uniform, speaking English smoothly. "You are not—with them?"

He pointed to the group.

"I am not!"

"You are—with who?"

Then she felt like Crispin Crispian in that old children's book by Margaret Wise Brown, the dog who belonged to himself.

"I am with myself."

He smiled broadly. "I am also with myself," he said. "I like to be with—myself."

His hair rolled back cleanly as a wave at the beach.

"You do?"

"Almost always."

"You don't get tired of your own self?"

"Never."

"You don't get lonely for other people?"

He looked around the crowded shop. "How could I? Other people are everywhere."

They both laughed.

"Do you go to school?" Liyana asked him.

"Of course," he grinned. "I am a—scholar. I do my homework every day. But right now—I am—eating lunch."

"So am I!" she said. "I am eating lunch, too."

Neither of them had any food.

"By the way," he said, "I can't read this tag either."

He called over a member of the Sandrouni family, who quoted something equaling about sixty-five American dollars. Too much! Liyana still had to translate prices into dollars in her head for them to make sense to her.

"Thanks."

"Do you want it?" he asked her.

"Well, I want it—but I can't afford it. Maybe they'll have a sale."

The Sandrouni man placed his hand on the cinnamon boy's shoulder. "Has he been telling you stories? Has he promised to give all my precious cargoes away for half price?"

Liyana laughed and thanked them both and

stepped back outside toward Abu Musa's where little cakes of *falafel* were frying. Abu Musa slid her crispy planets of *falafel* into pockets of warm, fresh pita bread and Liyana bit down hard. She was starving.

That night at dinner she said, "Poppy, today I fell in love with a lamp."

INTERVIEWING SITTI

Prepare for an unexpected visitor heading toward your door.

Back in the United States, Liyana's classes had oral history assignments where they were supposed to go home and ask their oldest relatives or neighbors what the world was like long ago. *What did you eat? What did you do for recreation? How did your mother cure a headache?* They could write the answers down or tape them, then choose the most interesting parts and compose a paper.

Of course Liyana always picked Peachy Helen, but Peachy would protest. "Honey, you think I remember that far back? I barely remember what happened yesterday! Let's just forget about it and share some scones with lemon curd, what do you say?"

Liyana would open Peachy's dresser drawers, pulling out a silver bracelet engraved with tipis and canoes, and dusty powder puffs, trying to jar her memory.

Usually she'd end up having to talk to Frank,

their neighbor in blue overalls who specialized in car engines and organic farming methods. He didn't remember much about childhood, or he wouldn't tell. But Sitti *remembered everything*. She even remembered when a Turkish tribe rode south past Jerusalem and the children were told to lie down in ditches so they wouldn't be run over by horses.

The problem was Liyana could only have a deep conversation with Sitti if Poppy were present. In Arabic class at school, Liyana was just learning the colors—*fidda* for silver, *urjawaani* for purple.

Anyway, Sitti loved when Poppy was present. She rubbed the back of his hand till he looked uncomfortable. He had been her last of eight children, born when she was past the usual childbearing age.

One Saturday in the village, with a light rain falling softly outside, Liyana tested her cassette tape and plopped down on a floor mattress beside Sitti, who was cracking almonds again by her fire in the oil stove. Liyana slipped off her blue Birkenstocks. Sitti picked one up, turned it over, looked at its sole upside down and said in Arabic, "It's too fat."

Tell me a story.

"About what?" Sitti laughed. She offered

Liyana an apricot. *The whole world was a story. Stories were the only things that tied us to the ground!*

Because she knew Sitti liked the subject, Liyana asked for "a story about angels." Poppy looked dubious even as he translated. He thought angel talk was foolishness.

Sitti stared at Liyana's cassette recorder as if it were an animal that might bite her with its tiny teeth. A thread of faraway music floated past and vanished.

Sitti placed both hands over her own eyes, as if casting a spell on herself, and began speaking. "Your grandfather, my husband, who died so long ago already, used to come home with his pockets full of a plump kind of dates, not those thin, dried-up ones that make you thirsty even in your sleep. He would present them to me as if they were coins or golden bracelets. He knew I loved them very much. We would place them in a white bowl covered with a cloth in the cabinet and we would eat them one at a time and I am not ashamed to say we did not tell the children they were there. Because one hundred little children from everywhere were always passing through this house. And there would not have been enough of them to go around, you know? But also, we wanted them ourselves!" Sitti laughed her throaty laugh.

"So one day I was taking a nap as your grandfather traveled up to Galilee and an angel appeared in my dream and said she would give me some important advice, because she was an angel. 'How can I be sure of that?' I asked her. I can't believe I was so rude to an angel!

"She said, *I will soon appear to your husband, who is carrying luscious dates in his pockets and I will ask him to share them with me and he will not be able to say no. Check with him when he comes back. That will prove it. Now here's the advice*—and she gave it to me. So the minute he returned I said, 'Did you get dates?' and he looked sorrowful.

"'Yes,' he said, 'but as I was standing in the *souk*—the marketplace—a young girl with strange eyes came up to me and said, *Please sir, I beg you for the food you are carrying in your cloak,* and as she seemed to have some extra power to see through cloth, since the dates were not visible, I felt obliged to hand them over. Then I couldn't find any more to buy before I came home.'"

Liyana asked, "What was her advice?"

"What? Oh. Not to buy the cow. Someone was selling a cow just then. We never have many cows around here, you know. There's only one right now, down the road in Hossaini's courtyard. Most people like goat's milk better. But I always liked cow's milk better so I wanted your grandfather to buy a cow that was for sale in the next village. He didn't want to. He didn't like cow's milk. Also, cows need more to eat than goats. And he didn't want it tied up in our courtyard at night taking up all the room.

So we didn't buy it. Good thing! Because we heard it died only a few weeks later. So the angel saved us from trouble! And all we lost was—a few dates."

Sitti cleared her throat and smiled. She stared at Liyana meaningfully. Poppy was finishing his translation. He still looked dubious.

Leaning over to Liyana, Sitti stroked her hair, the way you'd pet a cat or dog. "Always listen to the angels who find you," she said. She placed two fingers in the center of Liyana's forehead and closed her eyes.

So Liyana closed hers, too.

Maybe this was a charm.

⸻

When Liyana's aunt had to go to the hospital because her legs swelled up, Sitti said they swelled "because she has such a big and heavy head."

When Poppy told her that had nothing to do with it, she said, "What do you know? Your head is normal sized."

If a bird pooped on a clean white sheet while flying over the clothesline, that meant bad luck.

But if it pooped on your head, that meant your first child would be a boy.

Sitti wouldn't wear socks because cold feet would help her live longer. She thought Liyana should stop wearing socks, but Liyana couldn't stand it.

Sitti perceived messages everywhere. *You will soon go on a long journey to a place hotter than this place. Beware of a bucket.*

Liyana liked this stuff. She made a whole new notebook for it.

Poppy said he became a doctor because he grew up with such superstitious people. "They drove me crazy," he told Liyana in private. "I had to balance them out."

"Do you believe in heaven?" Liyana asked Sitti on the day of their interview, and she answered quickly, "Of course. It's full of fresh fruit." They took a short break to slice three Jericho oranges in half and share them. Sitti closed her eyes when she swallowed. Then she bustled around the room, muttering, sweeping the windowsill with her short-handled broom, straightening the bags of rice and flour and sugar on her shelves. She pulled a few strands of long hair out of her pink comb.

"What's she saying now?" Liyana asked.

Poppy said, "I think she's reciting the bees passage from the Koran."

Liyana sang out, "Ho!" to get her attention again.

Sitti jumped. "Sit down!" Liyana begged her. "Please! *Min-fad-lick co'dy hone!*" It was one of the first phrases she'd learned.

Liyana asked Sitti to tell more about her dreams at night and she said, with a mournful expression, "I dream of all the hard times I had in this life. And how mean the Jewish soldiers act to us. They don't even know who we are! And I dream of the way I felt when my most beautiful and beloved son," she paused dramatically, staring at Poppy, "went so far away from me I couldn't even see the tip of his shadow."

Liyana's father liked this conversation less and less.

Sitti ordered Poppy to give money to the poor before she died and more money to the grave digger and the women who washed her body. She insisted the people who buried her should leave lots of space in her grave so she could sit up to talk to the angels. She didn't like to talk to anyone lying down.

Liyana laughed out loud, but Poppy stood up, rubbed his hands together over the fire, and said, "Let's do something else."

RAFIK'S ESSAY ON KHALED AND NADINE

We have some new friends who live at the refugee camp down the little road behind our house. They have a bicycle and we do not and sometimes they let us ride theirs. The tire is rubbing the fender. Poppy says we can get a bicycle soon. Liyana says she hopes we can get two. They caught our chicken when it flew away. It is not really ours but we act like it is. Khaled thinks we live in a very big house because their house has only two rooms. When we visit them, Nadine, his sister, makes us drink this red juice made from pomegranates which makes my mouth go into shock.

Sometimes they come over and watch Abu Janan's television with us. They don't have a television and we don't either. Abu Janan says it makes him happy when people fill up his rooms. Liyana likes ancient reruns of "I Love Lucy." She says Desi Arnaz and his cute accent remind her of Poppy. I like "Tarzan," who reminds me of Liyana. I wish Abu Janan had a Super Channel so we could pick up "Star Trek," my favorite American show. Liyana has no interest in "Star Trek" at all. She hates the jumpsuits the characters wear and says their faces have seams. Also she says she has never seen anything green on that show, like a blade of grass or a tree. So she is glad there is no Super Channel and when I told her I would save up my change from my lunches so I could pay for the channel, she said she would steal my money and donate it to the refugee camp.

Khaled and Nadine like anything at all. They have lived in the refugee camp all their lives. They like whatever we watch. They roll their Rs when they speak English and we told them they do not have to do that. I'm sure they could tell us a lot of things, too.

Rafik Abboud

DONKEY
BY THE ROAD

*Emily Dickinson never had
to move across the sea.*

After a nurse appeared at St. Tarkmanchatz without warning and plunged a clumsy cholera injection into the arm of each student, Liyana stayed home from school for days with a raging fever. "I think she *gave* me cholera," Liyana mumbled, after falling asleep with a thermometer in her mouth. Her mother bathed her face with cool water and set up a water pitcher beside her. Her father gave her some medicine he worried wouldn't help much. They both said, "Rest, rest, rest."

From her bed, she could hear her family continuing their lives without her. Clinking. Opening doors. Rafik running water in the bathroom.

She was—*incidental*—to the planet's actions.

⸺

For one day she lay dreaming of the part in Jackson's hair. When she had told him she was leaving the country, a week after their kiss at the movies, he looked as blank as an ironing board.

Someone dropped a book down the hall. Someone banged a locker door. Why did she remember those sounds?

He put on a cowboy voice and said, *"Well—see ya later—pardner."*

That is what he did.

———

The second day she lifted her hand to flip open a book of poems by Emily Dickinson, trying an experiment. Each time Liyana read a Dickinson line she really liked, she'd close her eyes and make up a line of her own inside her head. I'm not copying, she thought. I'm being *infused*. It's like drinking water straight from Sitti's spring.

When she read, *I felt a Cleaving in my Mind— As if my Brain had split*—her own head answered, *A Canyon opened—where before there had been smooth land. Now where do I stand?*

———

The third day Liyana was sick, she watched the sun crawl through her room as the hours progressed. It does this every day when I'm not here to watch it, she thought. Light rays crept across the windowsill, touching the legs of the table, and her schoolbooks toppled like monuments beside the tangled sheets of her bed—she'd kicked the blankets to the floor because she was SO HOT.

Long fingers of sun inched across her mattress. When she thought, this is the same sun that strokes the faces of my old friends back in my earlier world, her eyes felt thick. What was Claire doing at this moment? Claire's recent letter told about the school spelling bee that Liyana had won the year before, a new singer that everybody liked, crushes and anticrushes. It also said, "Are you *all right?*" because the bad news of Jerusalem made it across the ocean more quickly than good news ever could. If Liyana answered at this moment, she would have to say, "No."

Sitti appeared that afternoon with a flushed face, looking upset. She kept repeating something so Liyana's mother called Poppy at the hospital to translate. Poppy had spoken with Sitti that morning by telephone and mentioned Liyana was home sick. Sitti was furious he hadn't alerted her right away. Was he trying to insult her? Didn't he know she could make Liyana well?

Sitti closed the door of Liyana's room and smoothed the white sheets out on the bed, muttering the whole time. Sitti made Liyana lie very still with her arms stretched out alongside. Plucking a handful of silver straight pins from her plump cloth belt, she stuck them one by one, standing up, into the sheets around Liyana's body. Liyana kept cracking her eyes open to peek at what Sitti did. She mumbled the whole time she worked. More and more pins appeared. There must have been hundreds! Soon the pins outlined Liyana's body like a metallic running fence.

Then Sitti said a series of prayers. She leaned over Liyana with a rocking motion, back and forth, rubbing her own hands together over Liyana's body and opening them wide. She flicked her fingers, as if she were casting the illness aside. Liyana felt spellbound. A cool current seemed to shoot through the pins around her. Were they breaking the circuit of the fever or what? She couldn't even tell how long all this went on. Twenty minutes? An hour?

Rafik returned from school and stepped into Liyana's room to say hello to Sitti. "Wow!" he said. "It's a voodoo bed!" Khaled and Nadine were downstairs sending *Get Well* greetings.

Then Liyana began sweating profusely. Sitti acted happy now. She took towels, wiping Liyana's face and arms and legs very hard. Liyana called to her mother, "I'm *starving!*" It was the first appetite she'd had in days. Her mother brought her slices of fruit and toast and soup.

All through dinner, Rafik reported to his sister later, Sitti chastised Poppy for not having let her heal Liyana earlier. She shook her finger and frowned, telling him he should have been smarter, especially since he was a doctor and all. She slept on the couch, and left early the next day, on the first bus back to the village.

The fourth day Liyana felt well enough to eat three bowls of tapioca pudding. She could have written to Jackson to say, "Guess what? I forgot your last name."

Instead she stood by the front window staring down on streams of cars passing by. A yellow license plate meant Jews and blue meant Arabs. When you stayed home for days in a row, it seemed strange to remember all the places you would have been going otherwise.

Liyana could see the old man, Abu Hamra, pushing his cart of lettuces and cabbages up to the crossroads where he sat with it. Abu Hamra didn't like you to peel back the outer layer of a cabbage to peek inside. The first time Liyana visited his stand with her mother, she idly tried to see inside a tight cabbage's head, but Abu Hamra snapped at her so loudly, she dropped it.

Poppy said Abu Hamra's family had their well closed in by Israeli soldiers a few years ago after his nephew was suspected of throwing stones at an Israeli tank. That could make you mad for a long time, Poppy said. Losing your water because of a rumor.

Beyond the lettuce cart, a donkey sprawled by the road on his side, head down, as if he were sick, too. Where had he come from? Had a car hit him in the night? No one stopped, or paid him any attention.

Liyana slowly pulled on her oldest, palest blue jeans. She hadn't been dressed in four days. She never knew blue jeans were so heavy. Her mother stood in the kitchen chopping vegetables for soup. The house smelled healthy, of celery and carrot broth. Her mother looked surprised to see Liyana up and about.

"Are you well?"

"Not quite, but I'm going down to see the donkey by the road. I think he's hurt or sick."

Her mother shook her head. "The fever must have affected your brain. No ma'am. Get back in bed, dearie."

For some reason Liyana started crying.

"He needs me," she moaned. Then, more logically, "What if he needs me?" She begged her mother to let her carry him a pan of water.

Mom examined her with a tipped eye. Then she dried her hands thoroughly on her apron. "I'll go with you," she said. "Put a sweater on, too. It's windy out."

They filled the bottom of the steamer pan with water and took along a saucer and spoon.

The donkey's velvety eyes were closed. He

breathed heavily and seemed to like their gentle stroking. His muscles relaxed. A man in a car slowed down and called out to them in Arabic. Liyana shook her head.

"I think he said the donkey's dead, but he's wrong," she told her mother.

"Is your Arabic really that good already?"

"No, but I have a better imagination in Arabic now."

The donkey opened one glossy eye to look at them, but stayed down.

They spoke soothingly to him, spooning water onto his dry tongue. He licked it slowly around inside his mouth and swallowed. "Sweet donkey, take it easy, have a little sip."

Liyana's favorite Christmas song had always been "The Friendly Beasts." In one verse a donkey speaks: *I, said the donkey, shaggy and brown, I carried His mother up hill and down, I carried her safely to Bethlehem town, I, said the donkey, shaggy and brown.*

Liyana asked her mother, "Do they have a humane society here?" Her mother didn't know. While they discussed it, the donkey opened both eyes together for the first time, stared at them, heaved his deepest breath yet, and died. He was suddenly, absolutely gone. They didn't see any soul rise out of his mouth or nose, though they were looking hard.

For the second time in an hour, Liyana cried. Even her mother was wiping her eyes. Where had he come from? She would ask Khaled and Nadine if someone was missing a donkey from the refugee camp. Liyana wanted to bring a sheet out from the house to cover him, but they only owned the sheets for their beds and one set extra. Her mother put a soft hand on Liyana's shoulder.

"Let's go on home," she said. "We did what we could. And we were with him when he left us."

In the night his body disappeared. Maybe someone with a truck carried him away. Liyana felt bad that nobody stayed with him till that happened.

The fifth and last day that Liyana was at home recovering, she thought about donkeyness all day. She tried to sketch a donkey in her notebook. Her drawing was hopeless. Some people say a donkey is a "humble" beast—unlike a proud Arabian horse, for example. She thought about the word "humble" because Poppy had told her it was something she needed to work on.

She did not feel humble. She didn't think she was *brilliant* or anything, but she *did* want people to like and miss her. She wanted more letters stacking up in Postal Box Number 898 that said,

"Nothing is the same without you" and "Please come home soon." She pretended they were on their way. Poppy would flip them out of his briefcase and say, "Jackpot!"

Then she thought about the boy she'd seen in the lamp store. His dark hair combed smoothly straight back.

They could meet again. It was a small enough city.

*D*ETECTIVE WORK

*We used to leave notes
on smokers' doorsteps saying,
"Excuse me, but did you know your lung cells are
shriveling up?"
Signed, The F.B.I.*

Liyana began visiting the Sandrounis' ceramics shop every other day, memorizing the intricate curls of vines on fancy tiles.

She pretended she had various missions: to collect the store's business cards to send to her friends back home, whose mothers had enormous interest in painted ceramics, or to purchase a small blue drinking cup, or to check again on the price of that green lamp which she would really love to see sitting by her bed. She wouldn't even mind learning how to electrify things. She studied cords and switches.

The Sandrounis soon greeted her as if she were their old friend.

"Ho—back again? We are irresistible!"

Mr. Sandrouni folded a newspaper he was reading very carefully. "You know what?" he said to

Liyana, who just happened to be standing nearer to him than anyone else. "I think it is better to use newspapers for wrapping than for reading." He placed the newspaper on his giant pile. "Always a bad story. Always something very sad."

She wanted to ask about the cinnamon-smelling boy—was he their son, or nephew, and where was he now? But she couldn't do it.

Finally, on the day she'd decided her browsing was getting ridiculous and she'd better stop hanging out in the shop or they'd put a detective on *her,* he appeared again, just where he had stood the first time, eating yogurt out of a cup.

"What's up?" he said to her, tipping his head and smiling.

"I was taking a walk." She coughed and grew courageous. "I was looking for you."

He raised an interested eyebrow. "Yes?"

"I think we might—have more things to talk about."

Liyana, she said to herself, *Poppy would flip!*

Here, in the land of dignity.

Here, where a girl was hardly supposed to THINK about a boy!

But he didn't flinch. He grinned even more widely. "I'm *sure,*" he said. But he wasn't making fun of her. "I think you are right." His spoon rattled around in his cup. "Shall we talk about—yogurt?"

She took such a deep, relieved breath it sounded as if she were gulping. "I eat another kind without so much writing on the cup," she said. "It tastes saltier and less creamy."

"I prefer it myself," he said. "This kind is more sweet. But the store was finished with—your kind. Do you like yogurt with fruit?"

"I hate it."

"I hate it, too!"

Mr. Sandrouni looked vaguely amused. "Shall we start a taster's club in here when business gets slow?" he said. "You could eat out of my bowls. Don't they have those things—people tasting cheese and wine together?"

Liyana felt a charge of enthusiasm as if such a dopey conversation were electrifying her.

The boy put out his hand. "Don't you think we should trade names now that we know so much about each other?"

She thought he said his name was "Omar" but he went by "Or."

"Why?"

"It's shorter."

When she told him hers, he smiled. "A nice name," he said. "I never heard it before." He said it twice. Liyana thought it rolled around on his tongue.

She asked, "Is your last name Sandrouni?" and he looked startled.

"Me? No way! I'm not related to these guys! I'm just—an old friend of their family!"

Mr. Sandrouni said, "He asked me to adopt him, but I refused."

Liyana and Or made a plan to meet for yogurt at Abu Musa's the next day, after discovering they had exactly the same lunch break.

———

At dinner that night, Liyana did not tell her parents about her new friend. But she asked Poppy, "Have we ever had anyone in our family named Omar?" and he looked puzzled.

"Well, I think way back when your grandfather was young and he used to ride his Arabian horse from the village all the way up to Galilee just to eat the tiny crispy fish that were caught in the sea— then I think we might have had an Omar. Why?"

"Did you know him?"

"No. Maybe I heard a story about him. It's a common name, you know."

Later, as they ate rice pudding, Poppy added, "I met the famous actor, Omar Sharif, in a tiny café in Egypt once. Did I ever tell you that? We shared a table because there weren't many tables. He asked me what I did and I said I was getting ready to go to medical school. Then I asked, 'What about you?'"

"I'm an actor," Omar Sharif said. "I'm getting ready to be a famous actor."

Liyana opened her eyes wider. "Wow, he *knew that? Before it happened?*"

Poppy said, "I had never heard of him. So I answered cockily, if you can believe it—*Isn't everybody an actor?*"

———

At Abu Musa's café, neither Liyana nor Or ordered yogurt. They ordered *hummus,* which came swirled with sprigs of parsley for garnish. They sat at a crooked table outside, dipping their breads into the same creamy plate.

"Did you always live here in Jerusalem?" Liyana asked him and he said, "Always—forever and ever—from the time of the—infinite sorrows—till now."

She liked how he talked. His English was very flowing.

"Do you hope to live in Jerusalem forever?"

She felt like an interviewer. Tiny gray birds poked around their feet for crumbs and pecked at a paper wrapper. Did it taste of salt, of pomegranate syrup, of sesame? Did they fly around the city together or had they met just now for the first time? Liyana tossed them a stalk of parsley.

"Where else would somebody go, after here? Omaha?"

For some reason that struck her funny. Not that she had ever been to Omaha, but just the fact he would think of the *word*.

"I'm sure there are lots of immigrants who have gone to Omaha," she told him.

"But a place is inside you—like a part of your body, don't you think? Like a liver or kidney? So how could you leave it? It sounds like big trouble to me."

She stared at the table. The patterned grains of wood in the scarred surface reminded her of currents in the Mississippi River. Would she ever smell that muggy air again?

"But what do *you* think?" he continued. "Didn't you come here from another place? Do you think I'm wrong?"

A sparrow landed right on her foot and jumped off again. "I'm from St. Louis," she said softly. "Just—a city. Like—Omaha. I don't think you're wrong. But—do you think you can get your kidney back?"

He tapped his finger on the tabletop. He stared at her in a soft way that made her feel warm. Then he said, "I hope so."

Old men were trudging up the skinny street with baskets of kindling tied to their backs. Liyana took a big sip of her lemonade. She felt saddened by their conversation but glad to be mentioning it, at least.

"What do you *do* all the time?" Liyana said. "Where do you go when you're not in school?"

He looked around. She liked the straight line of his jaw, his skin's rich olive tint. "Well, I walk. I walk a lot. I go to the Sandrounis', and the museums, and the libraries, and the soccer fields, and the beach sometimes in summers—do you go to the beach?—and the green country around Nazareth, where my mother is from—have you been there?"

They ordered a bowl of *baba ghanouj* because they were still hungry.

He said tentatively, "I'm also very happy to stay at my house and read books and listen to music."

He had careful fingers. He tore his bread into neat triangles, not ripped hunks, as Rafik did. He offered her more before he took any himself. Liyana realized she was staring at the subtle valley above his upper lip, the small elegant dip under his nose. Did everybody have one of those?

She was staring at his wrist, the graceful way it came out of his sleeve.

"Have you heard any of the new folk music over here?" he asked.

"No," she said. "But I would like to."

He invited her to meet him on Saturday at 1 P.M. at a coffeehouse called "The Fountain" where they had live local music on weekends. "They have orange juice, too—if you don't drink coffee."

She wished she had a pocket calendar. She'd fill in every day.

When they parted to return to their own schools, he took her hand formally and shook it. "Liyana, it was a real pleasure talking with you. Better than most days of my life! And I look forward to our next visit."

"Or," she said, hesitating a moment, because it felt like calling somebody "And" or "But." "Or—I enjoyed it—too."

He gripped her hand a moment extra.

Sometimes to hold a good secret inside you made the rest of a day feel glittery. You could move through dull moments without any pain.

All afternoon at her desk, Liyana felt lifted up by the glint of her secret. An invisible humming engine shone a small spotlight onto one corner of her desk, to the upper right of the geometry text, and the triangles they were studying all looked like bread.

$\mathcal{T}$HE FOUNTAIN

If you could be anyone,
would you choose to be yourself?

The day after Thanksgiving, which no one else in Jerusalem even mentioned, much less celebrated, Liyana's family sat on the low couches in the living room after dinner reading different sections of newspaper when she blurted out her plan.

"Fountain? Fountain? Never heard of it," said Poppy.

"You've never taken the bus alone into the city," said her mother, putting down her page.

"Well, it can't be very hard," Liyana answered testily. "I mean, I've taken it coming home, right? Is there a huge difference? On our road it only goes north to Ramallah and south to Jerusalem. I'll take the south one. Then, when I see the city, which I *do* recognize by now, I'll get off. Then I'll walk."

"Walk?" they said in unison.

———

Every day Liyana's father drove her into

Jerusalem, letting her off by Jaffa Gate so she could walk into the Armenian Quarter by herself and go to school. At lunch she hiked miles within the walled city, around curls and corners of tiny alleyways, up secretive staircases, along crowded thoroughfares smelling of oranges and rose water and damp, mopped stone. And now they acted as if she'd never walked before.

"How did you hear of this place? Do your friends at school go there?"

"Well—they *might* if they know about it."

Actually she hadn't mentioned it to any of them. She was still keeping it a secret rolled up tightly inside her.

"Was it in the newspaper?"

"Maybe." So she spread the back pages from both newspapers on the floor and started scouring them. All she found were ads for purchasing a "beautifully sculpted charm replica of the Second Holy Temple in Jerusalem" and a concert by the Jerusalem Woodwind Quintet (the Jewish paper) and giant obituaries and restaurant ads (the Arabic paper).

She stomped into her room and fell down backward on her bed.

A little later, Liyana's mom stepped into the

doorway of her room and smiled the motherly smile that says, *"I know where you are and I remember being there myself."*

Her mother said, "You know, I have a few errands in the city myself. Would that make things easier? If I drove you and dropped you off and came back to get you?"

"What are your errands?"

"Well, I need to go to a tailor, for one. The two denim skirts I bought right before we left the States are a little too big. I should have tried them on."

"That will take about ten seconds."

"And I'd like to find the vitamin store I heard about. We're running out of Cs and Es. And I need to explore more of the Jewish neighborhoods on foot because I want to find out what's—available. You know how Poppy only takes us around east Jerusalem because he doesn't *know* the other side? Well, I'm ready to discover it. All that might give you two hours or more."

Saturday arrived and Liyana rebraided her hair ten times. Then she brushed it and decided to leave it loose. It had little waves in it from all the activity. Her mother, who was not yet used to driving in the city, still pumped the gas hesitantly and everyone passed them. Even very old men passed them.

Liyana said, "Mom, I'm meeting a friend there."

"From school?"

"Not my school."

"A girl?"

"Not a girl."

Her mother's foot hit the brake a little. "You mean—this is—a date?"

"Not a date. It's an—appointment."

"Who is he?"

"He's Or."

"What?"

"For Omar. I met him—at the Sandrounis' ceramics shop. The place Poppy showed me. I was—just in there—a few times."

"He works there?"

"No. They're friends."

Liyana could see right then she had rounded the bend where conversations with her parents were no longer going to be as easy as they once were.

"Do you know what your father would say?"

"About what?"

"Liyana! This is his country. It is a very conservative country. Haven't you noticed? Remember the shorts? Remember his story about someone getting in trouble in the village simply because he talked to a woman in the street? People have supposedly even been killed! For little indiscretions! I realize you are not a villager and you don't have to live by their old-fashioned codes. Just remember your father won't like it if he knows about it. Still, I think you should tell him. Absolutely. Tonight at dinnertime. Or the minute we get home. And— oh Liyana, be careful. Be—*appropriate*."

There it was. The word she hated most.

They parked on a side street near the Old City. Or had described to her how to walk to The Fountain.

"Where's the tailor?" Liyana asked Mom, who was carrying her skirts bunched up in one arm, and her mother said, "Who knows? I'm looking for her."

Liyana struggled to remember Or's directions exactly—up one hill, past the odd windmill, to the right, then straight. The streets seemed wider on this side of town. They passed a store for watches, a bank, a gift shop full of antiques, a nursery school. Fewer sounds of Arabic drifted through the air now—just the husky, less familiar-sounding accents of Hebrew and languages they couldn't identify. Norwegian, Liyana thought. Polish or Russian.

She recognized The Fountain by the courtyard in front of it containing chairs, striped umbrella tables, and—yes—a fountain spurting water from two crossed jugs into a blue pool.

Someone in the cheery interior adjusted a microphone on a stage. A lady with a deep tan, bright lipstick, and a pink drink at an outdoor table turned her cheek up to the sun. Liyana didn't see Or anywhere.

"Are you sure this is it?"

"Yes." Two dark birds dipped into the fountain and splashed themselves.

Liyana didn't know how to make it sound sweeter, so she just blurted it out. "Could you please go on now?"

Her mother looked slightly hurt but not terribly.

They decided to meet by the windmill in two hours since there was only one and it was easy to find.

Just before Liyana stepped inside the café by herself, Or materialized beside her. "You made it! You remembered my directions!"

She could have told him she remembered even the smallest brown hairs on the back of his hand.

"There is bad news," he said. "The person I hoped was playing and singing is not here today. Another person is playing who, I am sorry to say..." he whispered into her ear, "is very terrible."

"Would you like to go to the Israel Museum instead?" he asked straight into her ear. "It's not far away." She had never been there. Poppy had talked about going one day, but they got sidetracked into visiting the tomb of Lazarus instead.

"Uh—sure." But she felt a little worried. Her mother and father never liked it when she and Rafik changed their plans without telling them.

The Israel Museum, largest in the country, displayed archaeological wonders and contemporary art. Liyana had been reading about its shows and lectures in the newspaper. One Saturday, sleepily thumbing through the newspaper at the breakfast table, she'd suggested to Rafik that he attend a youth workshop on "developing artistic talents."

He said he had all the talents he could handle right now.

Later he asked her, "Am I the only youth in this house?"

Liyana followed Or up the street. He waved at shopkeepers and said something to an old woman passing in a black dress and black scarf.

Then it struck her. He said it in Hebrew!

A yellow cat dodged a black car. Her heart was pounding. Two young women in blue jeans walked by chattering, pushing baby buggies.

She didn't know how to ask him this.

"Or," she stuttered, "did you—are you—what did you—say to her?"

"Her husband died a few months ago," he answered. "She's a neighbor of ours. We took food to her house during the first week of mourning, when she and her family were sitting *shiva*—that time when the family doesn't wear shoes or leave the house, when they cover all their mirrors. This is the first day I've seen her out in the world again. "

"Cover all the mirrors," Liyana repeated. "That's a—powerful tradition. It's a—Jewish tradition?"

He looked at her curiously. "Yes, it's a Jewish tradition. And I think you may have some similar Arabic traditions, too."

As her heart jogged and blipped, she said, "Well, they won't listen to music in the village, after someone dies. I don't know about the mirrors. Come to think of it, I don't know if they *have* any mirrors."

Liyana's mind flew forward at full speed. She realized there shouldn't be anything shocking about his being Jewish in a place made up mostly of Arabs and Jews. It's just that she hadn't even *thought* of it. And wasn't his name "Omar" an Arabic name?

When she mentioned this, stuttering, he laughed roundly so his fabulous teeth showed. "*Omer,* my friend," he said, "with an *e* not an *a*— which is a Jewish name. You don't like it as much?"

She thought, *It's stupid for my heart to race.*

"Could we sit down a minute?" she asked. They sat on a wall beside a cedar tree and she took a deep breath.

"Did you know I wasn't Jewish?" she asked him.

"Of course."

"How?"

"Well, you were carrying Arabic copybooks in your satchel, for one thing. Those little gray notebooks for homework? And you told me you live on the Ramallah road, didn't you? I don't have any *other* friends who live on the Ramallah road."

"Does that bother you?" she asked.

"Ha! Would I suggest we get together—if it bothered me? The question is—does it bother *you?*"

"Of course not," she said, startled, as words came out of her mouth that she could not predict from minute to minute. "I'm an American," she said. "Mostly." But that sounded ridiculous. He hadn't asked for her passport. "I mean, this fighting is senseless, don't you think? People should be able to get over their differences by this time, but they just stay mad. They have their old reasons or they find new ones. I mean, I understand it mostly from the Arab side because my father's family lost their house and their money in the bank and lots of their community when my father was a boy and the Palestinians were suffering so much, just kicked around till recently as if they were second-class human beings you know they couldn't even show their own flag or have hardly any normal human rights like the Jews did till recently and it's getting better only slowly you know my relatives have to get permits for things all the time and it wasn't that way when my father was little, things were more equal then and of course I know the Jewish people suffered so much themselves, but don't you think it should have made them more sensitive to the sufferings of others, too?"

Her mouth had become a fountain. Spurting waterfalls of words.

He stared at her quietly. "I do."

Birds jabbered in branches above them. Flit and bustle. What did people seem like to birds?

Omer took a deep breath and stood up. "It's a bad history without a doubt," he said. "Nothing to be proud of." He closed his eyes, turning his face to the side, right into the sun. "So what are we going to do about it?" Then he opened his eyes, made a little bow, and put his hand out toward the avenue, as if to offer her the street.

Liyana thought, *Now he'll hate me. I'm a talking maniac.* As a kind of finishing touch, Liyana blurted, "I have hope for the peace, do you?" And he stared at her closely. "Of course I do. Would you still like to go to the museum?"

⸻

They walked up the street without speaking, their arms brushing a few times. Liyana thought, *My mother's probably watching us from the window of the bank across the street, her mouth wide open with shock that I'm not where I said I would be.*

⸻

Inside the massive museum, Liyana and Omer stared happily at giant paintings, sculptures, and ancient lamps dug out of caves. They made themselves pay polite attention to the older art, though they both agreed they were more interested in the odd contemporary rooms.

Liyana liked how Omer stood back from pieces, then moved in to examine them closely, and drifted back again. She still felt breathless from her outburst. He seemed calmly deliberate, paying close attention. He shook his head over a painting that was nothing but bright red slashes, quick thick lines. He said, "My eyes don't like it. Do yours?" Liyana wondered why it was such a relief to dislike the same things your friends did. What did that tell you about a person?

"Do you mind," she asked, "if I call you by your whole name instead of your nickname?"

He said, "I don't mind if you give me a new name I never heard before."

Omer was wearing a thick, white, long-sleeved T-shirt with three buttons at the throat, blue jeans, and purple high-topped tennis shoes. She liked his clothes. She could easily have stared at him more than the artwork, but tried to keep her gaze on the walls whenever she was in his vision. Her eyes rose into a turquoise horizon. She floated on the ripe blue cloud an artist had painted crowning a yellow city. Was that Jerusalem? Sometimes Omer stood behind her and she heard his breathing as they viewed the same piece. She felt a delicious jitter inside.

One artist offered a giant bright installation titled "Underground Springs" made from tin cans roped together, painted flashing purple and silver, spilling forth from a map of Israel on the wall. Omer laughed out loud. "Do you worry about it?" he asked. "Where all the trash will be ten years from now? I worry about it every time I open a can of tuna fish."

"Tuna fish?" Liyana said. It was one of the things her mother had been looking for in their Arab stores, but Arabs didn't like tuna much. "Can you get it over here?"

"Of course. It's delicious with yogurt." He poked her in the side. Other foods the Abbouds missed crowded her mind. Should she ask? Lima beans! Lemon meringue pie!

When she finally remembered to glance at her watch, she exclaimed so loudly, a dozing guard over in the corner jumped. "Oh my! I forgot to meet my mother! I'm ten minutes late already!"

She and Omer sprinted toward the windmill, where they found her mother tapping her foot and staring at her watch, arms crammed with packages. When she saw them (about twenty-five minutes late by now) she said to Liyana, "I thought maybe you'd gone onto daylight savings time."

"Mom, I'm so sorry! The time—slipped away from us. We ended up going to the museum instead, I hope that's okay with you, you would have loved it!—you know that big one I've been wanting to go to? Anyway, this is Omer, my friend I mentioned."

Her mother greeted Omer with interest, but couldn't shake his hand since hers were loaded. Omer reached out and insisted on carrying almost all her bags to their car. Liyana could see she was impressed by his manners.

"I found it!" her mother said over her shoulder to Liyana. "Mayonnaise!" Omer raised his eyebrows. Liyana felt trembly and weak. She hoped her mother wouldn't say other goofy family stuff. But her mother smoothly turned her attention to Omer, smiling that generic mother smile.

"Have you always lived in Jerusalem? Do you like your school? Are you familiar with Liyana's school? Do you know other people who go there? What do you most like to do in your spare time?"

He said, "Wander. Both inside and outside my head." Her mother looked at Liyana as if she could now see how the two of them were connected.

In the car on the way home, her mother said calmly, "Liyana, I don't think he is an Arab."

Liyana said, "So?" which was not the way to answer your mother when you wanted to keep her on your side. But that's what came out.

They drove in silence for a mile, past the Universal Laundry and Abdul Rahman's shoe repair shop where Liyana's favorite beat-up American loafers were currently taking a vacation, awaiting new soles. Liyana said, "No one I go to school with is an Arab either. Did you know they made me an honorary Armenian citizen?"

Her mother looked sideways at her. "You know what I mean."

Liyana swallowed twice. "We already talked about it. He believes in the peace as much as we do."

A crowd of old women with baskets on their

arms waited for a bus. Her mother paused a long time before saying, "I just fear your father's response. Of all the boys you might find in this town to have a crush on…"

Liyana kept plummeting. "Can he come over? For dinner someday soon? He gave me his telephone number and I gave him ours!"

"Don't you start calling him, Missy," her mother said, and Liyana opened and closed her mouth like a fish. If she didn't, she might suffocate.

At dinner, Poppy said starkly, "What? Who? Where?"

Liyana said, "This isn't a book report, you know." Then she said, "Remember when you told us how you had Jewish neighbors and friends when you were growing up here? Remember how we had plenty of Jewish friends back in the United States? Why not? He lives on Rashba Street. Did you ever go to Rashba Street when you were little?"

Poppy said, "Sure." But a moment later he said, "Never, never, never."

All evening Liyana stood by her window staring west toward Jewish Israel. She had a new feeling about it. The guard at the museum quietly locked the galleries. The paintings slept calmly on their walls. Over there the Mediterranean's soft blue waves were scattering shells. Liyana had never yet been to a beach in this country. She thought she'd like to visit one with Omer. They could take their shoes and watches off and walk and walk for miles. They could sink their feet into the sand.

WE WISH YOU A MERRY EVERYTHING

Would a wise man please step forward?

At Christmas time, Jerusalem and Bethlehem felt crisp and cool, flickering with candles in windows, buttery yellow streetlights, and music floating from shops—thin threads of light and sound. But the holiday decorations weren't nearly as prominent or glossy as they were in American cities. "I don't think Santa Claus made it over here yet," mourned Rafik.

"Sometimes," Liyana mused, "when you're standing in the places where important things really happened, it's even harder to imagine them. Don't you think? Because video stores and Christmas pilgrims unfolding Walking Tour maps are getting in your way. History is hiding."

"Thank you," said Rafik. "Thank you for your wisdoms."

At midnight on Christmas Eve they stood with their parents in the long line at the Church of the Nativity in Bethlehem. Poppy had done this as a teenager himself, with his Arab Christian friends. Liyana and Rafik both had checkered black and white *kaffiyehs* wrapped around their necks against the chill. Irish nuns harmonized in wavery soprano voices. Liyana and her mother led a few verses of "Angels We Have Heard On High." A gold star on the floor inside marked the spot where the manger might have been. It was the one "official" spot that didn't make Mom feel like crying.

Liyana liked to remind herself: *Jesus had a real body. Jesus had baby's breath.*

And Jesus did not write the list of rules posted on the stone wall. There were many, but Liyana's eyes caught on the first: NO ARMS ALLOWED INSIDE THIS CHURCH.

$\mathcal{A}$ KERNEL OF TRUTH ON EVERY AVENUE

She really believed her parents
when they said, "Look both ways."

On one of the first warm days, Omer and Liyana licked pistachio ice cream cones as they sat on an iron bench near the Russian Orthodox Church with its onion domes. They were waiting for Hagop and Atom from Liyana's class to appear so they could go see a French movie at the British library.

Omer asked, "What religion are you?"

The Abbouds had never belonged to a church since Liyana was born, but it might have made things easier. Liyana's mother said they were a *spiritual* family, they just weren't a *traditionally religious* one.

Most people said, "Huh?"

They wanted you to say, "I'm this kind of letter and I go in this kind of envelope."

Omer knew exactly what she was talking about the minute she started to describe it. He said people always asked *him* if he was religious or secular. He would say, "I have Jewish hands,

Jewish bones, Jewish stories, and a Jewish soul. But I'm not officially observant of—the religious practices of the Jewish people. Got it?" His family did a few special-holiday things.

Liyana's family believed in God and goodness and hope and positive thinking and praying. They believed in the Golden Rule—*Do unto others as you would have them do unto you*—who didn't? A mosquito didn't.

Liyana's mother believed a *whole* lot in karma, the Hindu belief that what someone does in this world will come back to him or her—maybe not the day after tomorrow, but eventually. Liyana also liked the eightfold path in Buddhism, and the idea of the *bodhisattva,* the soul who does good for others without any thought for himself or herself. She hoped she would get to know some in her life, besides her parents. Rafik believed in sandalwood incense.

Liyana's entire family believed in reincarnation because it made sense to them. They didn't want to have to say good-bye for good so soon. Poppy said he'd like a thousand lives. Rafik wanted to be reborn in Japan so he could ride the bullet train.

"But what about all these *new* people?" Omer asked her. "Where did *they* come from? You know, the population explosion?"

"I don't know. Maybe souls can split or something." Liyana wasn't too interested in the details.

She just liked thinking of different lives as chain links, connected. She had always felt homesick for some other life, even when she was a baby standing in her crib wearing a diaper not knowing any words yet.

Liyana's parents did not believe everyone was an automatic sinner when they were born. Too dramatic! All people on earth would do good and bad things both. Poppy said every religion contained some shining ideas and plenty of foolishness, too.

"The worst foolish thing is when a religion wants you to say it's the only right one. Or the best one. That's when I pack my bags and start rolling."

He was always rolling, Poppy Abboud. Out of one good story into another one. He didn't like fancy church buildings either. "What *else* could they have done with their money? They could have helped the poor people, for one thing!"

⁓

Once in the United States some ladies came knocking at the Abbouds' door when Poppy was home alone. "We'd like to tell you about Jesus Christ," they announced, and he thought to himself, "I was born in Jerusalem, right down the road from Bethlehem, and they think they're just now telling me?"

But he said, "Come in, come in." Excusing

himself for a moment, he marched into his bedroom, tied on a long gray cloak that had belonged to his father, and a checkered *kaffiyeh,* the headdress that he never really wore, and leapt out of the bedroom into their startled gaze.

"But *first,*" he said, "may I tell you about Muhammad?"

They left the house that instant and never returned.

The Abbouds did not believe in the devil, except the devilish spirit inside people doing bad things. They did not believe in hell, or anybody being "chosen" over anybody else—which Liyana had to ask Omer about. He looked sober. He told her the Jewish idea of being "chosen" meant more than he could explain. "Maybe Jews are also chosen to suffer. Or to be better examples."

Liyana said, "It seems like big trouble any way you look at it. I'm sorry, but I don't like it. Do you *believe* you're chosen? It sounds like the teacher's pet."

He didn't know what that was. "It's not a question of *believing,*" he said.

"What do you mean?"

Omer said, "It's more like—history. A historical way of—looking at ourselves—and things."

Liyana felt gloomy. "And it's history that gave us all these problems," she said. "I think as long as anybody feels *chosen,* the problems will get worse."

Omer asked, "But what about your father's family in the village? Don't they try to make you become Muslim like they are?"

"No. Not yet, anyway."

Omer said, "I'd like to meet them. Do you think I could—go with you someday?"

"I hope so!" Liyana said.

Poppy knew from when he was a boy there must be a *kernel of truth on every avenue.* He *thought* about the reasons behind different beliefs— no pork, for example, came from the old days when pork was the first meat to spoil. "Does it make sense," Poppy said, "that any God would choose some people and leave the others out? If only Christians or Jews are right, what about most of Asia and the Middle East? All these millions of people are just—extras? Ridiculous! God's bigger than that!"

Any kind of fundamentalism gave Poppy the shivers. The Jews in Hebron called themselves "holy pioneers." "Fundamentalists talk louder than liberals," he said. "That's too bad. Maybe we moderate people should raise our voices."

When Liyana told this to Omer, he said, "Your father's right. Please, I want to meet him!"

⁂

On the other side of the earth, Peachy Helen's parents had believed their Christian denomination was "chosen" too. They were the only ones going to be "saved"—but Peachy refused to raise her own children that way.

Peachy Helen had often taken Liyana's mother to the art museum instead of to church. They would stare into blue and green paintings by Monet. "Look at the wavery edges of things! *That's* how we could live."

When Liyana's mother had measles as a girl, she lay in bed for a week in a dim room with lowered shades. She lay as still as a cucumber on a vine.

"Peachy Helen stood over me saying prayers of healing that she made up as she went along. She said, I hope they'll work if they're not official. First she cried, then we both laughed together. I promised her I would get well. And of course I did. But it was then I realized I had been grumpy sometimes for no reason. After that, I thought of every day as A FRESH CHOICE!" She talked about it in capital letters as if it were a feature at the grocery store. "My mother sang a song to keep me calm, "Look for the Silver Lining." The same one I taught to you."

Mrs. Abboud had told Rafik and Liyana to carry the song as a crucial part of their memory banks. Liyana had a stomachache when they learned it so she kept picturing the inside of her stomach coated with silver. They made Peachy Helen pay a nickel to hear them sing it. Sometimes Liyana thought of that song as their religion.

When Liyana and Rafik were little, their mother took them to the art museum *and* to a rich assortment of Sunday schools—Methodist, Presbyterian, Episcopalian, Unity, and Unitarian—where they signed in as "visitors," wore the yellow visitor ribbons, and sometimes kept coming back for months. They just didn't *join* anything. Poppy stayed home reading the newspaper or digging in the garden.

"Didn't the churches wonder where you went when you disappeared?" Omer asked.

"I guess we seemed like hoboes."

"What's a hobo?"

Then they talked about wanderers and gypsies and vagabonds longer than they talked about anything else.

Liyana's parents would discuss religion late into the

night in the living room when Liyana was in bed. She would listen to them till their words blended into a soft sheet of sleep gently spreading over her.

Their words made sense. Why *would* any God want to be only large enough to fit inside a certain group of hearts? God was a Big God. Once Liyana answered someone that way, but it didn't work very well.

"What religion are you?"

"Big God."

It sounded like the Big Sam Shop, where truck drivers bought new tires.

<hr />

Some people let their countries become their religions and that didn't work either. Liyana thought it would never happen to her. She never even felt like a Full and Total American, except maybe when her kindergarten class said the Pledge of Allegiance with hands on their hearts and she was proud to know the fat fruits of words between her lips— republic, nation, indivisible—what a pleasure just to say *words* that felt bigger than you were.

Liyana knew *indivisible* even when her friends still thought it was *invisible,* but she didn't tell them because there are things you have to find out for yourself.

WATER AND ASHES

*When we were born
we were blank pieces of paper;
nothing had been written yet.*

On Rafik and Liyana's birthdays, Poppy always brought flowers to their mother. He wanted to thank her for having had such wonderful kids. The day before Liyana's fifteenth birthday, he stepped through the door after work with a hefty bouquet of white roses, saying, "What do you think? Fifteen deserves something—regal!"

Their mother was still at the English radio station where she worked three days a week now. Rafik liked to say, "Our mother is a DJ," but the station was mostly news, interviews, and cooking programs. Liyana dug under the sink for a glass jar to put the roses in.

The phone rang and Rafik answered it. He called to his dad, "Quick! I know it's Sitti, but I don't know what she's saying! She's shouting loud! I think she's crying too." Liyana froze.

Poppy let the roses dangle upside down as he

listened. Liyana rescued them, her blood buzzing. Usually Abu Daoud conveyed Sitti's messages, or she yelled into the phone from a distance. She didn't like to hold the receiver because she thought it might shock her.

Poppy asked a few questions, then was silent a long time. Finally he slammed down the phone. He'd just told Sitti they'd be there right away. "What, what?" Rafik and Liyana asked him at once.

"I'll tell you in the car."

He was out the door already.

⸻

Driving too fast to the village, Poppy said Israeli soldiers had appeared at Sitti's house and demanded to see her grandson Mahmud, who'd been living in Jordan for the past two years. He was studying to be a pharmacist. Poppy had told Liyana she would like him because he had a good sense of humor, but she hadn't had a chance to meet him yet.

Sitti told the soldiers, "He's not home," because that was the way she talked about him— as if he might turn the corner any moment. "He's not home, but he might be coming soon." She could have said that about anybody, even her dead husband, the way she thought of things.

Poppy said the soldiers pushed past her into the house and searched it, dumping out drawers, ripping comforters from the cupboards. Sitti said, "He's not in *there*." They broke the little blue plate she loved. "What are you doing?" she screamed. There were four of them.

Then they went into Sitti's bathroom and smashed the bathtub with hard metal clubs they were carrying.

Rafik said, "Smashed the bathtub? Why?" Liyana felt nervous wondering, were those soldiers still around? What if they got into a—tango—with them?

Poppy said, "They smashed the sink so it cracked into big pieces on the floor and water streamed from the broken faucets into the room and Sitti was terrified. She thought she was going to drown. She thought water would fill up the whole house, but of course it must have poured into the courtyard and Abu Daoud heard her screams from next door and came running over. He turned off the water at the pipe, I think. Anyway, she said it's not gushing now. Then the soldiers smashed the toilet—"

Rafik interrupted. "WHY?"

Poppy swerved to avoid a sheep in the road. His voice sounded tight and hard. "THERE IS NO WHY. I am filling up to my throat from these stories. Do you know how many of them I hear every day from my patients at work? I don't tell you. I can't tell you. And I thought things were getting better over here."

Liyana said quietly, "I thought there was always a why."

Shadows stretched across the road, late afternoon, a softness falling down from the sky no matter what people did.

At Sitti's house, a small crowd of men and women had gathered tensely outside. They nodded at Poppy and his children as they passed. Rafik entered first and shouted, "Sitti's house is a mess!"

Sitti was mopping and crying all at once. Liyana tried to take the mop from her hand and she brushed her away. An old lady Liyana didn't recognize was down on her knees scrubbing the floor with pieces of rags.

Everyone kept muttering about the soldiers. Poppy translated. *The soldiers left in a truck. We hate their truck. We thought they weren't supposed to bother us anymore. We thought the peace said they would stay away.*

What did they want? They wanted Mahmud. WHY? For two hours Poppy talked to everybody. Nobody knew. Mahmud read books. Books could be dangerous? Poppy tried to phone the police in Ramallah, but the phone line was blank. The soldiers had cut it. Poppy put his hands to his head. He shook his head, saying, "They must do it because it's personal. It's insulting. And it's weird."

He tried to calm Sitti down, but she was inconsolable, whimpering like a cat. Liyana thought she was sadder about the blue plate than the toilet. Sitti kept fingering its pieces, trying to fit them together.

Rafik and Liyana sat in the corner, invisible as the lemons in the bowl on the second shelf. Bathrooms were not cheap. Sitti was not rich.

She reluctantly agreed to spend the night at Aunt Saba's house, folding a dress to wear the next day and her prayer rug and a towel. She mumbled something under her breath.

They walked with her through a stunned village. Even the scrappy birds seemed quieter. Even the children who usually called out from rooftops weren't making any sound.

━━━━━

In Ramallah, Poppy stopped at a store open late for plumbing parts, so he could engage a plumber to head to Sitti's house the next day. At home, their mother was frantic. She met them at the top of the steps. "No note? Do you realize what *time* it is?"

After Rafik told what had happened, she was silent. Then she shouted, "NO! That poor little bathroom! But why? Why the bathroom?"

Liyana quoted, "There is no why." It was strange how quickly someone else's words could come out of your mouth. Idly lifting the front section of the newspaper, she read that a Jewish deputy mayor of Jerusalem proposed two thousand Arab homes in east Jerusalem be torn down to make room for fifty thousand houses for Jews. It didn't say anything about pain or attachment or sorrow or honor.

Liyana slipped outside with the front page and the box of kitchen matches.

On a bare patch of earth, Liyana lit two edges of newspaper. They caught slowly at first, then burst into a cone of bright flame. The fire ate the words. Fire ate them inside and out. Liyana blew the ashes into the dust.

Later Sitti would tell them her new bathtub swallowed water with the sound of a cow.

FIFTEEN

Before anything was written, where was I?

That night Liyana dreamed a cake fell off its plate into the sea and floated away from her. She reached wildly with both her arms, standing knee-deep in the pull of powerful waves.

And it was Omer she was calling to. "Save it! Can you reach it?" but he was swimming too far out. Then she was shouting and waving, "I'm sorry! I wanted to share it with you!" but he could not hear her. He was swimming the other direction. And the cake was drowning.

When Liyana woke on her birthday, her mother was singing in the hallway. Poppy joined in off-key as he stepped into the bathroom and Rafik pretended to be playing a trombone. "Pancakes for breakfast!"

Liyana's place at the breakfast table was surrounded by cheerful hand-drawn cards with yellow Magic Marker daisies. "A decade and a half!" Rafik had written. "Is that an antique yet?"

Poppy wrote half his card in English and half in Arabic. "To my soon-to-be-bilingual daughter," the English said. Liyana could make out letters in Arabic by now—ones that looked like chimneys or fluted edges, but she couldn't really make out *words* yet. So he helped her read it. *"I'm proud of you. What a year it's been!"*

Mom's just said, "To my queen—at 15" in calligraphy. She was already stirring up batter for a pineapple upside-down cake, Liyana's favorite. "I had a weird dream about a cake," Liyana said.

When Poppy went downstairs to get his gift for Liyana out of the trunk of the car (fifteen new notebooks, including some fancy European ones, and fifteen new pens), he found a mysterious silver package sitting on the step. He carried it upstairs held far out from his body, saying, "Isn't it sad what one thinks about these days? Should we get a bomb-sniffing dog? In the old days people never thought about such things."

Since it had Liyana's name handwritten and spelled correctly on a card at the top, she opened it and gasped.

Inside was the green lamp she'd first asked Omer about, at the Sandrounis' ceramics shop, the one too expensive to buy for herself.

A tightly folded note was taped to it. "Don't worry, I traded labor, not cash. Happy birthday! Omer."

Liyana wondered how he got to her house so

early to deliver it. He must have taken a taxi from Jerusalem, dropped it off, and ridden the same taxi back.

Poppy said dourly, "Is this an appropriate gift for a young man to give a young woman?"

Her mother said, "It's fine! It's not jewelry or clothing. It's not silver or gold. Don't give her any trouble!"

———

All day at school, when Liyana described the scene of Sitti's bathroom smashing, the chips of ceramic and waterlogged rooms, her classmates shrugged. People got used to disasters. No one was even killed.

Liyana felt distracted during class. She always had mixed feelings on her birthdays. She gazed out the school window at the changing clouds, casting a flurry of words toward Omer's side of the city. *I miss you. I want to see you. You would never do something like those soldiers did.* But she wrote only five words down in her new notebook: *I love your amazing memory.*

$\mathcal{H}$ISTORY OF KISSING

*I would like to know
the story of every little thing.*

Rafik and Liyana dressed one of the sleeping chickens in the henhouse in a brocade tunic Liyana had sewn especially for her, from a wide silver and burgundy scrap her friend Bilal had given her. They imagined what it would be like for Imm Janan, their landlord's sleepy wife, to discover her hen wearing a lavish robe, as if she'd been crowned queen at midnight.

Liyana had had a hard time sewing the thing so the hen's legs could poke out where they needed to. She even "fitted her" once, in the dark. Rafik wanted Liyana to sew a bonnet as well, but she thought that might be a little much.

The hen mumbled cozily in their hands. Liyana said, "I hope this won't give her bad dreams or anything." Once the robe was tied on and the hen's legs came through the bottom, she rippled her body back and forth, as if to see how much she could still move. Did she think it was a new suit of feathers?

They photographed her with their mother's flash camera, which seemed to upset her more than the dress did.

Rafik said, "I don't think she likes having her wings pressed down." But she settled back into her nest and closed her eyes.

The next morning they were anxious to get to the American Library, where they often went on Saturdays to do their hideous homework. Afterward they'd meet Poppy for lunch and have minty ice cream at the YMCA next door. At breakfast, Rafik kept glancing out the window toward the henhouse. He said, "Drive us, Poppy, let's go now!" What if Imm Janan saw the chicken and screamed instead of laughed? They wanted to be gone when she discovered it.

———

At their gleaming library table, Liyana felt distracted. She kept getting up to pull reference books off the shelves and flip through their pages. She found some really old ones about Palestine with intricate drawings of the Old City in them. In a 1926 book called *Life in Palestine When Jesus Lived,* she read, "…the people were constantly at work… How many languages were spoken, what differences of color, look, habit, manner, dress, must have been seen!"

On her birthday after school, she had called Omer to thank him for the wonderful surprise, and his mother, who didn't speak English very well, answered the phone. Liyana had to ask for him three times.

Omer seemed shy when she raved over her lamp. He just said, "Read some good books under it, okay?" and asked what she had been doing lately. They hadn't been able to share their lunch breaks for a few weeks since he'd been practicing for a debate tournament with his team at lunchtime. Liyana had mentioned more than once that she and Rafik would be studying at the American Library in Jerusalem on Saturday. Now she kept hoping secretly Omer would show up.

So when the heavy green library door squeaked open again, after admitting nuns and the Italian man who ran the matches factory and his daughters and six blond tourists with turquoise backpacks, and Omer finally stepped through, wearing a checkered yellow shirt and looking quizzical, Liyana rose joyously to greet him and they hugged tightly for the first time. She pressed her face against his shoulder. It smelled like sun.

Liyana introduced Omer to Rafik, who said only, "Is it true you play soccer?"

Omer folded a small *origami* ball for him from a piece of notebook paper, and batted it across the table. "I made the ball so you make the goal," he whispered.

They tackled their respective heaps of homework, whispering, laughing, and joking till the librarian stood over their table, saying, "You will please keep your silence or I will be forced to ask you to leave." Then it was harder than ever not to laugh.

Liyana was writing about Mark Twain, since he too had lived in Missouri, her old state, and no one else in her class had chosen an American for their author's report. Everyone else was doing someone like Shakespeare, Dante, or John Milton. When she went to search for the library's tattered copy of *Huckleberry Finn* on the far shelves of "Fiction"—to compare the older edition with her own—Omer walked to the end of the same aisle to study the giant Map of the World on the wall, copying some town names from Russia in his notebook. "We have to write about the places our ancestors came from," he said. She had not known his grandparents were from Russia till now.

Liyana kept thinking how everybody was a little like everybody else and nobody was the *same*. She thought of those snowflake and fingerprint stories about the perfect uniqueness of each one and wondered, "Are we supposed to feel good about that?" She *wanted* one snowflake to resemble another one now and then. She even imagined she carried some essence of Mark Twain inside herself, which was why he appealed to her so much. Twain didn't like the Middle East, though. She wouldn't quote anything he'd said on his dopey travels through the Middle East.

Somehow she couldn't bear to return to their table while Omer still stood at the end of the aisle. She felt suspended, reading spines of other books, held fast by his presence close by. She whispered *chillywilly* under her breath. He turned, then, and caught her staring at his back. He came over beside her and whispered, "What are you thinking about?"

Her throat felt thick with a wish to say, simply, "You" but she said, "Mark Twain."

He touched her elbow gently, leaned forward, and placed his beautiful mouth on hers.

A kiss. Wild river. Sudden over stones. As startling as the first time, but nicer, since it happened in the light.

And bigger than the whole deep ache of blue.

It didn't go away right away.

It held, as Omer gently held her elbow cupped in his hand. Warmth spilled between them.

"Liyana," he said. "I—like you."

"Oh!" She said, "Me too. I like *you*."

He said, "You are not—mad?"

"No!"

He smiled, "I don't think the books—are mad." He kissed her again, on her right cheek only, delicately as a feather's touch, and the librarian pushed a cart past their aisle, not even glancing in their direction.

⁂

After they returned in their newly dazzled state to the cluttered table where Rafik was drawing an elaborate soccer field on four pieces of notebook paper laid out end to end, Omer leaned over him and said, "I have bad news, new friend. I have to go to my own soccer game—right now. Would you like to come with me?"

Rafik couldn't, because he and Liyana were meeting Poppy at the Philadelphia for a late lunch at two. But Liyana could tell he was pleased.

Liyana and Omer traded a long gaze as he left. They grinned easily. She placed one finger on her vivid lips. Rafik didn't notice.

Then she walked over to "Reference" and slid an encyclopedia off a shelf to see if "Kissing" had an entry, but nothing appeared between Kishinev, the capital of the Moldavian Soviet Socialist Republic of the USSR, and Kissinger, Henry, born in Germany and a naturalized American like her father. Well, she thought, sort of like her father. Her father didn't care for him. There was no "kissing" in the encyclopedia. She wondered, "Where did kissing come from? Who started it?"

She knew about the Eskimo tribes who liked nose rubbing more than kissing. She was glad she hadn't been born into one. She made a kissing list in her notebook:

> *Lemony lips,*
> *warm magnets pulling toward one*
>   *another,*
> *streets crisscrossed by invisible tugs,*
> *secret power fields.*
> *Electrodynamics.*

Then she wandered over to the "Newly Arrived" shelf (she thought she should live on that shelf herself) and placed her hand directly on a book called *A Natural History of the Senses* by Diane Ackerman. Flipping it open, she discovered a whole astonishing chapter called "Kissing" in the section called "Touch"!

She took the book to their table spread with Rafik's information on famous rivers of the world and shielded it from Rafik to read, *"There are wild, hungry kisses or there are rollicking kisses, and there are kisses fluttery and soft as the feathers of cockatoos."* Liyana had never touched a cockatoo, but she liked how it sounded.

She wrote down a "first line" that said: *Being good felt like a heavy coat, so I took it off.*

The author, Diane, talked about her memory of kissing in high school, using a rich string of adverbs—"inventively...extravagantly...delicately ...elaborately...furtively when we met in the hallways between classes...soulfully in the shadows at concerts...we kissed articles of clothing or objects belonging to our boyfriends...we kissed our hands when we blew our boyfriends kisses across the street...we kissed our pillows at night...." OH!

And Liyana knew this book was for her. Because last night, the very night before today, she had kissed her pillow and thought she might be cracking up.

$\mathcal{G}$OAT CHEESE

Drop in anytime and stay forever.

Poppy said their skins would feel so sticky after plunging into the Dead Sea, they'd have to lie down under freshwater spigots to wash off.

He drove Liyana, Rafik, Khaled, and Nadine on the descending road through sand dunes toward Jericho because Rafik had been bugging him so much. Mrs. Abboud had gone on a weekend retreat with her women's group. The women were going to hike ten miles through the wilderness to see some hermit nuns who wouldn't be hermits anymore once they got there.

Liyana and Rafik had bathing suits on under their clothes, bottled water, towels, and a basket of small bananas. Liyana hadn't worn her baggy old-man shorts after all. She'd decided to make them into a purse. Khaled and Nadine said they would go swimming in their clothes. They brought extra clothes rolled up and tied with a string.

Sunlight vibrated on the golden sand. Graceful dunes cast shadows on one another. There weren't any clouds. It felt wonderful to leave the clutter of town behind.

Around a curve, Rafik shouted, "Stop!"

Poppy hated when someone yelled in a car. He braked sharply and pulled over. The roads didn't have shoulders like they did back home. "Don't scare me! What is it?"

Rafik pointed. "I want to visit them."

Poppy and Liyana in the front seat hadn't even noticed the Bedouin tents perched far from the road in a crevice of shade between two dunes. They'd been talking about Sitti's new obsession for black sweaters. Though they had bought her two already, she still wanted one with *pockets*.

"You *said* we could visit the Bedouins!" Rafik's voice from the back seat was insistent. He didn't beg very often. "Please!" Khaled and Nadine jabbered in Arabic to each other.

Poppy looked at his watch. "If we visit them, we may not make it to the Dead Sea. They'll keep us all day."

"We'll just run away!"

Poppy said, "Khaled, what do you say?"

Khaled's voice was gentle. He never wanted to boss anyone around. "I say—*yes?*"

The minute Liyana's eyes focused on the flapping black tents, she noticed a small camel staked beside them, the first she'd seen in this country since they arrived. Poppy always included camels in his childhood stories and folk tales, but they'd mostly vanished from this land since then. Where had they gone? Had they all trekked away to Saudi Arabia or Abu Dhabi? She'd been wishing so hard to see one.

Liyana pitched in, "Yes! Let's visit them for just a minute! Come on, Poppy!" Nadine was laughing.

Poppy groaned, "A Bedouin's minute is an hour to you. Maybe two or three. Believe me."

But he pulled the car farther off the road. He said, "What if we get stuck in a sand dune? What if the sand shifts while we're visiting and swallows the car entirely?" But his children were relentless.

Poppy had said Bedouins, like their camels, were much fewer and farther apart than they used to be, but still as friendly. "I thought they were fierce," Rafik said.

Poppy said, "They are, but not to their guests."

The five of them hiked in toward the tents. Halfway there, Poppy returned to the car to get the basket of bananas. "You always bring a gift to Bedouins," he said. "Like a house gift. To people without a house."

The women of the tribe were off beyond the tents shaking dust from little rugs. Children in baggy clothes played a game involving sticks, balls, and large tin cans. Tall men with lean faces sat before the largest tent, wearing black cloaks and headdresses, stitching tarps together with huge needles. Maybe they were making a new tent, Liyana thought.

The camel shifted its feet as they approached. It watched them closely. Spectacular white cheeses lay lined like thirty perfect moons on a dark cloth, drying in the sun. Nadine pointed at them and babbled excitedly to Khaled. She said in English, "So much!"

All the men rose up as they approached. Poppy talked fast and heartily so that before they knew it, they were sitting in a circle with the Bedouins. Everyone was laughing and nodding and asking questions about America and the women were serving tea and slicing a cheese in front of Rafik.

He looked worried. He hated white cheese. Liyana grinned.

Poppy translated, "They're ready to adopt you. See? I told you. Get set for a long day."

He also said, "I told them we are Arab-Americans and they're shocked. They didn't know such people existed. We're the first visitors who've come by in a long time. In the old days people used to stop in more. Bedouins don't even wander as much as they used to. Nowadays they change places only once a year, instead of every few months. In

Saudi Arabia the Bedouins have all been settled in towns. It's a shame. It was a great tradition."

Rafik's eyes were huge. Did the woman think he was going to eat the whole cheese? Why were they focusing on him instead of Khaled? Maybe they liked his red and blue striped T-shirt. Nadine took four pieces of cheese, which helped him out.

"How do Bedouins live?" Liyana asked Poppy. "I mean, where do they get their money?"

"Money? Do you see any money? The goats are in a patch of grass over the dune somewhere. The people sleep right here. They eat right here. Their lives are extremely simple."

Now Liyana knew. She wanted to be a Bedouin when she grew up.

A woman with kind eyes produced two goatskin drums. Even though Poppy said Bedouin music usually happened after sundown, two young men began slapping quick rhythms and singing for them—the same words and notes repeated over and over. Liyana clapped her hands and hummed along. They liked that. Nadine snapped her fingers. A girl with tight braids swayed and bent hypnotically. Khaled accepted a drum and began playing with one swift, accurate hand. Rafik leaned backward on the tarp, as far from the cheese as he could. He nodded bravely when the women pointed at it again.

They sat within the graceful slopes of dunes, tucked away from the road and the few cars and jeeps going by. Liyana felt her thoughts drifting into the sky. Her eyelids drooped. Was this music putting her into a trance? She wished her friends from back home could be here. This was what they would call "an exotic moment." She wished her mother were here, too—hermit women couldn't be more interesting than *this*.

After the ninety-ninth verse of the song, Poppy stood up. The Bedouins protested. "Please," they said to him in Arabic, "you must spend the night!" Poppy laughed. He promised they'd be back. What could they bring them from the city? The Bedouins wanted Rafik to take a cheese home with him—a new cheese, not even the strong one they had all nibbled from. Poppy left the bananas and the basket both. The Bedouins liked the basket. They kept touching it admiringly. It was her mother's favorite basket. Liyana wondered, would she be upset?

Walking back to the car with the entire Bedouin tribe sadly watching them leave, Poppy said to Rafik, "Oh no, you didn't even ride the camel! You petted it, anyway. It's their last camel. Was it too small to ride? Shall we go back? You want to try?"

Rafik considered it. He turned and waved,

looking wistful. Liyana said, "Remember, camels can spit."

Poppy sighed, "And we might have to leave you."

The Dead Sea water was so prickly with salt, it stung Liyana's eyes. Her skin felt marinated after ten minutes.

"It's seven times saltier than the ocean!" Poppy called out. He strolled back and forth by the water wearing a white baseball cap pulled low over his thick hair. He hated swimming. "How do you feel at the lowest spot on earth?"

"Down deep!"

"Bottomed out!"

They were practically sitting on top of the water, as if invisible lounge chairs buoyed them up. Rafik called out, "Strange!" He was paddling fast like a duck. Khaled laughed harder than Liyana had ever seen him laugh. "Did you like the Bedouins?" she asked.

He said, "*Very* much. Did I ever tell you my *Sidi*—grandfather—was half Bedouin? Once when I was small he took me to visit, like today."

"Where is he—now?"

"He is dead. He and—my *Sitti*, too. When our village was taken away. I saw it."

"Saw what?"

"The Israeli soldiers—exploded a house. You know, like they do when they think you are bad. And the house fell on my grandparents. It was not their house."

A single puffed cloud drifted past overhead. Far away someone hooted and leapt into the sea.

"And then what? Did your family fight back?" Liyana asked. Khaled had never mentioned many personal things before.

Khaled said haltingly, "My family—does not like to fight. My parents are very—sad till now. They will never be finished with sadness. I—had a bad picture in my mind—a long time. For myself I never fight. Then my mind is sick and doesn't get well. Sadness is—better."

Liyana said, "I think I would fight. Not kill, but yell or something."

In the car going home, Liyana would tell Poppy what Khaled had told her and Poppy would ask him more questions in Arabic. For now the thick gray water seared a scrape on Liyana's knee. She said, "Khaled, nothing about this sea feels dead to me."

ALL OUR ROOTS GO DEEP DOWN EVEN IF THEY'RE TANGLED

She wanted another kiss—
her chapped lips were burning up.

In March, Poppy found three American evangelists lost in the Old City and brought them home for dinner. Liyana thought, "If I were his wife, I would say *Thanks a lot* and not mean it."

But her mother was in the kitchen humming happily and clattering pot lids as the visitors sat around the table toasting each other with glasses of mint tea and gobbling roasted chickpeas. Rafik showed them the new designs he'd been sketching for Star Trek phasers. He could tune in to planets X, Y, and Z. The two evangelist men, Reverend Crump and Reverend Holman, wore bright red-and-navy diagonally striped ties, and the woman, Reverend Walker, wore a long gray dress with a lace collar. Liyana asked the woman cautiously, "Are you married to…?" and nodded at the men, curious if one was her mate and she used her own name, but the woman declared, "Honey, I'm married to THE LORD'S GOOD WILL!"

Poppy said they had been wandering with dazed looks by the shoe shops where the streets get narrower when he stopped to offer directions. "Our countrymen!" But they didn't remind Liyana of anyone else she'd ever met in her life.

Reverend Walker said, "God told us to visit Mount Gilboa right now to see the blessed Gilboa iris that only blooms three weeks a year. So we packed our bags in Atlanta and *bought tickets! Amen!*"

Now they were waiting for further instructions from God because they hadn't received a complete itinerary. What were they supposed to do after they had visited the flowers and the Church of the Nativity and the other holy spots lined up like pearly buttons across the stony ground?

Poppy offered his advice. "I know a hospital that could really use some volunteers right now. It's in Gaza and all the orderlies have been quitting and the nurses are in an uproar and nothing is getting done. Just a day or two of help would be a—Godsend."

The evangelists looked at one another. Reverend Holman said, *"Praise the Lord!"* after Mom served the lentil soup and the coleslaw, which reminded them of home, and the stuffed grape leaves and the hot bread. But every one of them was quiet when Poppy mentioned the hospital.

Reverend Crump told Poppy he wished they could say a prayer in Hebrew for him. Poppy mentioned that he didn't know any prayers in Hebrew himself, but Liyana didn't think they got it. When Poppy went to the kitchen to get a fresh pitcher of tea, she leaned forward and said gently, "We're not Jewish, you know."

Then Reverend Walker asked Liyana if she'd been bathed in the blood of Jesus and she could see Rafik's eyes open wider. Luckily her tongue got stuck and her mother replied, "Um—we don't think—quite in those terms."

So everyone had some nut cookies and hot tea. Rafik said, out of the blue, "Do you know what our grandmother has in her collection? She has an empty tear gas canister that the Israeli soldiers threw at her house one day. It says *Made in Pennsylvania* on the side of it. The soldiers get their weapons and their money from the United States." The guests' eyes grew wide. They didn't know what to say. Then Rafik buttered his last pocket of bread.

Reverend Holman said to their mother, as if Rafik and Liyana weren't present, "Your children must feel alienated here, don't they?"

Mom said, puffing proudly, "I think they're doing quite well."

Rafik added, sighing in a melodramatic way, "But we *do* miss the school milk in little red cartons," which made his mother put her thumb and first finger together like an alligator closing its mouth.

After dinner the visitors went out on the front balcony to meditate on the hospital idea. Rafik and Liyana wrinkled their noses at each other and escaped into Rafik's room, where he put on his cassette tape of Japanese bamboo flute music. Liyana stared out the window where the heavens blazed like an orange bonfire, and wrote in her notebook:

The hills are dark with the shadows of night
But up in the sky is a brilliant light
of fire, fire, fire in the sky.

That day her geography teacher had said Arabs and Jews should trade places for a while and see what it felt like to be each other. But Atom said it would be too hard to do. She wondered. Could she even imagine exactly what it would feel like to be her own brother? Poppy's voice called them back to the living room. "We miss you in here!"

Reverend Crump asked for a last glass of water so he could take his "anti-panic pill" and Liyana stifled a laugh, pretending it was a cough. Poppy asked if the meal had upset him and he said, "Night brings on a brooding melancholia."

When Reverend Walker laid her hand on his back and said something that sounded as if she were speaking in tongues, "HIYA-hallah-wallah-kallah-mone," Rafik's eyes widened with interest.

Reverend Holman announced they'd decided to travel on into Jordan because they really wanted to see the famous carved city of Petra, so they'd better not take on any voluntary duties at that poor hospital in Gaza after all. But Lord have mercy, they'd keep it in their prayers.

Later, after he had driven them back to their hotel, Poppy was muttering, "Holy, holy, holy."

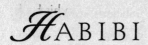ABIBI

*Darling: a dearly loved person,
a favorite, a charmer.*

For years the word floated in the air around their heads, yellow pollen, wispy secret dust of the ages passed on and on.

Habibi, darling, or *Habibti*, feminine for my darling. Poppy said it before bedtime or if they fell off their bikes—as a soothing syrup, to make them feel sweetened again. He said it as good morning or tucked in between sentences. He said it when they left for school.

Whatever else happened, Liyana and Rafik were his darlings all day and they knew it. Even when he stayed at the hospital past their bedtimes, they could feel his *darling* drifting comfortably around them.

Their mother called them "precious"—her own English version of the word. She fed them, folded their clothes even when they could have done it themselves, and squeezed fresh orange juice instead of opening frozen cans.

At Liyana's house they had fresh apple salad

with dates, baked yams, delicious stir-fried cabbage. They had a father who wrapped their mother in his arms. They had "*Habibi,* be careful, *Habibti,* I love you," trailing them like a long silken scarf. Liyana knew it didn't happen for everybody.

In Jerusalem they were living in the land of *Habibi*—Sitti rolled it off her tongue toward them and it balanced in the air like a bubble. They hovered inside the wide interest of these people they barely knew.

Their giant family offered them glasses of cool lemonade with sprigs of mint stuck in like straws. They handed them bowls of pastel Jordan almonds and the softest cushions to sit on.

In return, Liyana's family gave them oddities to think about. Liyana played the violin for them and told them, through Poppy, she would be in a symphony in Europe someday. They didn't know what a symphony was. Liyana wore blue jeans with paisley patches on the knees and her aunts pointed and whispered.

Poppy admonished her, "They think you're destitute if you dress like that."

Liyana said, "So?" She repeated the word inside her mind. "Des-ti-tute. Desti-TOOT." She started to like it.

Liyana smashed a potato in a bowl, mixed it with butter, milk, and salt till it was creamy, and offered it to Sitti. *"Mashed potato,"* she said, as Sitti carefully tasted it, and smiled. Sitti took the whole bowl from her hands and gobbled it down. She even tried to shape the words. *"Mash bo-tay-toes."*

It was the first English she'd ever tried to say.

———

Liyana's whole family seemed to be joining things. Poppy had joined a human-rights group to focus on treatment and services for old people. Rafik had joined an ecology club at his school—they would work with garbage and recycling. Their mother belonged to a Women's Communications Club—women of different backgrounds writing letters to editors and sharing optimistic ideas. She would probably be elected president soon. After their first meeting, the *Jerusalem Post* wrote an editorial saying if other people followed their example, the peace process might zoom ahead.

And Liyana? She belonged to nothing but Watchers Anonymous. She walked the streets of old Jerusalem muttering her new words in Arabic, sprinkling them down into cracks between stones. *Ana tayyib*—I'm fine. *Wa alaykum essalaam*—and upon you peace. *Shway*—a little bit. Watermelon

was *hubhub*. It wasn't any harder to say *Ana 'asif*—
I'm sorry—than it was to say other things.

But people acted like it was. Two taxi drivers
honked and honked at a jammed intersection,
refusing to budge. A boy threw a hard ball at a
geranium pot on Imm Janan's front step and it
shattered.

Liyana was no better. One day in Arabic class
she grew so irritated with the dull text, she ripped
a whole page out of her book. The teacher ordered
her to stand in the hall and wrote a mean letter to
her father. In Arabic.

Poppy said, *"Habibti, please."*

Liyana took a walk by herself down by the
refugee camp, standing for a long time in the
pinkish light soaking up the quiet motions of
evening. Women unpinned skirts and undershirts
from lines. Where were Nadine and Khaled
tonight? She always felt better when she talked to
them. Boys polished crooked bicycles with rags.
What pumped up their hopes?

"Poppy, do you think there will ever be a time
when all people get along just fine?" she asked
when she got home.

He was marking hospital charts at the table.

"Nope."

What would Liyana do if she could?

She'd touch Omer's shoulder lightly and leave a little *habibi* dust there. She'd place one secret red poppy alongside Sitti's pillow and disappear into the cool night air.

ℬANANA EASTER

*Who can guess
what the weather will bring?*

Jerusalem woke to a blizzard for the first time in fifty years on Easter Sunday. Poppy stood by the front window exclaiming, "This is just not something you expect to see here!"

The road out front looked strangely deserted except for a few kids in raggedy jackets and two disoriented goats. Rafik ran downstairs in his pajamas, opening his mouth to the sky. He said the snow tasted like icing without vanilla in it.

Mrs. Abboud had tried to bake hot cross buns, as she did every Easter, but they didn't rise. "Let's call them hot cross pancakes," she said. It was the first year nobody was interested in hiding any eggs.

The whole family drove slowly through swirling snow to the Garden Tomb, where Liyana's mother wanted to attend the sunrise service. She got ideas into her head and would not let go of them, no matter what the weather. How could she miss her first Easter service here in the place where everything had really *happened?* Arab families stood outside in their transformed yards staring happily up into the magical air. Did they even know how to make snowballs?

Recently, Liyana's mother had narrated a program at the radio station called "Debate Over the Tombs." Some people believed the tomb of Jesus was at a different location. Mom voted for the one on the cliff above the bus station, a cave in the craggy rock, where a small group of devout and frozen people was already waiting, shivering in skinny coats and scarves and hats and gloves.

The sun did not rise.

Or if it rose, no one could tell.

There was snow on the crooked branches of the olive tree. People crowded close among snow-capped stones while a priest with chattering teeth held his Bible and tried to speak. He said Easter gave human beings their highest hopes. It was the "greatest feast of the year, the victory march of the human soul." Poppy leaned over to whisper in Liyana's ear, "Jerusalem needs lower hopes, too; down-to-the-ground, pebble-sized, poppy-seed-sized hopes." She closed her eyes, trying to feel what it *meant* to be assured that dying did not just mean *dead.*

Many in the crowd were weeping. Maybe they had dreamed of being here for years. Maybe they had traveled from Spain and California and the tears would freeze on their cheeks. Near the end of the service, a tall, thin-faced lady toppled over backward into the snow and struck Liyana with her elbow on the way down. Rafik blurted, "Whoa!"

Poppy rushed to the lady's side. He carried smelling salts in his pocket for such occasions. He carried aspirins and nitroglycerin tablets and who knew what else. He leaned over and spoke to the fallen lady gently. She didn't seem very hurt. She kept arranging her hair. Poppy took her pulse and whispered to her while someone called a taxi to drive her back to her hotel. She said she didn't need to go to a hospital and that she fainted every time she got "emotional."

She had disrupted the final prayer. As a few Americans started singing "How Great Thou Art," to fill in the space, Liyana's eyes traveled curiously around the group. She felt startled to see her secretly famous banana seller standing off to the right, wearing a bulky blue sweater much too large for him. He'd been hidden behind someone till people began moving around. His hands were poked up high in either sleeve. Liyana had never seen him without his cart before. She poked Rafik and whispered, "Look who's here!"

Poppy helped the weak-kneed lady into the

car, then turned to Liyana as it disappeared. He was grinning. "You know what? She thought this snow was a miracle—it swept her away!"

Behind Poppy, the dwarf broke into the first smile Liyana had ever seen on his face. He said, in Arabic, *"Mabruk"*—"Congratulations!"

Liyana reached toward him to shake his hand.

"Fee mooz?" she asked, which meant something like, "Do you have a banana?" Or maybe it meant, *"Is there* a banana?" which sounded a little foolish if you considered it.

Miraculously, as miraculous as snow on Easter and strangers passing out onto the ground, the small, smiling man pulled a stubby banana from his pants pocket and handed it to her. She tried to press a coin from her wallet into his hand, but he waved it away, laughing heartily, saying Arabic words she couldn't understand.

Poppy looked startled by this odd transaction. "What's going on?" he said.

Liyana dangled her prize banana in front of his nose. A yellow banana in the white, white snow.

Rafik said, "It's an Easter egg."

A DAY
COULD UNFOLD

Teach me to sew a vine of stars.

One day at lunchtime, after buying a slightly tattered two-months-old American women's magazine at the newsstand as a surprise for her mother, Liyana heard her name floating above the idling taxis near the King David Hotel. She raised her head to the sky as if a bird had called her.

Then Omer appeared, sprinting up to her startled side, and said, "You didn't tell me your name means a vine! I found it spelled almost the same way in the dictionary—a tropical rain- forest vine. It roots in the ground."

Liyana grinned. "Where have you *been?*"

"Where have *you* been?"

He said, "I was going to call you last night." It seemed like a thin little lie anybody might say, but she liked it.

Omer wanted to invite her to a poetry reading by local poets at his school that evening. She said she'd have to see if one of her parents could drive her, since it was at night. He drew a map to his school on the back of a grocery list written in Hebrew from his pocket.

"Do you still have my number?" he asked.

Liyana thought, *Oh please.*

"Well," he grinned, "you did not use it recently, so I could not be sure."

He held her elbow for a moment before she ran off toward the Armenian Quarter and her Arabic class, which was already two minutes into its lesson on how to ask questions.

Again, as it had before when Liyana saw Omer at lunchtime, the afternoon puffed up lightly, joyously, a delicate pastry, a sweetened shell of hours.

On the local bus home, everything still shone in the light of Omer's smile. The cracked bus seats, squealing brakes, ladies with huge plastic bags of fresh bread, the bus driver's bald head, were shining, shining.

"*Shookran!*" Liyana exclaimed to the driver, climbing down at her stop. "*Thank you!*"

She was not usually so enthusiastic.

The driver lifted his hands from the wheel and shimmied them in the air, laughing at her. "*Alham'dul-Allah!*"

Praise be to God—that a day could unfold with surprise invitations. Liyana leapt upstairs two steps at a time.

But she was met by her brother with a stunned look on his face. "Khaled's been shot," he said. "And Poppy's in jail."

HOW MANY SIDES DOES A STORY HAVE?

A story is a seam in a dress—
some days it unravels.

"What?" screamed Liyana. "What do you mean? Where is Mom?"

She dropped her school bag onto the floor.

"Mom went off in a Palestinian police car. She made me stay here to tell you. She is *very very* upset." Rafik looked bleary-eyed.

"How do these things go together?"

"What things?"

"Khaled and Poppy!"

"I don't know," he sobbed. "I'm telling you everything she told me. Ismael's father dropped me off here after school and Mom was blazing out the door into a police car that was parked out back, this strange kind of car I don't even know the name of, and I didn't get any more details."

"ALWAYS get details!"

Liyana rushed into the kitchen and stared at the phone. She had no idea whom to call. In this country you didn't call 911. "Let's go down to the camp and find Nadine," she said. "Maybe Nadine can tell us something."

Liyana and Rafik galloped down the road without speaking. The refugee camp looked more topsy-turvy than usual. Beat-up cars sat at odd angles out front, as if people had jumped from them without parking. A sack of pita bread lay scattered on the ground. A heap of smoking rubber tires polluted the air. And a crowd of teenaged boys huddled together by the small house with the blue-painted front door where Khaled and Nadine lived with their parents.

"Hello!" Liyana shouted to the boys. "Please, *wane* Nadine?"

The boys yelled in unison, "Nadine!"

Nadine came to her window and peered out anxiously.

"*Yallah!*" Liyana yelled to her. "Quickly! We need to talk to you!"

Nadine came stepping out of the house with bare feet. She was shivering. Where were her shoes? Where was her shy mother, Abla, who often served small plates of delicious sweets and figs to Liyana and Rafik?

"Where is your mother?" Liyana said.

Nadine cried, "She went hospital with Khaled. He was bad, bad! Shot!"

"We heard that! It's terrible! But—who shot him?"

Nadine said the word for "soldiers" and covered her eyes.

Liyana stared at Rafik, baffled. "So how did Poppy get into this?" Of course she had never considered that their father, who could not even trap a mouse, had shot their friend, but the connections seemed jumbled.

"You father—he come run—from you house," explained Nadine. "He see the soldiers—no like it. He come run, he wave arms," she demonstrated, waving wildly. "The soldiers call *Khaled!—come out house!* Khaled no come out." She used the Arabic word for "scared." She was crying hard now. "The soldiers say, *Yallah! Yallah!* The soldiers mad! Khaled come out, turn round and the soldier shoot! Khaled fall down. Is bad, bad! You father run to soldier, say *No! No!* He stop him." She threw her arm.

Liyana was staring open-mouthed.

Rafik said, "He *hit* the soldier?"

"No, no, no hit, just..." She showed them. Poppy had pulled the soldier's arm back. Hard.

Liyana covered her mouth. Rafik asked, "The arm that had a gun in it?" but Nadine didn't understand. Nadine said the ambulance came for Khaled and the soldiers took Poppy. They pushed him into a car.

Now everybody was crying. Liyana was crying. "Which hospital?" she wailed. "And where is the jail?"

One of Khaled's cousins knew where the jail was. He'd been in it twice himself. He didn't look very happy about going back there. But he walked quickly with Liyana and Rafik to the Abbouds' house to call a taxi.

When they reached Jerusalem, after passing the usual daily things—vegetable carts, sheep, stores, family vineyards propped on poles—the taxi turned sharply onto a gray industrial-looking street.

At the grim-faced jail, Liyana strode up to three Israeli soldiers guarding the front and said, "Please, I need to see my father, Dr. Kamal Abboud. He hasn't been here long. He came— maybe an hour ago."

One soldier sitting on a crate lifted his eyes sleepily from the orange he was peeling. "Not possible," he said. She could smell the fragrant orange scent rising from his hands.

Something shifted inside her. It trembled and

could have turned her away. Her throat felt shaky. But she didn't turn. She stomped her foot on the pavement, raising her leg twice and pounding her foot down as hard as she could. Liyana stomped her foot at the soldiers. "Of *course* it's possible!" she said loudly. "He is my *father!* I need to see him! NOW! PLEASE! It's necessary! I must go in this minute!"

The soldiers looked her up and down. She was still wearing her navy blue school uniform with its rumpled white cotton blouse. The soldier with the orange sighed heavily, as if she were really irritating him. He dropped the peelings into a sack, wiped his hands, and said, "Come." But another soldier put his arm up and made Rafik stay out front, which made him furious.

———

The first soldier took Liyana into an office, shone a hot spotlight into her face, and photographed her. He asked her name, age, school, her phone number, and address, barking his questions. He asked two more times what she wanted and she repeated, "To see my father." Did he have a bad memory? The second time she spoke calmly and slowly. He took the embroidered purse Sitti had made and said she could not take it in. She watched him toss it onto a dirty table cluttered with empty coffee cups. He said she could not stay long.

Liyana followed the soldier down a gloomy hall, staring into dark cells as her eyes adjusted. Sleeping bodies lay wrapped in blankets on cots. Some cubicles had high slits for windows, but some had none. One man stood tall in the center of his cell, staring straight toward the hall where she walked, his hands held behind his back. His face looked blank. It was strange to walk through a jail. What were the prisoners' stories? How long had they been here? Had they done anything worse than her father had?

Poppy sat on a wooden stool in a cell bent over with his head in his hands. Usually he only sat this way when one of his patients was dying. Her mother was nowhere to be seen. A small moan escaped from Poppy's mouth when he saw her through the iron bars, but he wasn't crying. The air smelled dank and sour.

"*Habibti!*" he said. "*No no no!* What in the world are you doing here? How did you get in? This is no place for you!"

"Or you either," Liyana said, gripping a bar. It was strange how calm she felt the minute she entered his presence. "Poppy! We have to help you get out!"

He said, "I'm working on it. Liyana, don't

worry. I'll be out soon. It's a big mistake. Take care of yourself! *Go home! Stay safe!*" The soldier stood behind Liyana with his arms folded.

"Where is your mother?"

"I don't know! I thought she might be here. How bad is Khaled? Which hospital is he in?"

Poppy thought Khaled's leg wound would not kill him. "It was low down. I hope they wrapped it before he bled much. The soldiers whisked me away so I couldn't even help him! I kept telling them I was a doctor! I said, "Since when do you arrest doctors on the scene of an injury?" But they wouldn't listen to me. Oh, it certainly was a case of being in the wrong place at the wrong time. I know you hate that phrase." He shook his head. "I just keep thinking how we used to carve faces into acorns with our pocket knives. We would stick broken matches into them and spin them on the ground like tops. Now look where we are!" He waved his hand back and forth as if to indicate he was speaking about all the prisoners on the hall. And the soldiers too.

"But Poppy, what was *happening* at the camp in the first place?" Liyana asked.

He said, "*Habibti,* if I wanted to talk about first places, I'd have to go too far back. What was happening *today* was the bomb in the Jewish market-place—did you hear about the bomb?—near a school, which is terrible. The soldiers got a tip that someone in Khaled's camp had something to do with it. That's why they came into territory they're not supposed to be administering anymore. Maybe they thought Khaled did it! But we *know* how much Khaled hates violence....How could I stand by saying nothing? He's not a bathtub, for God's sake...."

The soldier stepped forward roughly, motioning that he was ready to escort Liyana out, but she held her hand up and said sternly, "WAIT." Poppy opened his dark eyes very wide. He raised his eyebrows. "Liyana, go!" he ordered. "Get out of here!"

The man in the next cell was praying loudly.

"Poppy, *we love you!*" she said, clinging to the bars with both hands by now. She could have thrown herself down on the ground like a little girl having a tantrum. But she held back, held tightly, saying only, "This is not *right*."

Poppy placed two fingers on his lips and blew a kiss at her. "Don't tell Sitti!" he said. "Promise me! She'll stage a revolution! Take care, *habibti!* And where's Rafik?" he shouted, as the guard marched her off.

"Outside! They wouldn't let him in!"

Liyana reclaimed her purse from the office and asked the soldier if he knew where her mother might be, but he pretended he didn't understand her.

Before jumping back into the waiting taxi with Rafik and Khaled's cousin, who both looked deeply curious about what had just happened inside the jail, Liyana stared hard into the face of the soldier who had escorted her. He was sitting on his crate again. She didn't blink. She wanted to see him clearly.

Then she stared into the faces of the other two soldiers guarding the prison door. They leaned into the wall, huge guns slung over their shoulders. They could have been handsome if they had smiled. She couldn't stop herself. Pointing at them with the forefingers of both her hands, she said loudly, "You do not have to be so mean! You could be nicer! My father is a doctor! My friend you shot is a gentle person! YOU DO NOT HAVE TO BE THIS WAY!"

The soldiers didn't say anything. But they looked surprised.

At the tall white hospital, which reeked of ammonia, but still smelled better than the jail, Liyana, Rafik, and Khaled's cousin were admitted to see Khaled without any trouble. Liyana and Rafik said they were his cousins, too. They let the true cousin do the talking until they got inside.

Khaled was still down in Emergency on a thin

little bed with his leg wrapped as tightly as a stuffed grape leaf. His mother sat beside him wringing water out of a washcloth. She was bathing his face. Khaled looked surprised to see his visitors and lifted partway up on his elbows.

"What!" he said weakly. "You find me! I am worried about your father! Where is he?"

A nurse refreshed a water glass beside Khaled's bed. She stared at his guests, then left. Khaled said he'd heard about the bomb on the radio and felt very sad. Then he said, "You know I know nothing else about it."

"We know."

Rafik stared at Liyana. *She* knew. He didn't know. He hated being cut out of things. Liyana said they'd both seen Nadine, who was very upset. She said Poppy was acting fairly calm behind bars. Khaled shook his head. "He was good to me. He tried to stop them. He hates fighting, too. He told me that when we came home from the Dead Sea. I can't believe they took him!"

"Doesn't this make you feel *more* like fighting?" Liyana asked.

Khaled sighed heavily, stretching his upper body as if his neck were stiff. He seemed very tired. "Believe me, I feel less. Ohhhhh..." He closed his eyes and sighed. "Did you know—it's my birthday?"

"NO!" Liyana and Rafik spoke together. "Is it really?"

Rafik shook his head soberly. "I'm starting to think birthdays are bad luck."

A black-and-white clock on the wall said six. The fragrance of cooking rice wafted down the hospital hall. At least *some* things still felt normal.

As they exited the hospital, Rafik said, "*Now* where are we going?"

Liyana whispered, "Home."

———◦———

She liked how the taxi driver waited wherever they asked him to. He was idling in front of the hospital. He knew they were having an upsetting day. In the car heading north, Rafik said, "Tell me every one of Poppy's words. Did he look scared? Did they have chains in there?"

Liyana said, "I didn't see chains," but Khaled's cousin, the one who had been in jail himself, said, "Believe me, they have everything."

It seemed strange to find their house sitting calmly where it always sat, lights in the first-floor windows and the upstairs dark. Their car was still parked outside, too. But their mother wasn't back yet. She rang them up from police headquarters in Jerusalem soon after they had entered the house and flicked on lights in every room.

"I have good news," she reported, brightly. "They say your father will be released tonight. I haven't seen him. I've been filling out papers in ten offices. This is the worst day of my life, but it will have a happy ending! Have you been home all afternoon?"

Liyana went downstairs to ask Abu Janan more about the bomb in the market. He shook his head. "People dead." Old men and women. Innocent, everyday people who had as much to do with politics as Liyana did. Shopping bags. Corn. Purses. Stockings. Shoes. Kleenex. Teeth. Earrings.

How could anyone do that? Liyana thought. Maybe it was done by the Arab father whose ten-year-old son was shot by Israeli soldiers last week. Maybe it was done by the brothers of the tortured prisoners Poppy met all the time, or the cousin of the mayor who lost both legs when the Israelis blew up his car. Did people who committed acts of violence think their victims and their victims' relatives would just *forget?*

Didn't people see? How violence went on and on like a terrible wheel? Could you stand in front of a wheel to make it stop? What if Khaled had been killed when he was shot? Would that have made Liyana or Nadine do something violent, too? It was better, as happened with Khaled's own grandparents and himself, if you were able to let the violence stop when it got to you. But many people couldn't do that.

The telephone rang in their apartment again and Rafik raced up the stairs to get it. "It's for you!" he shouted down to Liyana.

Her feet felt leaden on the stairs.

"Poetry reading?" Omer's voice said.

Liyana had forgotten completely.

$\mathcal{N}$EGOTIATIONS

Maybe peace was the size of a teacup.

"*Jail*," said Poppy soberly, settling himself on the couch with a large glass of water and tipping his head back, "is an experience I don't ever want to have again." He'd come home from jail at 11 P.M. in a taxi and the driver refused to take a cent from him.

Liyana, Rafik, and their mother were shocked when Sitti climbed out of the taxi after him. Where did *she* come from? Rafik and Liyana jumped up and down. "Poppy's home! Poppy's free!" He hugged them so tightly, Liyana felt surprised.

Sitti had appeared at the jail a few hours after Liyana did. The soldiers wouldn't let her in, though. As Poppy was being released, he found her outside shouting, waving a broom, and demanding to see the governor. "She still thinks it's fifty years ago," he said, shaking his head. "We had someone called a governor then." An old lady she knew at Khaled's camp had called Sitti's village to tell about Poppy being arrested.

Poppy said, "You can't keep any secrets over here."

A few nights later the Abbouds were eating cabbage rolls at the dinner table—Mom made Liyana a small casserole of vegetarian ones on the side, filled with nuts and raisins and rice—and everything was almost back to normal. Khaled was back at the camp with a heavily bandaged leg and a crutch. The Abbouds had been down to welcome him with molasses cookies that afternoon. Sitti had carried her broom home to its corner.

But Poppy seemed a little odd. He'd taken a few days off from work and kept sitting at the dining table scribbling notes and staring into space. He made an unusual number of phone calls and spoke only in Arabic. One day their mother reported he wore his pajama top till noon—something he *never* did.

When Liyana asked what was going on, he said he couldn't stop thinking about all the people who were still in jail—many for more ridiculous reasons than his own. He was becoming an activist in his old age. He was going to see the Jewish mayor of Jerusalem tomorrow. He'd heard a man coughing too hard a few cells down. The man obviously needed medicine. He put both his hands up in the air. He walked down to the refugee camp and talked to everybody. He rolled his papers and banged them on the table. "I'm trying to figure out how many things an ordinary citizen can do!"

But at dinner he asked Liyana, "Now what are *you* thinking about? The tables are turned. You've been so quiet tonight."

She dove in. "Could my friend Omer—Mom's met him—come to the village with us someday soon? He's never been to—an Arab village. He invited me to a poetry reading the other evening, but I wasn't able to go, since my father was just getting out of jail—so I thought it might be nice to invite him somewhere, too."

Poppy's hand went up to his forehead. "Right now? Oh, Liyana. He's curious about us? He wants to know how we do things? He likes our food?"

"You don't have to sound so defensive!"

Poppy was silent for a moment. That's what *he* always said to *her*. "Our family—wouldn't appreciate it. They wouldn't—understand. It would seem suspicious—or unsettling to them. The peace isn't stabilized enough yet."

"Understand? What's there to understand about having a friend?"

"Liyana—you know. You're just acting innocent on purpose."

"I *don't* know! I don't *want* to know! What good is it to believe in peace and talk about peace if you only want to live the same old ways?"

"Is his family orthodox?"

"No. He doesn't seem orthodox—anything. He seems very universal."

Poppy sighed. "They always seem—universal. Do you have any passages from your favorite prophet Kahlil Gibran you'd like to read to me just now?"

Liyana's mother tapped her water glass with a spoon. "Don't make fun," she said to Poppy. "Remember what my parents said when I fell in love with you? They said nothing, remember? And do you remember how cruel that was?"

Poppy reeled back in his chair. "Now she's in love?" he thundered. "Liyana's in love? I thought she just wanted to go to the village!"

Rafik was roaring. Liyana hated this.

"So is it okay or not?" she asked, pushing back two lonely green beans to the edge of her plate.

Poppy was quiet.

A bus roared by on the road outside.

Liyana said softly, "We want to write a new story," and Poppy said, "What?"

Mom, queen of her Communications Club, took a deep breath. "She's right, you know. What good is a belief in peace if it doesn't change the ways we live?"

But Poppy wasn't listening. "It's *inappropriate* for a girl to invite a boy anywhere in this part of the world. They'll think you're engaged or something. They'll think he's a spy. How will I explain him?"

Rafik groaned. "Could we talk about something else? Let's just invite him already! Who cares? Say he's MY FRIEND, not Liyana's! Say he's my mentor or something—like we had in school in the United States. I met him at the library. He's a nice guy. And Sitti invites everyone *else* on earth to our dinners—why not him, too? "

Liyana loved Rafik with all her heart.

Poppy said, "He was at the library, too?"

Then he said, "You're *stubborn,* dear Liyana. You're that fine Arabian horse again, constantly trying to get your own way. Why do you want to take him and not Khaled or Nadine?"

"Let's take them as well! Let's take everybody! Don't you want a coming-out party? And didn't you mention, last week, how wonderful it was when Mr. Hamadi, your favorite thousand-year-old patient, let the Jewish doctor work on his eyes and never once referred to his ethnicity? Didn't you say before you went in jail that it would be great if people never described each other as 'the Jew' or 'the Arab' or 'the black guy' or 'the white guy'—didn't you just SAY?"

Her mother repeated, "She's right, you know."

⁂

After dinner, Liyana was on the phone. Omer always laughed when she identified herself with both her names. "You think I can't tell? I told you you're the only Liyana I know!" His rich voice rang out, a rippling stream of energy across the wire between their rooms. The minute she heard him, she wished they could talk forever.

Poppy had told Liyana they shouldn't "set the date" for the village trip yet. He made it sound like a marriage. It would happen—"someday"—when the time felt better. When Khaled's leg was stronger. "Don't rush me," Poppy said. "Don't rush anything. Okay?"

Omer was so happy Liyana had taken his interest seriously.

But he called her back the next day, sounding downcast, just needing to talk. His mother didn't want him to go to the village with Liyana, *ever*, but he told his mother it was very important. "Then she took a long walk," he said.

"What does that mean?"

"It means she's worried. And I'm going. Just let me know when."

Omer was leaving for two weeks with his class on an extended field trip to a kibbutz in northern

Israel. They did this every year. He wasn't thrilled about it. He'd be picking cherries, boxing them, digging, and weeding. The thought of such a long gap till they might meet again made Liyana's heart sputter in her throat.

She wrote for two hours that night, putting the word "heart" together with every verb she could think of. Her heart tipped, it rumbled, it swelled. She tried to write a story in which she was not the main character, in which some person she had never heard of before did things and felt things. But she still had trouble imagining lives she had not lived.

NEW COUNTRY, OLD COUNTRY

For the first time these days,
she also felt like part of a sea.

When Liyana considered the echoes bouncing off the walls of Jerusalem, she felt like the dot on an *i* in an American alphabet book for babies. Nearly invisible.

When she turned a corner in the Old City, she was just a ripple of an ancient, continuing echo. *Going, going…almost gone.*

"Will we ever go home?" she asked Poppy after an evening walk up to the small grocery to smell the air and buy new wooden clothespins and a box of loose tea.

Poppy was whistling, so she figured it was a good moment to ask something like that.

He paused. "I would hope," he said, "that you felt comfortable here."

"Oh I *do*," she said. "I feel more comfortable every day. But I was just…wondering. Sometimes

I get incredibly homesick for…"

Then her mind went blank. What was she really homesick for? Those ugly green signs marking exits off the interstate? The sports sections of American newspapers that she never glanced at anyway? The chilled tapioca puddings in little tubs at the supermarket?

What was she really missing anymore?

———

Rafik told everybody he didn't miss anything. He had too much to think about over here to waste time with missing. He also said his Arabic was developing more quickly than Liyana's because he was less afraid of making mistakes. One day Liyana was trying to say "Excuse me" to somebody and she said something like "monkey's heart."

The sea. One wave running into another. But they had lived beside the Mississippi River, not beside a sea. She used to imagine the river running southward to pour into the Gulf of Mexico she'd never visited. Now, from this great distance, she felt closer to everything than she ever had before.

She did not feel like a foreigner in the Old City anymore. Now she had her own landmarks and scenes to remember. She had Hani, the banana seller, Bilal, the fabric seller, and Bassam, the spice man. She knew where a certain stone corner was chipped away. Maybe a vendor had bumped it with his cart long ago. She knew where the cabbages were lined on burlap in front of a radiant old woman who raised one hand to Liyana as if she were blessing her. She knew the blind shopkeeper who sat on a stool in front of his shop nodding and saying, "*Sabah-al-khair*—Good morning"— to the air. The Old City was inside her already.

"Did you ever think," Poppy said, "that some of us might stay and some of us go back—in the future, maybe, when you and Rafik are grown? Wouldn't it be strange if you were the one who stayed—and the rest of us moved back to the States? How can anyone know what the next day brings?"

The next day brought two good things. One, Liyana received a tiny present in the mail from Peachy Helen, a new four-inch-tall edition of Kahlil Gibran, and it was a volume she didn't have yet. Secondly, Mr. Berberian brought up the history of the "peace talks" at school, and suggested the students ask their elders' opinions about them.

Since Liyana's family was going out to eat *kousa,* stuffed zucchini squash, in the village that evening, she got Poppy to ask Sitti at dinnertime.

Sitti was wrapping the cooked *kousa* in white cotton towels to keep them hot on the plate.

Sitti looked surprised. She puffed up like a dove when it ruffles its feathers.

She pointed at her own chest and said, "I never lost my peace inside."

$\mathcal{E}$XPEDITION

Her father always told them
the Arabs were famous for their hospitality.

Finally one day when Poppy was in an especially good mood because a new wing at the hospital had just been completed and his dear old patients got to move into better rooms, he said to Liyana, "Okay, why don't you invite your friends? We'll go out to the village next Saturday as usual. The Jews and Arabs are talking better over in Hebron for a change. Maybe it's a good time for—your friend—to come along. And I'd like to get Khaled and Nadine out of that camp for a day."

On Saturday, Liyana kept watching from the balcony till the lumbering bus that carried Omer appeared on the hill. She ran out to meet him. He waved happily. He said he'd liked the bus trip north, which he'd never taken before. "Not understanding all the talk around me, but just picking up bits and pieces, made me feel—free."

"I guess I should be feeling free all the time, then."

Liyana's mother walked daintily down the

steps with her hand extended. "Hello again!" she said to Omer. She was wearing her pink embroidered Mexican blouse, which she usually wore on birthdays and holidays. Liyana had even dressed up in a maroon velvet vest.

Poppy was in the bathroom when they went upstairs, "shaving," Mom said. Liyana guessed he was really hiding out. "We'll be going to the village as soon as he's ready."

Rafik lay on his bed reading a recently arrived tome of Star Trek wisdom, the Vulcan dictionary. One of his strange extraterrestrial friends in the U.S. had sent it to him. Rafik told Omer, "It took a month for it to arrive surface mail, which means it came on a ship. Liyana says it was obviously not a spaceship."

Rafik mumbled some gobbledygook to Omer that probably meant "comrade." Then he stood up, extended his hand normally, and asked in English if Omer would like to play catch until they left.

When Poppy emerged from the bathroom, his skin looked raw. He came toward Omer with his hand out, a little too jauntily, and said, "Let's hit the road!" Liyana thought he looked at Omer curiously, in a good way. They picked up Khaled and Nadine at the camp. Nadine had a bundle of *za'tar* breads wrapped in a cloth for Sitti from her mother.

Driving up to the village, Rafik and Nadine, who were smallest in size, huddled on the floor of the back seat, laughing. Liyana was tucked into the center of the seat between Khaled and Omer. Today she didn't mind at all that they were crowded. She even liked the curves more than usual, when they made her lean in Omer's direction.

Poppy stopped at three different shops to pick up newspapers, bottled water, tins of apricot juice, a stack of two dozen pita breads, a bulging sack of fresh oranges, some with leaves still attached, and a special kind of white cheese. "Keep going, already!" Liyana's mother said. "The car is stuffed!"

Liyana thought Poppy was trying to stall.

As their car careened past a concrete Jewish settlement with its enclosures of barbed-wire fencing and military tower, Omer craned his neck to stare out the window and spoke soberly. "I have never before seen this part of the West Bank. I always wanted to see it."

He stared out at stony orchard terraces and banks of olive trees. Deep pools of shade. Cradled valleys. Flocks of stone-colored sheep. Poppy kept taking full breaths at the wheel, as if he were hyperventilating. Khaled had his face pressed to the window. Omer said, "These lands don't seem abandoned. The villages look very old. I *knew* it wasn't true."

Poppy said, "Who says they are abandoned?"

Omer said, "People—say."

Then Poppy asked Omer, "What do your friends think about the West Bank?"

Khaled looked at him. Omer stared and stared out the window. He said, "They feel—scared. They—don't know. They never came here. They think it is a different world."

There was a long silence in which Poppy echoed him, whispering, "Different world?" He didn't sound mad about it.

"I never imagined it—so beautiful over here," Omer whispered.

Liyana tapped her mother on the shoulder, speaking softly. "Remember? That's just what we said!"

Rafik whispered, "Are we in a spy zone or something? Why is everybody whispering?"

Liyana's hand brushed Omer's on the seat. He gave it a little squeeze.

***

Poppy changed the subject. "Has Liyana ever told you about when I met the actor Omar Sharif?"

Omer said, "Yes, but you could tell me again." Poppy laughed. He was loosening up.

In the village, the almond trees around Sitti's house had burst wide open with fragrant white blossoms. They hadn't been blooming the week before. Everyone breathed deeply and stretched as they stepped out of the car.

Swirls of children appeared around them. They carried blue marbles, rattles in an old tin can. Their faces hoped, *did you bring us anything? Gum, candies, what, what, what?* The only cow in town, hidden within a neighbor's courtyard, let out a loud *Moooooooo.*

Omer said, "Even the cows welcome you?"

"Of course!" Liyana said, and Poppy laughed.

Poppy pulled a handful of clinky loose change from his pocket and dropped it on the ground in front of three boys. "Oh-oh!" he shrugged, teasing them in Arabic. "Take it, take it!"

Rafik produced a pack of Chiclet chewing gum and peeled the wrapper back. He held out the box. Omer startled Liyana by pulling a plastic sack of orange balloons from the backpack he carried.

"What else do you have in there?" she asked.

He tipped his head and looked secretive. "Slowly!" he told her.

Around their heads, in the sweetness of a breeze

that already smelled of summer, a dozen children blew up their blazing orange bananas and planets. They huffed and giggled. Some had almost no air in their little lungs at all. Khaled helped them. Sitti stepped from her stone courtyard flapping her hands. She hated it when people stood around outside. She wanted them inside, sitting down. Sometimes the village felt like a kingdom with Sitti as the queen.

They stepped carefully over the crooked threshold of Sitti's house. Liyana liked watching Omer notice things. When his eyes fell on her own second-grade school picture with two missing front teeth poked into the corner of Sitti's picture frame, he pointed and made a question mark with his hand. *You?* She grinned. Balloons were bumping and plummeting against the ceiling as children batted them high.

Dareen, Liyana's second cousin ten times removed, appeared with a huge bouquet of mint. Omer stuck his face into it as she passed and she laughed. She was shy.

"I like *n'an'a*," he said, using the Arabic word for mint, which startled Liyana.

"You know some Arabic?"

He turned his finger in the air. "Language is one tiny shiny key!"

She felt a sudden regret—she didn't know

anything in Hebrew yet. "All I know is *shalom.*"

"That's a beginning," Omer said. Liyana thought how both Hebrew and Arabic came from such a deep, related place in the throat. English felt skinny beside them.

But if she tried to take on one more language, she thought, she might explode—like the almond trees with their billowy blossoms.

Sitti kissed Nadine and Khaled on both cheeks and leaned down to place her hand gently on Khaled's leg. She said a blessing over it. Then she shook Omer's hand, putting her face very close to his to stare at him. Moments later, she spilled her high-pitched siren again. Was she *that* glad to see them? Flapping her fabulous tongue way back in her mouth, she wailed and trilled.

Liyana said, "I couldn't make that sound for a hundred sheckels," and Omer clapped his hands. "I saw it in an Arab movie once! It's like the tongue is trying to fly!"

Liyana, Rafik, and their three friends decided to hike around the village. They walked slowly because Khaled was still limping, passing the post office and climbing among the cemetery with its unmarked graves. Poppy's father's bones lay somewhere in there. Maybe he was dust. They walked among the lentil fields to a mysterious mounded shrine encircled by large smooth stones. They all stooped and looked. Prayer rugs were rolled against one wall. A circle of half-burned candles in blackened glasses filled a corner. Nadine and Rafik crawled inside. Khaled sat on a stone to rest.

Liyana plucked the feathered head from a weed. "Omer, how old were you when your father died?"

"Five."

"How did he die?"

"A car accident."

"Do you remember him?"

"He's—cloudy in my mind." He paused. Then he spoke again, staring at Khaled. "My father did not think Arabs and Jews could ever get together again. My mother says that, too, when she reads the news. She's pretty upset today. That I came here. My father thought our break was—really broken."

Khaled looked off across the valley. "It's a bad story."

Liyana said, "That's why we need to write a *better* one."

Far away, a single donkey brayed. The note resounded through the valley.

Omer ran his hand through his hair and

continued, "Sometimes I try to think of my father's eyes still in the world, looking. What did he see? He needed to see more!"

Khaled said, "We all need to see more."

They were quiet, suspended in yellow light that falls onto hills when no one is watching.

Then Rafik broke the spell, galloping down the road toward the spring where he and Omer scooped cold water straight into their palms. They splashed their own faces. They splashed each other's faces. Liyana walked behind more slowly with Khaled and Nadine. They seemed a little sad. Khaled said, "We wish our family lived up *here*."

Later everyone washed their hands and sat on floor cushions in the big family circle as platters of steaming food traveled around. They scooped mounds of rice and cauliflower onto plates and Omer asked questions through Poppy. He wanted to know people's jobs, how they were connected. Poppy said, "Don't get started! They're *all* connected!"

Liyana whispered to Poppy, "Who do they think he is?"

Poppy whispered back, "Who knows? Maybe they think he's our next-door neighbor from St.

Louis, since he's only speaking English. I just said he was our friend."

Omer, Khaled, and Nadine ate so much that everyone was complimented. The aunts always teased Liyana's family about living on "crumbs of bread and mint leaves." No one seemed suspicious of Omer, as Poppy had said they might. In fact, they seemed flattered that any mystery person would want to spend time with them. When you sat around with people, regular people with teacups and nutcrackers, they just wanted to get to know you.

Sitti threw her head back to gulp a soda straight from the bottle. A scraggly cat leapt through the doorway onto the ledge above Sitti's bed. She waved it away, muttering and mumbling.

"What's she saying?"

"I won't even begin to tell you." Poppy sighed.

Khaled said, "She told him he is not invited and he can go cook his own dinner with the other cats on the roof."

They ate and ate and ate. The whole day tasted wonderful. Afterward, when matches were struck for the awful after-dinner cigarettes and steam rose in small clouds from coffee cups, Omer said something directly to Sitti in slow, broken Arabic, which made the whole room go quiet. Now they *knew* he wasn't from St. Louis. A little hush rolled around the room.

Sitti replied in a voice more booming and animated than usual. It made Poppy sit straight up. Liyana tugged at him. "What is she saying?"

Everyone in the room pinned their eyes to her face. Except for Abu Daoud, who stormed from the room looking angry, after blurting something sharp to Omer. "What happened?" Liyana pulled Poppy's sleeve.

Poppy spoke haltingly. He didn't like translating if the person who had spoken could understand him. But sometimes he had to. Omer had said how much it meant to be with them. He thanked them for their welcome and said they felt like family to him. He wished they didn't have all these troubles in their shared country. Sitti said, "We have been waiting for you a very long time." But Abu Daoud, who now realized Omer's identity, hissed, "Remember us when you join your army."

Later Liyana would try to remember exactly what the room looked like during the next few moments. Maybe the light changed. Maybe the sunbeams falling across Sitti's bed intensified, and the small golden coffee pot glittered on its tray. The day turned a corner right then, but you would have to have been paying close attention to see it.

Sitti plunged into a new story, her voice dipping and swooping energetically, hands fluttering around her face. Omer stared at her with complete attention. Poppy frowned as she spoke.

"She's saying," Poppy translated hesitantly, as if the story tasted slightly bad in his mouth, "that your friend here reminds her very much—of someone she used to know. Someone—she liked a lot. Nobody knew it, though. He played a little flute—called a *nai*—that used to be more popular over here. This was—forty, fifty years ago? He was a shepherd and—he slept in a cave. Shepherds do that. Or, they used to."

"Cool!" Rafik said.

"And she was—married for a long time already. So she kept her feeling for him—hidden. For years. Maybe I shouldn't be telling you this! Maybe she shouldn't be telling me! Hmmmmm. She says—he 'saved her heart.'"

Poppy put his hand to his forehead and pinched it, massaging the skin the way he sometimes did when he was trying to work out a problem. But Sitti kept talking. Khaled and Nadine looked mesmerized. Liyana's cousins' mouths hung wide open. Aunt Saba let a cigarette burn down to a stump between her fingers and flicked it into the air when it stung her.

Poppy cleared his throat loudly and continued translating. "The shepherd—had a healing power, she says. For *air!* He could make the air feel calm again when it felt troubled. You know—after something bad happens—it's like a bad note hangs in the air? Hmmm—She says he could fix it. He would walk up a road—playing his flute. His flute—fixed it. I wish he were still here!"

Liyana's mother said, "Where is he now?"

Poppy held up one hand. "Wait a minute, she's going *on and on.* She says—your friend—has her friend's—same kind of hair. He has—his exact same shape of head. He has—something in the way he turns his eyes to things."

Now Sitti opened both her hands to Omer and said, *"Khallas."* Finished. The story was done—for the moment. She also said *"Shookran,"* thanking him, and smiling widely.

Omer leaned forward to take both her hands in his and thanked her back, in Arabic. The room stayed entirely quiet. Sitti laughed her gutsy, throaty laugh.

Poppy said, "She thinks your friend is—the angel—of her friend, who was killed in the '67 war. He wasn't fighting either. He was standing in front of a fruit shop in Nablus."

"You mean—she thinks Omer is his reincarnation?"

Poppy didn't know the word in Arabic, but he tried. She shook her head. "No, she says, *the angel*. I can't explain. She thinks one person can carry the spirit of another person in—an angel kind of way. Omer, you've got a load on your back you didn't even know about!"

Omer spoke softly. "I'm happy to carry him."

———

Omer and Liyana slipped away for another walk before sunset without Rafik or anyone else. Liyana felt sneaky, but relieved to have a few moments alone. If Sitti could be a renegade, then she could, too. They climbed the highest hill above the village to the abandoned stone house where her uncle used to live. He had been a recluse and almost never came down.

The path rose at a steep angle. Omer offered Liyana his hand more than once. When they were out of sight of the village, he no longer let hers go.

Weeds had grown up tall around the house's pale sunbaked stones. A cool breeze drifted through her uncle's open windows. He had died five years ago.

"What did he eat?" Omer asked.

"What he grew in his fields. They say he was very thin."

Inside the vacant house, they took deep breaths.

Liyana said, "My grandmother is full of surprises."

Omer said, "Oh Liyana. I'm glad your grandmother isn't mad that I came."

"Hardly!"

Liyana's throat flickered. She gulped and stared at him hard.

Omer said, "Do you think I kissed other people before? Well, I didn't. It's a big surprise to me. I don't want you to get in any trouble," he said. He kissed her hand.

She laughed. "Maybe a *little* trouble. I can't see any way around it." She leaned forward and kissed him one time on the mouth, then they both looked out the window into the valley, side by side.

Liyana did not think her uncle's spirit was angry with them for being on his hill. Distant plowed fields seemed to steam and breathe. She felt a great peacefulness floating in the air.

Poppy was standing outside looking up into the night sky when they appeared in the dark. He shook his finger at Liyana. But she knew sometimes he just pretended to be mad because he thought he ought to be. "Where have you been?"

"On the hermit tour."

Rafik and Nadine were collecting the popped bodies of balloons from the ground and handing them to Sitti, who stretched out the elastic skins and let them spring back to flatness. She groaned and looked entranced. Then she poked them into her belt.

Omer took both Sitti's hands in his again when they said good-bye. She peered deeply into his eyes and said, "Be careful! Come back! Please come back!"

Omer said, "Thank you, thank you, I am so happy to know you."

Liyana didn't even need translations.

On the drive home, Liyana felt exhausted in a good, full way. Rafik had hurt his knee on a rock and kept moaning in the back seat. Khaled said, "Now you're like me." The two of them were eating a handful of pumpkin seeds, pitching the shells out the open window into the blackness. Some of them flew back in and hit Liyana on the forehead. Normally she would complain. But this night she didn't care. She just brushed them away and leaned in Omer's direction.

Poppy said, "Today was quite an experience. Nineteen people asked me if they could borrow money."

Liyana's mother said she'd had the best day *ever* in the village and had finally learned how to make *lebne* by straining yogurt through cheesecloth. She thanked Khaled, Nadine, and Omer for their kindness to the children. "I don't think they will forget those balloons for a very long time." Poppy said he would drop Khaled and Nadine at the camp and drive Omer home since it was too late to catch a bus. Liyana could come along for the ride if she wanted to.

The roads were deserted at this hour. A skinny moon lay tipped on its back.

# MAP

The calendar has a wide-open face.

Liyana lit one short candle in a blue glass cup and set it on the rug in front of her in her bedroom. Then she sat cross-legged before it. Everyone in her family had gone to sleep.

Flipping open an old notebook she'd written in just before she left St. Louis, she read, *It is hard to find anyone else who will admit they do not want to grow up. My friends say they're ready. Claire says it sounds great to her. Mom says she felt relieved to get older, even though she loved Peachy. Finally she was under "her own jurisdiction." That makes it sound like a court case. Poppy liked growing up because it meant he could travel "beyond the horizon." That makes it sound like "Over the Rainbow." Why does everything sound like something else?*

I want a map that says, "Here is the country of littleness, where words first fell into your mouths. Here are roads leading every direction. Some people will travel many roads. Some will set up camp close to their first homes. Some will stop loving their early words. Nothing will be enough for them. Keep your hearts simple and smooth

The entry ended there, in midair, without punctuation, after a sketch of a circle with squiggly lines extending out from it. Sometimes Liyana felt tempted to draw a large X over the pages in her notebooks.

Tonight she sat a long time before writing on the first page of one of the new blue notebooks Poppy had given her for her birthday. *There is no map.* She closed her eyes and waited. Then she wrote, *Every day is a new map. But it's just a scrap of it, an inch.*

Then she leaned back against her bed. *I like inches,* she wrote. *They're small enough to hold.*

The candle flame was swallowing itself. She tipped the glass to the side so the hot wax wouldn't smother the wick. In the other rooms of the house her parents and Rafik were wrapped in their deepest, dreamiest breaths by now. She stood, stretched, and stared out the window into the utterly clear night. A few tiny lights blinked from poles to the west and the south. People she would never know were sleeping in their beds and turning over.

An odd thought came to Liyana. Maybe this close feeling was a gift for growing older. Maybe this was what you got in place of all the things you lost.

How did a friend change your heart? Could

things still be simple? She didn't need *everyone* to know her—just a few people. That was enough. She needed her family, two countries, her senses, her notebooks and pencils, and her new devotion to—trade. When you liked somebody, you wanted to trade the best things you knew about. You liked them not only for themselves, but for the parts of you that they brought out.

It wasn't the beginning or end of any story, but the middle of—what felt rich.

$\mathcal{D}$OORS

There was a door in the heart
that had no lock on it.

Sitti wanted to show Omer her vineyard. She wanted him to tell her why her grapevines had dried up. Angels knew everything. She wanted to show him the treasures in her treasure box—the folded velvets and broken watches and golden buttons. She wanted him to travel with her to the Sea of Galilee.

"Why him?" Poppy asked. "Why don't you want to go alone with me?"

"Because he can speak Hebrew and you can't. And we may need it."

It was so rare for Sitti to leave the village. She wouldn't go to the Turkish baths in Nablus. She'd even decided to postpone her trip to Mecca again.

But she'd been having a craving for the little crispy fish that were caught and served at Galilee.

"No elevators," she said, shaking her finger at Poppy.

Rafik asked how she felt about boats.

"No boats!"

When they got to Galilee and found the old pink restaurant surrounded by a colorful clutter of buildings, they chose a green metal table near the water. Liyana's mother spoke to a waiter in Arabic even before they sat down, ordering water without ice for herself and hot tea for everyone else. Rafik ripped open a packet of crackers he had in his pocket and tossed them to three brown ducks who paddled up. He leaned over to feel the water.

"Yikes! It's cold. Sitti!" he said. "Let's go swimming!"

Liyana and Poppy pulled up an extra table so they would have enough room. The seaside breeze felt firm and cool. Sitti held her open hands toward the small waves as if she could push them back. She mumbled something. Poppy conveyed, "She's blessing—the energy. But she is also saying, Rafik, stay away from me!"

Reading the menu, Poppy said, "What do you know?" and shook his head. "The tourist industry has found this place! Too bad. It used to be so quiet and tucked away. Now the meals have biblical names."

They all ordered the same thing: *Disciple's Special.* A holy, purified meal. A picture on the menu showed crispy fish, moons of lemon, mounds of rice.

They drank their hot tea before the food came,

toasting the sea. Sitti gathered the empty teacups in front of her so she could read the grounds.

She waggled her finger at Rafik and yakked excitedly. Poppy sighed, "She says you need to study harder."

Liyana said, "I could have told you that without a teacup." Rafik lightly kicked her shin.

Next Sitti gazed into Omer's eyes, then his cup. She spoke in a deeper voice. Poppy translated, "You will need to be brave. There are hard days coming. There are hard words waiting in people's mouths to be spoken. There are walls. You can't break them. Just find doors in them. See?" Sitti's white scarf lifted in the breeze. "You already have. Here we are, together."

Omer said, "All that in my tea leaves? They're very talkative!" He smiled at Sitti.

Liyana's mother put her arm around Poppy and pulled his chair closer to hers. The sun was glistening on her head like a spotlight.

Sitti tapped the rim of Liyana's cup, tipping it back and forth.

"I think she's cheating!" Rafik said. "She's moving your leaves around so they say something better! Have you ever noticed how my cup is always bossy and your cup always holds a compliment?" He threw a hand to his forehead and Omer laughed.

Sure enough, Sitti said the leaves in the bottom of Liyana's cup promised her a beautiful future. "Revolting," muttered Rafik.

"Walk and talk," Poppy translated. "Walk and talk." He tipped his head and winked.

"She knows your specialties, anyway," Omer whispered.

Sitti touched her first two fingers to Liyana's forehead, and crooned. Poppy said, "She says you have a powerful world in there. Be strong. Keep letting it out."

Liyana looked down at her own hands folded on the table and said, very softly, "I'll try."

Their full plates were arriving. Sitti took a ravenous nibble before everyone else was served. She kissed her fingers. Another waiter collected the cups. Poppy sliced. He sliced and sliced. Was it tough? He took a tentative bite, beckoned to the first waiter, and pointed sadly at his fish. "I'm sorry," he said, his face crinkling good-naturedly, "but it's not *quite*—delicious."